Library of Congress Cataloging-in-Publication Data

Kornbluth, Jesse.
    Highly Confident : the crime and punishment of Michael Milken / by Jesse
Kornbluth.
        p.   cm.
    ISBN 0-688-10937-3
        1. Milken, Michael. 2. Stockbrokers—United States—Biography. 3. Securities
industry—United States—Corrupt practices.
I. Title
HG4621.M55K67   1992
368.1'68—dc20
[B]   91-43450
                                                                                          CIP

Printed in the United States of America

First Edition

1 2 3 4 5 6 7 8 9 10

BOOK DESIGN BY LYNN DONOFRIO DESIGNS

HIGHLY CONFIDENT

HIGHLY CONFIDENT

The Crime and Punishment of
Michael Milken

•

Jesse Kornbluth

WILLIAM MORROW AND COMPANY, INC.
NEW YORK

For My Mother and Father

There is no trap more deadly than the trap you set for yourself.

—Raymond Chandler

A NOTE TO THE READER

It has become common for reporters who covered the investigation of Michael Milken to say they've never encountered a story so shrouded in secrecy. I found something else: I've never worked on a story in which so many people had such selective memories. Again and again, the men and women I interviewed knew *exactly* what the other guy did wrong but couldn't recall anything questionable about their own behavior.

If selective memory disturbed me more than any penchant for secrecy, it was because I had greater opportunity to meet with the key participants in this story than any other writer. Since 1988, I have interviewed several hundred people who worked with Milken, competed against him, or brought him down. I have also spent hundreds of hours with Michael Milken, and hundreds of hours more with his family, his closest friends, and his attorneys. That unique access was immensely useful, providing both information and a privileged window into the man and his world.

But this cooperation was a mixed blessing. In 1990, after insisting on his innocence for three and a half years, Milken pleaded guilty to six felony counts and read a lengthy admission of his culpability in court. Despite that, his continuing preoccupations suggest that he still sees himself as a convenient target, an easy symbol of a misunderstood decade, and, in comparison with others, relatively blameless.

I welcome Michael Milken's decision to speak up at last. I applaud his willingness to participate in a project that he doesn't authorize or control. At the same time, I recognize the self-interest involved. In talking with Milken, I was constantly reminded of Gertrude Stein's dictum: Very interesting, if true.

What *was* true? The more interviews I conducted, the more I feared this book would be a pale retread of *Rashomon*—a many-sided account with no way for anyone to determine the truth. I was, apparently, not alone in feeling frustrated. Late in my research, people on every side of this case began to send me confidential memos, transcripts, and investigative reports. By the time I started writing, the leaks had become torrents, and I had ten thousand pages of previously unseen material.

This mother lode of documents was invaluable. And so, while I am grateful to everyone who met with me, I am particularly indebted to those sources known in my home as the Silent Friends. Their contribution allows me to dare to hope that what I have written here may someday be classified as history.

But history—even financial history—doesn't have to be a blow-by-blow dissection of deeds and transactions. In finance, as in any enterprise, character is destiny; motivation, relationships, and personality are perhaps even more important than numbers and dollars. In these pages, therefore, my intention has been to tell the human story behind a prosecution that was the biggest manhunt ever to focus on Wall Street.

This prosecution has, in recent years, been simplified to become a parable of white hats and black hats: saintly prosecutors versus mendacious billionaires, or, depending on the point of view, mendacious prosecutors versus saintly billionaires. But there are, as a federal judge has noted, "no angels in the guise of men who are prosecutors." By the same token, financiers who amass great fortunes are not necessarily devils. In this story, shades of gray are dominant. And in this story, complicated and conflicted people make their way through a drama that sometimes seems more like a sustained psychiatric episode than a criminal prosecution.

CHAPTER ONE

L.A.'s asleep. But not Michael Milken. Showered and dressed, he pads past the rooms where his children rest, goes downstairs, and presses a button. At the bottom of the dark driveway, the gate electronically opens. A few minutes later, there's a flash of lights, the low hum of the black Mercedes 560. It's 4 A.M. Larry Shamhart is right on time.

Shamhart, a pleasant man who resembles Curly of the Three Stooges, never intended to be a driver for anyone. He lives in Glendora, a half-hour drive from Milken's home even on a deserted freeway. But eighteen months ago, he was in a helicopter crash, and when he woke up, with his back and kidneys badly injured, his twenty-year career as a Pasadena police officer was over.

When Drexel's chief of security offered him a job as Milken's morning driver last spring, Shamhart didn't admit that he'd never heard of Drexel Burnham Lambert or the man responsible for its recent good fortune. Nor did he say that he considered this a temporary position, a holding action until something better came along. So in his second week, when he overslept, he was so nonchalant about it that he only called Milken because his boss told him to.

What happened next was unprecedented in Shamhart's experience—Milken wasn't angry. Just the opposite. He'd driven himself to work, no problem. And he was glad to hear from Shamhart; he'd been worried that something had happened to him. That episode, and the way Milken always asked about his family, changed everything for Shamhart. Now he no longer minds waking up at 1 A.M., driving to Beverly Hills, picking up the Mercedes, and getting the newspapers before driving another twenty minutes over the mountain to collect Milken in Encino.

The front door opens, spilling light onto the lawn and signaling Shamhart to hurry out of the car. If Milken has really been at it, he'll have as many as five canvas boating bags filled with reports and prospectuses. Shamhart hates those mornings—helping Milken lug all that paper strains his back. But there have been fewer bags the last few months.

If Shamhart asked, Milken would say that the era of mergers and leveraged buyouts and hostile takeovers is ending, and that the future will be built on transforming debt into equity. That is true. It is also true that some of the problems Milken has been pondering at home for the last few months cannot be set down on paper.

So far, the morning of October 1, 1986, seems as if it will be pleasant and uneventful. Milken emerges toting just two bags, looking like a taller, younger Willie Loman. He swings the bags into the backseat, settles himself, and glances at the headlines as Shamhart heads toward Ventura Boulevard and the freeway. The news is dull, so Milken and Shamhart chat about their families and L.A. sports teams, a conversation that is often so animated Milken never gets back to the newspapers.

Shortly before they reach Beverly Hills, Milken knots his tie. At 4:25, Shamhart turns off Wilshire Boulevard into the drive that separates Drexel's two buildings. And at 4:30 A.M., his usual arrival time, Milken is at his desk.

He does not stay there for long. His associates are starting to file in—there's a little competition to beat the boss to the office—and he likes to have the dozens of personal notes he writes each night waiting for them on their chairs. He reviews yesterday's trading sheets and adds a few more items to his to-do list, which usually averages four pages. And then it's time to call clients in New York and London before the market opens and the trading floor starts to sound like a disco.

A pleasant routine for Michael Milken. He's in his element, he's warmed up. There are the pencils that one of his assistants

12

has prepared for him with an eyebrow-pencil sharpener. There is the schedule of appointments taped at the top of his Quotron. There is the glass of water. And there, most important of all, are the two phones, and the circuitry that will allow him, for the next twelve hours, to earn another million-odd dollars on his way to a world-record salary.

All is readiness.

Then, at 5:30 A.M., the phone rings.

It's Ivan Boesky.

Boesky likes to call Milken from his New York office at this hour, badgering Milken's assistants, never taking no for an answer. If they tell him Milken will be busy for a half hour, Boesky tries again in twenty seconds. And in another twenty seconds. And another, and another, and another—he is nothing if not relentless.

Milken's assistants, not surprisingly, despise Boesky. Sue Cochran and Janet Chung sometimes play the child's game of rock-paper-scissors to determine who will have to humor him while he waits for Milken. Sometimes, rather than wonder how many calls he's willing to make, they do everything they can to get Milken to talk to him. Today, Boesky has to wait only thirty seconds.

"Good afternoon," Milken says, his standard greeting.

"Afternoon, Michael. How many hours you been up this morning?"

"Two and a quarter."

"Two and a quarter—it's time for lunch, Michael. What's going on with you?"

"Oh, just working very hard."

"That-a-boy."

There's the briefest pause.

"I saw your Salomon stock moved up yesterday," Milken notes, referring to Boesky's investment in Salomon Brothers, the investment bank that is Drexel's archrival.

"Yeah, I kind of remain optimistic about that. Do you think I'm crazy?"

"Not in the short run. I think the principals think it's worth, you know, somewhere between thirty and fifty."

"Yeah, but the world has changed since the first greenmail."

"Correct. We'll find out what happened shortly," Milken

says, leaving it to Boesky to guess if this is dry humor or dark prediction.

They discuss some other stocks, and then Milken tells Boesky that Charles Keating will be calling him.

"Who is Charlie Keating?" Boesky asks.

"You know, he purchased one hundred million of your debt—"

"Yes."

"And he bought it for his insurance company and his savings and loan."

"Right."

"And he needs an update for his due diligence standpoint."

Boesky bristles. "What kind of an update? I'm not inclined—"

"You started with what—two hundred twenty million in equity?"

"Yeah."

"You might give him a feeling where the equity stands right now. I assume it's at the same level."

"It's more than two-twenty," Boesky says quickly.

"Fine."

"Because we had infusions, you know."

"That might be a point you want to make," Milken says, in the thin, affectless voice that sometimes gives the impression he thinks he's talking to a child.

Milken has no other business to discuss, so Boesky turns to his reason for calling. "You remember some time ago we talked about the idea that it might not be bad to get together?"

"Yeah."

"And we never got together."

Milken asks Sue Cochran for his schedule—he wants to know when he'll be in New York next.

"Do you understand what I'm talking about?" Boesky asks, trying to nail down the topics of special interest without actually naming them.

If Milken thinks Boesky is talking only about the high interest rates on money borrowed overnight, he's kidding himself. In 1985, Milken and Boesky aides began to keep a scorecard of Boesky's trading activity with Drexel. Some of this was standard Wall Street practice—a way for a broker to remind a client that his ideas were profitable, a way for a client to see just how well his broker was doing for him. But much of it was something else: a running tab on stock that Boesky had bought at Milken's request and stock that Milken had bought for Boesky. In other words, stock they were "parking" for each other.

In March, when Drexel was raising $660 million for Boesky's arbitrage fund, Boesky decided that Drexel was charging far too much for its services—and he informed the investment bankers that he was reducing Drexel's fee by $5 million. Drexel New York screamed to Milken to get it back. And Milken decided the moment was ripe to make Boesky pay for a ton of uncompensated investment banking work Drexel had done for him over the years.

Ivan Boesky was a strange creature. To hold on to his money as long as possible, he liked to give his employees their salary checks after the banks closed. He fought over standard brokerage commissions. And he balked at paying investment banking fees. But he was generally good about compensating his partners in crime for the illegal services they performed for him. So what Milken described as a charge for legitimate services was, for Boesky, a settling of the parking account, pure and simple.

There was much argument over the amount—at one point, Boesky was convinced that Drexel owed him money—but on the day the old Boesky partnership was being dissolved and the new fund was being born, Boesky agreed to pay Drexel $5.3 million. Drexel's invoice couldn't have been shorter. "For consulting services as agreed upon on March 21, 1986," it read.

Prosecutors could have a field day with that. If Drexel had performed legitimate investment banking services, why weren't they itemized? And why this separate bill? Why hadn't Drexel simply added this fee to the $24 million it was already charging Boesky?

What was *really* going on here?

Along with some securities lawyers, Milken would say, "Nothing much." For him, parking was a gray area, "industry practice," at worst a minor infraction settled by the Securities and Exchange Commission without an onerous criminal prosecution by the U.S. attorney. In another time, Boesky would say the same thing. But now they have entered what Milken has called a "new environment." And the accommodations that once seemed harmless—Wall Streeters joked that the appropriate punishment for parking should be a fifteen-dollar ticket—will almost certainly be viewed by the government as serious violations of the securities laws.

Milken's attention is wandering, and not just because Boesky wants to discuss matters he'd prefer not to think about. He's juggling another call, and talking to a salesman, and reminding an assistant about a client he wants to talk to; there's always something else he has to do. But he pays just enough attention to this conversation to say—blandly—that, yes, he knows what's on Boesky's mind, and as for New York, he'll be there next on October 22.

Then Milken has a better idea. Boesky has been talking about selling the Beverly Hills Hotel, which his wife, Seema, and her sister, Muriel Slatkin, inherited from their father in 1979. Boesky himself owns just 4 percent of the stock, but as a celebrated financier, he makes many of the economic decisions about the hotel, and as he's been saying for a while, this looks like the top of the real estate boom, an ideal time to take a profit.

"If you're thinking of selling the hotel, maybe if you come out here, you and Kirk Kerkorian and I could spend a half hour together," Milken says.

"Actually, I was thinking of coming out and spending a few hours in L.A. next Thursday."

"Fine, you're on," says Milken, who has never liked to travel. He sets a date with Boesky at the Beverly Hills Hotel from two to four in the afternoon on October 9. "We'll meet with Kerkorian at the beginning," he suggests. "It only takes fifteen or twenty minutes to shake hands and say hi. And if he has some interest and a feel for the thing, maybe we can get him to make a higher bid."

"The next question is, ah, having kind of like a *private* meeting, no?" Boesky asks, determined to corner Milken.

Milken doesn't balk. He says he wants to take a look at Boesky's debt. In light of falling interest rates, he's not sure Boesky has the right capital structure.

Boesky is concerned about this, but not very. "Ah, I would also like you to kind of—"

"I understand," Milken says. "I think we can cover all issues."

"Ah, and if you could, ah, spend a little time recalling what we had talked about."

"I'll review all the points, don't worry."

"Good."

"Great." For Milken, who handles as many as a hundred calls a day, this conversation is over. "I'm going to jump."

"Thank you," Boesky says, as he hangs up and Tom Doonan, a criminal investigator in the employ of Rudolph Giuliani, the U.S. attorney for the Southern District of New York, disconnects the recorder that has taped this call.

Ivan Boesky hasn't been bothering Milken much since Drexel helped him set up the biggest arbitrage fund in the history of American finance. His comparative silence may be an indication that he really is as good as his 1985 book, *Merger Mania*, says he is—with his business up and running, he has no need for Milken. Or it may be that he wants to teach Milken a lesson; now he's truly important and powerful, and to prove it, he won't be doing much with Drexel until Milken decides he's as important as Henry Kravis, Ronald Perelman, Saul Steinberg, Boone Pickens, and Carl Icahn. Those men get billions in backing for transactions that rocket them onto the front page—why shouldn't he?

Or perhaps there's a darker meaning to Boesky's silence. In August, Boesky informed the employees of the Beverly Hills Hotel that he was being investigated by the Securities and Exchange Commission. But even before that announcement and the press reports that followed it, rumors were flying—mostly about Dennis Levine, a Drexel managing director who'd been nabbed for insider trading in May.

Levine is said to have told SEC investigators and prosecutors from the U.S. attorney's office that he and Boesky had routinely broken insider trading laws. Boesky has denied any wrongdoing, but then, he's denied even knowing Levine. In fact, he has been downright outraged by Levine's criminality. "Can you believe that guy?" he told Milken a week after Levine pled guilty to squirreling $12.6 million in illegal trades, using aliases and codes, in an offshore bank. "In a different world, he wouldn't be alive now."

Given the buzz about Boesky, the fact that he has arranged a meeting with Milken for the first time in three months is information to be ruthlessly guarded. For Michael Milken, this is no challenge—although he sits in the center of his trading room and never leaves his desk to take a call and even encourages his salesmen to listen in on his phone conversations, there is another level of information that is far from public knowledge. There's no file that holds it; Milken keeps it all in his head.

Still, for this meeting, Milken needs a few facts, so he turns to Charles Thurnher, the administrator in charge of record keeping. Thurnher, on his own recognizance, expands the circle, though not wantonly—he calls Cary Maultasch, the equity trader in Drexel's New York office who has the greatest contact with the Boesky organization.

Mike's going to meet with Ivan, Thurnher says. He wants an update on Drexel's commission business with Boesky. What's his trading been like?

Maultasch is high-strung and paranoid by nature, he's seen psychiatrists for years and sometimes has to take medication. Because he has a connoisseur's appreciation for equilibrium, he's been made exceptionally unhappy by the recent rumors and press reports. He cannot exactly see the future, but whatever's going down, he knows one thing: he doesn't want to put himself in a position that could force him to testify against Mike Milken, the man who set it up for him to make $1 million a year.

In this situation, Maultasch wouldn't dream of picking up a phone and calling Michael Davidoff, Boesky's head trader. Boesky might already have cut a deal with the government, and Davidoff may have followed him—Davidoff could be taping his calls, you never know. So the best Maultasch is willing to do for Thurnher is give him whatever information he has on hand. Then he calls Milken.

"Be careful," Maultasch says.

Milken, though surprised that Maultasch knows about the meeting, doesn't freeze him out. As Maultasch recalls it, he even confesses his greatest fear: "I assume I'll be speaking for the record."

Milken has no idea how right he is. In late July, shortly after Boesky got his subpoenas, he asked his lawyer what they meant. Harvey Pitt, who was once general counsel for the SEC, knew how to read these documents—not as demands for information, but as accusations of criminal behavior. "Ivan, the government does many things," he said, "but it's not likely they made this up out of whole cloth."

So Boesky pled. Just like that. One afternoon in August,

some assistant U.S. attorneys were sitting around in New York deciding there was no way they'd ever nail Boesky, and a minute later Harvey Pitt was on the phone, suggesting he'd like to come in and talk. When he hung up, the astounded prosecutors burst out laughing. By Labor Day, though, they had their game faces on again, and in exchange for the arbitrageur's willingness to help them make other cases, the U.S. attorney and the SEC let Boesky have a deal that looked good for all concerned.

On one hand, Boesky's punishment is astronomical: a lifetime ban from the securities business and a fine of $100 million, the largest in the SEC's history, practically equal to the agency's entire annual budget. On the other, he is allowed to sell off his positions in an orderly fashion before his deal with the government is announced—a sort of federally approved insider trading operation—and, after the announcement, he'll have another eighteen months to unwind the business. And the government is even going to let him take $50 million of the fine as a tax write-off.

Best of all, Boesky only has to plead guilty to a single felony count—and he can be sentenced whenever he pleases. In other words, under the current system of judge selection, he can, in effect, choose the judge who will sentence him. If that lenient liberal is impressed with his contrition and cooperation, he might get as little as a year in jail and be released long before he has to enter a federal courtroom and face a defense lawyer representing someone he's implicated.

And what does the government get for all that?

Michael Milken.

Well, it's not just Milken. Boesky also promises to provide damaging testimony against three other players, all major figures in the takeover game that's making a great many people crazy. But the others are gravy. The prize is Milken, the reclusive, practically unknown Californian who is said to have made a fortune backing outsiders like himself.

To stop Milken is to stop Drexel Burnham. To stop Milken is to stop takeovers fueled by junk bonds. To stop Milken—and then to turn him into a government witness—is to stop upstarts and outsiders like Kravis, Perelman, Steinberg, Pickens, and Icahn, and, perhaps, to put most of what is politely called New York's "Nouvelle Society" in jail. It is to make real the fondest dream of the American Establishment—Congressman

John Dingell, the Fortune 500, the Business Roundtable, and some of Drexel's battered rivals.

It is to roll back the 1980s.

There's only one catch.

Boesky's company must file a report with the SEC in mid-November. It's a routine document, but it's a public one—and, in it, Boesky must disclose any investigations or legal judgments. Every financial writer in America is working the Boesky story now; there's no way this document will lie unnoticed in the stack of filings the SEC releases daily. As a practical matter, then, whatever help Boesky can give the government must end on November 14, when the news of his plea and cooperation will have to be announced.

So there is a great deal riding on the October 9 meeting at the Beverly Hills Hotel. For Boesky, who has probably got only this one opportunity to be alone in a room with Milken before the news breaks, the incentives are obvious. If Milken incriminates himself for the benefit of the hidden tape recorder, Boesky can expect prosecutors to write an even more glowing letter to the judge. He can anticipate reduced jail time—or maybe none at all. A revealing tape might even help him get permission to return to the securities business.

But Boesky is not the only beneficiary of a successful taping. For the SEC, there's the chance to nail the financier hailed in the business press as "Milken the Magnificent"—and remembered less fondly at the agency as a man who has eluded three prior investigations. If Boesky delivers Milken, everyone on Wall Street will fear a freshly potent SEC. In Washington, no longer will John Dingell, who heads the congressional committee that oversees the SEC, use the agency as a punching bag, taunting its representatives in public sessions for their inability to make cases. Instant credibility, instant deterrence—Boesky can make it all happen.

And then there's Rudolph Giuliani, the U.S. attorney for the Southern District of New York. If Boesky hands him a tape filled with damning admissions, Milken might decide—maybe even right after the Boesky plea is announced—to make his own deal with the government. That would eliminate any need for a long investigation and a public trial. It would generate Lord knows how many new cases. It would establish the U.S. attorney's office as the preeminent crimebuster on Wall Street. And, without question, it would generate reams of great publicity for him.

No one has more at stake, though, than Michael Milken, who doesn't even realize he's the target. He's already the most powerful figure in American finance; if he keeps it up, he'll be the richest man in the country as well. From that vantage point, he will be better able to direct his energy and resources to the causes that are important to him: education, cancer research, minority businesses, and third world debt. In the process, he may finally satisfy his unexamined compulsion to do every possible piece of business—a hunger that used to be latent but now consumes him.

And yet, with all Milken has and all that promises to unfold at his command, he'll be at a disadvantage when he walks into Boesky's hotel suite. With the exception of his father's death from cancer in 1979, Milken has lived in a world that works almost exactly as he likes. Now he's in the situation he hates most—he's not in control, he's not running the show.

As Milken well knows, he's most effective when he's on his own turf. There, he's deliberately ambiguous; like a guru, he talks in parables, in fragments, in ironic jibes. Unless he's giving orders to buy or sell, he rarely makes direct, declarative statements. As a result, even the most astute businessmen in America often walk out of meetings with him certain only of his promise to get the deal done.

If Boesky ever turns on him and describes this conversation to the government, however, SEC investigators and U.S. attorneys who don't know how little Boesky means to him may soon want to examine him under their harsh and unforgiving microscopes. Far from his trading floor, it's easy to distort what he says and how he says it; in a prosecutor's office, literal-minded men can put their spin on his ambiguity. And that could be fatal.

But Milken is a poster boy for optimism, taking his philosophy from the southern California weather report: blue skies today, bluer skies tomorrow. All his life, he has hated confrontation and gone to extravagant lengths to avoid it. He is smarter and more credible than Boesky; he will find some way to put Boesky off. No doubt about it, he will prevail.

"Guilty," the Senate decrees, ordering federal judge Harry Claiborne removed immediately from office for tax evasion. The California Angels lose an error-ridden game to the Boston Red Sox in the American League playoffs. Eugene Hasenfus, shot down in Nicaragua, announces that his aircraft was carrying weapons to the contra rebels at the direction of the CIA. But the most important message the *Los Angeles Times* holds for Michael Milken on October 9, 1986, is in his astrological forecast, which he never reads. "If you are more concerned with details," it advises, "you can come to a better understanding with partners."

Details. Milken trades all day, he's working on five major financings, he has a family charitable foundation and other causes that interest him, and though he seems to be able to manufacture time, there's only so much a man can do. "My nightmare," he has told his wife, "is that as I'm being lowered into my grave, someone will lean over and say, 'Mike, please, just one more little favor . . .'"

And now, the night before his confrontation with Boesky, one more detail. Milken's wife, Lori, goes to Beverly Hills for dinner at the Ivy with Janet Chung and two other women he works with. They talk about Milken and Drexel until Janet, who spends eight to ten hours with him each day, can't take it anymore and asks Lori about her writing. As she is about everything, Lori is self-effacing, but Janet won't be put off—she wants to read Lori's short stories, and she makes Lori promise to put some in Michael's bag. After dinner, to show she's serious, Janet calls Michael at home to remind him to remind Lori. And, of course, everybody forgets—except for Janet, who ransacks Milken's canvas bags as soon as she comes in at 10:30 A.M., which is just about lunchtime on Milken's trading floor.

"I'm sorry, I have a lot on my mind," Milken says.

That's an understatement—with so much to juggle, he almost forgets about Charles Thurnher. Fortunately, Thurnher has looked at Milken's calendar for the day. Now he asks if Milken would like the update. Yes, Milken says, very rushed, but not now—ride with me to the meeting.

Thurnher has had these sessions before. They are treacherous. When Milken gets you alone, he bombards you with questions: Why are our Federal Express charges so enormous? Do lunches have to cost so much? Can't anything be done about the light bulb bill? Thurnher's not convinced Milken really cares about the answers. Sometimes, it seems, all he wants is to make sure he's the one asking the questions.

Today, for example, Thurnher has prepared a computer run that shows Boesky's recent stock purchases from Drexel. Milken won't look at it. He has only one question: Has Boesky increased his trading with Drexel since March? No, Thurnher says. And with that, Milken turns to more mundane topics, seemingly comfortable with the meeting to come.

At the Beverly Hills Hotel, Boesky is in a panic. Tom Doonan, Giuliani's investigator, wired him up almost an hour ago. Milken's surely on his way. And yet here he is, surrounded by maintenance men and their supervisors, all of them focused on fixing his telephones.

For a day and a half, workmen have been filtering in and out of Boesky's first floor suite, dragging ladders and tool kits—and still the bloody phone doesn't ring. The irony is killing. The microphone taped to Boesky's chest broadcasts everything that's said in this suite to another room, a floor away, but technology supposedly perfected long ago can't be induced to function. And communication within the suite works no better. Boesky has said he's about to start an important meeting, and the workmen have sworn they're leaving, but they're not doing anything about it; their big concern seems to be that the phones work for tomorrow's wake-up call.

"Five minutes," the repairman pleads, from his perch on a ladder.

"Two minutes," Boesky barks.

"The best thing to do is clean this mess up," the supervisor decides. "Put things together, Ivan."

Boesky blinks at the insolence.

"Not you, *this* Ivan," the supervisor says quickly.

"His name is Ivan, too?" Boesky asks.

"Yes."

For Boesky, this is like Abbott and Costello. And it's not over. Now someone from the phone company arrives, determined to review the whole problem. The other Ivan continues to dork around with a ladder as if he's got all day. Investigator Doonan is in a room on another floor with Harvey Pitt, who has flown out with Boesky to provide moral support and legal advice. Useless, both of them.

Boesky calls room service.

"Would you be good enough to bring a thermos of coffee and a thermos of espresso to my room. And some mixed nuts. And a couple of cups. *Merci*. And some grapes. Thank you."

23

At length, Boesky clears the room. He calls his office to find out how the market closed, and then, to his absolute astonishment, the phone actually rings. It's Milken, he's in the lobby. Terrific. Come on up.

The door opens. There they are, face-to-face for perhaps only the tenth time in their five-year relationship, both aware that the government has declared war on their corner of finance. Two of the most intriguing figures on Wall Street, now staring each other down in this Beverly Hills version of the O.K. Corral.

Only one looks the part, and that's the forty-nine-year-old Boesky, in his bespoke three-piece suit with the gold watch and chain he copied from Winston Churchill. The collar of his white shirt is too long, accentuating his scrawny body and narrow face—Ichabod Crane goes to Wall Street. It's the eyes that make him seem authentic: piercing, unforgiving, the eyes of a man who has only to look at his prey to calculate its weaknesses. Arbitrageur's eyes, seeking profit in the spread between appearance and reality.

Milken, in contrast, looks like an economics professor who will never be a panelist on a Sunday morning talk show. Everything about him screams off-the-rack. There's a second button on the cuff of his blue oxford shirt, a sure sign that it was bought at a department store. The blazer and gray flannels are standard-issue, the loafers are regulation Bally, somebody gave him the Hermès tie. At forty, he looks small and boyish, even though he's five feet eleven inches tall and wears a fairly obvious toupee. All he needs is a calculator clipped to his belt and a plastic nerd pack to hold his pens, and the picture of the unworldly genius would be complete.

"Michael."

"How are you, Ivan?"

"Happy to see you."

"Michael, want some coffee?"

Boesky has to be joking. The one thing everyone knows about Mike Milken is that he's the ultimate Boy Scout—he drinks nothing that contains caffeine, hard liquor has never touched his lips, he's had maybe one beer in his life, it's unclear if he's even been in the same room as a joint. All he likes is water or fruit juice, and, if you're going to serve him water, it better not be fizzy.

"A little tea?" Boesky asks.

"A little water."

"We have water."

The Milken-Boesky relationship, from the beginning, has been about power and dominance. In economic terms, Milken is the clear winner—he not only controls Boesky's access to financing, he's already much, much richer than Boesky could ever become. But power is also psychological, and here it's difficult to say who is dominant. Is it Boesky, who whines and nags and bullies and wheedles to get his way—a master manipulator who is fully capable of offering Milken a drink he knows he hates, just to try to unnerve him? Or is it Milken, who is disciplined and discreet—a gamesman who never tells you exactly what the rules are?

Today, Milken intends to control the conversation as much as he can, for as soon as they're settled, he launches into a discussion of the nominal business at hand—the sale of the Beverly Hills Hotel. One possible buyer, he suggests, is Steve Wynn, the Las Vegas casino owner and loyal Drexel client.

"That would be an incredible feeder, see, but I told you that a hundred years ago," Boesky says. "Did I not?"

"Yes," Milken admits. "You did."

"Run a helicopter from the hotel to Vegas—all he'd have to do is find one live one a night. Wynn buys this hotel, he pays it off in one year."

"It's not that easy anymore," Milken points out. "Sometimes gamblers win."

"*Very* rarely," Boesky says. But he's not about to debate Milken about the laws of probability in Las Vegas. Although the Beverly Hills Hotel will eventually be sold, Drexel can't possibly be the agent—there's not enough time for Milken to complete its sale before mid-November, when their relationship will come to an end. So the thing for Boesky to do is wrap up this bogus topic and introduce the real one. "The bottom line is that to do anything with this place, the guy has to be in a buying-an-art-object mood."

"We have a guy from the Middle East, Europe, Japan. Then you have the people in the United States—if I was selling, I'd have a little talk with Donald Trump."

"Donald has already made the call," Boesky says. "This should be reasonable for him."

Milken now takes another step to dominate the meeting—he picks up the phone and asks Kirk Kerkorian to come to room 136 in an hour. And then waits. Who will suggest a conversational stroll down Memory Lane? Not Milken. So all the pressure is on Boesky.

Boesky pauses.

"First of all, we have had some government inquiry," he begins. "That's not unusual. We always have inquiry. We had a subpoena. Our lawyers were able to get that withdrawn. Maybe they'll come back at some point, maybe they won't. The atmosphere being what it is today, they might. Not unreasonable. I might ask you, have you got any inquiry?"

Milken shakes his head.

"Any subpoena?"

Another shake of the head.

"Nothing? That's good. Okay. The question is, we go back to a long time ago. And we talked about a little item of business that we had. We've got to figure out what that is."

"It's done," Milken says simply.

"It is? That's good," Boesky says, boring in. "Tell me what it is, because I'd like to know."

"The issue was how do we get to the negotiation of all the fees on the deal and the lawyer fees," Milken says. "They have the data in New York."

"What data?"

"What data?" echoes Milken.

"We have to have a story that's the same."

"Well, of course, we have."

"What's the story?"

"I have a list and they have a list."

"What list do you have?" Boesky demands. "When I went back home after I visited you last, you said, 'Look up some of the things that happened this year.' I did, but if I'm asked, What did you pay Drexel for . . ."

Milken falters. "The five point three million was related to . . . well, for the old partnership."

"Which things though, Michael? You send a bill for five point three million, you've got to have documentation."

"They have that in New York," Milken repeats. "That's where the fees are. They have the data."

"Which things?" Boesky asks again.

*   *   *

This is not the way to pin Milken down. Milken hates to offend—asked for an opinion, he's likely to offer some banality, the better to get on to a topic that's concrete and safe. Asked for a fact, he will gladly talk for hours, impressing listeners with his mastery of detail even as he bores them to death. So a request for specifics is, for Milken, nothing less than an invitation to drown Boesky in minutiae. He leaps to the task.

First, he says, Drexel's New York analyst did considerable research on food companies for Boesky. That's worth, for billing purposes, $500,000. There was corporate finance work on restructuring of the Boesky partnership. Analysis of tax considerations. People flying back and forth for fifteen months. Add $1 million. Then there was a study on savings and loans, which interested Boesky for a time. Add another million. Not to forget research on entertainment companies.

"By the way, speaking of MGM," Boesky interjects, "do you know we still have Turner preferred in the portfolio? Is that residual joint venture, or is that—what the hell is it?"

"I think you should hold the securities," Milken says.

"*Hold* the securities?" Boesky asks, almost giggling.

"No kidding—next one was the energy field," Milken says, moving right on.

"Wait a minute. How much for movies?"

"Entertainment industry is like eight hundred thousand."

Energy research, Milken says, turns out to be worth $750,000. Real estate, add another $350,000. Looking for opportunities in bankrupt companies, $700,000. Research on high-yield bonds, somewhere between $200,000 and $500,000. And that's not all the uncompensated work Drexel did, Milken notes. There was a company in Michigan that Boesky looked at, and there was another business, and then there was—anyway, the amount Boesky owed actually comes closer to $5.6 million than the $5.3 million he paid. A small point, perhaps, but this is a relationship where no point is too insignificant to be scored.

"Okay," Boesky says, overwhelmed by Milken's recitation. "Now, when I wrote the check, I don't have anything I wrote it for. What should I have in my file?"

"Obviously, I will give you—have them send you a copy of all the backup data if you want."

"That would be helpful."

*   *   *

They are at an impasse.

With the possible exception of the comment about Boesky holding on to the Turner preferred—which might be an admission of a joint illegal stock ownership arrangement between Boesky and Drexel, or might just as easily be a suggestion that a prudent investor might not want to sell the Turner at this time—Milken has said nothing that indicates he thinks he's broken the law. Clearly, he is prepared to defend the uprightness of the $5.3 million invoice.

But as Boesky is well aware, Charles Thurnher kept the scorecard for Milken, and Cary Maultasch did much of the trading of the stocks on that scorecard. Milken will have a difficult time denying that. So Boesky begins a new line of questioning.

"Let me ask you something else," Boesky says. "Mr. Thurnher—is there anything he has in the whole world?"

"No."

"It's gone."

"Does not exist."

"That's right."

"How reliable is Thurnher?"

"Reliable."

"You also have what's his name, Cary Maultasch."

"Uh-huh."

"What's his reliability level?"

"The only one Cary speaks to at your firm," Milken replies, "is Mike Davidoff."

"Sometimes Maultasch will call Davidoff and say, 'That's for us, this is for him,'" Boesky notes.

This is exactly the kind of dialogue that plays brilliantly for prosecutors when it's spooled out in front of a jury. Milken shifts gears.

"He might have said . . . he might have been thinking, he doesn't recall, the truth of the issue. . . ." Milken's almost completely lost. Finally, a response comes to him. "Davidoff might have misunderstood something. Cary might have said he had other customers."

Boesky asks Milken again for a more detailed invoice. Again, Milken promises one. And, sensing that Boesky has run out of questions, Milken lays out his version of these events.

"If you remember," Milken says, "you told me, 'If I don't do some business, I'll pay you.'"

"Right."

"And when you were disbanding the partnership, you couldn't carry the thing forward, so you paid us."

"All right."

"Wasn't that our understanding?"

"That was our understanding," Boesky agrees. "And we've got to have an understanding, because if I'm asked the question and I say 'Blue jeans' and you say 'Khaki pants,' it's not going to sound right."

That last remark sounds like an admission—and if the settling of the parking arrangement inspired the $5.3 million fee, a puzzling admission at that. This is the ideal time for Boesky to say, "Mike, you don't have to sell *me* on that story. Sure, if we ever have to testify, we'll talk about legitimate investment banking fees, but we both know the truth—you held stock for me, and I held it for you." But Boesky doesn't say that, not any of it.

The phone rings. Boesky goes into the bedroom to answer it. The caller is his fifteen-year-old son, John, a boarding student at the Lawrenceville School in New Jersey. John wants permission to go to a classmate's house for Yom Kippur. Boesky thinks this is a fine idea. But something else has inspired this call—John is depressed. Other kids keep confusing him with his twin brother, Ted, who is also at Lawrenceville, so he has dyed his hair blond. That doesn't seem to have helped, so he just got a crew cut. "I don't feel I'm being me," he complains. "Why do I have to do this?"

Boesky couldn't be more sympathetic. "All I can tell you is, you shouldn't change John Boesky. John Boesky is a lovely boy," he says. "I'm gonna be home on Saturday night, and on Sunday. If you want to call me, we can have a nice long conversation about these things."

When Boesky emerges from the bedroom, only five minutes remain before Kirk Kerkorian is to show up. Boesky and Milken chat about the changed climate on Wall Street, about Boesky's crushing debt, about Milken's enthusiasm for the preferred stock of American Motors. As he always does, Milken inquires about Boesky's children, and Boesky, sounding like a concerned parent, tells him the story of the twins and the hair crisis.

A knock at the door. It's Kerkorian. Boesky welcomes him and apologizes—there's someone he has to see for just a few minutes. What he really has to do, of course, is go upstairs to have Doonan disconnect the microphone hidden under his shirt. On the way, a young man recognizes him. He sticks out his hand.

"Jeffrey Brooks."

"Pleasure," Boesky says. "Where are you from? New York?"

"I have a discount brokerage firm," Brooks replies. "If you ever need something that you don't want the whole crowd knowing what you're doing, I run Jeffrey Brooks Securities."

"Give me a call," Boesky says amiably, and if he doesn't have to suppress a bitter little laugh at how the secrecy-loving Jeffrey Brooks has just introduced himself to Rudy Giuliani and the whole white-collar unit of the U.S. attorney's office, he is not human.

CHAPTER TWO

"**I** got more done this week than I have in months!" Michael Milken exclaimed, ten days after the meeting at the Beverly Hills Hotel. But that was no reason to enjoy a lazy Friday. "Let's see if we can break our record today," he urged his assistant.

"Let's break our record"—it could have been Michael Milken's motto. To him, that was an innocent exhortation, all-American call to diligence, teamwork, and measurable achievement. In October of 1986, he would never have seen it as a denial of reality and a refusal to acknowledge that his world was slipping out of his control. Nor would he have understood how anyone might find in this remark a snapshot of a tragic transformation—a picture of a man whose love of accomplishment had grown to include a mad hunger for transactions and accumulation.

What was Milken thinking?

Years after the events that put him in jail, that key question still tantalizes. What drove the man who has repeatedly described himself as "risk-averse" to such high-stakes, high-risk confrontations with Wall Street, Congress, and corporate America? If he was really a genius, why didn't he understand that it's not shrewd to rile the Establishment while you're earning a salary that may stand in the *Guinness Book of World Records* without serious challenge deep into the next century? And, most of all, why did a man earning an honest fortune get himself in so much trouble for so little gain?

Those questions can't be easily or glibly answered. For the Milken story is not the saga of a poor boy who would do anything to escape his poverty or a desperado in flight from a soul-deadening past. This was someone who was raised in relative comfort, bathed in love and admiration, cherished anew for every fresh accolade.

As a child, he was—and he knew he was—the prodigy, the golden one. As a student, he was that rare event, an intuitive genius who nonetheless applied himself. As a young man starting out in New York, he was promoted rapidly and regularly. His wife loved him and accepted his passion for his work. Later, when he moved back to Los Angeles, he bought a house ten blocks from his childhood home, where he was, once again, surrounded by his family and his closest friends. Many of the giants in American finance were so eager to see him that they did so at his convenience, even if that meant meeting him in the predawn hours on a weekend.

Respected, catered to, deferred to, even revered—Michael Milken had it all.

What was missing? What went wrong?

For clues, start with Milken's childhood. Born on July 4, 1946, he was the first child of Ferne and Bernard Milken, a couple whose marriage was as rich with symbolism as their son's birthdate. Bernard, an accountant, taught his children the virtues of work, charity, and anonymity. Ferne, bubbly and civic-minded, was actually the more ambitious parent, constantly pushing her children to achieve and dominate. Their values met and merged in their first-born, producing an outgoing but straitlaced, aggressive but sentimental, arrogant but well-mannered young man who truly believed that the world beyond Encino would be as straightforward and predictable as he liked to believe his family was.

And, on the surface, the Milkens do sound remarkably uncomplicated—very much like a fantasy family on a 1950s TV sitcom. Many children of the postwar era will recognize the family structure. The strong but softhearted father. The nurturing but forceful mother. And the child who slaves to fulfill their dreams.

In these families, there was no domestic violence, sexual abuse, alcoholism, or addiction; here, there was massive parental interest and emotional support, if not outright coddling. As a result, in the most turbulent period of this century, these homes were spared the worst outbreaks of radical politics and drug experimentation—whatever their internal conflicts, these sons were carrying out their parents' agenda, not rejecting it. So it is hardly surprising that when Michael Robert Milken recalls his childhood, he suppresses all complexity and speaks instead of a Wordsworthian paradise where even the problems were happy.

"A lot of my father's family remained in Poland and died in the Holocaust, but my grandfather came to the United States in the early 1900s," Milken has recalled. "My dad's mother died in childbirth. When he was two, he got polio. When he was nine, his father was killed in a car crash, and he went to live with relatives."

Milken doesn't volunteer that the saga of Bernard Milkevitz—he'd change the name when he and Ferne moved to Los Angeles—was even grimmer than that. For some years, Bernard's address was an orphanage. And he'd carry the effects of his polio to the end of his days.

"When I was fifteen years old, a boy said to me, 'Your father has a terrible limp!'" Milken told Marie Brenner, of *Vanity Fair*, when she confronted him with some suppressed facts about his father. "I said to that boy, 'You're crazy!' He said, 'I'm not! Your father walks with a *brace*! He's *limping*!' I went home that night and I really looked at my father. The boy was right. It was then I realized my own father was handicapped."

Later in that conversation, Brenner mentioned Bernard's stint in the orphanage. Milken quickly corrected her. "It wasn't really an orphanage," he said. "It was a sort of home. . . . I prefer to think of it as a boarding school."

Bernard Milken put himself through the University of Wisconsin and law school by selling peanuts and working in a sorority house. He met Ferne there, and married her after her freshman year. Though this was a love match on both sides, it also brought Bernard into a family far more secure than his own. Ferne's family not only owned a business, but the business was profitable enough to send the children to California in the summers. These trips were compelling; some of Ferne's brothers and sisters moved west. At twenty-six, with his degrees in hand, Bernard followed with Ferne.

The Milkens lived first in downtown Los Angeles, and then, after Michael was born, near that part of Melrose Avenue where interior decorators and restaurants now thrive. Lowell arrived in 1948. (The Milkens' only daughter, Joni, was born in 1958, when Michael was twelve and Lowell was nine.) Bernard found a job with an accounting firm, worked hard and lived frugally. By 1953, he and Ferne were ready to buy a proper house, with a proper yard, in a neighborhood of families.

The San Fernando Valley was the inevitable choice. Framed by mountains on three sides, the Valley had been discovered by explorers in the 1760s and purchased from the Indians in the 1840s, but there had been virtually no development for the rest of the century. In 1915, a developer decided to sell "the largest body of land ever subdivided in Los Angeles." To lure potential home-buyers, he held a barbecue. By day's end, two tons of beef had been consumed—and Encino had begun its ascent from a sleepy farm community of one thousand to its self-proclaimed status as "the Beverly Hills of the Valley."

In the 1930s, this image of Encino as a sister city to Beverly Hills, only with better moral values, was craftily nurtured by the chamber of commerce. The chamber's brainstorm was to choose an honorary mayor from its celebrity population every few years, and have him appear at ceremonial events. This slim connection to Hollywood obscured the realities of life in Encino— children traveling to school on horseback well into the 1940s, and the occasional oxcart appearing on Ventura Boulevard as late as the 1950s.

The boulevard wasn't lined with shops when the Milkens moved to Encino, but even then, it was terribly important. In this otherwise progressive suburb, Ventura Boulevard was the closest thing to a demarcation line for Encino's two classes. The wealthy and the famous—Al Jolson, Spencer Tracy, Shirley MacLaine—owned large homes south of Ventura Boulevard on tree-lined streets that led up to the Santa Monica Mountains and, beyond, to Beverly Hills.

The ultimate south-of-Ventura resident was Clark Gable, who bought a twenty-acre hillside spread from film director Raoul Walsh in 1939, just after completing *Gone With the Wind*. For $50,000, he and his new wife, Carole Lombard, got a ranch house, a guest cottage, a barn, orange groves, and rolling fields. Gable savored the privacy; he equally enjoyed the fact that interviewers and photographers came to see "The King" milking cows and gathering eggs. He fled when Lombard died in 1942, but he returned two years later and lived quite contentedly in Encino with Kay Spreckels until his death in 1960.

In the 1950s, Encino's biggest attraction for celebrities was still that it wasn't Beverly Hills. "To live in Encino was a deliberate choice," says Steve Allen, a south-of-Ventura resident who served as honorary mayor in 1961. "We wanted to raise our children in a middle-class environment, and the Valley was middle-class heaven, what people in New York would call 'suburban living.'" The middle-class mentality ran quite deep. "When my son, who was Michael Milken's age, was nine, I used to pick him up at school in a Rolls-Royce," Allen says. "He finally told me, 'Dad, please don't do it again. The other kids tease me.'"

The Milkens knew none of this when they went house hunting. It was merely a matter of economics and circumstance that they found a modest ranch house on a small lot in an undistinguished subdivision on the north side of Ventura Boulevard. In summer, it is blazing hot in these flats—so hot that some visitors are, tellingly, advised, "It gets better after the Jewish holidays."

Across the boulevard, in the shaded hills to the south, an August afternoon seems cooler, almost comfortable; on days when other parts of Encino are sweltering, you can hear the *thock* of tennis balls and the laughter of children in swimming pools. Visiting these adjoining neighborhoods, it's hard not to be reminded of Philip Roth's *Goodbye, Columbus,* and the distance between the muggy apartment where the narrator lives with his aunt and the lush and breezy home of his beloved, just minutes—and light-years—away.

Bernard Milken couldn't have been less interested in finding out what it would take to move his family across Ventura Boulevard. Nor was he keen to be a regular at the Sunday brunch at the Pink Pig on Van Nuys Boulevard, where the cooler fathers listened to jazz piano and snapped their fingers as their children bounced on the padded Leatherette seats. Bernard was a good accountant, he umpired for the Little League, he spent time with his family. It was enough, it was more than enough.

A brilliant son doesn't acknowledge reality, and his family rewards him for it—that scenario is hardly unique. But the denial in this family was of a very high order. Michael Milken never discussed his father's withered leg or his years in an orphanage; from his early childhood, he ignored the obvious, noticing only the below-the-surface value that others might never appreciate.

This lesson in nonjudgmental behavior was reinforced by Bernard's work. Some of his clients were wealthy but irresponsible, jetting off on expensive vacations even when their finances were in disarray. Bernard Milken was the fixed point in their lives: always available, always willing to look at the numbers again in search of a fresh solution.

At tax season, the entire family helped Bernard, and, at an early age, Michael learned some of the unreal qualities of money. For Bernard's clients, money was of primary importance. They were intent on keeping it, the better to preen and indulge. So they weren't shy about encouraging Bernard to be aggressive in his analysis—to create an appealing reality on their tax forms and save them money.

For himself, Bernard Milken was far more risk-averse. Moving close to the edge appalled him; a deeply conservative man, he scorned anything "easy" or "sharp." As a result, he rejected many business opportunities that came his way, not because he didn't think they'd work but because they were "risky." Better, he thought, to make less and sleep peacefully.

Bernard was just as rigid at home. The Milken children, on tight budgets, had to account for every penny. At the same time, they were taught to share—to help others, to participate in school and community activities. But they were never, Bernard insisted, to seek recognition for their efforts.

He took this point of view very far. One summer, the Milkens were driving through the Grand Teton National Park on a family vacation when a guide flagged them down. "We were the umpteenth million visitors, and they were going to honor us," Milken says. "My father told them they'd made a mistake, that it was the car behind us. My brother and I had to push him to accept the free dinner and the raft trip."

The Milken family and his friends were always aware of Michael's intellect, but their reaction was far from awestruck. "My mother is somewhat like Auntie Mame, she has a high energy level," Milken recalls. "She was driving me somewhere, and we had an accident. My head hit the radio knob. I got a small scar." Then comes the family joke: "My mother told me the accident created my intelligence."

Whatever the cause, school seemed remarkably easy for him. From early childhood, he was a math whiz, mastering multiplication in the first grade and algebra and geometry soon after. At ten, his father asked him to help out at tax time. At first, he sorted checks, but he was soon checking the math and assisting in the preparation of the forms.

His academic prowess was never a burden for him. He was, until early adolescence, both fascinated by sports and extremely good at them; at fourteen, having reached his full height earlier than most of his classmates, he made the local all-star basketball team. With girls, he was known as a good dancer, who "could dance close and not count with his lips."

In those years, Milken's literary taste ran to *Thor* and *Silver Surfer* comic books, "stories that made you conceptualize." His real interest was the neatly cataloged collection of pop records that was piled high on his side of the ten-by-twelve bedroom he shared with his brother. He could remember who recorded a song and when, the color of the label, the publisher, and the name of the song on the flip side.

He was equally acute about social distinctions. The north-of-Ventura, south-of-Ventura division may have eluded his father, but it was not lost on precocious Michael Milken, just as it was not lost on the future actress Sally Field or the future superagent Michael Ovitz. When Marilyn Rosenthal LaMonte, a newcomer to the Hesby Street Elementary School, met the ten-year-old Michael Milken, he had lived in Encino for just two years. He was, however, quite the expert on the relationship between geography and status.

"He asked me where I lived," she has recalled. "I said Encino. He said, 'What part of Encino? South or north of the boulevard?' I said I lived in the hills. 'You sit in that group,' he said."

"He slept so little and did so much I didn't think he'd live to be twenty-one," says Harry Horowitz, Milken's best friend since fifth grade. That combination of brains, good manners, social awareness, and enormous energy made Milken successful in every area of school life. He was prom king in ninth and twelfth grades; he was also in the National Honor Society. He wrote a sports column for the school paper, represented Encino in "knowledge bowls," and competed in speech contests. In recognition of his academic work, his zeal for after-school sports, and his participation in service organizations, he received the Junior Chamber of Commerce Award.

But Milken's greatest recognition as a teenager among teenagers came when he was elected head cheerleader, a significant honor at a time when Birmingham High School was a football powerhouse. Here, at last, he was in the limelight. And here, for the first time, he got into trouble—the local paper criticized him for calling for more points when Birmingham was already leading 42–0.

Did Milken really want more of a rout, or was he putting the crowd on? It was hard to tell, for he loved to stage pranks. With a fake machine gun pointing out the car window and Horowitz as his wheelman, he'd race past restaurants and pretend to spray the patrons with bullets. When his physics instructor was absent, he delighted in volunteering to set up the experiments and then, to the substitute teacher's chagrin, putting the ingredients in the wrong order. And during fund-raising drives, he and Horowitz—already famed for their Mel Brooks and Carl Reiner routines—might turn a sales pitch for chocolate bars into an endless dialogue that destroyed the daily schedule for their entire class.

This spontaneity was immensely attractive to Lori Hackel, a quiet, studious, appealing girl who also lived north of the boulevard. She and Michael dated a bit in the ninth grade—his parents drove—and picked up again, more seriously, in the eleventh. "I never spoke out, I never did anything for fear people would look," she recalls. "Michael was free of that, and I envied him."

When the 142 members of the midyear class of 1964 graduated from Birmingham High, Milken was ranked fourth, with a 3.70 grade point average. He wasn't the valedictorian. Nor was he voted "most likely to succeed"—that honor went to Lori. But if he had to settle for "most spirited" and "friendliest," he wasn't crushed. "I was," he says, without irony or boasting, "the male image of my class."

Milken graduated from high school on a Friday in January and, on Monday, enrolled at the University of California at Berkeley. It was the height of the Free Speech Movement, which was, he says, one reason Berkeley was the only school he applied to. "I wanted to experience different things," he says. "I thought you had to go away from home to become an individual, I thought kids who went away matured more."

Though Milken promptly joined Sigma Alpha Mu and became president of the fraternity's pledge class, he wasn't isolated from the anti-Vietnam protests that were a staple of daily life on the Berkeley campus. "SAM wasn't as conservative as many fraternities," he recalls. "I went to certain political rallies. Sometimes members were arrested and I'd have to raise bail, or I'd need to talk with them about what to tell their parents."

It was at his fraternity that Milken first tested his prowess as a financier, investing money for classmates at potentially ruinous rates—he would take 50 percent of any profits, but absorb 100 percent of any losses. He not only made money for everyone, but he found time to serve as exchequer of his fraternity. "A great deal of money was raised," he reports, lapsing into the passive rather than use a personal pronoun. "The facility was upgraded."

He'd entered Berkeley as a mathematics major, but he soon found that math was no more difficult here than it had been at Birmingham High. "I didn't always study methodically, and there was even a time I didn't buy the textbook for a course until the night before the exam," he says. "At two A.M., I realized there was no way I'd get through the entire book, so I just looked at the chapters I thought had the important data." In his sophomore year, he transferred out of math into business. "As you go higher, math becomes more theoretical," he explains. "I was more intrigued to use my knowledge."

That is: to make math make money.

Much later, after he'd banked his fortune, Milken would insist that the last time he knew his net worth was in the 1970s, when he had to produce a financial statement. On the subject of money, he would echo his father, defining it as a by-product of useful work well done. "Money is a very fleeting emotion," he'd say. "I prefer things you can see and touch."

But in his teens, he was quite clear of his ambition—he was going to be a millionaire, and he was going to do it by age thirty. On a visit to his uncle, the former chairman of Hartmarx Corporation, he announced, "I expect to make a success of my life." And, back then, success was synonymous with wealth. At a certain age, he told his wife, you really should have made a certain amount of money. And he knew how he'd make it—by stepping closer to the edge than his father. For this was the big difference between

Michael and Bernard Milken: Michael believed his father was overly cautious, that you could be more aggressive without becoming a hustler or a gambler.

In every other way, Michael Milken did more than acknowledge his parents—he adopted Bernard's philosophy and Ferne's energy as if they were the Ten Commandments. Had he spent more time outside a neighborhood he had known for most of his life, he might have examined those views, changed them, or even rejected them. But he remained in his own little world, believing—as his father had—that as long as he lived right, no one would point a finger at him.

From his new perch, in a home across the boulevard, he would reach across Ventura and honor his parents. Their work ethic, their commitment to community, their refusal to call attention to themselves—in their son, all these would remain the same. As Michael Milken naively imagined his future, only the address would be different.

The year that Milken transferred from math to business, Lori transferred from the University of California at Santa Barbara to major in business at Berkeley. Milken settled into a pasha's routine: a few classes, the frat house, investing during the day, meeting Lori at the library at nine each night. He became president of his fraternity; she was elected president of her sorority. Somewhere else, a war raged.

The catalytic event in Milken's intellectual life occurred in 1967, when he chanced upon one of the five hundred extant copies of *Corporate Bond Quality and Investor Experience*, W. Braddock Hickman's study of bond yields from 1900 to 1943. The prose was arid— "It was pure statistics, not at all like *Catcher in the Rye*," Milken says—so he only read the summaries. He found them more thrilling than Salinger; Hickman's landmark effort suggested that a carefully chosen portfolio of low-grade bonds outperformed bonds with better ratings. For Milken, Hickman provided more confirmation than revelation: "I'd been following these bonds, and I thought they were good risks. What Hickman showed me was that results held up even through the Depression."

It's a commonplace of investing that the stock and bond markets are "perfect"—that is, they have absorbed all relevant information about a company and factored it into the price of the security. In this view of markets, there are no unexploited opportunities. What is, is right.

In the bond market, in particular, it was easy to follow this conventional wisdom. For decades, two bond services—Moody's, and Standard and Poor—had determined which bonds were "investment grade." The designation was important; many fund managers were only allowed to invest in firms blessed with this "investment grade" rating. As a result, companies with lower-rated bonds had a difficult—if not impossible—time raising capital at low interest rates.

Bond traders were not, as a rule, much concerned with the societal implications of the bond-rating system, but then, intellectually, they were not much concerned with anything. Bond trading, like the trust-and-estate departments of old-line law firms, was a place for amiable men who didn't have the mental equipment or the drive for more demanding work. Traders bought "steel" or "oil" for their customers and filed the bonds away. Their biggest challenge was remembering to clip the coupons regularly.

It's not surprising, therefore, that until Michael Milken came on the scene, America's most famous bond trader was a fictional character—Nick Carraway, the narrator of F. Scott Fitzgerald's *The Great Gatsby.* Carraway was bright and urbane, but when it came time to choose an occupation, he lacked conviction: "I decided to go East and learn the bond business. Everybody I knew was in the bond business, so I supposed it could support one more single man."

At Berkeley in 1967, Milken had an insight that would, in time, support an entire firm, overthrow conventional wisdom, and put a great many outsiders in executive offices—the bond services' seal of approval was less than accurate. All Moody's and Standard and Poor seemed to factor into a company's rating was its past performance, as reflected by the ratio of debt to equity on its balance sheet. The rating services didn't seem to care much about cash flow, which, as Milken saw it, said everything about a company's ability to service its debt. And the ratings services weren't even mildly interested in intangibles that couldn't be easily judged, but were crucial to a company's future—bold dreams, ambitious plans, dedicated managers.

Because the criteria used by the ratings services favored well-established, cash-rich businesses, barely one thousand companies were deemed worthy of the coveted "investment grade" designation. Most were well-known, Fortune 500 corporations. None were the brainchildren of blacks or Hispanics or women, few were headed by Jews.

This dichotomy wasn't lost on Michael Milken. "Unlike other crusaders from Berkeley, I have chosen Wall Street as my battleground for improving society," he wrote in an op-ed piece in 1970, two years after his graduation. "It is here that government's institutions and industries are financed."

The New York Times didn't publish his manifesto, but Milken was undeterred. These neglected, little-understood bonds were not just the means to his millions. They were his response to the challenge that Mario Savio and Jerry Rubin had hurled across the Berkeley campus: Which side are you on?

Michael Milken graduated *summa cum laude* from Berkeley. He was elected to Phi Beta Kappa, and to Beta Gamma Sigma and Beta Alpha Psi, honor societies for business and accounting students. He could have gone to any business school.

He applied only to the Wharton School at the University of Pennsylvania, and possibly, though he's not sure about this, to Harvard. But Wharton was his first choice—it allowed students to substitute business experience for some course work, and it rewarded him with a Joseph Wharton Fellowship, worth $1,000.

In August of 1968, Milken celebrated his good fortune by marrying Lori. They avoided the Kahlil Gibran, tie-dye route—the ceremony was at Temple Beth Hillel in Sherman Oaks, the reception was at the Sportsman's Lodge, the honeymoon was in Hawaii. After that large dose of familiarity, their first encounter with the East Coast was a violent shock.

"We arrived in Philadelphia with eleven suitcases at a motor inn that had a manually operated elevator and no phone in the room," Milken recalls. "We rented a car and headed out of town in search of something familiar. When we spotted a McDonald's, we knew we'd found civilization." They rented an apartment near Swarthmore—"The large black water bugs weren't as bad as Lori's screams"—and set about furnishing it. Four hundred dollars later, they were finished, and they turned on the television set to see people who looked very much like them getting beaten by the Chicago police.

At Wharton, Milken signed up for three majors—information

systems, operations research, and finance. As ever, he made an extraordinary impression. Eight months after he arrived in Philadelphia, two of his professors introduced him to the directors of Drexel Harriman Ripley.

Milken relished the provenance of this venerable Philadelphia firm. For their part, the Drexel executives were equally taken with Milken, who'd been described by one of his professors as "the most astounding young man I've ever taught." His assignment that first summer was to make some sense of Drexel's back office, then losing money because of excessive delivery costs. His solution, an overnight delivery system, saved the firm $500,000 a year. The back office was, however, of little interest to Milken—Drexel's research department was his target. Lower-rated, higher-yield bonds weren't much of a focus there, but Drexel researchers were willing to discuss them, and in 1970, as he was deciding where to work full time, they were finishing a report that couldn't have been more favorable about these bonds.

Before Milken made a decision, he factored in his wife's situation. After working as a buyer at a Philadelphia department store, Lori had enrolled as a graduate student in elementary education. She'd also taken an interesting part-time job as a research assistant to a University of Pennsylvania professor writing a history of the institution. She'd made friends in Philadelphia. As much as they'd ever be rooted on the East Coast, Philadelphia was home.

Given all that, Michael Milken was quite happy to accept an assignment as assistant to the chairman of Drexel. Several executive changes later, Milken was asked to research bonds—in the New York office. This job meant a two-hour commute each way, but it was only temporary.

Milken's six-month stint in New York became permanent when, at twenty-four, he was named head of bond research at Drexel. More compellingly, he was given a little capital and allowed to trade. Thus began a streak that is the envy of those who know how hard it is to win consistently—in seventeen years of trading, Michael Milken would have just three losing months.

Trading was, for Milken, a matter of doing his homework and being unafraid to go against the market. New York was more complicated. He was temperamentally unequipped to charm his way through Drexel's tricky politics—not that there was any polite way for one of the firm's three Jews to buy and sell bonds regarded by his colleagues as swill.

Drexel's president soon decided that Milken had to be fired. Charles F. Huber II, then head of the Institutional Department, asked why. "The traders don't like him—he calls on their accounts without telling them," the president explained. Huber pointed out that Milken was on straight salary, with no commissions. True, the president said, but he embarrasses everyone: "After the customers have talked to Mike, they don't want to talk to anyone else." Huber saved Milken's job by convincing the boss that the entire bond department would follow Milken if he were fired.

Milken's lot seemed unlikely to improve in 1973, when Drexel merged with Burnham and Company, a full-service brokerage firm. Fortunately, I. W. "Tubby" Burnham made it a point to meet him. And Milken gave Burnham his pitch.

Most non-investment-grade bonds, Milken explained, were "fallen angels," issued long ago by companies that had—or so the rating services liked to believe—slipped from grace. But it was wrong to think of them as "junk" bonds, for their problems were more about perception than reality. Many of these businesses, Milken believed, were actually quite good. And because of the market's misperception, their bonds were, from his point of view, even better, for they were both undervalued and thinly traded.

Milken did not need to point out the obvious—there was no New York Non-Investment-Grade Bond Exchange, no published record of the daily bid-and-asked for these bonds. No one really knew what these bonds should sell for; no one even knew what they did sell for. All anyone could tell is that bonds originally issued at 100—the offering price for all new bonds—were trading as low as 20 or 30 cents on the dollar. So Drexel's opportunity was really quite amazing. If the firm built an inventory and a customer base, there was potential for plenty of profit—for everyone.

The way Milken talked, it was obvious that he had thought a great deal about these bonds, visited hundreds of companies, devoured untold prospectuses, and read financial reports in his spare time; it was equally obvious, though impossible to contemplate, that he had gone on to master the complex material in the footnotes that even corporate lawyers avoided. Burnham was no fool—he agreed to fund a non-investment-grade bond-trading operation and reward Milken with a bonus agreement that was, though generous, hardly unprecedented on Wall Street.

"Mike's salary was twenty-five thousand dollars," Burnham has recalled, describing a compensation formula that would remain unchanged for all the years that Milken was at Drexel. "I gave him a two-million-dollar position and agreed that, after he covered his overhead, his group got thirty-five percent of the profits. We didn't care how much he made. We got all the rest."

The word soon got around that Milken's department was earning an unheard-of 100 percent return on investment—every year. "I know someone who's even smarter than Jeff Tarr," a friend told one of Laurence Tisch's sons in the mid-1970s. "That's not possible," the young Tisch said, for Tarr was perhaps the brightest young Turk in the arbitrage game. Out of curiosity, Tisch did call Milken, and, without preamble, asked him who held Loew's bonds.

Computerized records didn't exist in those days, and there was no ticker tape to record bond trades and help brokers identify buyers and sellers, but Milken had an excellent onboard computer—without any pause, he rattled off bond owners and prices as surely as if he'd been reading them from a chart. His friend was right, Tisch concluded. Milken really did know who held every bond, at what price he'd bought it, and the price at which he was willing to part with it.

As much as Milken loved trading, he seemed to love research more. In 1975, for example, he called Saul Steinberg, the controversial New York entrepreneur who had become proprietor of an insurance company—not because Milken wanted to sell Steinberg some bonds immediately, but to get a better understanding of the cash flow of Steinberg's company. I don't get it, he told Steinberg; your bonds should be trading higher. They met and talked. Several weeks later, Milken called again. His pitch was courtly: "May I present some bonds for you to buy?" His selection of bonds was impeccable, and Steinberg placed a $500,000 order, Milken's largest institutional transaction to date.

And once Milken had made the sale, he didn't disappear. It was as if he had all the time in the world; he'd spend hours discussing companies with his customers, talking over obscure or bankrupt firms that seemed rich in possibilities. He was inexhaustible. He not only kept the history of the entire high-yield market in his head, he was also a genius at credit analysis—he had merely to look at a company's financials and talk briefly with its managers to get a sense of its prospects and its credit worthiness in the future.

Best of all, Milken had a sense of decorum that was novel and refreshing. Traders can be foulmouthed, sexist, racist, and just generally crude; to compare a Wall Street trading floor to a pro football locker room is, in many instances, to slander the football players. But Milken never cursed or told dirty jokes, never suggested extramarital adventures. And he never oversold; if you asked him about a bond, he told you its attractions, pointed out any negatives, and then, like a gentleman, left it to you to make your own decision.

By 1976, his knowledge, drive, and salesmanship were making Michael Milken a fortune. No one would have known it. Although he now was a father twice over—Gregory was two, Lance had just been born—he still lived in Cherry Hill, New Jersey. He still commuted by bus. And he still dressed like a trading assistant who had decided the only luxury he could afford was a toupee that looked as if it had been welded on. For a man making an estimated $5 million a year, he was quite a study in incongruity.

Milken's colleagues were intimidated by his ability and wealth, so it fell to others to humanize him. In what was either a recognition of his work ethic or an office joke, a retail salesman gave him a miner's helmet with a built-in headlight, ostensibly so he could read more easily on the bus. That this has become a recurring anecdote in books and articles about him annoys Milken no end. "I may have used it *once*," he says, weary of the story. "Buses *do* have lights."

The miner's helmet does, at least, shine light on a larger question: Why did Milken continue to live near Philadelphia? "We looked at apartments in New York, but they were so expensive," Lori recalls, acknowledging her discomfort at spending what was, to her, a great deal of money on shelter. "And Michael actually enjoyed the commute. It gave him uninterrupted work time."

Only illness would make Michael Milken rethink this pattern, and in 1975, illness struck—Gregory had the first of the seizures that would come to afflict all of the Milken children. Michael and Lori had never seen a seizure before. They thought their son was dying; they had no idea that epilepsy ran in her family.

Not that the doctors at their local New Jersey hospital asked. Assuming that Gregory had spinal meningitis, they administered an unnecessary series of spinal taps that doubled him over and shot him full of antibiotics he was allergic to—and, this time, he did almost die. For ten days, Lori wept by Gregory's bedside, while Michael interrogated the doctors.

A month later, Gregory had another seizure. This time, the Milkens took him to Children's Hospital in Philadelphia, where parents were allowed to spend the night in their children's rooms and doctors were capable of identifying epilepsy. Once the diagnosis was made, Milken set about becoming the world authority on the condition.

A year later, Milken had to add a more serious disease to his studies. His father had noticed a swelling on one of his toes, but did nothing about it. The swelling darkened, the toe became painful, but he continued to ignore it. By the time Bernard Milken got around to seeing his doctor, the cancer was already moving through his body.

Michael went on a full-court press. Doctors, of course, were consulted—there was no specialist his father didn't see. Bernard and Ferne also were sent on a trip to Europe, with their sons and their sons' wives tagging along. The diversion was only momentary. Despite everything his son tried on his behalf, Bernard Milken was going to die.

Michael couldn't absorb it. There was something he wanted, and he wasn't going to get it. Impossible. Inconceivable. Michael Milken stymied? In all his thirty years, there had never been a problem for which he couldn't find a solution. There had to be an answer.

And there was. Not for cancer; Bernard was doomed. But Michael Milken had, at least, found something he could do. The idea was outrageous—altruism so egocentric it really wasn't altruism at all—but no matter. The decision, for Milken, was ridiculously easy, practically a no-brainer. To be close to his father and to have his children grow up in a healthier climate, he would move his entire department to Los Angeles.

Fred Joseph, ten years older than Michael Milken, had brushed gray hair and Paul Stuart suits and an easy way of throwing a leg over a chair arm. Add his quick smile, self-deprecating humor, and Boston accent, and it wasn't surprising that some people at Drexel Burnham in the mid-1970s thought he might become the John F. Kennedy of finance. That anyone made the comparison was, in itself, a kind of triumph for Joseph. Even at Drexel, Corporate Finance executives tended to have not only flair but pedigree—and Fred Joseph was the son of a Boston cab-driver.

Joseph had, however, graduated from Harvard, where he'd proved himself a potent counterpuncher on the boxing team, and Harvard Business School. And he had worked at Shearson and Hutton, two higher-ranked investment banks. But he was as much of an anomaly as the bond trader who would become his greatest asset.

Although Joseph had rocketed out of nowhere, he had no great desire to be rich. And although he looked and dressed the part, he could have cared less about an investment-grade social life. He had a 260-acre farm, but it was, he liked to say, "in a part of New Jersey where they don't hunt foxes"—while others socialized, he preferred to shoot deer with his bow and arrow and beat metal into sculpture at his forge.

What Joseph did want was to build, from scratch, an investment bank as successful as Goldman, Sachs. That was a dream of considerable magnitude—and it made him a perfect partner for Michael Milken. Like Milken, Joseph was compulsively competitive. Like Milken, he cared not a whit about Wall Street's low opinion of his firm. Like Milken, he was obsessed with finding an edge. There was even a personal connection: Three of Joseph's four children had epilepsy.

In 1977, Lehman Brothers and Goldman, Sachs underwrote, for a company called LTV, the first bonds issued as non-investment-grade—bonds that were "junk" from day one. Milken examined the deal and found it wanting. (It was; the issue later defaulted and traded as low as 35 cents on the dollar.) Surely, Milken thought, Drexel could do original junk deals, and do them much, much better.

For Fred Joseph, the idea of issuing junk bonds was electrifying. Underwriters of high-grade bonds charged 7/8 of 1 percent for their services; for lesser bonds, Drexel could charge 4 percent. For Milken, the idea was equally exciting—he knew how and where to sell these bonds.

"There was a lot of high-yield activity in the mid-70s," Milken explains. "By '75 and '76, there was a forty-percent appreciation in high yields. By 1977, everyone who had participated had been successful. Bonds that had been forty were now trading at eighty. People had seen that these companies were strong and successful." And people had seen Drexel. "There was competition for this market, there was someone who traded every security we did. But we were the dominant force."

Drexel did six original-issue junk deals in its inaugural year, raising $124.5 million; in 1978, it raised $439.5 million, almost $300 million more than its nearest competitor. Given the immense profitability of those deals, one would think other firms would have rushed into high-yield issues. But just the opposite happened; other firms withdrew, leaving the field clear. "Nineteen seventy-seven, 1978, 1979," Milken would muse, years later. "Back then, life was easy."

Milken chose the High-Yield Bond Department's Christmas party in 1976—a celebration of Drexel's first surge of massive prosperity—as the place to introduce his colleagues to the idea of moving to California. "This time zone will be better for families," he told them. "If a father leaves home at five A.M. or seven A.M., it makes no difference to his wife and children—they're asleep. But leaving two hours earlier means he's home two hours earlier. He'll have a lot more time for his family. And that's better for work, too. The stronger your family life is, the happier you'll be in your job; the person who doesn't have a happy home life or some other positive reinforcement is sometimes looking for too much from his job. If you need every idea applauded, you'll edit yourself, but if you know your wife and kids love you, you might be more willing to suggest new ideas."

With that, his head trader's girlfriend, a recent escapee from New York, stood up and seconded the idea. Soon his coworkers were suggesting cities—Santa Barbara and Newport Beach were the favorites—and wondering when the move would occur.

In 1977, Milken decided that Los Angeles, home to every member of his and his wife's immediate family, was the ideal location. That July, he bought a house—a special house—in Encino. Clark Gable's ranch had been subdivided, but his home was intact, set atop a group of streets that a developer had, predictably, named Clark Gable Estates. Many of the new houses were mock-

Tudor hulks, large as manors, with barely enough space in back for the obligatory swimming pool. The Milken home, which cost $700,000 and was bought without benefit of a mortgage, was the real thing. Set at the apex of a short, dead-end street called Tara Drive, it was not the largest in the area. It did, however, have unique charms: age, trees, coziness. And it had guaranteed privacy—the house couldn't be seen from the street.

That Gable's house was also south of Ventura might have had a certain appeal for Milken. He was a movie buff, and the identification with the confident, virile Gable may have amused him—it is certainly an irony that, a decade later, some of his coworkers were said to have called him "the King." But as he recalls it, the real attraction was prosaic. "What we liked best about the house," he says, "was that it was less than a mile from a good hospital."

Milken doesn't remember much of a debate within Drexel about his plan to move his department three thousand miles from Wall Street. "I mentioned it a long time before we did it," he says, with a shrug. There was certainly little argument in his department—of its thirty members, only two decided to remain in New York, and in both cases, they did so for reasons unrelated to Milken or Drexel.

In Drexel's executive offices, there also wasn't much to discuss. Fred Joseph was just starting to turn the Corporate Finance Department into a moneymaker. Michael Milken was, as he had been for years, making 100 percent of the firm's profits. If the tail wanted to wag the dog, so be it.

CHAPTER THREE

Michael Milken made sure his associates would be happy in Los Angeles. Before the move, there were neighborhood tours, discussions of schools, offers of financial assistance for those buying their first homes. And then, at last, there were photographs taken of the New York office—pictures so detailed that when the members of the High-Yield Bond Department reported for work in their new Century City offices after the Fourth of July holiday in 1978, their new trading room was a mirror image of the old one.

"The first day, a man representing Moveable Feast showed up with sprouts and tuna and whole wheat bread," Milken recalls. "This was a shock to guys who used to watch grease drip from their pizza." But that was the least of the changes brought by the move west. There was, for one thing, no name on the front door. Some have suggested that the absence of a Drexel logo was a conscious decision, a signal of Milken's declaration of independence both from Wall Street and his employer. This was a trading operation, Milken explains; customers had no reason to be there.

He made sure that his employees did, though, working them much harder than he'd suggested when he proposed the move west. As he'd warned them, the day did start earlier in Los Angeles—to prepare for the opening of the markets in New York, he needed everyone in no later than 5 A.M. But for a man who swore that his family was all-important, Milken had an odd habit of working until seven or even eight in the evening. Because he led by example, a few of his colleagues also stayed late, accepting the trade-off of "quality time" at home in exchange for quality money at Drexel.

"A lot of what happened, people brought on themselves," a Milken veteran says. "Mike understood that we were mortal. If you said you needed to have a certain amount of time off, he was quick to accept that. If you wanted to work sixteen hours a day, that was also fine—he took from you what you were willing to give."

There was one additional incentive for Milken's people to give more in Los Angeles, and that was the hiring of his brother Lowell. Brilliant, intense, and impatient, Lowell seemed to have little in common with his older brother. Michael, for one thing, never spoke ill of anyone. "We're not here to sit in moral judgment on our clients," he liked to say, and he extended that blanket acceptance to his employees—when he hired them, he all but announced that the job was for life. "No" seemed not to be in Michael's vocabulary.

Lowell was at least as sensitive and sentimental as his brother. At Drexel, however, people who didn't know him thought he was cold and fierce. Part of that was due to his appearance and manner—he wore wire-rimmed glasses and a toupee brushed to military precision, and he rarely revealed his private side to Drexel salesmen and traders. The Milken foundations were his idea, but his interest in charity didn't extend to business; it was as much a reflection of his character as it was a measure of his legal training that his response to almost everything was "What could go wrong?"

Although Lowell's duties were vague and broad, some of the salesmen and traders were quite sure that Michael's little brother was Big Brother, an all-seeing hatchet man. This soft-cop, hard-cop routine wasn't Lowell's idea, or even Michael's. It was largely a reflection of temperament—Michael had trouble delivering bad news, Lowell had no problem confronting the realities that surface in any business.

Before the move to Los Angeles, for example, Michael had made loans to his colleagues, charging no interest or the prime rate. He kept very casual track of these loans. When Lowell came on board, Michael asked him to make the financial terms clear—so Lowell handed each man a schedule of his indebtedness, his interest, and the dates of his anticipated repayment. Very few were grateful.

Lowell was also the supervisor of the employee partnerships. Following the example of other investment banks, Michael had started these partnerships as a way to help his associates as well as to protect the firm's profits and his own bonus—if his people didn't have to monitor their private investments, he believed, they'd be more inclined to focus solely on their work. For him, the partnerships were just another aspect of an employee-friendly management style: Let us have your excess capital, we'll invest it with ours, and you'll reap the rewards.

That, anyway, was the theory. And in the early days, when the Milkens began loaning money to employees so they could invest, the partnerships worked beautifully. They made money for traders and salesmen, and just as important, they conferred status—an invitation to join one was the Drexel equivalent of being tapped for Skull and Bones at Yale.

And, like Skull and Bones, a Drexel partnership was also a kind of secret society. The only information a Drexel employee could get was about the partnerships he was in. Some people, however, wanted to know how their coworkers were doing, or how other partnerships were performing; Lowell, correctly, refused to say. And that too was not endearing.

If Michael put Lowell in a position that caused him to be disliked, it didn't seem to trouble him—he did it all the time. Because he hated unpleasantness, Michael routinely passed supplicants on to his brother. That was rarely a happy experience for salesmen and traders who sought backing for their investment ideas. Indeed, they had only to appear in Lowell's doorway for him to turn over the papers on his desk. In short order, he would assess the proposition—which, more often than not, was a sure loser—and bluntly reject it. And if he and the employee happened to be leaving his office at the same time, he wasn't shy about letting the man see him locking his briefcases.

Despite the many services he performed for Michael, Lowell wasn't his brother's keeper. Like Michael, he'd graduated *summa cum laude* from Berkeley; he went on to edit the law review at UCLA law school and become a tax whiz at Irell and Manella, a top-drawer Los Angeles firm. There, his greatest pleasure was the occasional tax-study lunch, where a partner would present a problem of immense sophistication. Sixteen people would talk while Lowell listened and thought. And then he would suggest a novel approach that, on occasion, really did unlock the solution.

Lowell found Michael's trading room a loathsome contrast to his law firm. When the salesmen weren't talking business, their conversation veered toward topics—prostitutes, drugs, and gambling—that Lowell found repellent. He was equally unimpressed by the Drexel investment bankers from New York, who struck him as not altogether bright. And although Lowell regarded Michael as a genius and a visionary, it was hard for outsiders to see that; Lowell was the one person who could be direct, even curt, with Michael.

The death of their father, in 1979, might have produced a moment of revelation that led to a closer collaboration, but Michael and Lowell were, by then, very different people. Michael would schedule early morning meetings; Lowell would reply that Michael's hours were insane and unnecessary, and refuse to show up. Michael worked six or even seven days a week and took phone calls at any hour; Lowell made it a rule to do no business at home and only attended weekend meetings under duress. Michael lived in the Valley; Lowell and his wife Sandy bought a seven-thousand-square-foot home in Mandeville Canyon. Michael liked to believe he left the office for every school conference and athletic meet; Lowell really did.

What kept Lowell at Drexel was what lured him to join his brother's firm in the first place: bankruptcies, distressed situations, and real estate. There, everything he knew came into play. Mulling tax structures, government policy, business prospects, and debt obligations was almost like being back at Irell and Manella—only at Drexel, there was the added excitement of being able to commit enormous sums in anticipation of a mind-boggling risk-reward ratio.

"The day after Thanksgiving, my office was closed so I'd go to Drexel," recalls Stanley Zaks, chairman of Zenith Insurance and Milken's cousin. "I'd bring bagels and sit and watch the screen with Mike. It was like going to the theater. I remember Mike calling out to a new guy, 'Here's a security, I think Joe would be interested in it.' A half hour goes by. 'Did you talk to Joe?' Mike asks. The kid says, 'It's a holiday. He's not in the office.' And Mike gives him a look: 'What's the matter, don't you have his home number?'"

Soon, Zaks had seen enough of Milken's abilities and work ethic to introduce him to his friend Steve Wynn. And Milken had, in turn, delighted the Corporate Finance Department by landing Steve Wynn as a client at a time when Wynn needed $160 million for a casino in Atlantic City. In time, he would do much larger financings for Wynn, but he always retained his affection for that first deal—not because it was his debut as an investment banker, but because of its size. Nothing pleased him more in those days than to provide a boost to smart and struggling outsiders; that was service, that was functional idealism, that was what his father would have done.

But the financial markets were changing, and, with the election of Ronald Reagan, revving up for one long, unregulated wallow. In this new Wall Street, traditional alliances were suddenly meaningless. All that mattered was an ability to make money—without concern for risk, without regard for regulation. In this Wall Street, any firm that was first with an idea capable of producing towering yields was destined to roar to the head of the pack.

In 1981, at a brainstorming session, Drexel's Corporate Finance executives found an idea of that magnitude. There was no reason to limit high-yield bonds to small and mid-sized businesses seeking new financing, they concluded. There were also any number of CEOs of public companies who would be interested in financing for leveraged buyouts, or LBOs.

In the textbook version of these transactions, the company's executives buy up all of their company's stock, take the company "private," and, in the process, become owner-managers. The massive debt they've taken on acts as a discipline. They trim expenses, run a lean and mean operation, pay strict attention to their core business, and pay down debt—the LBO is, like the study of Latin, good for the soul. A few years later, the leaner, meaner owner-managers take the company public again. But now they are holding big chunks of equity—and once it's converted to stock, this equity makes them very, very wealthy.

The biggest challenge for the would-be owner-managers is clearing the first hurdle: finding the money to buy all the stock, often at a premium. But what if they didn't need a lot of money? What if their company's existing assets could be used the same way a house is when a would-be homebuyer applies for a mort-gage—as collateral in the transaction? What if all they had to pony up was the down payment?

The junk-bond-financed LBO was a quantum leap in corporate financing—a kind of small-money-down, thirty-years-to-pay proposition. It was certain to be attractive to CEOs and their key associates. But when John Kissick, head of Drexel's West Coast Corporate Finance office since 1975, outlined the idea to the firm's star salesman, it wasn't immediately attractive to him.

"Michael was concerned about the incremental risk," Kissick recalls. "He was afraid that if we expanded too quickly and had bad experiences, the demand for high-yield bonds could suffer a setback. 'Let's be careful,' he was saying. I told him, 'The potential return for investors can be fifty to one hundred percent greater; if we get enough deals going, the investors can live with the greater risk.' He said, 'Okay, as long as we can do LBOs and have no defaults.'"

And Michael Milken, already going full-bore, now acquired another set of responsibilities.

By 1983, backing LBOs had proved to be such good business that a Drexel brainstorming session was dedicated to producing another big idea. Five Corporate Finance executives and five representatives of the High-Yield Bond Department—including Milken—gathered in Beverly Hills that November to figure out a way to harness Milken's muscle to deals that weren't LBOs. They were soon discussing junk bond financing for what were then called "unsolicited acquisitions"—transactions in which one company bought the stock of another until it had acquired enough to become its master.

Such transactions were not new. But investment banks were squeamish about them—the hostility of these takeovers suggested a kind of corporate warfare that wasn't quite respectable. "We prefer not to call them unfriendly takeovers," sniffed Robert Greenhill, the Morgan Stanley investment banker who, despite his firm's high-mindedness, wasn't above wearing suspenders monogrammed with dollar bills. "Just because the management doesn't go along doesn't mean the deal isn't in the best interest of the stockholders, and we would never get involved in a deal that wasn't." Only one investment bank—Goldman, Sachs—cut through such self-serving rhetoric and announced it simply wouldn't represent clients intent on unfriendly acquisitions.

Drexel wasn't too proud for such transactions. And Drexel, as ever, found the edge. In the past, there had been two unshakeable rules in hostile takeovers. One, the deals had generally been bank-financed. The second followed from the first: Larger companies acquired smaller ones.

The 1983 brainstorming session at Drexel stood that tradition on its ear. With junk bond financing involved, it didn't matter if the acquiring company wasn't loaded with cash. What did matter was the balance sheet of the target company—the more cash it had, the more it could contribute to its own demise. "We take a minnow, identify a whale, and then look to its assets to finance the transaction," as a Drexel banker later explained.

Fred Joseph and other Drexel investment bankers were wild about the idea. The potential fees were enormous. So was the satisfaction of routing the competition on Wall Street. As a very senior Drexel executive recalls, the attitude at Drexel headquarters in New York was "Hey, guys, check *this* out."

Michael Milken's position on hostile takeovers financed by junk bonds is harder to pin down. Some corporate finance executives remember that he opposed them. "Mike believed that the Establishment would kill us if we did them," a high-ranking Drexel investment banker says. "We told him, 'That's fine for you to say, your franchise is established, your future is made. But what about us?'" Fred Joseph and others, however, remember Milken as an enthusiastic supporter of the first series of takeover deals. For his part, Milken suggests that he would have preferred to do more of the firm's straightforward financings—like 1983's $1 billion for MCI Communications and $400 million for MGM/UA Entertainment. According to Milken, he often told associates, "If there are never any more mergers or acquisitions, there are thirty thousand American companies to finance, and, if you include the debt of nations, trillions of dollars of securities to trade."

There was another reason why Milken might have opposed Drexel's entry into hostile takeovers. In 1981, he had collapsed at work. An ambulance was called, but he insisted on walking off the trading floor without assistance. Still, for the next few days, he had to wear a heart monitor. Later that week, a friend drove him home. "You're killing yourself, your body can't keep up with your mind," the man said. "Don't worry about me," Milken told him. "It's under control." The next week, although he now had three sick children—his daughter, Bari, born in 1980, was also afflicted with epilepsy—Milken was, once again, grinding away at full power.

There was even a financial incentive for Milken to oppose hostile takeovers—now that he had a franchise, he might have wanted to protect it. That year, after Drexel had declined to buy a building on what may be the most desirable corner on the Beverly Hills strip of Wilshire Boulevard, the firm asked Michael and Lowell to purchase it; they did, then leased it to Drexel for its new Los Angeles headquarters. Over the years, Milken had bought enough Drexel stock to qualify as one of the firm's largest individual shareholders. And in 1983, when Drexel's pretax profits were about $150 million, selling straightforward debt deals and trading bonds earned Milken $123.8 million—a level of compensation that would inspire very few men to wonder, "How can I do better next year?"

Just the ratio of his income to the firm's pretax earnings suggests that Michael Milken was far more important than his senior vice president title indicated. Very clearly, if Milken had said he had no intention of raising money for hostile takeovers, the idea would most likely have died right then. But Milken could never have said that—whatever he privately thought, he was constitutionally unable to tell his colleagues they couldn't pursue their business plans.

And—in 1983, anyway—junk-bond-financed hostile takeovers looked far from crazy to Milken. He saw them for what they appeared to be: the first transactions to come along that were vastly more profitable than daily trading. Back then, he couldn't see that they might attract cash-poor egomaniacs whose skill was self-promotion, not management. Or that they'd produce a class of asset shufflers who accomplished little more than heaping crushing mounds of debt on the companies they shuffled. Or that they would make Washington and Wall Street agree that Milken represented the most dangerous economic thinker since Lenin. In 1983, Milken saw the surface reality: *These deals paid*. And Milken was, by 1983, not good at refusing money and pushing clients into the arms of other firms.

For a man who opposed financing hostile takeovers after 1985—and who begged the firm to stop doing them after Boesky's plea—Milken was shockingly passive about turning his views into corporate policy. Although Drexel bankers have confirmed that

Milken complained hostile takeovers were "taking years off my life," he never refused to work on them and never memorialized his misgivings. For someone who says he opposed hostile takeovers, the evidence is voluminous: For the next four years, Michael Milken sold every deal he was asked to sell.

The first High-Yield Bond Conference was held in 1980. Its attendees fit easily into one room. The refreshments were doughnuts set on a table next to a coffee urn that wouldn't have been out of place in a teacher's lounge at an urban high school. No one could accuse Michael Milken of gladhanding his customers or splurging on entertainment.

By 1984, though, two thousand people were making their way to the Beverly Hilton Hotel for what deal makers, deal seekers, and deal backers saw as the ultimate networking session—a kind of countercultural Bohemian Grove. Here, fund managers and corporate executives pursued clients and jobs, collected reams of prospectuses, and figured out what to invest in next. And here, amid the pitches for money, the glossy handouts, and the expensive dinners, Michael Milken staged his version of Plato's Academy.

Although few understood what he was doing the first few years, Milken's greatest joy at these conferences was inviting educators, professors, and politicians to discuss topics of international importance. He would sit like a schoolboy, intently taking notes as these experts discussed the changing work force, the shrinking globe, and the role of business in creating social change. In his own speeches, he referred often to the challenges these speakers posed; all we are here for, he said, is to make the world better for our children.

But the conference was not all intellectual sermons and corporate presentations. This was the year's only blowout, and Drexel bankers were determined to spend money. Some of the elite took their clients to Valentino's, the best Italian restaurant in Los Angeles and the cellar for several collections of junk-bond-financed wine. Younger clients uninterested in more refined fun were sometimes led to mud-wrestling clubs. And there were two events that were pure entertainment, one for everyone, one for the inner circle of very important clients.

The event for heavy hitters was the cocktail party held at Bungalow 8 of the Beverly Hills Hotel—a private party that Milken never attended. According to the legendary "Madam Alex," some of the female guests there were professionals. Like other facts that Milken considers unpleasant, he finds this implausible.

The other event was the Friday night dinner, an end-of-the-conference celebration. Milken's old Encino friend, Harry Horowitz, had joined him at Drexel, in part to coordinate the conference. With David Dreyfus of Broad Street Productions, Milken and Horowitz wrote the skits and brainstormed the commercial parodies and music videos that introduced the celebrity entertainer.

In 1984, there was an announcement at the conference that dwarfed even the moment when Frank Sinatra stepped on stage as the surprise performer; Drexel was going to back hostile deals. Ronald Perelman, Saul Steinberg, Carl Icahn, and many others perked up. So did Ivan Boesky.

As an arbitrageur, Boesky's business was all about betting on the outcome of mergers and takeovers. Boesky understood what this announcement forecast—a bonanza for the arbitrage game. The more mergers and takeovers, the more opportunities he'd have to place his bets.

But, even better, Drexel's move offered him a new way to step off the sidelines and become a real factor—with very little of his own money at risk, he could now bid for companies, become an owner, call himself a "merchant banker." And if he didn't actually get control of a company, he could, at least, buy enough stock in one so it would get the heebie-jeebies and pay him a premium to sell his shares back and disappear.

As excited as Boesky was by the prospect of big scores ahead, there was some smaller money to grind out. He embarked on this quest right at the conference, pulling some well-heeled Drexel clients aside and asking them if they'd like to do themselves a favor. He'd already snapped up all the CBS stock he could afford, he said, and the price had moved up a bit; if they helped him out by buying another big chunk, the stock would go up much more. At that point, the members of his little group would average out their costs, unload their positions, and make big profits.

There was a beat missing for these men. Anyone buying more than 5 percent of a stock must notify the SEC. If we share profits, we'll have to file as a group, one said—we'll have to reveal our trading. Boesky, who had not waited until this moment to commit his first felony, grinned. We won't file, he said—we'll do this on a handshake. Astonished, the men made their apologies and hurried to tell Milken about Boesky's blatantly criminal proposition. Their warning was unequivocal: Mike, you must not do business with this man.

Maybe you didn't understand what Ivan said, Milken replied, characteristically refusing to judge the arbitrageur.

These investors weren't the only ones who read Ivan Boesky correctly but couldn't convince Michael Milken to turn away from him. A few months later, Boesky called the Milken home on a Friday evening. Lori answered the phone. "Is Mike there?" Boesky demanded, without any pleasantries. Lori explained that Michael was driving around the neighborhood, showing some salesmen he'd been interviewing how much more they'd enjoy life if they traded New York for the Valley. "And you *believe* that?" Boesky hissed. Another wife might have been amused. Laid low after the death of her mother and sick in bed with pneumonia and mononucleosis, Lori heard only the sneer in Boesky's voice.

Around that same time, Boesky had his first conversation with Lowell Milken. In the past, Lowell had a bad habit of not taking Boesky's calls or returning them, but Boesky was contemplating a change in the structure of his company; Michael suggested that Lowell set up a meeting with Boesky, his lawyers, and his accountants. So, reluctantly, Lowell took Boesky's call. At one point, Boesky put his secretary on the line. When the woman was slow to produce his schedule, Boesky went wild. "You fucking idiot!" he screamed. "Can't you do the *smallest* fucking thing right?" And that was all it took for Lowell, like Lori, to resolve to have as little contact with Boesky as possible.

Michael Milken didn't see that Ivan Boesky was, as a Wall Street executive who knew him well once said, very much like AIDS: once he was in your bloodstream, you couldn't get rid of him. Nor did Milken understand that there are only two ways to deal with a man that intrusive. You either take the Lowell Milken approach and refuse to have anything to do with him, or—like Dennis Levine and Martin Siegel—you give him what he wants. Michael Milken, seeking harmony above all, tried to strike an impossible balance. He'd handle Boesky, helping him in some ways, refusing him in others.

So Michael Milken heard the objections of his clients, his

wife, and his brother; that is, he watched as they opened their mouths and let the words fly. But it was too late. In the spring of 1984, although Ivan Boesky showed no signs of completing a single investment banking transaction and had bought not one high-yield bond, Milken took Boesky's constant calls—and, within months, he did him a favor that turned out to be illegal and asked for one in return.

Perhaps if Milken had had time to reflect, he might have turned away from Boesky. But Drexel had, by that time, already achieved warp speed, raising hundreds of millions of dollars for Saul Steinberg's bid for Disney and T. Boone Pickens's raid on Gulf, among others. In this charged environment, Milken was a high-performance machine, best at execution, worst at introspection. There was, for him, nothing to be gained by thinking about such unprofitable issues as character.

That November, after reading an article in *Forbes* by Allan Sloan and Howard Rudnitsky, Lori made an effort to get her husband's attention and slow him down. She had always believed that Michael would do well, and he had. Now she could not only pay her bills, she could satisfy her deepest fantasy—she could buy any hardcover book she wanted. For Lori didn't crave diamonds, wouldn't own a mink, had no thought of collecting art; no one could accuse her of urging her husband to make money so she could put on a show.

And yet here was an article with the unflattering title of "Taking in Each Other's Laundry" and the unsettling news that her husband had made at least $15 million the previous year. It looked as if Michael had assembled a network of buyers and issuers that was dizzying in its interconnections and somewhat terrifying in its collective power. And it seemed this group had only just begun to show its stuff. "Drexel and Mike Milken are running what almost amounts to a private capital market," the authors concluded. "Barring a real financial crash, they are likely to go on reaping the rewards for a long time."

A few nights later, as the Milkens were getting dressed for a charity event, Lori popped the big question: Do we really have all that money?

Yes, Michael replied.

Get rid of it, Lori ordered.

I'm sorry if I'm so successful, he said.

It doesn't look good, she insisted. Get rid of it.

Michael reminded her of the $5 million that he had already given to his foundation, the millions more he hoped to give, and the millions he paid in taxes. But he didn't remind her that when she signed their 1983 income tax return she might have noticed his compensation that year wasn't $15 million but $47.5 million. And he didn't suggest that this year, he'd earn even more–$123.8 million.

Leon Black, just thirty, was brilliant and outspoken and, for an investment banker, eccentric. Unlike most of his colleagues in the mergers and acquisitions game, he wasn't preoccupied with packaging himself in the armor of his trade—he hadn't gone the suspenders-and-yellow-tie route. Nor had he worshiped at the shrine of Schwarzenegger. Black's physical development ended at his jaws. At Drexel, he was called Pizza the Hut, in recognition of his voracious consumption of Italian take-out during the long nights of negotiating.

Black's greater hunger, though, was for deals, and the fees and prominence they brought. He and Peter Ackerman, his counterpart in Beverly Hills, were the Rosencrantz and Guildenstern of Drexel—day and night they labored, teeing up companies, running the numbers, showing some Johnny-come-lately that it didn't matter if he had no money, he was creditworthy, this deal could be done. Then they presented the package to Milken, who, they hoped, would make it all come true.

Black didn't regard himself as Milken's functionary. The press failed to understand that—all anyone ever wrote was Milken, Milken, Milken. But in New York, as other investment banks were exploring ways to attract Drexel clients that didn't involve competing directly with Milken, it was Leon Black who came up with the phrase that left the competition in the dust.

It all began in late 1984, when a Drexel client—in this case, Carl Icahn—was making a run on Phillips Petroleum. Icahn was not someone who came to mind as the owner and operator of a major oil company. His metier was buying enough stock in a company to make a nuisance of himself, and then getting its nervous CEO to buy him out at a premium. He had never taken control of a company; if he got his hands on Phillips, his debt would be hernia-inducing. Unless, that is, his dream was to find himself some $11 billion in hock.

The board and management of Phillips didn't want any part

of this New York greenmailer's hallucination, but to Drexel and Icahn, that was of no concern—true to the spirit of junk-bond-financed hostile takeovers, Icahn would buy Phillips with its own assets. If it succeeded, the next time Drexel could try this same kind of deal with someone hungrier and, possibly, even less presentable than Icahn. This was leveling the playing field, alright; this was the democratization of capital in action.

Still, before Milken went out to sell a single bond, someone was going to have to sober up long enough to commit some hard cash to this transaction. Typically, that's what commercial banks did. But Icahn versus Phillips was light years from a typical deal, and no one much believed the banks would line up to support a lark like this.

Icahn, one of the smartest, cash-conscious operators ever to hit Wall Street, had a solution. Not surprisingly, it involved Other People's Money. Drexel's, in fact—he wanted the firm to make a "bridge loan," which was nothing less than interim financing from Drexel's own capital. That put the ball back in the court of Leon Black, the point man on this deal.

In February of 1985, Black had a better idea—Drexel would write a letter to advise the banks it was "highly confident" it could raise the money for Icahn. There was nothing legally binding about this letter; it was an expression of faith in Milken's ability to raise a fortune for this Drexel client from Drexel's other clients. But because Milken was known to be a maniac about keeping his promises, the simple fact of his involvement might give the commercial bankers all the courage they needed.

Over the weekend, Black presented the idea to Fred Joseph, who was then running the Corporate Finance Department. It seemed like yet another quantum leap to Joseph. Drexel's president agreed that the lack of a legal commitment made the letter an interesting experiment—if it worked, great; if not, nothing significant was lost.

Icahn still balked, this time over fees. He had no interest in paying Drexel ⅜ of 1 percent for committing money he doubted he'd ever have to spend, so he asked Milken to start by raising $1.5 billion of the $11 billion purchase price. That comparatively modest sum was still more money than anyone before Icahn had ever wanted from Drexel. Still, Milken raised it. And, just for the hell of it, he raised it in forty-eight hours.

In the end, Icahn didn't win control of Phillips, but that's not to say he left the match in tears. Along the way, he'd bought $175 million worth of Phillips stock; when he sold it, two and a half months later, he'd earned a tidy $52.5 million profit. Phillips paid him another $25 million in "expenses"—no one wanted to call it greenmail.

Because the "highly confident" letter had demonstrated the awesome power of Milken's sales force and the near-religious faith his clients had in him, Drexel was an even bigger winner than Icahn. Since the Phillips triumph, Black and his M and A team had found half a dozen occasions to trot out the letter. To their apparent unconcern, it had struck terror in the boardrooms of the target companies, forcing restructurings, mass firings, and the sudden appearance of billions of dollars in fresh debt on formerly pristine balance sheets.

Now, where Drexel walked, the earth trembled, and companies scurried to sign on as Drexel clients, the better to keep the "highly confident" letter from their doors. Meanwhile, the money kept pouring in, bringing Drexel the biggest annual profits in the history of Wall Street. So as a new wrinkle in financial engineering, there was no doubt about it—"highly confident" was a stroke of genius.

As an exercise in human relations, however, "highly confident" was something else: an off-putting slogan, a frighteningly blunt statement of an insensitive, don't-give-a-damn corporate culture, a maddening, in-your-face taunt to other investment banks. Bullies and blowhards talked like that, not industry leaders. The real bottom line on the "highly confident" letter was that it rivaled bridge loans for the distinction of being remembered as the most boneheaded, shortsighted, counterproductive financing device of the 1980s.

Until Black concocted this letter, Drexel was a mildly disliked investment bank with one big profit-center its rivals chose mostly to ignore. "Highly confident" made that characterization downright quaint. Very simply, it stripped the intellectual content from the complicated issue of hostile takeovers, giving corporate America a potent emotional incentive to band together. As Andrew Sigler of Champion Paper and the Business Roundtable noted, "Today, thanks to Drexel Burnham Lambert, no company is immune from raids, and no manager can afford to ignore the short-term value of his shares." In a single stroke, Drexel had created a holy war, dividing America into Us and Them—predator and prey, upstart and Establishment.

Milken now finds the mere phrase "highly confident" so repugnant that he speaks of it as if he had never encountered it before. "No one is highly confident," he said, very forcefully in 1991. "There's *always* uncertainty. The person who's highly confident in most cases is the person who's the braggart—he doesn't know what he's doing."

A remarkable opinion, particularly considering that otherwise knowledgeable people on Wall Street believe that Milken—not Black—invented the phrase. Or that he came up with the idea of including it in a letter. Or that his signature could be found at the bottom. Which it essentially was, even though he never signed one.

Wall Street noticed. Soon an investment banker from a rival firm flew out to Beverly Hills. Milken thought he'd been sent to suggest that his company and Drexel co-manage more offerings. That was not the message his visitor had come to deliver. Instead, the man named a company that was one of his firm's prominent clients and hissed, "If Drexel backs a hostile raid against us, you are *dead*, and so is your family."

But Milken was, by now, a dynamo in perpetual motion, unable to slow down or reverse direction. No one could keep up with him. And because his and Drexel's lust for deals had become insatiable, the people who knew him best were coming to feel that he could no longer keep up with himself.

This concern for his welfare was expressed in a very narrow way—his friends and colleagues were terrified that Milken would kill himself in a car. It wasn't just that he was known to be a marginal driver, famed for getting four traffic tickets the first day he was legally allowed to be behind the wheel. There was also the matter of his inattentiveness; when Milken drove, he also tended to read.

That was to be preferred, though, to weekends, when Milken was a more exuberant driver. On the spur of the moment, he would decide to take family and friends to the movies. He'd pile everyone in the car with Kennedyesque abandon, a signal for his passengers to clap their hands over their eyes, slide under their seat belts, brace their legs, and just generally commit their souls to the Lord. Seconds before the start of the film, the car would drift into the parking lot, and the Milken contingent would rush into the theater. More often than not, the only seats were in the very first row. Looking up at the screen from an impossible angle, Milken would exclaim, "Isn't this fun!"

For him, it all was. And it all made sense, even the harrowing trip to the theater. It took six years before friends convinced him not to drive, and the only reason they prevailed was because he finally came to believe their argument that it would cost a great many people he loved many millions if something awful happened to him.

But almost more remarkable than Milken's lack of judgment behind the wheel was his philosophy of driving. "If you can see it, you can make it," he would say, looking ahead to a tiny gap in traffic. When he was approaching a traffic light that looked as if it would be red by the time he reached the corner, he had another stock phrase: "You can't run a yellow light."

It may go too far to regard Milken's terrifying driving or his remarks about it as metaphors. But at least one member of Milken's Encino circle recalls Milken's cavalier attitude about driving in a way that others have spoken of his business practices. "Michael always liked to play the edge," this friend says. "And Michael always got away with it."

CHAPTER FOUR

Eight months after Ivan Boesky was born, the leader of Detroit's "Purple Gang" died. As exits go, this was a splashy one: Harry Millman was shot to death. Although the Boeskys had no link to Millman's criminal enterprise, his murder passed quickly into the lore of the family—the scene of the crime was a restaurant owned by Ivan's father.

All his life, Ivan Boesky craved the highest highs and the lowest lows, either mass acclaim and wealth or an apotheosis as violent and dramatic as Millman's. For some who worked with him or closely observed him, the fact that it took him fifty years to achieve both of his ambitions doesn't suggest his was a divided soul. Evil didn't wrestle with good in him, they say; with Ivan Boesky, evil always prevailed.

Boesky sat on SEC panels when he was committing his most outrageous crimes. He did nothing to discourage his guests at the Harvard Club from believing he had spent years in Cambridge. He charged his investors high management fees and then defrauded them by making some of his most profitable trades through an entity that siphoned their gains to his account; later, in order to pay his lawyers, he may have defrauded his employees by draining $5 million to $10 million out of their salary-and-bonus account. He listed himself as an adjunct professor at Columbia University's Graduate School of Business when he was no more than a guest lecturer. He presented himself as a friend of the powerful when his one true intimate was a mysterious and uncouth Iranian who was on his payroll. He pretended to be a devout Jew while requiring one of his Jewish employees to work on Yom Kippur. He claimed to be passionate about charity while secretly hitting his wife's family up for contributions that could be given in his name. He posed as a devoted husband when he was pursuing many other women.

How did Ivan Boesky evade discovery for so long?

It wasn't because he had genuine financial acumen. Ivan was no Carl Icahn or Warren Buffett, a key associate explains; he understood transactions, but he didn't know when to sell his positions in one field and buy in another. His signature—huge stock purchases at a critical moment in a deal—turned out to be a function of information, not genius.

Nor was Boesky successful because of any deceptive charm. Employees say that he was impossible—"a raving maniac"—when he was doing well, and that it took adversity to make him tolerable. His wife describes him as an "iceman" to outsiders and secretive even within his family. Her sister, Muriel Slatkin, long ago told anyone who asked—and many who didn't—that he was "an arrogant and avaricious piece of sewage, the worst kind of bully." In 1984, then-Congressman Tim Wirth had a casual meeting with Boesky; his revulsion was physical. "We walked out of the conference room, looked at one another—and went 'ooof,'" Wirth's colleague recalls.

If wisdom about finance and a beguiling veneer don't account for Boesky's success, a lack of conscience does. Boesky lied. He had no problem with lying. He was adept at it—Boesky, lying, attracted more positive attention than more talented men who told the truth.

Boesky lied so often that, in the end, his very identity was a lie. But that is to apply a moral judgment to a man motivated by consistently pragmatic considerations. It would be more correct to say that Boesky was an actor playing a role. It was an exhausting performance—he had to maintain his persona for as much as twenty hours a day—but it was a satisfying one. It gave him recognition, money, and power; each day he wasn't caught, he won another Oscar.

As an investor, Boesky was a crank, a crook, an impostor; as an actor, he was authentic. For six weeks in 1975, he performed in a revival of *Abie's Irish Rose* in a downtown New York theater. In 1980, he had the lead role in a reading of *The Man in the Glass Booth*. Those performances sealed his love of the stage; he became a trustee of the New York Shakespeare Festival.*

In 1982, Boesky auditioned for his biggest role, and he got the part—he became a Drexel client. In 1983, Drexel did its first Boesky transaction, underwriting $96 million in debt. Around the same time, he and Seema invested in Reliance Capital, a private fund formed by Drexel and Saul Steinberg, with Michael Milken, Steve Wynn, Victor Posner, and Meshulam Riklis's daughter Marcia among the limited partners.

Tall and sharp-featured, with striking china-blue eyes, Seema Boesky seems like an overdressed suburban mother. In fact, she is a rich and willful striver who, in the mid-1970s, bankrolled her husband's first business. She was Ivan's first and most faithful cheerleader; her dream, she says, was for him to be regarded as an American Rothschild. To her, Michael Milken wasn't someone the Boeskys' friend Jacob Rothschild would ever receive—she was, she insists, an unwilling member of Reliance Capital.

It was quite uncanny. Michael Milken's wife hated Boesky. And, without even meeting her husband's new idol, Ivan Boesky's wife counseled him not to do any business with Milken.

In 1983, when Michael Milken first thought seriously about Ivan Boesky, he saw what most of Wall Street did—the king of the arbs. Such a man would make an excellent client. First, for the commissions Drexel could make on his giant stock trades. Second, for the investment banking fees Drexel could charge as Boesky bought companies and became a merchant banker. Third, for the window Boesky could provide on Wall Street. And, not least, for all the junk bonds Boesky might buy once he abandoned his riverboat gambler mentality and settled for a more predictable yield.

None of that came to be.

Boesky did most of his stock trading away from Drexel. He never completed a transaction. He was more intent on gathering

---

*In 1987, when Boesky was about to be sentenced, he solicited a character reference from Joseph Papp, founder of the New York Shakespeare Festival and the Public Theater. "As Marc Antony found Caesar, I found Boesky faithful and just in his dealings with me," Papp wrote the judge. "He kept his word and followed through on his promises."

information than sharing his insights. And he consistently refused to buy junk bonds.

And yet, long before there was an exchange of illegal favors, Boesky was getting far more attention from Drexel than clients who generated much larger fees. After President Reagan signed a bill liberalizing the laws regarding savings and loans in 1982—a regulatory change that then-Vice President George Bush thought would pump $40 billion in increased income to Americans over the next decade—a number of Drexel clients told Milken salesman and S&L expert Jim Dahl that they were interested in acquiring a California bank. Dahl did a thorough study, and concluded that Financial Corporation of Santa Barbara, owner of Santa Barbara Savings and Loan, was "the best acquisition candidate."

Dahl offered it only to Boesky, who leaped at the opportunity. Fortunately for the American public, Boesky didn't get control of an S&L with its vast, government-insured leverage. Not that he was actually turned down by the regulators—they just allowed Boesky's application to languish, without ever formally rejecting it.

While Boesky was still an active candidate for ownership of this S&L, he looked for a way to acknowledge Dahl's help. Boesky's idea of a reward was, Dahl says, to invite him to join his illegal network. Boesky was then accumulating stock in Gulf, and, as usual, he had bought so heavily he couldn't buy any more. And, as usual, Boesky had a criminal solution to this dilemma—Dahl would encourage his clients to buy Gulf. After the stock had run up, Boesky suggested, he would be quite happy to split the profits with Dahl and Dahl's clients; should there be losses, Boesky said he'd absorb them all.

Dahl, then making $3 million a year and not entirely dissatisfied with his prospects at Drexel, says he immediately reported this conversation to Milken. According to Dahl, Milken did not tell him, "That's crazy—what Ivan wants you to do is against the law." Instead, according to Dahl, Milken said, "That's crazy. If Gulf goes down, Ivan won't be able to make it up to anybody—he'll be broke!"

Milken doesn't remember either version of this conversation. But anyone's memory of this particular episode is less important than its implications. For the arrangement that Boesky proposed is eerily similar to the one that would later appear in Milken's plea bargain.

Undeterred by his S&L setback, Boesky plunged deeper into a relationship with Drexel in January of 1984. Fred Joseph didn't want the firm to buy a 1 percent stake in his arbitrage fund for $1.1 million, but to comfort Boesky, he asked Milken and the High-Yield Bond Department to invest. The conflict-of-interest possibilities were not large; years later, when it seemed shrewd to sell the position, the profit was $2 million, a trifle in Drexel dollars. Still, the closeness to Boesky's operation doesn't suggest that anyone at Drexel was very sensitive to appearances.

Dealing with Boesky, everyone at Drexel seemed to know, was a matter of give-and-take; the investment of a mere million dollars put the firm in excellent position to make many millions more. And not in the distant future, either. On January 23, 1984, as Drexel was about to raise money for the new Boesky fund, investment banker James Schneider sent Fred Joseph and Michael Milken a memo proposing a new fee structure. "Ivan seeks a quick response," Schneider suggested. "This is the time to raise our fee to two and a half to three percent for the debt placement [of some $50 million] and also charge three percent for the ten million dollars of Preferred Stock we seek to sell."

Boesky balked at the fee increase, and so, that April, Drexel placed $82 million of debt for him at the old rate of 2 percent. The hope was that Boesky would, with this concession, use Drexel as his primary investment banker. In the spring of 1984, this was something Boesky was happy to do—with Milken in his corner, he could see himself effortlessly snatching up undervalued companies and making a fortune.

Two weeks after Boesky got his $82 million, Boesky took the first step: He formally hired Drexel to raise another $80 million so he could acquire a company named Scott & Fetzer. In May, however, Scott & Fetzer turned its back on his offer. Rather than pursue a hostile takeover, Boesky dropped out of the bidding.

Still undeterred, Boesky asked Drexel for $70 million in financing so he could make a run at *U.S. News & World Report*. There were only three weeks left before bids had to be submitted; Drexel bankers worked frantically to have Boesky's ready. The night before bids were due, the Drexel banker masterminding the transaction flew to Los Angeles. But his 5:30 A.M. meeting with Milken never happened—a Boesky executive called to say there would be no bid. Boesky had explored buying the company not because he was passionate to own it, the Boesky executive said, but for a tax loss; when he realized it wouldn't be large, he lost interest. Fuming, the Drexel banker returned to New York and "thanked" Joseph for giving him the assignment.

Busy, busy, busy—and that was just the surface activity. On a more intriguing level, Milken was about to begin a series of accommodations for Boesky that would result in a smorgasbord of securities offenses. But for all the guilty pleas, Milken and Boesky rarely agree on the origins or facts of their crimes.

Some facts are indisputable. In 1980, Victor Posner, a perk-loving Drexel client who later became close to Milken, had bought more than 20 percent of an electrical contracting company named Fischbach. At that time, he signed an agreement that he wouldn't increase his position beyond 25 percent unless another bidder acquired 10 percent of Fischbach stock and filed a 13(d) report—a statement that the buyer has purchased more than 5 percent of the company's stock—with the SEC. Late in 1983, Executive Life Insurance, headed by Milken's friend Fred Carr, did just that.* Posner claimed that the Executive Life purchase voided the standstill. Fischbach, however, insisted it was still in effect.

Milken's response was to buy Fischbach stock. So did Boesky. Soon he too made a 13(d) filing. Now Fischbach could no longer insist that its standstill agreement with Posner was still valid.

Boesky has told the government that he accumulated Fischbach stock at Milken's direction. Milken disagrees: "I'm sure I told Boesky that it seemed like a classic arbitrage situation, in that you had two potential buyers of the company's stock." But as Fischbach and Posner continued fighting and litigating, the typical scenario of a classic arbitrage situation—a bidding war—didn't unfold. In this case, the price of Fischbach stock plummeted.

Boesky began to complain that it was all Milken's fault. And more: that Milken should make up his loss.

---

*The SEC investigated Executive Life's investment in this transaction and found it innocent. The insurance company, it turned out, invested in a number of Posner deals.

"Blaming his problems on someone else—that wouldn't be an unusual thing for Boesky to do," Milken has said. "It's not unusual for many people in the investment business to do this. However, few, if any, have the tenacity of Mr. Boesky."

Milken agreed to help Boesky make up his losses through other investment opportunities—a practice that's hardly unprecedented on Wall Street. But such an agreement is supposed to be recorded on the books of each firm. Here, no official record indicated that Milken had agreed to recommend securities with the understanding that Drexel would guarantee Boesky against loss. And without such a record, this parking arrangement—which continued for almost two years—was a clear violation of the securities laws.

"To deal with Michael was as simple as a phone call. We're thinking of this, we need to finance it, what do you think? He'd say, 'It sounds like two hundred fifty million. Go ahead and have the lawyers write it up.' I would call my attorney and tell him to prepare a document, and a week or two later, it would be over. Bang. *Period*."

But when Steve Wynn, the chairman of some of the most successful casinos in Las Vegas, looked back on Milken's career in 1989, it wasn't the $1.65 billion in financing that he remembered. "The first thing he would always ask me is, 'How's your wife? How are the kids?' And Michael's attention to personal information wasn't unique to me, because I've discussed this same peculiarity with other fellows who have done business with him. Everyone always was amazed how Michael seemed to have an almost complete grasp on the details of everybody's personal life. I've never had the feeling that it was because it served his purpose in business. I've always felt it was because he had a very sincere and genuine personal interest in people."

That personal interest was long-standing and deep. The casino owner helped Milken get big-name entertainers for the Drexel bond conferences and, later, became partners with Milken in an investment group that included singers Lionel Ritchie and Kenny Rogers. So when Wynn was ready to make a logical transition—from Las Vegas to Hollywood—Michael Milken paid close attention.

In the spring of 1984, Wynn's initial interest was in Walt Disney Productions, a bleeding hulk with a great name and management that was too unimaginative to exploit it. To help him evaluate Disney, Milken sent Wynn information about two other entertainment companies, MCA and ABC. The implicit message was that Disney was a comparatively poor investment. Wynn understood—he spent $91 million to buy 2,214,800 shares of MCA.

When Wynn took that position, there were vague rumors about MCA in the air. MCA chairman Lew Wasserman had had some health problems; it was thought that he might be willing to sell his stake in the company. And Wynn had an in—he was a social friend of Felix Rohatyn, the Lazard Freres partner who was on the MCA board. On the theory that something could happen and that he might cut to the head of the line, Wynn's investment made some sense.

But if Wynn thought he was going to mount a takeover campaign, he was seriously deluded, for Wasserman wasn't likely to be swept away by a mere casino operator. Wasserman was famously tough and well-connected, and his board of directors was in his pocket; in an industry that thrived on sudden power shifts, he alone was secure. He had seen whiz kids like Wynn before—they were breakfast. "Lew Wasserman is the most powerful and influential man in Los Angeles," Milken said, years later. "In 1984, no one in the investment business would have thought Wynn could do something to MCA."

For all that, Milken sat back in late June as his friend and client Merv Adelson, acting at Wynn's request, alerted Wasserman that Wynn held 4.9 percent of his company's stock. Wasserman did not pace the floor nights worrying about a Milken-backed raider. Instead, he turned the matter over to Felix Rohatyn. "At four point nine percent, we welcome you—at five point five percent, you are the enemy, and it will be violent," was the message that Wynn says Rohatyn conveyed. According to Wynn, Rohatyn delivered a second message—"That was Marty Lipton talking"—clearly intended to let him know Wasserman had brought in the biggest name in antitakeover law.

The king of Las Vegas found those to be fighting words. In a sudden loss of proportion, he decided he wasn't about to take this lying down. And, maybe, he wouldn't have to. On a plane, Wynn had found himself sitting next to Jules Kroll, the corporate investigator. Kroll mentioned that he'd once been hired to investigate Wynn. That gave Wynn an idea: He hired Kroll to investigate Wasserman, and soon had ten volumes of material. And

Wynn had Milken. "When they threatened me," Wynn recalled, "I said, 'This isn't Russia,' and I went and got big brother."

But in the summer of 1984, Milken, though no less head-strong than Wynn, wasn't going to back *any* run on MCA. Fortunately, Wynn was a friend—he would understand. Unfortunately, his understanding might cost him a fortune. There was no buyer crazy enough to want to take Wynn out in one block sale. The only way to sell without dramatically depressing the stock price was to dribble it out into the market, chunk after chunk.

A friend in need—how could Milken not respond? And so, as Wynn assured *The Wall Street Journal* he was hanging on to his MCA position, Milken began quietly selling some of it to Ivan Boesky, who often bought stock in communications companies. He never told Wynn the buyer's identity.

Soon enough, Boesky was bored by MCA. Worse, as he began to sell his stock, the price fluctuated. Once again, Milken's most contentious client was moaning that he was losing money. And, once again, Milken guaranteed him against loss. Deeper and deeper went the obligations.

There were other transactions, most on the same theme—in the interest of what he thought of as customer satisfaction, in the pursuit of what he regarded as an orderly market, Milken reached to the most darkly shadowed patch of what was then regarded as a gray area. For him, though, this activity wasn't particularly shady. "There was no cheating of the Fischbach shareholders," he has asserted, to cite a representative opinion. "The only people who were hurt were the Posners, who paid too much for Fischbach."*

But the government wouldn't have given Ivan Boesky a sweetheart deal for turning in a man who parked stock and caused little economic harm. In the 1980s, parking wasn't uncommon on Wall Street; when lawmen stumbled onto it, they generally handled it as a regulatory matter, not as a criminal offense. So when Boesky was caught, he had to give the government something sexier—and in 1986, there was no better way to push the prose-

---

*Judge Kimba Wood, who sentenced Milken, ruled that he had caused no economic loss to the Fischbach shareholders.

cutors' hot buttons than to suggest that Milken shared inside information.

Boesky's accounts of the Occidental Petroleum/Diamond Shamrock and MGM/Turner Broadcasting transactions looked like textbook cases of insider trading—but prosecutors could never prove that Drexel's "tips" occurred before public announcements of these proposed mergers. Insider trading wasn't, however, Boesky's only major blast at Milken. He also told the government that Milken had directed him to buy shares of Pacific Lumber after Charles Hurwitz, a Drexel client, had announced his intention to buy that company.

For the SEC enforcement lawyers and assistant U.S. attorneys who investigated these transactions, this was the most damning of Boesky's charges—if true, it was an instance of Milken blatantly screwing his own client. For by purchasing shares, Boesky helped drive up the price of Pacific Lumber. Because Drexel's fee was tied to the purchase price, the more Hurwitz paid the more Drexel made.

Milken has argued that the government and Boesky's theory of this transaction is absurd. Hurwitz was a prickly customer with a reputation as a greenmailer—he was likely to walk away from the deal if the price went too high, and then, instead of collecting $20 million from Hurwitz, Drexel would have made nothing. As Milken tells it, Boesky couldn't have played any useful role for him. If anything, he says, he did better with Boesky miles away from this stock.

Still, one could understand that Milken might want to give Charles Hurwitz an uncomfortable moment or two. Hurwitz looked cold as ice—black hair slicked-back, expressionless eyes, a mouth that appeared not to have smiled in decades—and he had a personality to match. He flew commercial, and coach at that. His limousines, he liked to say, came in an unusual shade of yellow and had lights on top. For a native Texan, he had uncommonly little flash.

Hurwitz had moved slowly up the food chain of corporate clients and, as the owner of Simplicity Patterns, he had at last acquired a company with a delightful cash flow. Once he commandeered the Simplicity pension fund, he was in an even more delightful position. Now, as chairman of Maxxam, Hurwitz was—almost—the ideal Drexel client. He bought junk bonds. He knew Milken. He had money to invest. All he needed to join the club was to swallow a whale. For this purpose, Drexel raised a pool of capital for him. The only question was: What to buy?

Salomon Brothers had shopped a company called Pacific Lumber to more than one hundred prospective buyers; none was enthusiastic about the company at a high price. Hurwitz knew nothing about harvesting redwoods, but he was willing to bid higher than any competitor, and there was every hope his first acquisition might be a friendly one. Drexel wrote a "highly confident" letter. And on a pleasant day in September of 1985, Boyd Jefferies, the broker who often assembled blocks of stock, called Hurwitz to offer him $15 million in Pacific Lumber stock—at $4 a share *less* than it was selling on the New York Stock Exchange.

So much happiness apparently went to Hurwitz's head, for he balked at paying Drexel the fee it requested. Drexel—not Milken, but the Corporate Finance Department in New York— wanted warrants entitling it to buy 500,000 shares of Maxxam. Hurwitz didn't want Drexel anywhere near those shares. He was quite insistent, and the deal looked about to evaporate—or so Hurwitz threatened when he called Milken. That soothing monotone from Beverly Hills worked wonders, and Hurwitz eventually agreed to give Drexel warrants that could be transformed into 250,000 shares of Maxxam.

But then, on the horizon, loomed a familiar figure. Tall, thin, even less attractive than Hurwitz—here came Ivan Boesky, suddenly desperate to harvest redwoods in northern California. He'd already made one foray into Pacific Lumber, buying and selling a splinter's worth of stock through Jefferies before Hurwitz announced his intention to buy the company. Hurwitz made his announcement when Boesky was out of the country. In his absence, his chief analyst, Lance Lessman, saw the deal as a bad bet—Hurwitz had never completed a transaction. If he aborted this one as well, the stock price of Pacific Lumber might drop as much as ten points. On that logic, Lessman saw profit coming from its fall, and he shorted the stock.

Boesky heard of this and—he says—conferred with Milken. He then ordered his traders to buy shares of Pacific Lumber, thus canceling out the short. Lessman did more analysis, confirmed his initial impression, sold the Pacific Lumber stock that Boesky had just bought—and shorted it a second time. Boesky returned to the office, and, again, ordered his traders to cover the short.

You're wrong, Lessman told Boesky.

To show him why, Lessman created a strongly reasoned six-page memo that might have convinced any honest arb to short Pacific Lumber.

Boesky read it, rejected it, and gave his trader another order to buy. Lessman then made one last effort to stop Boesky.

You've got sixty seconds to make your case, Boesky said.

Lessman did, telling him exactly how many points the firm stood to make or lose in the various approaches.

And you'd be dead *wrong*, Boesky snapped, glaring at Lessman.

Boesky went on to buy more heavily, eventually filing a 13(d) statement with the SEC to indicate that he owned more than 5 percent of the company.

With that, Hurwitz sweetened his offer. Soon there was a happy ending for everyone. Boesky made a marginal profit, but he won his bet with Lessman. Hurwitz got the company—though he had to pay $4 more per share than his original offer. And Drexel's fee rose a bit as well.

Was Charles Hurwitz—as the government alleged—defrauded by Milken? If so, he never complained. For a man who was portrayed as a Milken victim, he was a loyal client for years to come.

In the summer of 1990, when his probation officer asked Michael Milken how he and Boesky came to form a criminal alliance, Milken characterized himself as overbusy and distracted and dominated by Boesky—as a victim. Between 1984 and 1986, Milken said, he and his associates traded in seven thousand securities and carried two thousand positions each day. During that period, Boesky called "thousands of times . . . yelling and screaming and accusing."

Boesky, he had come to feel, was an acute judge of character who knew how to exploit everybody's Achilles' heel. And Milken now believed he dimly recognized his own. He didn't confess to greed. He didn't talk about a drive to become the richest man in the world while insisting on the right to pass through life as an anonymous private citizen. He didn't admit to a need to control every player in every deal. He didn't even acknowledge the common failing on Wall Street, a passion to prevail in every transaction.

His weakness was, Milken implied, the product of a deep

insecurity. He needed to be needed. He was the Candy Man—in a dysfunctional world, he'd make everything right for everybody. In essence, he agreed with John Gutfreund of Salomon Brothers, who said, "Milken thought he was in the church business, but he was in the money business."

"I had a hard time not taking care of people," Milken told his probation officer. "In my desire to please customers, I went too far. I personalized too much. I had to be all things to all people. I've always preached that wealth comes from solving the needs of society and is not an end in itself. It's hard to reconcile what I've said with my behavior."

His behavior with Boesky, he concluded, was the result of the client's incessant assault: "The easiest thing was to say, 'I'll make it up to you.' Then I could get on to three or four calls on hold and two people standing nearby waiting to talk to me. I just got him off the telephone and didn't hurt anyone. . . . I believed so much in what I was doing, and that it was right and just . . . I concentrated on what I wanted to do, and thought, 'Okay, if you want to make money, I'll find you money.'"

Boesky's employees agree that Boesky was infuriating and a nudge. But, they point out, Boesky never really made money with Milken. In groping for an explanation, they conclude that, perhaps, he wasn't supposed to.

It wasn't until after Boesky's plea, these employees say, that they understood Boesky was merely a pawn on Milken's "to-do" list. Ivan worked for Mike, one Boesky associate said—theirs was a pusher-addict relationship. Milken had the buying power, Boesky the hunger for size.

So while it thrilled Boesky to get insider information from Martin Siegel and Dennis Levine and then make tens of millions, Milken could give him something that those middle-level criminals never could. It didn't matter that his relationship with Milken was an exercise in frustration. There was one big consolation—as he once told Levine, "Michael Milken is the key to the capital markets."

Boesky may have been sustained in his unprofitable relationship with Milken by that realization. And he may well have hoped that, after years of trading small favors, he'd collect in one giant swoop. If this was his scheme, he played Milken perfectly—in

1986, the fund that Milken financed for Boesky gave him a billion dollars of buying power at ten-to-one leverage.

As Drexel bankers worked on this new fund early in 1986, it didn't bother Boesky that they believed it would be three times bigger than was prudent. Or that Seema begged him not to do it. Or even that his most trusted employees proved beyond any argument that all he had to do was break even in any given year, and his expenses and overhead would wipe him out. They didn't understand, none of them understood. Aloft on the incredible lightness of leverage, Ivan Boesky felt truly and deeply alive.

CHAPTER FIVE

The first call to Ned Kennan came in 1983. As long as anyone could remember, it had been all but impossible for Drexel to recruit at the better business schools; suddenly, Wharton students were camping out in the halls, begging for jobs. "We want to know: what *is* Drexel?" Chris Anderson, a puzzled managing director, asked Kennan. "Who are we? What are we becoming?"

Anderson explained that Drexel had already hired two consulting firms to answer those questions, but he was interested in adding Kennan to the firm's growing roster of advisers. Kennan, he had heard, was eclectic, maybe even crazy. Such a man might understand Drexel Burnham.

Dr. Ned Kennan was not, on the surface, at all "eclectic." If anything, he was exactly what people who have never seen a mental health practitioner think one looks like. He had an accent. His beard was trimmed to look like the master's. He wore twinkling wire-rimmed glasses. He smoked unfiltered Gitanes cigarettes. He wore tweeds. It wasn't until Kennan spoke that he smashed through stereotypes—he mixed mythical references and street talk, boasted that he'd worked in Israeli intelligence for five years, and openly relished his access to corporate boardrooms.

Ned Kennan was an untapped resource throughout 1984. Then came the watershed event in Drexel's history—the decision to back Boone Pickens in his bid to take over Unocal, the fourteenth largest company in America, then topping $11.5 billion in annual sales.

Pickens, a distant relative of Daniel Boone, was a showman of the first rank. When he railed against corporate jets and top-heavy management structures of Big Oil, he sounded like Billy Graham describing hell; when he had to talk about his own values, Pickens liked to dwell on his boyhood paper route ("one hundred papers in forty-five minutes, using both hands") and his down-home common sense. To hear him tell it, he was just an updated version of Robin Hood—a champion of the little guy whose sole concern was something called "shareholder value."

New York loved Pickens. He was amusing, he looked good on the cover of *Time*, and he made investment bankers so rich that Mayor Edward Koch honored him when his contribution to the economy of lower Manhattan passed the $50 million mark. At Drexel, as Corporate Finance licked its collective chops in anticipation of Boone's next takeover effort, Fred Joseph found no reason to disengage from this battle.

To Joseph, Unocal was a classic energy company squandering its resources—a sorry contrast to Drexel, which had no limousines and no corporate apartments and yet somehow managed to produce $2 billion in pretax profit. As Joseph would later admit, he very clearly didn't understand the real issue here.

Lowell Milken did. Why are we backing this guy? he asked. He goes home and looks like a folk hero, we get the shit kicked out of us.

Lowell Milken seemed to be the only Drexel employee to understand that the gentleman administering those kicks was no ordinary specimen of entrenched management. Fred Hartley, the sixty-eight-year-old chairman of Unocal, was bloodless, watery-eyed, foul-mouthed—and adamant about running the company until he graduated to that nineteenth hole in the sky. Signs of his domination were ubiquitous. His yacht was named *My Way*. He'd had the corporate plane opened up—at a reported cost of $50,000—so his piano could be installed. Asked when Unocal would have a woman on its board, he remarked that he "had one lady in mind, but she died." After the great Santa Barbara oil spill, he wondered why people were so upset about the fate of a few birds.

Fred Hartley met Michael Milken once, at a charity lunch.

On that occasion, Milken recalls, Hartley launched into a tirade against Mexican women—he called them wetbacks—who were, he claimed, lowering morals in California by screwing everyone in sight. "In one hour," Milken says, "Hartley had attacked every race and every business that didn't take its money from the earth."

That sounds like Hartley—he loved to drill people and he loved to drill for oil. When anyone asked about the fortune he was plunging into a risky oil-shale plant in Colorado, he cursed the questioner and just spent more, until he'd pushed almost $1 billion into this sinkhole. So to describe Fred Hartley as one of the biggest pricks ever to occupy a chairman's office was to give him enormous pleasure.

Fred Hartley didn't like junk bonds. "Paper that's been run through a printing press," he called them. He didn't like LBOs or hostile takeovers. "A so-called legal method of stealing," he suggested. And he didn't like Michael Milken. "He doesn't invent anything, doesn't create anything," he said. "He just takes money from party A and gives it to party C, and he's in the middle as party B, getting a fee for having arranged the transaction. And if the deal fails, he brings in party D, which is the government of the United States, the taxpayers, to repay party A—what a racket!"

It follows that Fred Hartley didn't like investment bankers very much—in fact, he thought most of them were thieves. But he took to Dillon, Read, the whitest of the white-shoe firms, and Nicholas Brady, its chairman. Brady had never been described as the brightest bulb on Wall Street, but he was most assuredly the best-connected, and in the spring of 1985, he put his Rolodex at Fred Hartley's disposal. Very quickly, Unocal had hired some powerful Washington allies—former Senate Majority Leader Howard Baker, Jr.; former Assistant Secretary of the Treasury for Tax Policy John Chapoten, and the public relations firm of Hill and Knowlton.

Whether Brady shared his views on Boone Pickens with his good friend then-Vice President George Bush is not known, but Brady was certainly visible in Washington. "The first time I heard 'junk bonds' used in a negative sense was in 1984, when Clark Clifford, who was a director of Phillips Oil, came to my office to lobby me," a former congressional aide recalls. "That was a big deal—it was like your grandfather and the President rolled into one showing up to tell you these bonds were being used to destroy fine American companies. I thought that moment would be hard to beat. Then I saw Nick Brady lobbying for Fred Hartley at the Senate in 1985. As a former senator, he had rights to the cloakroom, and, believe me, he used them."

That spring, the Business Roundtable—an association of two hundred CEOs who form a kind of corporate version of the College of Cardinals—also joined the fray. Its position on "shareholder value" had long been clear. A corporation, it noted in its 1981 Statement of Corporate Responsibility, "must be a thoughtful institution which rises above the bottom line to consider the impact of its actions on all, from shareholders to the society at large." In other words: Don't judge us on our quarterly earnings, because management—which doesn't own much of its own stock—isn't going to do anything to drive the stock price up just to satisfy shareholders we've never met.

In March of 1985, Andrew Sigler, chairman of the Corporate Responsibility Task Force of the Business Roundtable and CEO of Champion International Corporation, went a bit further. Wall Street has gone crazy, he said. Seventy-five percent of all stock market transactions are by institutions. Sixty-five percent of all portfolios are turned over every year. The pressure on corporations to generate short-term gains is enormous. Takeovers have fueled those short-term gains. There's a great deal of money in play, and precious little deliberation.

"We are talking about probably the most immense accumulation of wealth in history—it makes the robber barons look like corner muggers," Sigler concluded. "We say, let's stop the person who is just playing. Let's stop the person who gets the greenmail. Let's stop anything other than someone with enough money to come in and tender for the whole company."

Fred Hartley now had every pillar of the American Establishment speaking on his behalf—his grievances struck a universally responsive chord at corporate headquarters around the country—but that still wasn't enough for him. When he discovered that Security Pacific, his own banker, was backing Pickens, he sued the bank. "The money changers are in the temple!" he shouted, upon learning that the American Lutheran Church had committed $10 million to Pickens. And in testimony at a congressional subcommittee, Hartley compared the Pickens bid to the 1964 Kitty Genovese murder in New York. "Dozens watched, but no one was willing to get involved," he said. "It was a national scandal—and this is no less. Now is the time to call a halt."

To the great surprise of Boone Pickens, that is exactly what happened. With the unexpected help of the Delaware courts, which ruled that some investors are less equal than others, Unocal offered its shareholders—but not Pickens—$72 a share, $18 more than Pickens was hoping to pay. The stockholders intelligently accepted, sending Pickens home with an estimated $100 million loss.

Despite the overnight quadrupling of Unocal's debt, Hartley claimed victory: "We're under a bit of an anchor, but we're still sailing." Dillon, Read and Goldman, Sachs, with less fanfare, banked $25 million in fees. And, in Washington, Drexel competitors seized the moment to move in for the kill.

"Very large pools of money are managed by arbitrageurs looking for rapid returns, and some of these pools are financed by junk bonds," Felix Rohatyn, the high-profile senior partner of Lazard Frères, told the Senate Committee on Banking, Housing, and Urban Affairs that spring. "Very large pools of money are in the hands of raiders, similarly financed. This creates a symbiotic set of relationships which has as its basic purpose the destabilization of a large corporation and its subsequent sale or breakup. It creates, at the very least, the appearance, if not the reality, of professional traders with inside information, in collaboration with raiders, deliberately driving companies to merge or liquidate."

Rohatyn had done everything but call for the immediate arrest of Michael Milken, Saul Steinberg, Boone Pickens, Sir James Goldsmith, Carl Icahn, Nelson Peltz, and Ronald Perelman. Congress, which did not have that power, did what it could. Congressman John Dingell, the scourge of Wall Street, declared that Drexel client Carl Icahn was "a chronic violator of securities laws rather than an American hero" and asked the SEC for a full record of enforcement actions against him, Saul Steinberg, Boone Pickens, Victor Posner, Irwin Jacobs, and Ivan Boesky. Meanwhile, Dingell's colleagues introduced thirty-four bills in 1985 alone to limit junk bond financing of hostile takeovers and cripple Drexel Burnham.

"There haven't been any unfriendly offers since the Unocal ruling," a momentarily cowed Fred Joseph told reporters in June. But backpedaling furiously wouldn't be enough, so Drexel belatedly hired lobbyists, who arranged for its more personable executives to swarm over Capitol Hill. Milken wasn't among them. "Normally, Michael likes to stay on the desk, and we like him to stay on the desk," Joseph explained. Other Drexel executives agreed—they estimated that it would cost the firm $30 million in lost income a *day* for Milken to go to Washington.

Still, Milken had some input. That year, Drexel clients bankrolled an organization that called itself the Alliance for Capital Access, and its director, a savvy Washington lawyer and congressional veteran, ventured west to meet the junk bond king. David Aylward had never met a mind that worked as fast as Milken's—or understood so little of the world beyond the trading floor.

Milken had anticipated a response to hostile takeovers, but he didn't have much of an idea how to mount a counterattack. And in the absence of any direction from Beverly Hills, the best idea at Drexel to combat the hatred flowing from Washington and Wall Street was unashamedly crass. As more than one Drexel banker put it that year, "Why don't we just write somebody important one big check?"

Fred Joseph became CEO of Drexel in the spring of 1985, and he began his tenure a worried man. His concern was not Drexel's enemies—he was troubled by the firm itself. New employees were flooding in, departments were expanding in all directions, and, as often as not, the person you called for some crucial task was someone you scarcely knew.

Where was Drexel going? What could be salvaged from the old Drexel? How were he and Mike Milken going to build an institution that outlasted them?

Once again, Fred Joseph reached out to Ned Kennan.

Joseph wanted Kennan to begin by seeing Milken, who was the embodiment of the Drexel culture. Kennan resisted. "I knew everyone admired him," he said in 1990, recalling events from five years earlier. "I didn't want to walk in too early and just hear the gospel." Instead, he started interviewing in New York, where he quickly learned that Milken was regarded as a god. In the late spring of 1985, he moved on to Beverly Hills, where he interviewed Milken associates he regarded as "the key disciples."

Michael Milken was Kennan's last appointment.

Starting late one afternoon, Kennan says he spent four hours with Milken in a Drexel conference room. Kennan asked if he could tape-record their conversation; Milken declined. "Milken did most of the talking," Kennan recalls. "He stood up, leaning against the wall. The thrust of his conversation was that, with the exception of some research capability on the East Coast, he had no need or use for Drexel Burnham. As he saw it, the whole corporation was there to serve him. He was in a position to share the spoils—not that the others deserved any. Finally, he suggested that he was plotting directions to new horizons. His general attitude was: Fred Joseph doesn't have to know, the client doesn't have to know, only I have to know."

This was not the Michael Milken who would describe himself after his guilty plea in 1990 as a passive, nonconfrontational man with a deep need to please. To Kennan, Milken was arrogance personified: an aggressive, egocentric leader with a deep need to be served, a contempt for his employer, and a compulsion for secrecy that bordered on the fanatical. And Milken, Kennan felt, liked it that way. For all his much-reported humility—he refused to be photographed for the annual report and insisted that the department Christmas card list the names of every employee, in alphabetical order—he seemed to Kennan to have an almost pathological enjoyment of his apparent divinity.

"Milken has an enormous drive that impels him to be in front of the crowd at all costs, whether it's cheerleading or controlling his department," Kennan explains. "He didn't have anger so much as the energy of anger. I sensed that he was a borderline schizophrenic who reintegrates reality in a way that best suits him. He reminded me of my girlfriend when I was fourteen. She said, 'My conscience is very clear. I never use it.'"

Michael Milken says that Ned Kennan has considerably re-written history. As he recalls it, he spent no more than an hour with Kennan. In fact, for him to have four hours to give to anyone in 1985 would have been unlikely; for him to commit so much time to someone in Kennan's profession would have gone against his penchant for privacy. Milken says he didn't understand why Fred Joseph would hire an outsider to plumb the firm's secrets; if this was a job worth doing, it might be better done by someone who had been brought on staff and was likely to remain on staff. Because Kennan struck him as someone who might be consulting for another investment bank the following week, Milken says he revealed as little as possible.

There was another reason Milken might have cited for what he describes as a distrustful attitude toward Kennan—for him, even a little psychological examination was too much. Growing up, no family member or friend went to a therapist. At Berkeley, "every guy who was nuts was planning to be a psychiatrist." And as an adult, he had kept his distance from anyone who wanted to analyze his behavior or motives. As everyone at Drexel knew, Milken hated talking intimately about himself.

On this one point, Kennan and Milken agree—Milken's reaction to his first encounter with a mind doctor was destined to be negative. Nonetheless, Kennan says he was stunned by how quickly Milken expressed those feelings. After their meeting, Kennan took the red-eye back to New York. He went home and showered. At 8:30 A.M., he was preparing to go to his office when Fred Joseph called to say that he had just heard from Milken—and that Milken wanted him to cut Kennan loose.

"I didn't bite his nose, Fred, I was nice," Kennan said. "What do you want me to do?"

Joseph said he was indeed firing Kennan, but asked him to hold on. With that, Chris Anderson, the investment banker who had originally discovered Kennan, came on the line—and rehired him, but at a lower profile. That sidestep, that small act of rebellion, was a metaphor for the real power hierarchy at Drexel, Kennan decided, and that troubled him. But when he started writing, he says, he was no longer thinking about Milken's hostility or its possible effect on his work.

For Kennan, Drexel wasn't a business, it was a religion. Milken was God, Joseph was his prophet, and the Corporate Finance and High-Yield departments were disciples. But the religion had become so successful it was in trouble.

"If there's one dissatisfied customer, one company that defaults, or if the greed becomes too great, the firm could bring on its own downfall," Kennan concluded. "However it might happen, I predicted the end of Drexel at the end of the 1980s."

Kennan's language was as apocalyptic as his conclusion. "I wrote: 'Beware, you're a one-product company, and without it, you're dead. Beware, you've stepped into the holy chamber of Wall Street and called the others liars and made money—you haven't many friends. Beware, there's a vacuum where you should have an image; you've left it for others to define you. If there's any downward movement, there will be an avalanche, for you'll have no control of your destiny.'"

On the subject of Milken, Kennan rang what he believed was a warning bell. "His life is all transactions, there's no connection between the man and the investment banker," Kennan advised Joseph. "If there's no disaster, Milken will develop clinical symptoms."

In August of 1985, Kennan submitted his report, which ran to one hundred single-spaced pages. Joseph stashed it in his desk. As Kennan recalls it, Joseph was horrified by the bluntness of the report—and he thought it was all wrong. Especially about Milken. Joseph didn't think he was arrogant. He did think Milken liked money, but surely not to the point of greed. As for Milken being a quasi-schizophrenic moving toward a full-blown freakout, that was completely ridiculous; if anything, the problem with Milken was that he was so normal as to be uninteresting on any subject but business.

Because Joseph dismissed this report, he never told Milken about its conclusions and never suggested that there was any concern about his mental health. Worse, ignoring Kennan's warning, Joseph encouraged his investment bankers to find more deals, more clients, more work for Milken. And in his own monomaniacal desire to create a great institution, he set about hiring men he considered the brightest minds on Wall Street. His choices were Martin Siegel, Dennis Levine, and Bruce Wasserstein.

Siegel, as we now know, took cash from Boesky while Levine was feeding Boesky illegal tips. Wasserstein, then responsible for most of the merger and acquisition business at First Boston, would come to help an emotionally unstable, cash-poor Canadian real estate developer named Robert Campeau go $11 billion in debt to buy the Federated and Allied department store chains, a pair of transactions so obviously ill-fated that it took just six months for Campeau's empire to go bust and the junk bond market to crash with it.

And yet, well beyond the moment that reality ripped the scales from his eyes, Joseph liked to believe that these three men—two rabidly avaricious felons-in-training and an investment banker nicknamed Bid 'Em Up Bruce for his disregard of prudent limits in takeover wars—would have helped Drexel become the premier *service* company on Wall Street.

Serving whom, one might ask?

Untethered in Los Angeles, Michael Milken basked in adulation, wealth, and approval—everything he had known as a boy. With one critical difference: He had no one looking over his shoulder to hold him in check. His brother's attention was elsewhere, his wife knew what he told her, his boss had an agenda that was counterproductive to his stability.

The internal neglect showed. In New York, Drexel's investment bankers had taken his carefully maintained anonymity and painted a face on it that was just as rapacious as their own. Then, when clients balked at paying the fees they demanded, they justified their greed with explanations that began with "Mike says"—even when they'd never consulted Milken. This went on and on, until even Milken heard about it and had to react. And he did—he told himself that these practices were unfortunate, they ought to be stopped, and somebody ought to do something about it. As for speaking up or taking some action himself, that was out of the question.

When Milken did speak—in a room where he was not aware that reporters were present—he was distressingly out of touch. "The force in this country buying high-yield securities has overpowered all regulation," he reportedly told a gathering in 1986. If he said that, he wasn't bragging—that year, he and Drexel were bigger than the government.

So it's completely in character that while the sky was falling, Michael Milken would conduct business as usual in the fall of 1986. For him, there were more compelling problems than Ivan Boesky to ponder—how to solve the third world debt crisis, when to start a fund to invest in businesses in Mexico, what to do to help the Russians in their painful strides toward capitalism. He had broken free of temporal concerns, he was standing on top of the world and looking into the future, he was contemplating vast acts of global transformation.

In that scheme, if Ivan Boesky had a problem, it was Ivan Boesky's problem, not one that involved him. Anyway, Boesky was an insignificant factor, a marginal customer who didn't have the power to hurt him. So Michael Milken turned his attention back to the problems that interested him. There, fully engaged, he could be confident. In his own way, he could even be highly confident.

CHAPTER SIX

A psychotherapist who had sex with his patients as a way of accelerating their cure, high-level political corruption, a borough president found with mysterious knife wounds on a heavily traveled highway—it sounded like a Dashiell Hammett novel or a parlor game, but it was the Parking Violations Bureau scandal, and early in 1986, it had the full attention of the U.S. attorney for the Southern District of New York. "Jeez, how'd you get this case?" Rudolph Giuliani asked the associate who briefed him on the doings of Donald Manes and Stanley Friedman and Geoffrey Lindenauer. "This is a great case!"

As a prosecutor, Rudy Giuliani was a man in a hurry—either to get great cases to court or to get himself on the nightly news, take your pick. "We need momentum," he'd tell his staff. "I want an indictment in ninety days, I don't want witnesses to disappear, I want one hundred fifty grand jury subpoenas to go out." The obvious attractions of the PVB case generated even more urgency for Giuliani, and many was the night that he and his staff looked up at seven or eight o'clock, ordered pizza and burgers, and went right back to work.

The Honorable Whitman Knapp had a surprise for Rudolph Giuliani—he too wanted to move fast. In fact, he wanted the trial of Bronx Democratic leader Stanley Friedman and his three co-defendants to begin just six weeks after Giuliani's office secured their indictments. That was a bit sooner than Giuliani had in mind; he had pushed his assistants so far so fast they hadn't quite prepared the case.

Giuliani had another trial coming up at the same time, this one involving the Mafia families of New York. It promised to be historic—and, partly for that reason, he'd decided to try it himself. But that no longer seemed fair. The Mafia case, built around secretly taped conversations, was straightforward; the Friedman trial demanded a talented prosecutor with the facts at his fingertips. The choice, as Giuliani put it, was between being a disc jockey and a trial lawyer—so he did the right thing, withdrew from the Mafia case, and announced that he would try Stanley Friedman.

Seen as a reflection of character, this decision also made perfect sense. Rooting out political corruption had been the throughline of Rudolph Giuliani's career, the issue that galvanized him and made him a civic hero. As he told *Vanity Fair*'s Gail Sheehy, "I don't think there's anything worse than a public official who sells his office, except maybe for a murderer." In this, he was not only a true New Yorker but very much the diligent child of Harold and Helen Giuliani.

His father, a Brooklyn bar-and-grill owner who taught him to box at an early age, had been equally quick to tell him what was worth fighting for—your grandfather, he told Rudy, chose to close several cigar stores rather than pay "protection money" to gangsters with political connections. Meanwhile, Giuliani's mother so imbued him with the idea of service that from age ten to twenty he seriously considered becoming a priest; he wanted to do something more with his life than just make money. To that point, the biggest difference between the home life of Rudolph Giuliani and Michael Milken was that Giuliani was an only child.

In 1970, after graduating from Manhattan College, making law review at New York University Law School, and clerking for a federal judge, Giuliani joined the U.S. attorney's office in Manhattan, which was then beginning an unprecedented series of prosecutions of New York City police. He had a key role in these cases, convincing one rogue policeman to tell all in language that sounded as if it had been lifted from a 1930s Warner Brothers movie: "It's over for you now. You have to decide to come to one side or the other. And I'll not hate you no matter what side you choose, but you are welcome on my side, and that is where I want you." He could also drop the priestly pose and crack a harsh whip, as he did in the 1974 trial of a Brooklyn congressman—his cross-examination was so withering the man stopped the proceedings and pled guilty. In 1975, when he left the U.S. attorney's office, his record was immaculate: forty wins and no losses.

Giuliani, a registered Democrat who had worked for Robert Kennedy's senatorial campaign and voted for George McGovern, became a Republican around the time he was invited to join the Justice Department during Gerald Ford's presidency. During the Carter years, he retreated to New York, and, at thirty-two, was made a partner of Patterson, Belknap, Webb and Tyler. When the Republicans returned to power in 1981, he returned to Justice, this time in the number-three job.

At Justice, Giuliani worked hard to gain favor with his superiors ("He has a great way of dealing with people and getting things done," said Attorney General William French Smith) and to dominate his underlings ("He was personally responsible for hiring all of the ninety-three U.S. attorneys, and he hired them all in his image," William Weld, then head of the criminal division, has recalled). His industriousness was legendary. In 1981, soon after he arrived in Washington, he was planning a narcotics task force that became the premier criminal justice initiative of the new administration; in 1982, at a trial in Miami, he enthusiastically testified on the administration's behalf that the two thousand Haitians seeking political asylum in America faced no danger of reprisals if they were shipped back to the most violent and despotic island in the Caribbean. By the beginning of 1983, Giuliani was grandly telling Connie Bruck, then reporting for *American Lawyer*, that he would have no interest in being named U.S. attorney in New York: "It would not make sense anymore to be in that job—that's something I've sort of passed."

Just a few weeks later, though, John Martin, Jr., informed Giuliani he was planning to resign as U.S. attorney for the Southern District. As is the custom, Giuliani then met with New York senator Alphonse D'Amato to talk about Martin's successor. And, out of the blue, D'Amato suggested that the best candidate was none other than Rudolph Giuliani.

This may have been less spontaneous an offer than Giuliani thought. Freshly divorced in the early 1980s, Giuliani had dated up a storm, and he had not excluded his secretary at the Justice

Department. He was, some colleagues thought, a rather too frequent guest on television news programs—and having just become engaged to Donna Hanover, a television newscaster based in Miami, he did not seem to be tiring of the media.

Giuliani was, moreover, more ambitious than Madonna. That had been apparent as far back as 1981, when Giuliani's mentor, Harold Tyler, had propelled him into the associate attorney general job. Within a year, Giuliani had managed to freeze one of his key associates—an administration favorite—out of the decision-making process. This news filtered back to Attorney General Edwin Meese. And when the U.S. attorney's job in New York opened up, Meese encouraged D'Amato to back Giuliani—even though D'Amato had already recommended John Keenan, a highly regarded New York prosecutor, for the post. D'Amato, who knew all about political favors, took a deep breath and threw Giuliani a bone.

Giuliani's mother opposed the offer, calling it a demotion. His fiancée, thinking of the opportunities for career advancement in New York, pointed out that Manhattan might be ideal for both of them. Romantic love triumphed over filial obedience; Giuliani "got excited" and took the job. Hanover was hired by a New York television station. Ahead lay marriage, family, two salaries, engrossing work. If he made his mark in the next few years, Rudolph Giuliani could soon be mayor, or senator, or, as he would unashamedly propose at a dinner party soon after he arrived in New York, President of the United States.*

When Giuliani arrived at the U.S. attorney's office on St. Andrew's Plaza, New Yorkers had no reason to think he would blossom into the best-known crusader against crime since Batman. His equipment was hardly ideal for the work. Giuliani had a receding mane that he raked and channeled until it looked ready to achieve liftoff, a faint lisp, and a sense of righteousness that overwhelmed his warmth and humor.

But he hit the ground talking, appearing in court soon after his arrival to make a personal plea for a severe sentence in a comparatively unimportant heroin case. The judge was impressed; the man got fifteen years. In short order, Giuliani was cutting a swath

---

*Rudolph Giuliani did not respond to repeated requests for an interview.

across New York. The upper tiers of New York's Mafia families, street dealers and major narcotics suppliers, Chinese youth gangs and tax-evading rabbis and extortionate building superinten-dents—Giuliani nailed them all.

There was one constant in all this: Giuliani's media presence. "The only way to deliver a deterrent effectively is to publicize it," he explained. "I want to send a message." Shortly after he moved into the largest and most visible federal prosecutor's office in the nation, Giuliani asked a lawyer and close friend, Dennison Young, Jr., to come on staff and help him send those messages. "Denny would review press releases as though they were indict-ments," a Giuliani staffer has noted. "He'd cross out assistants' names and put Rudy's in . . . Denny had a phenomenal devotion to press releases."

What Young didn't do for him, Giuliani was quite happy to do for himself. When *The New York Times Magazine* decided he was worthy of a cover story, he gave the reporter six uninter-rupted hours of his office time—and that was not his only inter-view for the profile. For a New York business magazine, he and his wife allowed a photographer into their bedroom. In 1985, when Carlo Gambino was murdered, Giuliani petitioned a judge for three days running to lift an order forbidding a press confer-ence. The judge refused—and later called the U.S. attorney a press hound. Giuliani was immune to such criticism. "I never cause press coverage," he liked to say. "I announce things."

In the first few years of his term, those Giuliani announce-ments had less to do with lawlessness on Wall Street than on Main Street. The message from Washington was blatantly pro-business, and Giuliani—who liked to wear his presidential cuff links—heard it. Indeed, he had helped craft that message. "The previous Administration had one priority, and that was white-col-lar crime," he told Connie Bruck in 1982, when he was riding high at Justice. "I think there was almost a McCarthyism to it. It had gotten to the point where these people had become zealots rather than prosecutors."

Just before he moved to New York, Giuliani was just as dour on the subject. "People have been chasing rainbows, spending two or three years chasing a white-collar case they can never make," he said in 1983. He felt the same way in 1984, when Arthur Liman—a graduate of the U.S. attorney's office and now the most visible partner at Paul, Weiss—called him.

The purpose of his call, Liman said, was to alert Giuliani to a client's strong sense that his company's stock was being manipulated. Someone was spreading rumors that the company was on the verge of being taken over; as the rumor mill drove the stock to new heights, the rumormonger was shorting it, thus locking in a nifty profit for himself when the truth came out and the stock price made an inevitable dip. Giuliani, Liman recalls, more or less laughed it off.

Very little that occurred in the next two years changed Giuliani's mind about the relative unimportance of Wall Street criminality. Early in 1986, in fact, a concerned executive at a small Wall Street firm blew the whistle on an insider trading ring that reached into both Drexel Burnham and Paul, Weiss; the U.S. attorney's response was to release the whistle-blower's name to the press. This error, which never would have occured in a Mafia case, guaranteed that no one on Wall Street would ever again volunteer to help the U.S. attorney build an insider trading case. For Giuliani, that was, in early 1986, no loss. Before Levine was caught, before Boesky was even on the horizon, Rudolph Giuliani had put his bet down—on Stanley Friedman.

At the height of his popularity—that is, in late 1985 or early 1986—Rudolph Giuliani made an appearance at the offices of the *Village Voice,* the weekly New York paper with a long libertarian history. The entire editorial staff seemed to be there; the room was packed. That wasn't surprising. As Nat Hentoff, a columnist whose career amounts to a passionate defense of the Constitution, has written, Giuliani was "the best friend the New York press ever had in any prosecutor's office." That day he proved it all over again.

Some years later, when Giuliani was running for mayor, Hentoff decided this off-the-record session was too important to be kept from the public. As Hentoff wrote, "Giuliani agreed to play a game that could be called 'A Journalist's Dream.'"

He was given a list of names and public figures. After each name was intoned, Giuliani was asked whether this person was about to be indicted, whether he might be indicted somewhere down the line, or whether the United States attorney had no interest in him. Giuliani obligingly placed each name in one of those categories.

There was a stillness of anticipation, a frisson of impending doom in the room that gave me a sense of what it might have been like to be in Robespierre's office as he and his colleagues decided who would be riding in the tumbrils to the guillotine.

This invitation for journalists "to go on a fox hunt," as Hentoff put it, tests the furthest definition of what is sometimes known as prosecutorial discretion. But not for Giuliani. "There is absolute right and wrong," he often said, and he was never unsure which side he represented. "I use my office as a pulpit," he would tell reporters, "to alert society and political systems to changes that have to be made."

Changes that have to be made—those are the words of an activist, even a visionary. But the man who rings a fire bell in the night isn't always best at communicating with underlings. And in their efforts to please him and advance his cause, his staff may become zealots and act in ways that would disgust him. Or his assistants may, as children sometimes do to their fathers, fulfill his unspoken desires, revealing an agenda of which he is unaware. Whatever, a moralist and a bureaucracy are a dangerous combination; it's usually only a matter of time before sparks fly.

In Giuliani's case, the catalyst had nothing to do with the law. On January 30, 1986, he became, at forty-one, a first-time father. "When it happens late," he told a reporter, "you appreciate it a little more." This may have been his greatest understatement; associates have recalled that parenthood sent Giuliani "over the moon."

And while Giuliani looked away, the mice did certainly play. Just ten days later, at 7 A.M. on a Sunday in early February, four federal agents arrived at the Long Island home of sixty-two-year-old Simon Berger. Like the Giulianis, Berger was in bed at that hour. But not for long—within minutes, he was handcuffed and on his way to the U.S. attorney's office. There, he was led to a chair facing a blackboard. On it were written the words "Arbeit Macht Frei."

Berger did not need a translator to tell him the meaning: "Work Shall Set You Free." He had seen the phrase before—when he was an inmate at Auschwitz, the concentration camp where almost all of his immediate relatives were killed. That morning, he couldn't help but make a certain connection between his childhood horror and this. For although he had no criminal record and had lived in the same community for thirty years and had responded fully to a Giuliani subpoena, government agents hadn't merely brought him in for questioning—they had arrested him for bribery, then humiliated him, for the apparent purpose of getting him to cooperate with the prosecutors and incriminate others. Berger had it almost right; the one thing he didn't know was that the offensive slogan had been on the blackboard for a month.

Ten months later, a jury needed only an hour of deliberation to acquit Berger on all charges.* But that wasn't the end of the matter—Giuliani ordered an investigation of the incident. Despite the enormous success of his office in penetrating vast conspiracies created by career criminals, he was never able to discover which of his men had written the offending phrase.

Charles Carberry, the soft, jowly bachelor who headed Rudolph Giuliani's securities fraud division, couldn't have had less in common with his boss.

Giuliani wore crisp white shirts and bright red ties; Carberry, according to the office joke, sent his suits to the cleaners to be freshly rumpled. Giuliani made his reputation battling organized crime and urban fraud; Carberry had always worked in the securities area. Giuliani grumbled if his press conferences didn't lead off the nightly news; Carberry hated personal publicity.

In fact, Charles Carberry was the only prosecutor in Giuliani's office who said he never read anything written about him—and meant it. "Once an article appeared, and though my name wasn't mentioned, someone outside the office had pontificated, and he was wrong, and I got upset," he recalls. "I went to Rudy and showed it to him. 'It's never going to be true,' he said. 'It's either not true or too good.' So I decided never to read anything again."

The low profile suited Carberry, who had studied at Colgate, St. Johns, and Fordham Law, and had also worked as a bank teller and a guard. The New York accent, the blue-collar back-

---

*In 1989, when Giuliani was running for mayor, the Berger incident finally surfaced. At first, Giuliani had no recollection of that long-distant event. Later he called it "reprehensible," a term he also used to describe the reporting of the story.

ground, the messy desk, the apparent shyness—these concealed a massive intellect, memory, and wit. They also hid his belief that he was at least as clever as his opponents.

This isn't to say Carberry thought much of the white-collar criminals he prosecuted. "I remember my first case, prosecuting Michele Sindona," he says. "He was on top of the world, the Michael Milken of his day—more so, really, because he was a public figure and European, so people thought he was cultivated. At the end of the trial, I saw him eating a piece of pie from the cafeteria. He ate without a fork, like a squirrel. I realized: He was just a guy. And, to a large extent, white-collar defendants *are* just regular people. Their criminal moments aren't great moments—this isn't *Richard III*."

Dennis Levine, as banal a thief as ever lived, came to Carberry's attention five months after he became head of the securities division. Between 1980 and 1986, neither the New York Stock Exchange's computerized surveillance unit nor the SEC had noticed that this investment banker was flagrantly trading in stocks that became both newsworthy and profitable soon after he bought them. It took an anonymous whistle-blower in Venezuela to start an investigation rolling by writing a letter—with atrocious penmanship and worse spelling—to the Merrill Lynch compliance department in New York. In his note, he called attention to a batch of suspiciously successful stock picks that came through his office. Surely, no one in Caracas could be that astute; the buyers had to be piggybacking on the trades of a wise and well-connected investor.

Soon those trades were, belatedly, traced back to a Bahamas branch of Bank Leu, where bank officials handling Levine's secret account had been so impressed by his stock-picking skills that they bought alongside him. SEC scrutiny was more than these bankers had bargained for, and they promptly contacted their wise and well-connected investor, who was, as luck would have it, now employed by Drexel Burnham Lambert in New York and writing "highly confident" letters.

Levine, though suddenly sweaty, was still confident. For Ivan Boesky, the biggest buyer of his insider tips, had once bragged that his lawyer used to be the general counsel for the SEC. "Harvey Pitt," Boesky claimed, "could convince the SEC of anything." Levine now told the bank to hire Pitt. And he instructed the bank to give Pitt as little information as possible.

"The consummate stupidity of Levine was that he didn't realize I'd insist on knowing the truth," Pitt says. "If he'd advised the bank, 'Tell them you've got an American client who's cheating, and you traded on his information but you want to insist on the sanctity of Bahamas bank secrecy laws,' I might still be litigating the case—and Ivan Boesky and Michael Milken might never have happened."

Pitt's aggressive stance forced the bank to produce Levine's name. After that, it was only a matter of time until Levine was arrested by the U.S. attorney in New York. Levine's lawyers were Arthur Liman, who had Carberry's job when he was an assistant U.S. attorney, and Liman's partner Martin Flumenbaum, who had worked shoulder to shoulder with Carberry and was still his close friend. Such men sometimes believe that a shared history counts for something. But when they came to see him shortly after Levine's arrest, Carberry laid it out for them, omitting the niceties.

"Here's how it works," he told them. "If you come in before I have a case—one count. You come in early and cooperate—two counts. If you come in when you're dead, like Levine, you take what I let you take—four counts. With Levine, I can take one racketeering count, good for twenty years, or these four counts. There's some sentiment in the office to go for racketeering, but I'll be satisfied with these four—if it's done quickly. I want to wrap this up and get the cooperation."

And then Carberry honored the long tradition of the U.S. attorney's office—he turned over all the incriminating evidence on Levine to Liman and Flumenbaum. "Here are the files, Arthur," he said. "If you're a magician, tell me what the magic is. If you're not, talk to your client."

Liman immediately understood the import of that gesture. "When I worked in that office, it was always considered the professional thing to make it clear when you had a cold case," he says. "Unprofessional behavior would be a trap play—not showing your hand in order to force a trial."

On the advice of his lawyers, Levine toppled quickly and turned over the biggest fish to date: Ivan Boesky. With that, the SEC—which had developed the Levine case and, as a result, had reason to claim priority status in the Boesky investigation—began to prepare its subpoena for Boesky trading records.

The commission was far from optimistic. "We thought Boesky would force us to long and drawn-out litigation with an uncertain result," recalls John Sturc, then the associate enforcement director of the SEC. "The stakes were large, Boesky had a lot of money, and we had, as a lead witness, a guy [Dennis Levine] who pled guilty, among other things, to perjury."

When the SEC subpoena went out to Boesky on August 7, Carberry was so certain nothing would happen soon that he went on vacation to the English Lake District. He returned to New York on August 31, the Sunday of Labor Day weekend. On his answering machine was a message from John Sturc: "Be down here tomorrow."

What had happened in twenty-four days?

Quite a bit—and much of it has to do with some truly clever maneuvering on the part of Boesky's lawyer, Harvey Pitt. For a brief moment, Pitt and his associates at Fried Frank had entertained the idea of encouraging Boesky to fight the SEC. "If it had been a straight insider case, Ivan could have defended himself," Pitt explains. "Levine wasn't a credible witness; no money had passed hands. For a lawyer—though not for the client—this would have been an exciting effort."

Pitt's experience isn't as a criminal lawyer, so Fried Frank reached out for Norman Ostrow, who was known to abhor plea bargains. Ostrow was in Carmel, California, vacationing with his fiancée, Barbara Grohman. Ostrow has since died, but Grohman, who is also an attorney, vividly remembers an unusual series of phone calls.

"Harvey Pitt wanted Norman to fly to New York immediately," Grohman recalls. "He couldn't be there that night; the earliest he could make it was the following morning. They said there was a time problem. I have a recollection of being surprised—what was the difference between 10 P.M. and 6 A.M.? It made no sense to us. But they called Norman back and told him not to come."

After that, the entire Fried Frank effort—conducted with ungodly haste—was to negotiate the best possible plea bargain. Pitt's explanation for the rush is as curious as the on-again, off-again calls to Ostrow. "I was petrified—this shows how naive I was—that Michael Milken would beat Boesky in," he says.

*   *   *

Another explanation for Pitt's urgency might be found in Rudolph Giuliani's schedule that August and September. Once Boesky decided to plead guilty, Pitt was quite clear—his client would settle with the SEC and U.S. attorney at the same time, or there would be no deal. Pitt, a savvy judge of character, knew whom he was dealing with. The way to get a good settlement with the U.S. attorney was to whisk Boesky through Giuliani's office fast, before Giuliani could take over the case or fire up his Xerox machine.

And as Pitt had to know, that was far from impossible. On July 8, *The New York Times* had reported that the Stanley Friedman trial—with Giuliani as the lead prosecutor—would begin on September 8. Thanks in part to Giuliani's penchant for pretrial publicity, the judge had moved the trial to New Haven, where the public was presumably less wired to the U.S. attorney's media hot line. For Pitt's purposes, that relative isolation was an answered prayer—Giuliani would be less available to his staff.

On August 6—the day before Boesky was subpoenaed—the *Times* noted that the trial would be delayed one more month; Giuliani would make his first courtroom appearance on October 6. For Pitt, that was no setback. As long as he had a Boesky plea agreement on Giuliani's desk while Giuliani was distracted by the Friedman trial, he might do wonders for his client.

When Pitt began the negotiations in early September, he acted as if time was unimportant. First, he asked Carberry to give Boesky immunity. "I said, 'I'll ask, but I know the answer is no,'" Carberry told him. "Rudy will never go for that. The best he'll go is one five-year felony."

Pitt promptly agreed to that. As he should have—for crimes far more serious than Levine's, Boesky was pleading to three fewer felonies, and the crime he was admitting left him with minimal exposure from civil suits. True, Boesky still faced a jail term, but with the right to choose the judge who'd sentence him, he was getting away with more than anyone who'd committed sustained and systematic felonies had a right to expect.

With the legal business out of the way, Pitt proposed a fine of $35 million. "We made it plain that there were other instances and problems," he says, "but the theory of the settlement was that whatever new we gave them wasn't going to be counted.

We settled solely based on what they had—which was Dennis Levine."

Here, the motive for speed was clearly economic. In 1982, Boesky had courted Martin Siegel, a Hollywood-handsome young investment banker at Kidder, Peabody. Siegel was one of the reigning geniuses of an emerging field: defending corporations against takeovers. But his innovative schemes on behalf of his clients were far more successful than his schemes to manage his personal budget—all he and his wife knew how to do was spend. A fancy house in Connecticut. A New York apartment. Children and nannies. No matter what he earned, it wasn't enough; the hottest investment banker on Wall Street was trapped in the upper-middle-class poverty cycle. In short, he needed to moonlight.

And that meant hooking up with Ivan Boesky.

In exchange for betraying his clients, Siegel got cash—$700,000 or $800,000 between 1982 and 1984, paid in briefcases, with couriers and code words, just the way it's done in second-rate spy novels. Boesky would have happily continued, but Siegel got cold feet. And then, in early 1986, Siegel too moved on to Drexel Burnham, where he began earning so much money legitimately that he might never have to traffic with the likes of Boesky again.

In the summer of 1986, there were still rumors about Siegel and Boesky in the air. Charles Carberry didn't have to hear them to believe them. "I'd read a book about the Martin-Marietta takeover fight," he says, "and the description of Siegel and Boesky was telling. You *knew* Siegel was a pig."

But Carberry had no proof.

If prosecutors had nabbed Siegel before Boesky made his plea bargain, Boesky's fine would have been far more painful—the best estimates of Boesky's illegal profits from his arrangement with Siegel are in the $80-million to $100-million range. With double or triple damages, Boesky's cost from Siegel-related crimes alone could have come to as much as $300 million. But with Siegel uninvolved, the cost of a guilty plea was dramatically reduced. Indeed, because he got to keep whatever he made with Siegel, Boesky may well have settled with the government without feeling *any* financial bite.

With Carberry limited to the Levine-Boesky crimes, the biggest fine he could insist on was $100 million, a nice round number that suggested double damages. Again, Pitt quickly agreed. But in the fine print, Pitt did something fiendishly bright. The $100 million actually called for two $50 million payments—one as a fine, the other to an escrow account that would be depleted in civil suits. For the fine, Pitt got the SEC and U.S. attorney to accept stock in two Boesky companies. Because those companies had invested heavily in Boesky's arbitrage fund—the partnership that Boesky's plea agreement would force him to disband—their value was certain to plunge after the announcement of Boesky's crimes.

The government might have scored its full $50 million if it did what it allowed Boesky to do: sell stock before the announcement of his plea. Instead, the SEC waited to unload it. By then, its value had dwindled to some $37 million, reducing Boesky's losses once again.

Fines and penalties weren't the primary point of these negotiations. The key was cooperation. And although Pitt didn't make a formal proffer until everything else had been settled, he'd been explicit about Boesky's assistance much, much earlier.

Was the government perhaps interested in Michael Milken? In Boyd Jefferies?

In a certain investment banker whose initials might be MS? And in another Wall Street figure?*

Yes, yes, yes, yes, the government men replied, sensing more cooperation, more plea bargains, more headlines—the great good place at the end of the long hard road.

When the SEC signed off on the Boesky deal, all that was needed was Giuliani's imprimatur. And Giuliani was—what a surprise!—extremely distracted, for he was just days away from the start of the Friedman case. "I only had access to Rudy on weekends," Carberry recalls. "I told him, 'We have a two-year investigation ahead, this will save us time.'"

With no opportunity to reflect, Giuliani agreed. On September 17, 1986, Ivan Boesky became an undercover agent for the government. And on September 22, Rudolph Giuliani went into a New Haven courtroom to do battle against Stanley Friedman.

---

*Although this man wasn't named, the prosecutors understood him to be Carl Icahn. After a long investigation, Icahn was exonerated.

CHAPTER SEVEN

When Michael Milken flew to New York for a weekend conference with Drexel's equity traders in October of 1986, they were expecting praise. Instead, he blasted them. "I get depressed when I come to Sixty Broad," he said, in the first criticism of his colleagues at Drexel's New York headquarters that anyone could recall. "You must understand *value*. Don't get too caught up in emotion, don't let ego get in the way. Why not go on making money with our mouths shut? Let the other guy be real big. The rest of the world will eventually come to us if we have the best ideas."

November found Milken on another plane, this time to Tokyo for Drexel's first-ever pitch for Japanese money. On the twelve-hour flight, as his colleagues slept, he sat on the floor of the first-class cabin, happily reading his way through prospectuses that filled half a dozen boating bags. He was back at his desk on November 12, just starting to consider the possibility of luring some of Japan's $100 billion in surplus capital to American companies. Mostly, he was exuberant about the "invigorating" Tokyo-to-Los Angeles flight—he was able to work all the way across the Pacific and then, after crossing the international date line, work the same day all over again.

Both trips were statements of vintage Milken philosophy—surface humility, hidden pride, accomplishment the world perceives but can't quite see. And work, always work. The more the better, filling all the time.

Ivan Boesky was also busy in late October and early November, playing the role of double agent with considerable verve. As was his recent custom, he sold some stock to Drexel and bought none. At the same time, he successfully prodded the firm to buy a five-thousand-dollar table at an upcoming benefit for the Circle Repertory Company.

To prove that he was serious about selling the Beverly Hills Hotel—and to lull any suspicions of Milken's—Boesky had a representative send Drexel an engagement letter and confidentiality agreement. And as he moved closer to the November 14 deadline, he looked after his own interests and decided to profit from the almost certain tumble that would hit the market in the days after the announcement of his plea bargain—he quietly began to increase his fund's short positions in stock index futures.*

There was one more task awaiting Boesky, and in early November, he finally got around to it. For years, he'd been impeccable in one respect—he never told his wife any of the secrets of the business that her fortune had bankrolled and that he'd named in her honor. At the same time, though, he had never taken much trouble to hide other aspects of his double life from her. As a rule, in fact, he went out of his way to make sure Seema knew about his extramarital activities.

In this, if nothing else, she was his enabler. Ivan's never home, and when he is, he sleeps with the light on; he's just not interested in sex any longer, she told herself. But sometimes the evidence was just too blatant. Like the time Seema found a girlfriend's panties in their Paris flat, a bit of "carelessness" that she jokingly shared with Fred Joseph when the Boeskys ran into him at an airport.

It was more difficult to ignore the time she was snubbed by

---

*Despite the soundness of this idea, Boesky began to sell off these short positions on November 11. Considering that the Dow Jones average fell 56 points in the first two trading days after the Boesky headlines, his decision to bail out early cost him millions of dollars in missed profits. Why did Boesky, for once in his life, turn away from a sure thing? Possibly because he had never been comfortable going short. Perhaps he correctly perceived—or was astutely advised—that public discovery of post-announcement profit-taking might play very badly. But this missed profit may, once again, suggest that Boesky was no genius.

the designer who did their Manhattan home—when she pressed him for an explanation, she learned he was miffed not to have been hired to decorate a $100,000-a-year suite at the Mayfair Regent that her husband had never mentioned to her.

And then there was the ultimate humiliation, which came her way courtesy of a neighbor in the Boeskys' building at 400 East 56th Street. "Oh, Mrs. Boesky," the neighbor chirped in the lobby, "I was surprised by the decor of your new apartment!" Another woman might have asked "What apartment?"—but Seema played along. It was true, there was a new Boesky flat, just a few floors from hers, making it easy for Ivan to see the vastly younger woman he had installed there. The punch line was so awful Seema had to share it. Ivan wanted it all, she told her friends—he'd instructed the decorator not to make the place too plush, so the girlfriend wouldn't believe he might get a divorce and marry her.

A wife of twenty-four years might have suspected that Ivan Boesky was up to more than hanky-panky in the early fall of 1986. Certainly, there had been hints. In August, he started the Ivan and Seema Boesky Family Foundation. He took many more trips, never announcing his destination. He moved his and his family's bank accounts from Merrill Lynch to Citibank. He brought some art back from the apartment he and Seema had recently bought in Paris. And he signed his ownership interest in the Beverly Hills Hotel over to Seema.

But Seema was so accustomed to being frozen out by the mystery man who shared her bed that she saw no significance in any of this—and she was absolutely clueless when Boesky sat her down and dropped the bombshell. In just ten days, he said, his picture would be on every front page in America. His net worth would undergo a sea change. He would probably go to prison. In any event, the reputation that the two of them had so carefully cultivated would be destroyed, probably irrevocably.

At his office, where Boesky had been equally covert, employees had a much better idea something awful was coming down the pike. It was impossible not to see that—every day brought fresh signals of imminent disaster. First, Boesky decreed that no new accounts could be opened. Then the firm began selling securities and not buying any. In short order, people began to suspect that Boesky was about to downsize.

Or so Boesky's employees thought when they were looking at the bright side.

When they were gloomy, they remembered the scary accusations they'd heard about Boesky on Wall Street over the years. How Martin Siegel, in the days before he joined Drexel Burnham, used to be called "Boesky's vice president at Kidder Peabody." How Siegel's $3 million home on the Connecticut shore was rumored to be "the house that Boesky built." Right after the Levine arrest, a well-informed arbitrageur had told a Boesky analyst, "I know for a fact Ivan routinely keeps bags of cash in the office." Cash? In bags? Why would a man with chronic margin and net capital problems keep anything more than small change around?

A few senior members of the Boesky staff started putting these stories together, and they recalled other unusual moments. Stock buys that seemed just too smart. Phone calls that galvanized Boesky to take large positions. Research reports ordered only after he'd placed big stock orders.

And then, as Boesky's secret countdown accelerated, a Boesky executive had an unsettling conversation with one of Ivan's closest advisers, a man who had always seemed immensely sophisticated about the securities business. On this day, though, he seemed to go out of his way to establish himself as a rube, for he asked a series of surprisingly naive questions about insider trading—wondering, in essence, if the kingpin of such a scheme could enlist others without ever telling them what was up. Why was he talking this way? Was he sending a message? Or was he aware of impending disaster, and desperately seeking some distance from it?

By mid-November, Boesky had been a one-man recording studio for almost two months, taping more than a dozen investment bankers, arbs, and traders. The results were mixed. Boyd Jefferies, head of the brokerage firm that made its reputation by trading twenty-four hours a day, had accommodated Boesky by parking stock for him—and he compounded that lack of judgment by taking Boesky's calls and incriminating himself. Martin Siegel was more astute. He seemed to sense the presence of Boesky's electronic memory; when Boesky phoned him, he was noncommittal and in a hurry to be anywhere else.

Milken was just as elusive, but that may have been because,

by November, Boesky had less and less finesse as a government agent. On November 6, for example, Boesky blatantly tried to get Milken to recommend a company then under a takeover threat from a Drexel client.

"I don't know, I don't know what to tell you," Milken said blandly. "In my opinion, the company is going to have to protect itself."

The stock is a buy, Boesky insisted.

"I'm just making a comment, guy," Milken snapped, moving Boesky on to his second reason for calling.

"Ah, ah, Michael, you may remember, ah, you were going to send me some things?" he babbled. "I have received none."

Okay, Milken replied, they will be on the way.

"I beg your pardon," Boesky said.

"They will be on their way," Milken repeated.

Next, Boesky called Jim Dahl, the Milken salesman he'd tried to turn into his operative, and asked for hot stock tips. "Everything I've bought recently has gone down," Dahl replied. "I know better," Boesky said, but Dahl was so skittish the call dribbled to an end soon afterward.

These conversations certainly conveyed an atmosphere of paranoia, but from the point of view of a prosecutor looking for hard evidence against Milken, Boesky had been something of a dud as a secret agent. In all the phone calls to Drexel, he'd come up with nothing. And in the entire 123-page transcript of Boesky and Milken's face-to-face conversation at the Beverly Hills Hotel, there was only one possible nugget—Milken's remark about "holding" the Turner preferred. That wasn't the kind of evidence Boesky had promised.

And it wasn't a matter of Milken sensing Boesky had gone over to the government. Conversations have two sides, and Boesky simply hadn't held up his end. He hadn't pushed. He'd been guarded. He'd needlessly pussyfooted around his own misconduct. Had he just wimped out? Or had he promised the government more than he could deliver and didn't want the prosecutors to learn that he'd cheated them?

With the clock ticking, the prosecutors wanted more. On the morning of November 13, they had Boesky call a Drexel salesman to discuss several million shares of the security that all but obsessed them—the Turner preferred. After all, it's Drexel's position, Boesky told the salesman, hoping to get a reaction. Instead, he got a bid.

That wouldn't do. And that left, for taping purposes, only Boesky's employees. They might not be so tight-lipped about the Boesky-Milken schemes, particularly when the boss put some questions directly to them. So later that morning—just a day before Boesky's deadline—prosecutors had him summon Michael Davidoff to his office.

Talk about a Faustian scene. Boesky's inner sanctum was built for the Shah of Iran and, later, occupied by financier Marc Rich, now indicted and living as a fugitive in Switzerland. Forget Boesky's toys: the Quotrons on his desk, the two-way video system and Ozlike intercom that earned him the nickname God, the legendary phone console with three hundred direct-dial buttons. What really mesmerized visitors was what they saw as they faced Boesky. There, through the vast window and seeming almost to frame his vulpine profile, were three giant numerals on the next building—666, the satanic number.

That number seemed particularly appropriate as the nervous, timid, thoroughly hassled Davidoff entered. "I know you've never hurt any people," he began. "But some people feel they'll be the last to know if anything is going on."

"You know there have been inquiries," Boesky replied calmly. "You know that's a subject of some concern."

"Yeah."

"Let me ask you a little question about history," Boesky said, uninterested in making Davidoff comfortable before he started. "Do you have Turner preferred?"

"Right."

"It was part of 'our position,' right?"

"Uh-huh."

"When I say 'our position,' that was a so-called joint venture with Drexel?"

"Yeah, we carried it for them," Davidoff acknowledged.

"Do you remember if Mike said it was a joint venture or Maultasch said it?" Boesky asked, getting right to the heart of the matter.

"I guess Maultasch. I don't know if I ever spoke to Mike."

"Not Milken?" Boesky asked, practically prompting Davidoff.

But Davidoff didn't get it. "Well, isn't Maultasch somebody—"

111

"Maultasch *is* Milken," Boesky snapped.

Davidoff still didn't get it. "I assumed *you* had a conversation with Milken," he said.

"Right. . . . You know that. . ." Boesky paused. Feeding Davidoff the desired answer would be pointless. He dropped the subject. "Whatever I. . ."

"You don't want to tell me anything, that's okay."

"You know every effort I would make would be to do the best we can under any circumstances," Boesky said.

"Absolutely," Davidoff agreed.

Recalling that Davidoff had once said he wanted to go into the ice cream business, Boesky suddenly got enthused. "The downside risk is the ice cream business. Wouldn't be so bad, would it?"

"No."

"You know what I thought about the other day? There's no such thing as a drive-in deli. We got a drive-in everything. Why have we never created a drive-in deli? I haven't figured that one out yet. But, who knows, maybe you and I are going into the drive-in deli business . . . or find an ice cream stand someplace. What kind of ice cream were you going to sell?"

"Steve's is pretty good," Davidoff replied.

"Steve's is excellent. . . . Alright, let's get to work. Go back up there and trade, Mr. Davidoff."

"I don't know what you want me to do."

"Huh?"

"About the talk."

"What do you mean?"

"I don't have an answer to it, you know, but with all these questions people are asking, an explanation is necessary."

"As soon as there's something to say," Boesky replied evenly, "I'll be the first to say it."

To the surprise of everyone on his staff, Boesky said it the very next day, entering the conference room shortly before the close of the market on Friday afternoon. Flanked by lawyers, he briefly explained his settlement with the government and what it meant for them. He said that he alone was responsible for his transgressions. He dared to hope the call for reform that would surely follow the news of his guilty plea would produce some good.

112

Because Boesky glossed over just what it was he had done to merit such extraordinary punishment, the speech played beautifully—some wept, many hugged him, all wished him well. This is, one employee thought, like the Shah getting thrown out and the palace guard kissing his feet. The analogy was more accurate than he knew. For Boesky, like the Shah, had beefed up his security force at the end of his reign.

Who was Boesky afraid of? As it turned out, he had reason to fear John Mulheren, the manic-depressive risk arbitrageur who had been one of his closest friends—six months after Boesky pointed prosecutors in his direction, Mulheren grabbed an assault weapon and set off to assassinate him. But Boesky wasn't thinking about Mulheren in the fall of 1986. He was totally focused on the completely absurd idea that Michael Milken would have him killed.

At first, his lawyers thought he was paranoid. Then, as the deadline came closer and Boesky's concern increased, they weren't so sure. They knew how powerful Milken was in finance; maybe he was that well-connected elsewhere.

But in focusing on Milken, whom they didn't know at all, they overlooked the man they had come to know fairly well. There was every reason for Ivan Boesky to believe that Michael Milken would put out an order to have him killed. It was, perhaps, what he might want to do if the situations were reversed.

CHAPTER EIGHT

The people closest to Michael Milken say you didn't really know him if you never saw him at the end of a busy week. His voice might be a whisper, his eyes could be bloodshot, but there he'd be, pressing on—and, despite his exhaustion, hanging in long after everyone else had gone.

Some of Milken's salesmen and traders were bachelors in their twenties, interested in women and not averse to parties. They had no chance to go out during the week, when workdays that started before dawn meant dinner at 6 P.M. and an early bedtime. That left the weekend. Actually, it left Saturday night; on Friday nights, few were up to socializing. For most of them, Friday evening was a measuring device to gauge how much Milken had drained them—if they could stay up until the opening sequence of *Miami Vice*, it hadn't been a killer week.

As the market crawled toward the close that second Friday afternoon in November, few appeared likely to make it to 10 P.M. Not only were there half a dozen deals to be completed before the end of the year, but Ronald Perelman, who'd taken over Revlon in 1985 and had recently been stalking three companies simultaneously, had just announced a $4 billion offer for Gillette. So in addition to the daily grind—which included, in the late morning, the Boesky organization selling Drexel its block of Turner preferred—there was a frenzy of phone calls all that Friday, lining up commitments for Perelman.

At 1 p.m. Beverly Hills time, the stock market closed in New York, and there was the inevitable release. Then everything changed forever. "Look at the tape!" someone shouted, as the Boesky news started crawling across the video screens. People clustered around Quotrons. And what one of Milken's assistants would describe as a "weird feeling" came over the trading floor.

It's impossible to know how Milken reacted. One story has it that a Drexel client with no knowledge of what had occurred called Milken right after the announcement to buy some Boesky debt. In that improbable version, Milken is said to have screamed over the phone, "Don't you know? It's all *over*! Ivan's *dead*! There's nothing left!" Someone else insists that Milken jerked back in his chair. Others have recalled him stammering, almost drooling. Jim Dahl, who sat across from him, says the news had virtually no effect—Milken was quiet and reflective, but he kept on working.

As the market closed, forty of Drexel's senior line executives and their wives entered a conference room at the firm's New York headquarters. It wasn't a social gathering. It was a meeting designed to help Drexel's leaders—and, for the first time ever, their truest partners—think strategically about the years ahead, which Fred Joseph believed would be marked by harsh and incessant challenges from competitors and regulators.

A Harvard Business School professor began by showing a film about a media attack on a utility company. The attack was memorable, the company's response was futile—in the movie, the press saw to that, emphasizing the negative and turning a minor blunder into a major scandal. The moral was clear: If a company wants to avoid grim headlines, it must identify troublesome situations early and eliminate them.

With that, the seminar leader divided the group into teams. Pretend you're Citibank, pretend you're Salomon Brothers, he said—how will you hurt Drexel's business?

Fred Joseph was just leaving his office to join the panel discussion when Martin Siegel called. Siegel sounded distressed. And this disturbed Joseph, who had dreamed of having Siegel at Drexel for almost two years before he made the first call to him. Siegel had been at Drexel just six months. Was he already considering a better offer?

In fact, Siegel said he was thinking of resigning, but not to take another job. He had just received a subpoena demanding records that had nothing to do with Drexel. He'd need time to comply with it. He feared his work would suffer.

Did you do anything wrong? Joseph asked.

No, Siegel said.

Don't do anything premature, Joseph told him. Let's sleep on it.

Joseph didn't get much of a chance to share doomsday scenarios at the seminar. Shortly after the role players began knocking Drexel, he was motioned out of the conference room and told about Boesky's plea, the sheaf of subpoenas it had spawned, and the TV crews waiting downstairs. Joseph was staggered by the news and by the suddenly ironic fantasies of danger being concocted in the next room.

What did it all mean? Joseph couldn't say. But he didn't need to watch a film to know how to handle the crisis at this stage: He dispatched lawyers from Cahill Gordon—Drexel's outside counsel—to talk to Charles Carberry, head of Giuliani's white-collar crime division.

Lowell Milken wasn't in the office when the Boesky news broke. A week earlier, while he was visiting the chancellor at Berkeley to talk about a project involving the Milken charitable foundations, he suffered what felt like a heart attack. He rushed back to Los Angeles, saw his doctor, and was sent home to rest. On Monday, he started a week of tests; all he saw were doctors, hospitals, and his bed.

At two-thirty on Friday afternoon, he arrived at a gastro-intestinal specialist's office for a full examination. After waiting, being examined, and learning he had a hiatal hernia, Lowell went with his wife, Sandy, to pick up a prescription. By then, it was well after four, and Lowell, who hadn't gone to the office all week, thought he might at least pick up his mail. Certain he could get in and out of the office quickly at that late hour, he had Sandy drive him to Drexel.

Richard Sandler and Craig Cogut were sitting in Lowell's office when he arrived. As the lawyers who did a great deal of work for Milken's department, they spent their days establishing partnerships, reviewing investment opportunities and working on Drexel deals. They were bright and meticulous, and Sandler, in particular, was as conscientious as a brother to the Milkens—which wasn't surprising, as he had been Lowell's closest friend since childhood and now lived around the corner from Michael. This afternoon, though, Sandler was drained and gray.

We need a few minutes, he said.

A minute only, Lowell replied. I'm not feeling well, and I've got Sandy waiting.

Boesky's taken a plea, the lawyers reported. Subpoenas have been issued to Mike and Cary Maultasch and Charles Thurnher—and you. The marshals have been here.

Kevin Madigan, the lawyer for the High-Yield Bond Department, entered. He explained how he had accepted the subpoena, and what it demanded—massive submission of documents, and in just a week. What they needed now was to get criminal lawyers for the people who had been subpoenaed.

For Lowell, there was nothing to discuss—there were criminal lawyers, and then there was Edward Bennett Williams. A legend in the profession, the sixty-six-year-old Williams had almost single-handedly raised the reputation of defense lawyers from fee-grubbing shysters to high-minded dragon slayers. He had tenaciousness and guts to spare—ever since he'd represented the Teamsters in their battles with Robert F. Kennedy, he was known for his fearlessness in confronting the government.

Although Williams hadn't been trained as a securities lawyer, Lowell knew that he'd been an amazingly effective advocate for businessmen. In 1979, he had persuaded federal prosecutors not to indict oil man Marvin Davis. That same year, the SEC charged Gulf & Western founder Charles Bluhdorn with numerous violations of the securities laws; Williams led the SEC into a maze of negotiations that ended, years later, with the case being dropped. He had defended Central Intelligence Agency chief Richard Helms and former Treasury Secretary John Connolly. He represented *The Washington Post*. He was even saving Victor Posner from himself.

Cogut and Sandler found Williams in Washington, still at his office, and faxed him the subpoena. When Williams called back, he was all questions and snarls. "I'm not sure I can get started in a week. Who authorized Drexel to go to the government? We're gonna have to get some organization here."

For all his apparent displeasure, Williams couldn't have been happier to represent this client. He'd had a recent bout of the cancer he'd been fighting since 1977, and the distraction of a big

117

case was welcome. And it didn't hurt that his opponents would be the SEC, an agency he had often bested, and Rudy Giuliani, a man he did not quite like.

For years, important friends in New York had been telling him, "Michael, slow down, you're going to get in terrible trouble." His reply never changed: "I haven't done anything wrong." That exasperated a few old-timers who'd had scrapes with the SEC in its more activist years. "Don't you understand how it works?" these veterans shot back. "If they want to nail you, you don't have to do anything wrong."

In fact, there was much Milken and Drexel had done that would be fuel for those who wanted to nail the firm. None of these business practices revealed criminal behavior, but each suggested a way of operating that was rough even by Wall Street standards. Taken together, they stripped the veneer of idealism from Milken's operation—for a so-called visionary, he didn't seem to mind sitting back and letting those closest to him act like sharpies.

Hostile takeovers financed by junk bonds, for example, were sheathed in the rhetoric of patriotism; in the Drexel version, the raiders they backed were kicking out entrenched management, revitalizing companies, and creating jobs. This anti-excess rhetoric obscured the fact that some of these deals were excessive, and, far from creating employment, caused thousands of workers to be laid off. But in 1984 and 1985, those considerations mattered only in factory towns. At the height of the takeover boom, what would-be titans saw was that Milken could raise money for almost any deal at almost any price—with his help, they could outbid all competitors. Drexel investment bankers cheered the raiders on, unconcerned that they might be paying too much for companies; the loftier the cost, after all, the more Drexel could bill for investment banking services.

And stiffer fees for the corporate finance boys in New York were only the beginning. Out in Beverly Hills, there were other ways to profit from a transaction—Milken might demand equity, in the form of warrants, to sweeten the deal for his bond buyers. Milken made this demand right up front, but he wasn't shy about increasing his demands at the eleventh hour. In either case, the names of those who needed the equity in order to feel comfortable about buying this risky debt were not disclosed. That was

"Drexel policy." It was also shrewd politics—Milken never had to reveal that he was, on more than one occasion, the bond buyer.

After all those machinations, Milken might still raise more money than the transaction required, putting the client in the odd position of being offered excess capital. But "offered" isn't quite the word. Milken firmly believed that the best time to raise capital is when you can get it—and he strongly encouraged his clients to take an extra $50 or $100 million. And then, because their interest rate was high, he advised them to invest the excess in some junk bond issue Drexel was just bringing to market. The yield was high, the new issue was sure to be successful, and, anyway, what was a better place to put your money than Milken's bonds?

Some clients heard the sermon and got religion. Others resented being asked to join what critics would come to call the "Drexel daisy chain"—a network of clients who bought one another's bonds so faithfully that they formed a kind of high-yield universe. No matter what they felt, though, many clients went along with the Milken program. "We wrote it off as the cost of doing business," an otherwise assertive Drexel client sighed, when asked how his portfolio had come to include the bonds of some truly wretched companies.

Even in more straightforward financings, Milken had an agenda. In Wall Street tradition, one investment bank serves as lead underwriter in an offering of securities, and several firms sell the stocks or bonds. When Drexel was invited to sell bonds for other firms, it often got screwed; when it was Drexel's turn to lead, Milken returned the favor.

To one Drexel executive, the most egregious example of this screwing was a $3.2 billion Occidental Petroleum financing that was supposed to be sold by Drexel, Salomon Brothers, and Shearson. "The bonds the other firms got—their share was pitiful, just incredible," he said. "Their salesmen and traders didn't get fed. It was embarrassing."

It was worse than that—it was stupid. In the past, upstarts had challenged the Wall Street pecking order, but, for the most part, they worked hard to mend fences and become part of the Establishment. For Drexel, winning wasn't enough; Wall Street was unending war, and satisfaction lay in crushing the opposition.

Fred Joseph was an eager general in this conflict. By necessity, this empire builder had some relationships with CEOs of other investment banks, but they never became social. At night, he rushed home to New Jersey. And his weekend pursuits couldn't have been more solitary.

Milken cherished an isolation so total that he made Joseph look like a gladhander. Although he was the most powerful American financier since J. P. Morgan, Milken was an alien on Wall Street. He didn't have a single relationship with the head of another firm; even when he worked in New York, he made no effort to get to know anyone who couldn't become a client. The only community he could live in was one he created and dominated—one reason friends cite for his eagerness to move his operation to California was his fear that his troops would hang out at Wall Street watering holes after the trading day and, in the glow of alcohol-induced good fellowship, give away useful information.

Values flow from the top, and Milken's hunger for deals and control soon spread to those who worked most closely with him. In 1985, a company called Green Tree Acceptance saw Milken's department sell 71 percent of its newly issued securities to just six investors—including 22.6 percent to Reliance Insurance, headed by Saul Steinberg. Was this, a Green Tree official wondered, the same Steinberg who'd made a run at Disney? "Yeah, but he didn't beat up Mickey Mouse, he just greenmailed him," Milken lieutenant Jim Dahl replied. His lack of empathy led to a lawsuit.

This misunderstanding, if that's what it was, wasn't an isolated occurrence. A few weeks before the Boesky news, representatives of Staley Continental discussed a stock offering with Dahl. Staley was considering using several other investment banks and bringing the offering to market on a co-managed basis. Drexel responded by quietly buying 1.5 million shares. And then—just a day before the Boesky announcement—Dahl threatened Staley. "It's very important for us to sit down and talk," he reportedly said, "before you do something that hurts me and I do something that hurts you." But before that chat, Staley believed, Drexel sold off its stock, driving the price down and killing the offering. And that led to another lawsuit.

Until now, all this and more had been kept private. But thanks to Boesky, that would change. Prying reporters would turn lore and rumor into anecdote and fact. And Michael Milken and his world would be nailed in the court of public opinion.

*   *   *

Michael Milken never wanted to meet the press.

"It's not modest," he'd say, when friends told him that he should explain what he did all day. He avoided media, he told others, because he wanted his children to have a normal childhood. For a client, he put it in economic terms: "No one ever made a dime off publicity."

Milken did believe all those things. But as he indicated in a deposition just a month before Ivan Boesky took a plea and pointed journalists toward Drexel, his overriding view was that the press was self-serving and ignorant. Journalists, he said, "want to sell magazines and need to create something on the cover so someone would buy it." Magazines that called his clients "corporate raiders" also ran articles "telling me that the stock market was dead, and then it subsequently ran up a hundred percent; that utilities would never be able to borrow again, and they subsequently proved to be a most attractive investment. I also read articles that gold was a great buy, only to fall fifty percent in value; that interest rates were going down, only to go up, et cetera, et cetera. . . . You have to ask whether anyone pays attention to journalists or considers their opinions worthwhile."

Now the very journalists he scorned would hold his years of silence against him. They'd shred his privacy, critique his business practices. And here was the beauty part: The press could say whatever it wanted about him. By temperament, he was never going to welcome reporters into his life. And thanks to the unwritten rules of criminal law, he couldn't now even if he wanted to—no respectable criminal lawyer would advise a client to talk about his case to the press. He was the safest of targets, a potential defendant whom no one knew and who couldn't speak up and defend himself.

So as the Mercedes ferried him home that cool Friday evening in November, Michael Milken wasn't just concerned or pensive or upset. Every wall he had worked so hard to erect was going to be knocked down; he was going to be the creature he most despised, a public figure. And that devastated him.

When Janet Chung arrived at the Drexel office at 10 A.M. on Saturday, she expected to see the usual weekend faces. Typically, four or five people would be there, finishing old projects, getting a jump on new ones. On those mornings, the room glowed with an inner-circle feeling. On Rodeo Drive, storekeepers were preparing to welcome the first of the day's customers; here, behind thick tinted glass, these happy few had the satisfaction of doing Mike's Work.

Chung was generally among the first to arrive on Saturday. The morning after the Boesky news, someone beat her—and she was glad to see that Milken was in fine spirits. Unaware that his good mood was an act, Chung quickly settled down to work. An hour later, she got up to do some photocopying. Milken followed. As the machine hummed, he asked her for his office calendars—he wanted to know when Ivan Boesky had come to see him.

Chung made a face. Sue Cochran, who didn't know how to type and didn't like to take Boesky's phone calls and hated filing and worked fewer hours and rarely came in on Saturdays and nonetheless made much more money than she did, had thrown the calendars away. Typical.

Then she remembered her own diary, in which she recorded even the most trivial events. There was a lot about Boesky there. On the phone, waiting for Milken to pick up, Ivan had quite the little flirt with her, and, to lighten him up, she'd acknowledged one mutual passion—for chocolate. The next time Boesky came to Beverly Hills, he brought her some. Before his next visit, he warned her that he expected a kiss—so she gave him a bag of Hershey's Kisses. Harmless stuff, but worth noting. And useful now, for those entries would, as she told Milken, tell her the dates of Boesky's visits.

A little later, Milken suggested that they talk. What about? A private conversation, he said. Her salary review.

Chung was puzzled. In 1985, her first full year working for Milken, her annual review was so memorable she didn't have to consult her diary to date it—it was six o'clock on Christmas Eve, everyone had left, they were completely alone. He'd started the review by lecturing her about the importance of getting along with people. What do you mean, she'd replied, I get along with Boesky, and nobody can stand him, not even you, and nobody tells you, Oh, Mike, Ivan's a client, please get along better with him.

Then he gave her the really bad news—she would get a $5,000 bonus and a $10,000 raise. Most twenty-four-year-olds just two years out of college could live with that. But Chung knew that was much, much less than Sue Cochran and the other assistants would be getting. And so she ran into the ladies room, weeping, while he stood outside the door like a doofus, calling Janet, Janet, until he realized she wasn't coming out and he went home to his family.

This was much different.

Not only was the review a full month before she expected, but he said he was delighted with her work and that she'd be receiving a $40,000 bonus. And that was it. Three minutes, in and out. Did that make her happy?

I'm not sure, she replied, coquettishly.

Milken got the joke and smiled. That cheered her. She wasn't at all annoyed when he asked her to come in on Sunday.

I'm not going anywhere, Lowell said. If you want me at the meeting, we'll have to meet at my house. And that ended that conversation, not only because Lowell was still feeling unwell but because Lowell said exactly what he meant and hated repeating himself. Okay, Michael agreed, and called New York to alert Fred Joseph to the change in plans.

Joseph wasn't flying out alone; that wasn't the way investment bankers liked to work. Like nuns, they traveled in pairs. Tough cop, soft cop, to be sure, but there was a better reason—finance really was subtle sometimes. It took more than one set of ears to catch all the nuances; it took several points of view to arrive at the most creative solution.

Still, Joseph's choice of a companion was interesting. He hadn't picked Bob Linton, Drexel's chairman and Joseph's predecessor as CEO, or Ed Kantor, head of trading in New York and, on the chart of organization, the executive in charge of supervising Michael Milken. Instead, Joseph chose Leon Black, author of the "highly confident" letter. It says something about Black that he could, in just two words, alienate every right-thinking CEO in America. And it says something about Fred Joseph that this is the man he'd take to California to plot Drexel's defense strategy with the Milkens.

"Did you do anything wrong?"

Forty-eight hours earlier, Fred Joseph hadn't hesitated to ask Martin Siegel that question. In Lowell Milken's living room, with Leon Black and Peter Ackerman and Richard Sandler looking on, he never considered putting Michael Milken on the spot like that.

For more than a year now, Milken had barraged him with ethical and legal questions. Milken couldn't be more careful, Joseph was sure of it.

On Sunday afternoon, Milken spoke at length about very practical concerns. He would have to spend time with lawyers, he said, and that would take him off the trading desk. In his absence, he feared deals would slip through that weren't really creditworthy. If they tanked, clients who bought those bonds would be less prone to participate in the next deals. The franchise might be eroded.

To prevent that, Milken said, the firm should throw more bodies into credit analysis for deals already in the pipeline. During the investigation, it should slow down the deal flow. Just to be on the safe side, Drexel should cut back its inventory of high-yield bonds—he sensed a drop coming in the junk bond market. And, above all, the firm should call a halt to the hostile takeovers that were making Drexel a pariah.

Milken had delivered some of this sermon before. Joseph, Black, and Ackerman hadn't been convinced then, and they weren't convinced today. Milken seemed not to understand that the firm wasn't just a trading desk in Beverly Hills, that dealmakers also had to eat. The hostile deals would continue.

After the meeting, Joseph—who had traveled with Boesky and attended the bar mitzvah of one of his sons—pulled Lowell aside to bitch about their new enemy.

"I don't think we should have done business with Ivan," Joesph said.

"Why tell me?" Lowell shot back. "I *never* thought he was someone to do business with."

At the annual event that Drexel called the High-Yield Bond Conference and everybody else called the Predators' Ball, Michael Milken liked to show a photograph of a man knocking a woman over. Then he projected the same picture—uncropped. The woman was stepping off a street corner, a car was bearing down on her, the man who seemed so obviously to be a mugger was actually saving her life. "Perception and reality," Milken announced. Just like our junk bonds, he didn't have to add.

Perception and reality were very much on Cary Maultasch's mind when he flew in from New York on Saturday, his nerves shot, to see Milken. He didn't know what was happening; Milken might have answers. Over the weekend, when he cornered Milken for a minute, Milken mentioned a fee Boesky had paid Drexel. That only fueled Maultasch's paranoia—he'd never heard of this payment, but he wasn't inclined to believe it was innocent. In that brief conversation, Maultasch got in one direct question: "When you met with Ivan, were you careful?" Yes, Milken said. But that didn't reassure Maultasch—when it came to Boesky, Maultasch knew, you couldn't be too careful.

At 4 A.M. on Monday, Maultasch had a more extensive audience with Milken. Despite the hour and the security guard station just across the hall, Milken was behaving very oddly, communicating in whispers or by jotting on a legal pad. Maultasch understood. All weekend, there'd been jokes about Boesky—"Ivan's only paying five million of his fine; Mike's doing a junk bond offering for the rest"—but none about the government. People who hated music were now playing radios loudly in the office. Milken, who had iron kidneys and routinely sat at his desk for eight hours without discomfort, had discovered the kitchen and bathroom, where conversations could be muffled by running water.

And now this.

Milken had brought a stack of papers into the conference room. Maultasch could see only the top sheet—a photocopy that looked like a document Charles Thurnher had once sent to him in New York, with a column of company names and the dollar amounts of Boesky's profits or losses in those stocks. Milken would consult the list, then scrawl a name on a yellow pad. What about this stock? his eyes would ask. Maultasch, who'd brought his subpoena along, would check it, then nod or shake his head. And then Milken would erase the name from his pad and scribble another.

When Milken had to talk, he favored terse whispers. There really aren't any limits on your ability to trade, Milken suggested. You have authority to buy stock up to $100 million. Your supervisor is Alan Rosenthal.

Well, this was nonsense. Maultasch did have authority to trade up to $100 million—when he had worked in Beverly Hills and traded convertible bonds. But he'd been in New York on the equity desk for more than a year, and whenever he was going to make a trade of any consequence, he checked first. And Rosenthal was his supervisor only in name.

Mike Milken—villain or victim? As he left the conference

room and stepped into the elevator, Maultasch didn't know what to think.

Monday was National Amnesia Day on Wall Street. As reporters discovered by midmorning, nobody—including reporters who once regarded the fallen arbitrageur as a trusted source—knew Ivan Boesky. Or if they knew him, they hadn't talked to him about deals. Or if they talked to him, they never shared nonpublic information. In any event, this conversation was off-the-record, on deepest background, and it had to end abruptly, because, though this wasn't said, it was necessary to engage the services of an attorney before there was no one left to hire—as the joke had it, Ivan Boesky had single-handedly enacted the Wall Street Criminal Lawyer Full Employment Act.

In Beverly Hills, certain Drexel employees were behaving like children lost in a forest and dropping crumbs; they seemed determined to create a trail. Terren Peizer, the young salesman who sat right next to Milken, walked in Monday morning and announced he'd had a serious car accident the night of the Boesky news. That was true—but he didn't have a mark on him. That day, Peizer asked the department's lawyer so many questions about Boesky that, by midafternoon, several colleagues told Milken to watch out for him. Soon, Milken was convinced that Peizer was a mole, a government spy.

Jim Dahl, never known as a fresh-air enthusiast, now developed a burning desire to have a walk in beautiful Beverly Hills with Charles Thurnher. Dahl was extremely concerned about rumors of a Boesky "scorecard," for he had kept some scorecards of his own. As the principal salesman for the savings and loans, he'd kept running tabs of trading by his biggest customer, Thomas Spiegel's Columbia Savings, which then had $2.33 billion—or 28 percent of its assets—invested in junk bonds.

Columbia, Dahl told Thurnher, was "nothing like Boesky." That is, the Columbia trades were designed to reduce taxes. Insurance companies did this kind of thing all the time, selling off positions at the end of the year to create losses, then buying the stocks back in January. In every case, Dahl emphasized, there was risk—this wasn't parking. "I'm concerned about civil suits," Dahl said. "We should stick together." Thurnher, who had learned over the years to listen and not judge, said nothing.

Milken, Maultasch, Dahl, Peizer—four men who acted strangely, either because they were afraid or because they sensed they might be guilty of some unspecified crime. Only Milken, after his initial paranoia, snapped back quickly to his usual self. By Monday afternoon, he was even reassuring. This was, he said, going to be "a short investigation, just a couple of months."

Then he opened *The Wall Street Journal* on Tuesday morning. Under the byline of Daniel Hertzberg and James Stewart was an article that chilled the blood—the SEC was investigating insider trading in hostile takeovers. Its focus was on twelve transactions. Drexel had been involved with eight of them. The SEC's investigation, Hertzberg and Stewart wrote, was "dramatically wider" than the Boesky news had suggested.

Wider? To Michael Milken, it couldn't have been narrower. The SEC probe was aimed right at him.

Four days after the Boesky announcement, Rudolph Giuliani delivered his first summation in New Haven. It lasted five hours. "Giuliani had spent dozens of hours in recent days preparing," the *New York Times* reporter noted in an article relegated to the front page of the metro section, "and its presentation had almost a choreographed look about it."

As well it might have. "When I'm on trial, I'm pretty much out of it," Giuliani once admitted, and that was New Haven in a nutshell. In the evening, he worked with assistants on the case. For entertainment, he watched television news segments about the trial. For dinner, the main course was analysis of the witnesses. At midnight, when his aides left, he was still working.

For all his preparation, it didn't look like much fun being Rudolph Giuliani as the trial wound down. For weeks, he had received great coverage. Now, all anybody seemed to care about was Ivan Boesky. Giuliani's prosecutorial debut—a story that should have built to a front-page climax—had turned into a meaningless digression.

The effort wasn't entirely wasted; Friedman was convicted. But had Giuliani's eight weeks in New Haven been worth all the effort? In the past ten months, he had appeared at twenty-one press conferences; in the Boesky matter, he was, for all practical purposes, invisible. Did anyone care about civic corruption? Was the big story now greed run amok on Wall Street? And if it was, how was Rudolph Giuliani going to catch up to the SEC?

CHAPTER NINE

"**T**his defense works as long as everyone locks arms," Edward Bennett Williams was saying. "But if the chain breaks, this will turn into a Greek tragedy, and the U.S. attorneys will sit in the front row and watch us kill one another off."

Richard Sandler and Craig Cogut were in Washington, five days and seven lawyers after Boesky Day. They had saved Edward Bennett Williams for last, a choice both diplomatic and wise, for the Williams message was all about the Others and Himself—while it was important to pick first-class lawyers to represent the lesser Drexel people, the most crucial decision was the choice of the lawyer who'd lead the defense.

Williams emphasized this last point because Sandler and Cogut had indicated that Milken had a dilemma. On one hand, he was impressed by Arthur Liman's vast experience in securities law. On the other, he knew he couldn't top Williams's expertise in a courtroom. Unable to choose, he wanted both.

"Nothing against Arthur Liman," Williams said, "but when it comes time for surgery, two people can't operate."

As Williams kept referring to murder and surgery, it seemed to Sandler that he was talking around a subject he couldn't directly address. All week long, lawyers had said, "Ed's a god, but is he well?" Someone had to confront the obvious. Sandler, mild-mannered by nature, had been holding back, letting Cogut lead these conversations with defense lawyers. But Cogut wasn't taking the lead here.

"How's your health?" Sandler asked, gulping at his own bluntness.

"I've had cancer for nine years, I've had three mini-surgeries, and I've never missed a day in the office," Williams answered matter-of-factly, relieved to have been asked. Then he leaned forward and returned to his favorite themes, the wretchedness of the government and his insistence on being lead counsel. "And after all the surgery, I have more wounds in my back than in my belly."

That was good enough for Sandler, and he and Cogut rushed back to Los Angeles and briefed the Milkens. That Saturday, Sandler and Michael Milken flew all night, spent Sunday morning with Edward Bennett Williams, went on to New York, and met with Arthur Liman on Sunday afternoon. In both meetings, at Sandler's suggestion, Milken took his lawyers aside and told them what might be the most material fact of the case—his salary.

Milken was back in the office on Monday, as fresh as if he'd spent the weekend playing with his children. But this trip only looked like a typical Milken blitz. There was a new reason for the breakneck schedule; Drexel's leaders in New York thought it was key for customers and rivals alike to know that Milken was still on the trading desk and selling deals. The idea of placing Milken on administrative leave—putting the interests of ten thousand employees above its biggest profit-maker—was never seriously considered.

In the first few days after the Boesky announcement, as Drexel New York was well aware, a thousand retail customers closed their accounts. More significant, two corporate clients called rival investment banks to chat about moving their business. Worst of all, an ominous buzz swept Wall Street: Milken had committed suicide. Drexel's chairman was about to tell reporters "no comment" when a Milken lawyer intercepted him—"This isn't a 'no comment' issue," he all but screamed.

By the time the suicide rumors ended and the reports merely suggested that Milken had resigned, Chairman Robert Linton knew what to do. "I'm amazed such rumors exist," he told the press. "It's like the presidential assassination stories that make the rounds periodically."

That didn't stop the talk, though, and, the following afternoon, Drexel had to issue a statement that it was still "highly confident" it could raise $3 billion for Revlon in its takeover bid for Gillette. With that, Gillette stock rose 4 points. "We've never fallen down on a 'highly confident' letter when asked to perform—I mean *never*," Leon Black told *The Wall Street Journal*. "You have to separate the rhetoric from the fact."

Revlon withdrew from that fray, just as Sir James Goldsmith, an international raider with a gambler's knack for knowing when to fold, walked away from Merrill Lynch's promise to back his bid for Goodyear with $1.9 billion of its own money. No matter—the week after Boesky's plea, Milken's sales force placed $1.5 billion in debt, including a billion-dollar issue of Safeway Stores bonds.

Even the usually skeptical James Grant, editor of *Grant's Interest Rate Observer*, had to be awed by that, for Drexel sold every dollar of debt in this transaction by itself—no co-managers for Mike Milken this time, thank you very much—and banked $40 million in fees for its efforts. "An audacious piece of corporate finance," Grant all but gushed. "For this to be done on a day of tears says a lot about Drexel's institutional strength."

Outside the financial press, there was less respect for Drexel's macho performance. "The fantasy of many businessmen right now is that Boesky implicates Milken and Perelman and Icahn, and they all go to jail," a corporate vice-chairman told *The New York Times* in December. That was also a fantasy bubbling slowly toward the consciousness of writers and editors in New York. They kept it at bay—there were still openings to attend and legends to burnish—but the theme beginning to surface in the aftermath of Boesky was one that would come to be known as "Wall Street excess."

The term was a blunderbuss, referring to anything from kids fresh out of business school getting paid ridiculous salaries to hunting parties where financiers who had only recently discovered horses drank Lafite out of silver stirrup cups. It also referred to the unanticipated rise to social prominence of three men—all Drexel clients—who were tall only when they stood on their wallets: Henry Kravis, Ronald Perelman, and Saul Steinberg. These men and their wives, along with their decorators and caterers and florists, cultivated a small but influential quadrant of the New

York press, until everyone who cared about these things—and in 1986, a great many people did—knew that Kravis had his new apartment totally decorated in just forty days so he could be married there to fashion designer Carolyne Roehm, that Steinberg occupied a thirty-five-room triplex once owned by John D. Rockefeller in the same building, and that Perelman was never seen without an unlit cigar so long you really couldn't call it a phallic symbol.

In that heady time, when Reagan's economists talked about the "trickle-down effect," New Yorkers had a special understanding of the phrase. They saw, as few others could, where the spillover of deregulation went—a reputed million dollars to Sister Parish just for the curtains of a certain Fifth Avenue apartment, five-figure bills from Glorious Food for a dinner party, $25,000 for couture dresses that were never intended to be worn twice, the florist Marlo charging $1,000 for a single vase jammed with more precious roses than a Fantin-Latour. In Paris, a French jeweler dazzled his society guests when topless models displayed the merchandise between courses; in New York, his dinner guests at the Plaza seemed equally satisfied when fully clothed models showed off the costly sparklers.

To outsiders, it sometimes seemed that the consumers were, in all this getting and spending, forgetting to remove the price tags. To insiders, those price tags were the point of the exercise. "You can be at a party, and someone will walk in and say, 'Oh, there's Mr. So-and-so,' and everybody says, 'He's worth six hundred million' or 'He's worth a billion,'" Dominick Dunne recalls. "And so, before dinner, we find out how much people are worth. Before dinner's over, we find out that the apartment we're in was sold to this very rich person by Alice Mason for $7 million or $9 million. And we know what everything in it cost as well. These people talk about money all the time. It is the main topic of conversation in this world."

"Green smog." That's what they called it in Los Angeles, where the wealth settled over the western part of the city like heavenly haze and the average price of a house in Bel Air rose to $4.6 million. In New York, the prevailing ethic—only money matters—was buried under euphemisms, and the press glorified the men who made the money that bankrolled the show. Now they were no longer raiders or greenmailers but "takeover artists."

131

So glossy magazines produced in the media capital didn't note that the Tissots chosen by the personal curators of the freshly monied had originally been owned by *parvenus* exactly a century earlier—or that, before dinner parties, these curators sometimes showed up, flashcards in hand, to prep the hosts in case the guests asked for an art tour. No one invited to dinner at the home of John Gutfreund, then high in the saddle at Salomon Brothers, publicly derided his wife for getting rid of formal place cards and writing the names of her guests in gold ink on freshly plucked leaves. No society profile revealed that one wife was mad for any artifact owned by Madame de Pompadour, or that another—a photographer's darling—left a child home with possible appendicitis while she made an appearance at a key fashion gala.

One night, Ronald Perelman—the new owner of Revlon and, as luck would have it, Bill Blass perfume—gave a cocktail party in honor of the highly regarded designer. Two old-school social arbiters, Pat Buckley and Nan Kempner, came and went without acknowledging their host or hostess; their snub rated nary a mention in publications grateful for Revlon advertising. But then, so great was the admiration for Croesus wealth that a major financial player could announce on a summer evening in Southampton, with perfect confidence that the media folk in attendance would never run with his remark, "If you have less than seven hundred fifty million, you have no hedge against inflation."*

Milken bankrolled much of this excess, but he had no personal connection to it. He and Lori loved the simple life: meals in the kitchen, a photograph of the family over the mantel, a social calendar that called for black-tie only at charity events. In the long march of shopping and showboating that characterized the 1980s, there was only one time that any Milken spent money in public—and, when it occurred, the motivation was charity.

This historic event took place at an art auction at the synagogue. Michael had said he'd attend but, as usual, he was late. And, for the first time in their marriage, Lori made a major financial decision without her husband's endorsement—to enrich a charity, she bought two Renoirs for $500,000.

---

*On the other hand, when the father of one of the Kravises' decorators died and the *New York Times* obituary erroneously described him as a "baker," a correction was quick in coming, restoring the missing *n* in his occupation.

Saul Steinberg, one of the Big Three in New York and an art collector of considerable sophistication, returned to his apartment late that evening to find an urgent message: "Call Mike Milken—*important*." When he did, Milken's concern was about art, not finance; he wanted someone to appraise the paintings, as he intended to sell them. So Steinberg called Richard Feigen, the New York art dealer whose specialties included Old Masters and New Money.

The next time you're in Los Angeles, Steinberg said, please see Mike Milken. Don't worry, he's not going to buy.

When Feigen next visited Los Angeles, Milken personally came to the Beverly Hills Hotel and drove him to Encino. There, Feigen inspected the Renoirs and pronounced them "terrible." Milken had just one question: Can you sell them? Feigen thought he could—in Japan. Milken, immensely relieved, wandered off to play with his children. Soon Feigen sold the paintings; Michael and Lori Milken had some of their children's art framed and hung in their places. And that was the end of the Milkens' public spending.

Once the investigation heated up, the media's infatuation with the Drexel Rich and their possessions would fade just as quickly. Suddenly, it was not quite so wonderful for this Manhattan group to have made all that Milken Money. But Milken never understood that the glossy stories about his free-spending clients might hurt him. "The world is *not* three guys in New York," he'd say, and move right on to what he considered more important topics.

And yet the way these *arrivistes* tried to turn their money into social acceptability was not just a constant subject of magazines that even prosecutors liked to read, it was deeply offensive to those who regarded themselves as cultural arbiters. Frustrated by what appeared to be a lack of moral clarity, economist John Kenneth Galbraith decided to put this scene in perspective. Asked whether Ivan Boesky was the 1980s equivalent of Richard Whitney, the New York Stock Exchange official who was jailed in the 1930s, Galbraith—born poor, but now a patrician—blew right by the dull financial stuff to speak as a social commentator.

"Whitney was a member of the Porcellian, one of the most distinguished Harvard clubs, and he went to Sing Sing in a custom-made suit; I don't think Mr. Boesky is quite in that league—make sure you print that," Galbraith sniffed. He was just as scathing about Milken's form of finance. The Boesky scandal was predictable because of "the belief that new forms of financial activity involve new forms of genius." In fact, this was "euphoric insanity." Galbraith's conclusion was withering: "Anyone who buys a junk bond known as a junk bond deserves to lose."

In the old days, Fred Joseph kept a joke picture of a fully armed guerilla fighter on his office wall. But that was before Boesky's fall. Spending and bragging were suddenly out, prudence and humility were in. Drexel was, belatedly, going to quiet down and rejoin the rest of humanity.

In July 1986, for example, Drexel signed a $3 billion deal for office space at a new building adjacent to the World Trade Center. It marked a great expansion—but the chairman boasted that Drexel would outgrow even this two-million-square-foot space within five years. Now, just weeks after Boesky, Drexel canceled the lease.

Fred Joseph took the next step at the annual conference of the Securities Industry Association in early December, when he made a disclosure that approached self-abasement. In three takeover situations in 1984–85, he said, the firm had devised yet another new wrinkle in raising money for would-be acquirers. It had sent sealed envelopes with confidential information to its clients. A cover letter explained the rules: If you want to help us finance this transaction, open the envelope. But if you open the envelope and decide not to participate, that must be the end of your involvement; you cannot trade on this information, for it is not yet known by the public. In other words, open the envelope and buy the stock, and you're an insider trader. Which, apparently, was just what occurred—as Joseph sheepishly admitted, there had probably been some leaks.

The Boesky news had a bracing effect on Drexel in other ways. In a stunning about-face, it started working overtime to resolve the Green Tree and Staley disputes. In mid-December, Drexel hired Akin, Gump—the law firm of Robert Strauss, former chairman of the Democratic party and one of the highest-profile influence peddlers in Washington—to run interference on Capitol Hill. And, for the next six months, there were no hostile takeovers or "highly confident" letters.

When Fred Joseph sat down to write the annual year-end letter to clients and employees, he made the obligatory sounds of disappointment about Levine and Boesky. But he couldn't downplay the good news—a $1.5 billion increase in revenues, the right to claim that this was the most strongly capitalized private firm on Wall Street. In a numbers business, nobody could argue with those.

But Fred Joseph was also unnerved that December. "I can't match the government investigation," he told a reporter. "We don't have as much muscle. I'm pretty much shell-shocked."

Milken's lawyers saw that in the press and wondered. In a white-collar case, the keys to a winning defense are controlling information and never showing weakness. Why was Joseph so candid? Or had he been scared silly by Thomas Curnin, the lawyer principally handling the defense team at Cahill, Gordon?

If Curnin had told Joseph horror stories about the government, it wouldn't have been out of order—he had been there before.

Curnin's biggest white-collar case had involved E. F. Hutton, Fred Joseph's alma mater. In 1980, Hutton had discovered a way of making money that produced even more impressive profits than junk bonds—kiting checks. Hutton would deposit money in a distant bank in the form of a check, but before the deposit had cleared, Hutton would write a check on that account for about the same amount of money and deposit it in another bank; this game of musical chairs invariably ended with Hutton winning and each bank in turn looking at a huge, if momentary, overdraft.

"A certain branch in our retail system has been earning thirty thousand dollars per month in interest just from overdrafting of the bank account," a manager reported to Hutton president George Ball, who sent it on to hundreds of vice presidents and regional sales managers with a cover note: "A point well worth remembering, and acting on." The branch managers complied, and in just two years, Hutton gained the use of some $10 *billion* by shooting checks through some four hundred banks. By 1982, Hutton's biggest profit-center had nothing to do with stock trading, investment banking, or customer service—check kiting was king.

Inevitably, the scheme was found out, and Curnin was called to lead the defense. "He seemed like the right man," Robert Fomon, Hutton's CEO, later remarked. "He had a reputation for being tough." To the young Pennsylvania prosecutor working the case, however, "tough" meant "condescending"—Curnin first resisted his demand for documents, then blizzarded him with seven million pages.

Three years later, the prosecutor had chastened Tom Curnin. Now the lawyer who had sworn this case could be defended walked into Hutton's boardroom and outlined the firm's choices: a plea to two thousand felony counts and fines totaling $2.75 million, or a prolonged legal and media assault leading to a trial that might well see the conviction of at least three Hutton executives. The Hutton board was divided. Curnin advised settling and putting the trouble behind the firm, avoiding several years of bad press. And because Curnin had wrung what seemed like an important concession from the government—the company would plead guilty, but no one would be indicted—his recommendation carried the day.

What happened was the opposite of Curnin's prediction. With the exception of Attorney General Edwin Meese—who insisted that "this makes it clear to the business world white-collar crime will *not* be tolerated"—Washington screamed that guilty individuals were going unpunished, that the fine was a pittance. Hutton customers and star performers fled; several public agencies declined to do business with the firm. The press vilification was excruciating: "The criminal fine . . . in a bank heist of this size is like putting a parking ticket on the Brink's getaway car," William Safire wrote in 1985. "Hutton beat the rap."

In 1988, E. F. Hutton—an eighty-year-old firm reputed to have the strongest retail department on Wall Street—was dead, absorbed by Shearson.

In 1986, it was far from clear that Hutton had been fatally wounded. So Tom Curnin was, for the second time in half a decade, ordering up documents at the government's behest. And over at Drexel, Fred Joseph was increasingly dependent on the lawyer whose counsel had, he thought, saved Hutton.

Peter Fleming had never heard of Michael Milken.

"There was a revolution going on," he recalled in 1990, "and I was working like an asshole and not getting rich." Fleming's hand moved from his omnipresent can of diet soft drink to his ubiquitous filter cigarette, and he let loose a baritone laugh, for his version of not getting rich means being paid some $600,000 a year as the senior litigation partner of Curtis Prevost-Mallet. "Then my brother-in-law called me one November Friday and said, 'I hope they put that SOB Milken in jail forever.'"

Fleming was soon in a position to learn a great deal about Michael Milken—in one of his best machinations, Edward Bennett Williams had lobbied for him to be added to the Drexel defense team. It wasn't that Williams suspected Curnin would, once again, induce his client to fold; he just wanted to make sure that a lawyer who loved to go to trial was in the Drexel loop. And the fifty-seven-year-old Fleming, he knew, not only loved the courtroom but was intellectually convinced that much of what the government liked to call white-collar crime was really standard business practice.

At trial, Fleming got away with this contrarian approach because he was tall, silver-maned, elegantly suited and immensely confident. He defended his clients with blinkers on; the government's case didn't exist for him. He strode into court, did whatever business was necessary with the judge, and then turned his attention to the jury. Listen to me, he'd say to the jurors, and I'll tell you a story you've never heard before—the story of what really happened.

While jurors were mesmerized by that alternative truth, they rarely guessed that this unusually accessible blueblood was really an Irish Catholic from the wrong side of the tracks in New Jersey. Fleming had gone to Princeton and Yale Law, and he had married a debutante, but what he recalls of those experiences is that he pitched varsity baseball at college and his wife was "also a radical like me."

At the U.S. attorney's office, he was quickly famous as the most fanatic New York Giants fan anyone had ever met—and as the most brilliant courtroom interrogator of the last two or three decades. Once he left the government, Fleming distinguished himself for his passionate representation of white-collar defendants, including Attorney General John Mitchell and financier Marc Rich. In short order, the New York equivalent of Edward Bennett Williams was working alongside Edward Bennett Williams.

"I remember once going to see Giuliani with Ed," Fleming recalls. "Ed said, 'Rudy, I haven't negotiated with as tough a prosecutor since I went up against Tom Dewey.' Giuliani ate it up. Later, I asked Ed how he could have known Dewey—the age gap made it impossible. 'Yes, but Rudy didn't know that, or care to,' he said. 'I tell you, never in my lifetime or yours have we seen such a naked lust for power.'"

Fleming and Williams became friends as well as allies. From his days at the U.S. attorney's office, Fleming had known and liked Arthur Liman, now representing Michael Milken, and Michael Armstrong, now handling Lowell. And he had worked closely on a case with a young Liman associate named Martin Flumenbaum. Now a partner, Flumenbaum was assisting Liman on the Milken defense.

These lawyers made a natural team. They all preferred the courtroom to the negotiating table. And they all had the sense that Tom Curnin—who'd done his best to keep Peter Fleming from being hired by Drexel—was not experienced enough to handle what lay ahead.

CHAPTER TEN

"**F**irst he sold his friends to the government, and then he sold his stocks to his friends." That was just the printable reaction to the news of Ivan Boesky's sweetheart deal with the SEC. Arbs who took a huge bath in the days after the Boesky headlines were outraged to discover that Boesky had, "in the interest of an orderly liquidation," bought some stock the week after his announcement. And not just any stock—Boesky had bought stock in takeover candidates momentarily depressed by his news.

What *had* they been smoking in Washington?

In the weeks after the Boesky blowout, it wasn't just Wall Street asking that question. Securities lawyers noted that the Insider Trading Sanctions Act of 1984 authorized the SEC to demand triple damages—that is, 300 percent of the $50 million in illegal profits that Boesky had acknowledged. This suggested to some lawyers that the SEC should have leaned on Boesky not for $100 million, but for a heftier $150 million. "Very unusual," a former SEC official commented. "It seems pretty generous to me."

As it did to Capitol Hill. Senator William Proxmire recommended that the Senate Banking Committee hold hearings about Boesky's deal. And that was just a warm-up to the reception that SEC Chairman John Shad and Gary Lynch, the chief of the commission's enforcement division, got when they appeared before

139

the Subcommittee on Oversight and Investigations—John Dingell's committee—on December 11, 1986.

"I'm just a poor Polish lawyer from Detroit," Dingell likes to say. That's a joke; Dingell is probably the most powerful man in Congress. Certainly, he's one of the most effective. Reagan advisers, navy admirals, and military suppliers—"Big John" Dingell, 220 pounds solid and six feet tall, and his staff of more than one hundred investigators laid them all low. "I love a good fight," Dingell has admitted. "I love to swing the meat ax."

From the beginning, the Democrat from Michigan—who took over his father's congressional seat and intends to pass it on to his son—used that ax to attack every industry but one. He has not been overly interested in air bags or reduced automobile exhaust or better gas mileage, and the slowness of Congress to pass legislation improving auto safety has reflected that lack of enthusiasm. Dingell is unapologetic about his positions on passenger safety and cleaner air; Ford's headquarters is in his district. "Tailpipe Johnny's" commitment to the Big Three is also personal; his wife, Deborah, is an heiress to the Fisher Body fortune and, in her own right, a former lobbyist for General Motors. She thinks her husband is a "great big teddy bear."

No one in the Reagan White House would have agreed. "The President is a failure," Dingell declared in 1983. And that went double for John Shad. In 1982, when he had investigated Shad's finances and "congressional sources" leaked the story to *The New York Times*, Dingell didn't cry foul. That investigation led nowhere, so Dingell began railing against SEC budget cuts. And he certainly didn't miss noticing that when Shad defended junk bonds, he wasn't exactly hurting the cause of his good friend and former colleague Fred Joseph.

"The system is capable of detecting and prosecuting one-time offenders who make one illegal investment based on insider information, such as the psychiatrist, the football coach, and top Defense Department officials," Dingell thundered at the start of the December hearing, "but it has not been able to catch or make a case against major institutional insider traders."

Dingell didn't care that Levine begat Boesky and Boesky would beget other cases—for him, the key fact to emerge from this epic event was the revelation that, at the time of his plea bargain, there were *twenty-four* "open" investigations of Boesky at the stock exchange and *eleven* unresolved SEC investigations.

What *would* it have taken, Dingell wondered, for the SEC to bring Boesky down? Wasn't it riveting that Shad, who'd started at the SEC with a pledge to come down on insider traders "with hobnail boots," was only *now* willing to ask for a budget increase?

"Man bites dog," Dingell sneered. "Will wonders never cease?"

Shad was agog—he'd had a childlike fantasy of being praised by the committee. "We've come from silent movies to Technicolor operas, and I thought we were here for the Tony Awards," he said dolefully, and stepped aside to let Gary Lynch take the congressmen's questions.

For the popular, low-key Lynch, this was also like a bad dream. Months ago, his seventy-hour work weeks had moved into the one-hundred-hour range. Full-tilt CIA secrecy had been in effect. Not even wives were told that Levine, once known around the SEC as "Moby Dick," had led to an even bigger catch.

So when the news broke, a party was in order. That weekend, on two days' notice, Lynch's wife, a professional caterer, prepared stuffed veal and focaccia for sixteen jubilant SEC staffers. Her husband personally made the spaghetti carbonara.

And that wasn't the end of the good feeling. In the following weeks, the SEC glowed with World Series fever. With Levine, the commission had won a division title; with Boesky, it had taken the league pennant. The world championship lay ahead and, with it, the dazzling possibility of a sweep—in January, Michael and Lowell Milken were slated to be deposed. Such was the confidence in the halls of the commission in December that many truly believed the Milkens, too, would come in and tell all they knew.

And now, Dingell and his comrades were second-guessing the SEC. The questions were harsh, and escalating: When would the SEC make a big Wall Street case without an informant? How could the SEC be sure Ivan Boesky hadn't secreted a fortune in Swiss and Bahamian bank accounts? Had the SEC gotten far enough into Boesky's financial picture to ascertain that Boesky wouldn't be a rich man when this is all over?

"We are judge, jury, and prosecutor," John Shad had crowed in his salad days at the SEC. Hearing the facts of life from John Dingell, he no longer felt so cocky—Shad was, an associate recalls, "affected by the criticism and not dealing with it well."

141

Some of that despair, the associate continues, "had to filter down to Gary Lynch."

But Lynch was, in a way, tougher and more realistic. He knew how to work the press. And he knew how to work his enforcement team. Like Rudolph Giuliani in New York, he would do whatever it took to topple the man Ivan Boesky had told him was the king of insider trading.

It was mid-January of 1987, and this was the first meeting of the first team.

Edward Bennett Williams brought Robert Litt. Arthur Liman brought Martin Flumenbaum. Michael Milken brought Richard Sandler.

In the Williams & Connolly conference room, Edward Bennett Williams was the one you'd notice right off. The room was set up that way, with Williams at the head of the table, but he would have been the dominant figure in any setting. His decades of deposits and withdrawals from the favor banks of Washington had aged him and given him the stature of a senator, at least—power and political savvy radiated from him.

Self-importance, though, wasn't in the visible equation for Williams. He went into court wearing a not too good blue suit, white shirt, and black tie; he understood that standing in front of a jury has nothing to do with great personal style. Even in his conference room when he was just chatting with a client, his ego was ruthlessly suppressed. Instead, there was a Rotarian kindliness about him, an evenhandedness that, however cultivated, seemed rooted in his character. Williams was a man who held the secrets of a great many powerful people, and one way he'd become their confessor was his ability to sit back and watch and listen without making them feel judged. And then he'd say something so salty and profound and sensible that it was hard to believe he was, at the same time, suggesting a line of legal defense.

Liman was Williams's second. That he was the first to say it suggests how shrewd he was. People sometimes missed this shrewdness and, after a brief exposure to him, concluded that he was some otherworldly creature—so brilliant that arrogance and condescension had to come in the same package. Certainly, everything about Liman indicated that his cognitive functions had, long ago, taken over his being. He seemed always at sixes and sevens, the lawyerly version of the absentminded professor—the suit jacket was occasionally improbably buttoned, the hands sometimes fumbled for a pen that wasn't there, the Execu-hair was parted low and finished with a full swirl.

This Lawyer McGoo image, though genuine, also served a purpose that he had to be aware of: the concealment of a Liman who was calculating, a sharp judge of character, and an excellent businessman. In the courtroom, Liman dropped this knowing, worldly side of his personality and presented himself as a friend of all parties in a bipartisan search for truth—in the nicest possible way, he tried to shanghai the proceedings.

And he tended to get away with it, for lawyers and judges were overwhelmed by his intelligence and his credentials: Harvard, first in his class at Yale Law, a stint at Paul, Weiss, two years at the U.S. attorney's office prosecuting securities fraud and winning a reputation as the greatest trial lawyer of his generation, and then, at thirty-one, back to Paul, Weiss. In 1980, he was the odds-on favorite to succeed Robert Fiske, Jr., as U.S. attorney, but he withdrew his name from consideration. For Liman, the job really would have been a demotion—he was, by then, not just in the $1-million-a-year league, he was a power broker, a corporate matchmaker, a behind-the-scenes potentate.

Sandler, who had never been involved in a criminal case, presented himself as Milken's second set of ears—the phrase "general counsel" made him uncomfortable. He held that position because the Milken brothers drafted him for it; they weren't about to let some stranger invade their lives. For them, Sandler's lack of experience was less important than his good judgment and loyalty forged in three decades of friendship.

That left Bob Litt and Martin Flumenbaum to jostle for supremacy among the bag carriers. Of the two, Litt had the greater presence. He favored worn blue shirts and gold wire rims, he worked out, he was still in his thirties—he looked like a product of the Harvard of U.S. attorney's offices, which is how graduates of the Southern District of New York think of their affiliation. But he had also graduated from the real Harvard, and Yale Law, and he had clerked for Supreme Court Justice Potter Stewart. Litt's background made him somewhat impatient with slow thinkers; at the U.S. attorney's office, he'd been most impressed by two of the quickest minds, Marty Flumenbaum and Charles Carberry. Though he was still an associate at Williams & Connolly, there was little doubt Litt would soon be a partner—and he wore his future on his face. "Six years in the Southern District make you cocky," he once explained.

Martin Flumenbaum, born the year Liman enrolled at Harvard, had followed the same career path as his mentor: after starting out at Paul, Weiss, he'd won a string of convictions at the U.S. attorney's office, then returned to a partner's office at the law firm. Like Liman, he was a prodigious intellect—he had been Junior Phi Bete at Columbia, editor in chief of the Columbia newspaper, and a whiz at Harvard Law. Like Liman, he gave the impression that only mental firepower mattered. Unlike Liman, he had no otherworldly qualities; in him, passion and conviction sometimes came across unvarnished, looking very much like arrogance and inflexibility.

When these four men turned the meter on, the collective tab was north of $1,400 an hour. Not that cost was a factor–Drexel was footing the bill. Still, Michael Milken was the kind of man who made a point of turning off calculators and desk fans for less conscientious associates when he left the trading floor at night. Given that, one would expect that a session with his lawyers would find him with his yellow pad out and his pencil at the ready—the attentive student eager to master the new lesson.

But Michael Milken was shuffling paper.

Throughout the meeting, Milken would reach into a canvas bag, remove its memos and reports, sort them, and place them in another canvas bag. Then he'd start again. Rarely did he make eye contact with anyone.

"For chrissakes, Michael, you're driving me crazy!" Williams finally shouted. "Will you *please* pay attention!"

"I'm sorry," Milken said, looking down at the table. "But I was listening."

"I know you hear me," Williams retorted. "Just let me know it, okay?"

Milken nodded, stopped, paid rapt attention for almost an hour—and then resumed sifting the paper in his bags.

Williams didn't say it, but Milken's behavior at this meeting and in their preliminary conversations had led him to wonder how helpful a witness he would be at trial. The guy had miles to go before he was fit for the stand, Williams thought; at this point, he was way too quirky. "Some guys can't see the forest for the trees," Williams told Litt. "This guy can't see beyond the moss on the bark."

*   *   *

Michael Milken's distraction was inevitable. Everywhere he looked, he saw the alliance of old-line Wall Street, the Business Roundtable and the front page of *The Wall Street Journal*. Now, in Ivan Boesky, this conspiracy had acquired a new and deadly ally. The Protestant elite using Wall Street's Sammy Glick to do its dirty work—that was a painful irony. But it wasn't an irony Milken could dwell on, for it dealt with Boesky. And he couldn't focus on Boesky.

"For Mike, contemplating Boesky was an invitation to see the faces of Lori and the kids," a friend says. "And not in some pleasant family portrait—if he had to consider what he had done with Ivan, he imagined his family, weeping and brokenhearted, as he was led away in chains."

That was an impossible, unbearable picture for Milken. He'd never do anything to hurt his wife and children; they were his strength. And now, in his time of need, they would be even more—for him, and later for his friends, they'd be the proof of his innocence. If he'd never do anything to hurt Lori and the kids, then obviously, he hadn't. He hadn't hurt his family. He'd done nothing wrong. He wouldn't, therefore he hadn't. It was just that simple.

Milken's love for his family—the one fact he could always acknowledge—pushed him to make the final illogical leap that banished complexity and set in motion the most expensive legal defense in modern history. Now he was innocent not only of major crimes like insider trading, he was innocent even of minor regulatory crimes. Boesky lied, that was it. He'd never suggested anything illegal to Boesky, never crossed a line on Boesky's behalf. Whatever he and Drexel did wasn't criminal; it was Wall Street practice, and if the prosecutors didn't believe that, it was because they were carrying out some political agenda. And why? Because of his junk bonds! Because he encouraged men and women to tell him their dreams!

There it was, the case in microcosm. On one side, the canonization of Michael Milken—a socially conscious approach to criminal defense that, if nothing else, lay the groundwork for martyrdom. On the other side, prosecutors racing to corroborate Boesky's testimony. In the center, the undiscovered facts, chief among them the truth about that $5.3 million payment, an oyster waiting to be opened.

*   *   *

And there were any number of people hot to open it. Drexel and its lawyers mounted an investigation. So did Milken and his lawyers. So, of course, did the U.S. attorney and the SEC. Very quickly, all was chaos, as the opposing sides raced to secure—or neutralize—witnesses.

Drexel's first stab at an investigation was the briefest. It seemed that Cahill Gordon attorneys didn't want to barge right in and start asking questions, so they asked Leon Black to deputize someone to conduct an in-house investigation. Black chose David Kay, co-director of Drexel's Mergers and Acquisitions Department since 1978.

Why did Black select a man who was unaware of the $5.3 million fee until he read about it in *The Wall Street Journal?* In part, because Kay was fifty-six years old, had trained as a lawyer, and had been successful at another investment bank before coming to Drexel. In part, because he understood that the negotiation of client fees is often a shockingly unbusinesslike, imprecise calculation settled at the end of a transaction for a variety of investment banking services that may be completely unrelated to the deal.

But there was an even better reason to involve David Kay. He'd dealt with Boesky. He knew everyone at Drexel who had worked on Boesky's busted deals. He'd been the one to realize that, as Boesky's primary contact at Drexel, Milken ought to try to collect some compensation for the wasted time and effort. And Kay had developed a succinct point of view about Drexel's former client: "Ivan was a tire kicker."

For those who had suffered through Boesky's searches for the perfect company to buy, that told the story plain and simple—Boesky talked big, but when it came time to make the transition from stock speculator to corporate owner, he lost his nerve. At the last minute, without exception, he'd find some reason to back out of a transaction. And yet, because "he made the right noises," Drexel kept presenting him with new opportunities.

Kay's wasn't an extended investigation. He talked with the banker who had worked on Boesky's aborted purchase of *U.S. News & World Report.* He spoke, in passing, with Fred Joseph. He never contacted anyone in the High-Yield Bond Department. And he pointedly avoided calling Michael Milken—he didn't think Milken would be interested.

But Kay did talk with Steve Conway, a key Boesky assistant from 1981 to 1986 and no fan of his boss. Their conversation was narrow: uncompensated work Drexel had done on Boesky deals. Kay had a list of transactions, and Conway confirmed the list.

Kay didn't ask Conway if he was aware of any wrongdoing by Boesky or Milken. But then, Kay didn't press anyone—he regarded himself as a fact finder. When he presented his report, no transaction filled more than a single sheet of paper.

Burdened by the government's demand for 1.5 million documents, Drexel's lawyers were slow getting out of the blocks. Milken's lawyers, in turn, were hampered by Drexel's inability to produce its Boesky material in one swift submission. Rudolph Giuliani's investigative unit was having a hard time getting up to speed on the complexities of high-powered takeover transactions. As a result, first blood was drawn in Washington, by John Sturc of the SEC.

Sturc's father had worked for the International Monetary Fund, and he inherited that interest in civic service; he wrote his thesis at Cornell on congressional debates over postwar economic organizations, and had worked in the public defender group at Harvard Law with Marty Flumenbaum. Sturc was small, balding, tightly strung; his humor was dry as a martini. But he loved a story that made sense, and under his questioning, Steve Conway had one to tell that was a stunner.

Boesky was, according to Conway, a megalomaniac who craved money but lusted even more after power—so much so that he'd asked Conway to look at Unocal, an acquisition about $10 billion out of his league. Even if Boesky could have afforded this company, he wouldn't have bought it; he was too afraid of a high-profile failure. And, Conway said, Boesky knew he was a coward—he never attended one of the weekly meetings of his merchant banking department.

Conway believed that Boesky had been motivated by tax considerations to dissolve his corporation and form a limited partnership. Originally, he'd hoped to do it in late 1984. But when Boone Pickens backed away from his run on Phillips Petroleum, he was hit by a whopping $50 million loss. Instead of moving forward on the conversion of his business structure, Boesky resolved to make up that loss—which may explain his decision to join forces with Dennis Levine in the spring of 1985 and ride every takeover stock to the sky. By the end of that year, Boesky was near enough to the heavens to feel he could go forward with his recapitalization plan.

Conway told Sturc that he first learned about the $5.3 million payment on March 21, 1986, the day Drexel was completing the Hudson Funding deal. As he recalled it, Boesky lawyer and longtime confidant Steven Fraidin pulled him aside in the afternoon and advised him that a back-office employee said the $5.3 million was for "commissions." That had raised a red flag for Steven Oppenheim, of the accounting firm Oppenheim, Appel & Dixon—without documentation to support that claim, OAD couldn't sign off on the deal.

Conway and Fraidin called Boesky, who was at a dinner party, to tell him the bad news. Boesky was furious. "It's *not* for commissions!" he screamed. "It's an agreement with Milken for consulting!" And he immediately called Oppenheim. "If you don't sign off on the payment, you're fired!" he bellowed. But Oppenheim held his ground.

Fraidin then called Milken, only to learn that he was flying to New York on a plane without a phone. With time running out, the accountants asked to be transferred to Lowell Milken, who said he was only generally aware of the services being billed here. The accountants prepared a short, nonspecific letter, and Lowell agreed to sign it.

Was the payment really for consulting fees? "Boesky *never* paid for investment advice," Conway said. He liked the "soft dollar" approach—paying higher fees for stock purchases, making good a little at a time. Even if Boesky had been "evening up the score" for work Drexel had done in the past, it didn't make sense for that fee to be structured as a separate payment.

But there was no need to give Sturc a theoretical reply, for Conway vividly recalled a mid-1986 conversation he'd had with Set Mooradian, Boesky's keeper of back-office records. "I did a lot of things for Ivan because he told me to do them," Mooradian reportedly said. "It was dumb. I knew it wasn't for commissions. You didn't know what was going on between Boesky and Drexel. A lot of trading, stocks and bonds that weren't going on the nightly sheets—Ivan made me keep those records."

That rang a big bell for Conway, who vividly remembered that Milken had suggested buying stock in Harris Graphics and Fischbach, two stocks that had showed up on the nightly trading sheets. As Boesky kept accumulating the Harris stock, he told Conway, "Make your analysis look as good as you can." And when Conway pointed out that Boesky was holding unprofitable Fischbach convertible bonds for an uncommonly long time, Boesky replied, "We're doing a favor for Drexel, for Milken. Don't worry, we're protected—we won't lose money."

Having confirmed the parking arrangement, Conway next told the government about David Kay's investigation. There had been several calls, he said. One was on a speakerphone, he thought, perhaps so Leon Black could listen in. All Drexel wanted was confirmation of Boesky's busted deals. Still, no one at Drexel suggested that he adopt the firm's explanation for the $5.3 million payment.

But that, as Conway would tell the SEC a few months after his first interview, was only because he hadn't seen any of Milken's men since the Boesky news. At the 1987 Drexel Bond Conference, that changed—after an uneventful lunch with David Kay, Jim Dahl invited Conway to his room. There, Dahl explained that some of the $5.3 million was a "nuisance fee." It wasn't until Conway, who'd worked on Wall Street for many years, looked back on that meeting that he realized this was the first time he had ever heard the phrase.

On the defense side, the investigation undertaken by Milken's lawyers got off to the most fruitful start. The setting was right: Beverly Hills. So was the timing: December 31, 1986. How clever of Martin Flumenbaum to understand that Milken worked his staff hard, and that prudence dictated he not take anyone away from the trading desk except on the year's slowest day in the financial markets.

Inside the fortress, Milken's colleagues couldn't have been more glowing. David Sydorick, for example, swore he'd never seen anything like Milken's operation. When he worked at Bear Stearns, everything was secret; at Drexel, everyone got a printout listing every trade the department made that day. In five years with Milken, Sydorick said he'd never seen Milken leave his desk to take a phone call.

Jim Dahl—who'd had the most frequent access to Boesky—sounded even more convinced of Milken's innocence. "If Mike were involved in insider trading, twenty-five people would have to know about it," he told Flumenbaum. To improve his staff's sales technique, Dahl said, Milken encouraged other salesmen to listen in on his phone calls at any time—not something a man committing felonies via telephone would suggest. Despite this openness, Dahl emphasized, information about takeovers and LBOs was kept strictly confidential. "I never overheard conversations involving nonpublic information with clients," Dahl said.

Late in January, another Drexel employee sounded like an equally useful defense witness. Alan Greditor, a Drexel managing director based in New York, was Drexel's best analyst, with a particular expertise in food stocks—which happened to be an interest of Ivan Bocsky's. Starting in mid-1984, he recalled, Boesky's associates had bombarded him with questions and sought his recommendations. He never learned what Boesky did with this information, for Boesky rarely bought stock through Drexel.

In the fall of 1985, Greditor—along with Michael Milken, Leon Black, Peter Ackerman, and a few other Drexel higher-ups—attended one of Fred Joseph's beloved brainstorming sessions. We want to do more business with arbitrageurs, someone said. How do we go about it?

"How much more business *can* I do, given all the business I already do with Boesky?" Greditor snapped.

"What business?" Milken asked, clearly amazed.

Greditor told him about the hundreds of phone calls.

Milken was livid. "We have to get paid for this," he said. The days of Boesky buying stock through Drexel at a commission of five cents per share were over. From now on, he swore, Boesky would pay twelve cents a share—or he would pay a fee for the research that Drexel provided.

Greditor heard nothing more about a Boesky payment until late March of 1986, when he visited the Drexel office in Beverly Hills. Milken gave him a warm greeting, said that Boesky had paid up, and that Greditor "was a big part of it." When you get your bonus, Milken said, you'll see what I mean.

A few months later—on the very night in May that Dennis Levine first made front-page news—Greditor was scheduled to have a drink with Ivan Boesky at the Algonquin Hotel. Upset by the arrest of a colleague, Greditor wanted to reschedule; Boesky urged him to show up. "Come on, Alan, I even paid Drexel for you," Boesky said, endearing as ever.

Over drinks, Boesky sounded bored by the Levine news. His

focus was on the future—he wondered if he had to buy stock through Drexel New York in order to get recommendations from Greditor. No, Greditor told him, just be sure to do business with Mike. And throughout the spring and summer, Boesky lied to Greditor and said he was doing just that.

A few weeks before his guilty plea was announced, Boesky's mood changed again. Boesky was selling a large block of Quaker stock through Drexel, but he called Greditor to say he had no intention of paying any commission.

"Sorry, Ivan," Greditor replied. "We don't do business that way."

At this, Boesky went wild. "I'm losing my shirt!" he shouted. "They're killing me!"

Greditor kept his cool, pointing out that his stock picks had always been profitable for Boesky and that a nickel a share commission was standard. "If you won't play by the rules of the game, I can't deal with you anymore," Greditor said. "But I'll call Mike and ask him what he thinks."

No, no, Boesky told him, I'll be happy to pay, a courtliness so abrupt that it took the headlines of November to make Greditor understand the call had probably been taped, another in Boesky's efforts to provoke Drexel personnel to blurt out something incriminating.

The Greditor interview looked like another big win to the Drexel and Milken lawyers.* And now the defense team was actually beginning to think the government case would never get off the ground. For Tom Curnin and Ed Williams had talked with Charles Carberry, and Carberry had assured them that the government's investigation wasn't going to be finished anytime soon.

You can come in to see me, but I have nothing to tell you, Carberry had said. Maybe in May or June, I'll have an idea of the case. Right now, it looks like a two-year investigation.

Williams had pressed him: What kind of case are you talking about?

---

*Like all Drexel victories, the Greditor triumph was unavailing. In December of 1986, Greditor received his bonus check. He'd been expecting $75,000. He got $200,000. For your work on Boesky deals, he was told. In August of 1988, Greditor testified powerfully in the firm's behalf at the grand jury; four months later, the thirty-eight-year-old analyst died in a one-car crash on a New Jersey highway in the early morning hours. Ever since, Drexel conspiracy theorists have asked one another: Who killed Alan Greditor?

"I'm not going to make the little case, I'll only make the big one," Carberry replied.

In other words, Carberry was looking for the gross market manipulations that sometimes go along with takeovers—not minor, technical offenses that were the province of the SEC. That was good news. For Williams, Liman, Curnin, and Sandler all believed that if Michael Milken was smart enough to get his hands on more insider information than anyone else in the last half century, he was smart enough not to use it.

"It's not terrible," Arthur Liman insisted, early in 1987. "It's only for a few months." And they weren't crucial months, he reminded Richard Sandler. The work to be done now was mostly mechanical; it didn't need his oversight. Anyway, if something important came up, Ed Williams would want to handle it himself. So there really was no weakening of the defense if he accepted the appointment as special counsel to the Iran-contra investigation.

What could Sandler say? Off Liman went—not for the few months he expected, but for a year. Now, more than ever, Edward Bennett Williams was in charge.

Williams seemed up to the role when he met with the Milken brothers in Beverly Hills that January. "People will do what they have to to protect themselves," he warned. "Giuliani is raw political meat—he's a mediocre lawyer with all the drive necessary to get to the top in a shitty place like New York. So don't be surprised if the methods of the government create an atmosphere in which people perjure themselves. That's why it's critically important that very strong people represent Drexel. With Peter Fleming in there, we've got a chance."

A week later, Williams was on the phone from Washington, and his tone was very different. "You know I've been taking radiation treatments," he told Milken and Sandler. "Well, now there's some problem with my liver. I'm having some surgery. I'll only be away from the office for two or three days, but I'll send Litt out."

Cancer. For Michael Milken, it was not only a life issue—he'd lost seven members of his family to cancer in the past decade—but a business and philanthropic priority. Some years earlier, a local doctor named Bernard Salick wanted to start a twenty-four-hour walk-in chemotherapy facility, and Milken had raised $40 million in junk bond financing for him. But soon after he got his money, Salick phoned with terrible news: His daughter had contracted cancer, he was looking wildly for the right treatment, he would never get his facility up and running in time to pay down his debt. Don't worry about the money, take care of your family, Milken told him—and found Salick another $35 million. Meanwhile, through his foundations, he was beginning to reward cancer researchers with stipends totaling $2.4 million. People at Drexel knew: Mention cancer in Milken's presence, and you owned him. Williams, unaware of any of this, was about to get the full Milken treatment.

"Ed, Ed, it's okay," Milken said. "Take care of yourself. My problems can hold. Don't send Litt, don't think about this—we'll wait for you."

When Milken hung up, he turned to Sandler and flashed the smile only the inner circle ever got to see.

"They're dropping like flies," he said, with a nervous giggle, and as Sandler realized that the lawyers in charge of the defense were now the relatively unknown Flumenbaum and Litt, he too had to be concerned.

While Milken and his lawyers were worrying about their Maginot Line of a defense, the government was attacking on a whole other flank. Not that they knew they were, in this instance, going after Drexel. To Giuliani and Lynch, they were simply attacking systemic corruption on Wall Street—with Martin Siegel as the informer.

Siegel, a classic insider trader, knew he was doomed the moment the Boesky news flashed across the tape—he agreed to cooperate with the government less than a month after Boesky was unmasked. And Siegel also made a sweetheart deal: He would plead guilty to two felony counts and turn over $10 million owed him by Drexel, but he'd be allowed to keep his homes. Better, he'd have time to sell them and move to Florida—where state laws make it difficult to attach assets—before his plea became public.

Siegel threw himself into the task of taping former associates with even greater zeal than Boesky—his was a full conversion. But unlike Boesky, Siegel got trapped in the war that was heating up between the SEC and the U.S. attorney. For Giuliani was not content to mop up after the SEC. More and more, he wanted center stage.

There were several tried-and-true approaches to the challenge of gathering evidence in sophisticated white-collar criminal schemes. One was to let the SEC do the brunt of the work and, if appropriate, seek civil penalties. Another was for the SEC to investigate and, upon the discovery of significant criminality, bring in the U.S. attorney. A third was for the U.S. attorney to launch his own investigation; if he encountered resistance, he could always convene a grand jury to compel testimony.

But the way Giuliani was moving in February of 1987, all this was far too slow. For him, a highly publicized, scantily investigated arrest on Wall Street required no more soul-searching than the hasty indictment of Stanley Friedman. In fact, it required less. Compared with dealing with real bad guys—the Mafia, in particular—this white-collar stuff was a very low-risk game. "It's a lot safer and [the Wall Street figures] roll a lot easier," Giuliani boasted early that month. "By that, I mean they cooperate a lot easier. They cooperate against each other."

On February 11, Giuliani tested his theory by having federal agents arrest Timothy Tabor, who'd had the misfortune of working with Martin Siegel at Kidder, Peabody. Tabor had phone relationships with Richard Wigton, another former associate of Siegel's, and Robert Freeman, who headed the arbitrage department at Goldman, Sachs. In the Giuliani plan, Tabor—a tall, thin, former Rhodes Scholar who appeared to have a low tolerance for personal discomfort—would roll within minutes.

Tabor proved to be Giuliani's first surprise. Believing himself to be innocent, he refused to make phone calls for the prosecutors, thus earning a night in jail. The following morning, Giuliani upped the ante. Richard Wigton, certain that the two postal inspectors who announced his arrest were part of some practical joke, threw them out of his office—and was, for his mistake, handcuffed and frog-marched in tears across Kidder's trading floor. Robert Freeman got off lightest; he wasn't handcuffed until he reached the elevator.

By day's end, none of the "Wall Street Three" had rolled. Commentators now attacked the U.S. attorney with a passion that Giuliani usually reserved for his targets. Wigton and Tabor were unknowns, but Freeman—one of just 106 partners at the investment bank so respected that all Fred Joseph wanted was to clone it—was widely regarded as the embodiment of everything that was good and decent on Wall Street. For ten years, he and his wife and their three children had lived in Rye, next door to Capital Cities/ABC Chairman Thomas Murphy. He managed a Little League team; he jogged with his wife. In the summer, he and his family rented the New Hampshire house where *On Golden Pond* was filmed.

Rudolph Giuliani wouldn't admit what knowledgeable sources cite as the real reason for the arrest of Freeman and the others—he wanted to move against these targets before the SEC could serve them with subpoenas. He could never acknowledge that there may have been an adolescent, turf-war motive at the heart of this improbable event. He could, however, recast the incident in terms that never played badly wherever people hated the rich and the privileged.

"This is about the hundredth time I've been accused of going too far—I'm getting a little less sensitive," Giuliani said. "We've got to bring a whole new ethic on Wall Street. That's what this is all about."

In April, the U.S. attorney secured the indictments of Freeman, Wigton, and Tabor. The defendants petitioned for a speedy trial and the judge was happy to schedule one—for May 20, just a month away. But the indictments were defective. In May, a day before the trial was to begin, the prosecutors had to ask the judge to dismiss charges.

Giuliani had gone too far to turn back; no sooner was his deputy out of the courtroom than he was sticking a finger in the defendants' faces. "This is just the tip of the iceberg," assistant U.S. attorney Neil Cartusciello insisted. "We'll be back in record time."*

Then, without any preamble, Charles Carberry resigned as head of the securities unit—not because of the bungled arrests, he later explained, but because of Drexel and Milken. "I was

---

*Cartusciello never returned. There never were any new indictments. Two and a half years later, after Giuliani had resigned and was running for mayor of New York, Freeman pled guilty to a single felony count, and the investigation of Wigton and Tabor formally died. Giuliani offered a weak apology; his successor's sole comment was that the arrests might have been "premature." As he had all along, Tabor declined to speak to the press. Wigton did: "I will certainly never read again about someone being prosecuted and assume the government is right."

looking at two years of going through Drexel documents, then a third year to try that case," he says, ticking off the reasons. "I'd be in my forties, and I'd be in the U.S. attorney's office going on eleven years. I was getting married. I'd been offered a partnership in the second largest law firm in the country without looking for a job. And I could see the securities unit was going to grow in size. I would have more administrative responsibilities—which I never liked. The entertaining parts of the job were disappearing fast."

Perhaps. But Carberry was also taken aback by the coverage of the February arrests. "I was surprised by the lies after. The postal inspector arresting Wigton wasn't a six-foot-one guy tossing him around; he was five-four—and as for cuffs, they're *required*. From a prosecutor's point of view, you had to wonder about the class bias of the press: a guy doing a Medicare fraud gets arrested at home in front of his kids."

Distress over bad publicity and a disdain for administrative duties don't quite explain Carberry's sudden decision. Some have suggested that Carberry was pushed, that Giuliani lost confidence in him after the charges against Freeman, Wigton, and Tabor had to be dropped. But that assumes Carberry was the architect of those arrests—and as Carberry has made very clear, "I wouldn't have arrested Wigton."

Defense lawyers who know Carberry tend to believe he left precisely because he made arrests that he never would have authorized. "The office rule was: 'Never sink to the level of the defendants,'" one says. "That was the critical dialectic when we were all coming up. By 1987, that was gone. The mentality was now: 'Win at all costs, we'll worry about the appeal.' The assistants were no longer protecting the judges from error, Giuliani was thinking about politics, decisions were being made through the filter of 'How will this look in the press?' And I think Charlie looked at all that, and he looked at the Drexel case—which, come on, was the biggest case anybody had ever seen; you'd give two years of your life to it without having to agonize over your decision—and he said, very simply, 'This isn't me. I don't want any part of this.' And, good soldier that he is, he very quietly got out."

Whatever the reason, the resignation of Charles Carberry was a blow not just to the U.S. attorney's office, but to Drexel and Milken. For Carberry was succeeded by Bruce Baird, who had spent the last five years prosecuting organized crime *capos* and would come to regard Milken more like John Gotti than like J. P. Morgan.

In June of 1987, however, Bruce Baird was not a name Michael Milken was much aware of. He was thinking about other issues—the need for Drexel clients to change the capital structure of their companies, the copycat deals that rival investment banks were pushing, Latin America. The legal case was not in the foreground for him that season—Edward Bennett Williams was on the mend.

And that fact loomed over all others. Months before, he and Lowell had gone to the SEC's Washington headquarters to be deposed. This session was certain to be unenlightening for the SEC inquisitioners, for neither Milken had the faintest thought of answering any substantive questions. It was, however, a splendid opportunity for everyone to take everyone else's temperature.

For Lowell, the SEC encounter produced a single, terrifying insight: There had been a mind-meld between Boesky and the enforcement division; the commission had completely bought his story. Michael came to a different conclusion. "I can't believe," he said, "how deferential they were to Ed."

CHAPTER ELEVEN

"**Y**ou get out there, you make the introductions, and you get the hell off the stage," Harry Horowitz ordered. Michael Milken obeyed, for the persistent fear of his closest friends was that federal marshals would cart the junk bond king away in front of his two thousand best customers at the height of the Friday-evening festivities.

And Horowitz wasn't the only paranoid at the 1987 Drexel Bond Conference. Marty Siegel's guilty plea, the arrest of the "Wall Street Three," and, just the other day, a plea bargain from Boyd Jefferies, whose brokerage firm had accommodated so many of the raiders who were also Drexel's clients—the government seemed to be on a roll. Even inside the heavy security of the Beverly Hills Hilton ballroom, no one felt safe.

Harry Horowitz had it all wrong.

The government investigation had stalled.

To date, there hadn't been a single Drexel defection. Charles Thurnher had indicated that he would cite the Fifth Amendment at the grand jury and decline to testify; realizing Thurnher's importance, Charles Carberry had granted him immunity, thus compelling his cooperation. But Thurnher was an "outside" guy, and his knowledge, though vast, would be ultimately useless to the government; he knew enough about the ways of the High-Yield Bond Department to do his job without drawing conclusions. For that reason, his new status as a government witness worried no one in defense circles. It did, however, worry the SEC—in the enforcement division, the feeling was that Thurnher was a Trojan horse, sent in to befuddle the investigators and gather information for the defense.

The government's inability to move forward quickly was bracing to Drexel's leaders. And as the conference began, so was the presence of Steve Ross, the chairman of Warner Communications. Ross was then at the height of corporate stardom; his fleet of jets carried only the most powerful celebrities, he was widely beloved by people Drexel executives never dreamed of meeting, a handshake from him was better than a contract from anyone else. And he adored Michael Milken.

All this was of less importance, though, than the fact that Ross had survived a harrowing investigation of a Warner-owned theater in Westchester. In the newspaper accounts, at least, there seemed to be some clear links to the Mafia—but Peter Fleming had engineered a victory almost no one had predicted. Now, at the bond conference, Ross pulled Fred Joseph aside for a pep talk about Fleming.

"1 know how difficult this is," Ross said, echoing advice that Fleming had been giving Joseph all along. "Stick with the lawyers. They know how to do it. You won't like it—it's going to take a long time—but trust them."

After that, Joseph was considerably less agitated. And as he surveyed the new "Drexel Helps America" theme, broadcast here for the first time, it was almost possible for him to fantasize again. "If this investigation hadn't occurred, Drexel would be growing faster than Citibank," he confided to a Milken associate.

What might have been—it was Fred Joseph's persistent theme that week. "Sometimes I wake up and think: If it wasn't for the investigation, we'd have Dennis Levine, Marty Siegel, Joe Perella, and Bruce Wasserstein—we'd be the killer firm on Wall Street," he told another Milken associate during the conference.

Both men thought Joseph had lost his mind. Who wanted to be Citibank? Who wanted a mergers and acquisitions team that wouldn't quit until it had brokered the world?

Joseph was calmer when, invoking Fleming's advice, he tried to cheer up Harry Horowitz: "This will be over in two years." Horowitz was unimpressed. "Yeah, that's what the Jews thought in Poland," he replied dourly. He felt like sneering at Joseph: "Sure, right, it's only for a few years, it's only armbands, at least we're still together."

But nothing would have placated Horowitz. Five months into the investigation, he felt everyone was missing the big point: The government knew nothing about finance, so it would seize on common business practices and declare them to be crimes. Someone needed to speak out for Milken and Drexel—and as Milken's best friend, he thought he could get a forum.

Horowitz's plan was to leave Drexel and start an educational campaign that would teach Americans how the world really works. "More than fifty percent of all securities are controlled by pension funds," he saw himself saying. "When they want to sell, that's good stuff. When Mike wants to sell, it's different. Well, indict Mike or leave him alone."

And that was just for starters. He also wanted Milken to reveal, at long last, the man inside: "Mike should screw all other work and move to New York. He should get out on the street, start working with the homeless, live through six weeks of bad publicity, and then start solving problems. Then people could see what we do—the legend of Mike Milken is just that, a legend. People don't expect the guy to be humble and self-effacing. If he were out there, they'd see how he is: You have a problem, you call. He's the father, the father with ideas."

The lawyers didn't understand what Horowitz was talking about. "I was left to hurt in silence," he says. "The attorneys all went, 'No, no, don't let's tell anyone today why this is absurd, let's save it for court.'"

Harry Horowitz was slightly out of the loop. The lawyers did have a plan for Milken: He wasn't going to say one word about the case. And Milken had a plan for himself: He was, two or three years too late, going public.

In New York, the public relations experts were streaming through Drexel. Corporate favorite Gershon Kekst, political veteran David Garth, crisis manager John Scanlon, global consultants David Sawyer and Scott Miller, campaign heavyweight Roger Ailes, former Mobil spokesman Herbert Schmertz—before the final crash-and-burn, every spin doctor with a big reputation was dragged in to suggest ways for a terminally arrogant and universally hated company to change its image overnight. In southern California, there were fewer candidates for this kind of work; the clearly superior consulting firm was Winner/Wagner.

Chuck Winner and Ethan Wagner told Milken they weren't comfortable with the demands he might make on their time and energy. They didn't have a clear sense that anyone in particular was in charge. And they preferred to work in the background, doing research and developing a strategic plan—they feared that the client was looking for a quick fix.

"It didn't feel like a match," Chuck Winner concluded. "There was a feeling: This is what we want done, how much will we have to spend? It was difficult for them to realize that having the facts on your side doesn't make all the difference."

Their objections were not new ones for Michael Milken. He said he understood; he also asked to meet again with Winner and Wagner. "He was a wonderful salesman—he told us it could work," Winner recalls. "He said he was the ultimate decision-maker. And he said there was a positive story about him that wasn't being told, and another story, about Ivan Boesky and Rudy Giuliani and how they had made him a victim of circumstance."

Winner and Wagner signed on, but not before extracting one guarantee: no work on nights or weekends. They'd been involved in political campaigns and they were used to long hours, but something about the way Milken and his colleagues talked about their work ethic was troubling—they seemed to spend a lot of time at the office just to be working.

Winner explained that he wouldn't produce immediate results; he had much to learn. He threw all thirty-five people in the office into this project; under the direction of Lance Brisson, they conducted a few polls in New York and arrived at a handful of conclusions. Some words—"takeover" and "junk bonds," most dramatically—turned people off. Anti-Semitism? The polling couldn't find any. Drexel and Milken? For both, the slate was surprisingly blank. The absence of any hardened feeling about Milken was, the consultants thought, a considerable asset.

New Yorkers had clearer, if somewhat divided, feelings about Rudolph Giuliani. They weren't sure if he was the right man for a high public office, but they did feel positively about him as a crimefighter. That eliminated one possible media angle; in a Milken versus Giuliani fight, Giuliani would prevail.

Almost everyone who was polled knew Ivan Boesky. And almost everyone thought he was scum. So although Winner and

Wagner weren't able to learn much about the criminal case, they were comfortable making Boesky the enemy: People needed someone they disliked more than Milken, and because that couldn't be Giuliani or the government, it had to be Boesky.

The positives were trickier to select. Showing the world what kind of person Milken was would require more time with the press than Milken could probably handle. A sensible compromise was to showcase the social benefits of high-yield debt. If the public could be made to understand that junk bonds—at least in their original form, as financing for small and mid-sized companies—were good for America, the product might redeem the man. Still, someone had to deliver the facts to the public. An elder statesman? Clients? Milken himself?

In 1985, Milken had switched from a toupee brushed flat like Lowell's to one with a more casual, curled look. That it was all black amused some clients, who teased him about it: "Mike, you're almost forty, you can get one with a *little* gray." And in recent bond conferences, the producers had brought in Richard Nixon's lighting man to figure out how to deemphasize Milken's overhanging brow and sunken eyes. Changes in his appearance, however, could only take Milken so far. What remained to be addressed was the problem he had faced throughout his career—how to talk English to strangers.

"Mike was a terrific student," Winner recalls. "He wanted to learn and do better, he wanted to be graded after each performance." But the videotapes didn't lie: Milken had trouble making eye contact. And while he could be articulate and caring and immensely human, he could—particularly when he was preoccupied with the investigation—be unfocused and rambling.

What had happened to the high school debater? Why was Milken such a charismatic figure in his business and at his annual conferences, and so flat everywhere else? Why did he need an environment that he completely controlled in order to express himself naturally? Or was there another reason?

Winner had no time to work through Milken's psyche. Reluctantly, he decided Milken couldn't be his own spokesman. Maybe, he thought, the problem was that Milken couldn't overcome a trader's professional resistance to disclosure. If so, there was very little for him to do, for the philosophy of Milken and his lawyers seemed to be the same: Acknowledge what you must, but not a word more.

"We had to beg and plead for them to let information out," Winner says. "As a result, we had to react often to other people's moves. And surprises help no one."

"Who owns the corporation?" journalist Edward Jay Epstein asked in 1986. Not the shareholders, he concluded, in a paper that had been commissioned by the Twentieth Century Fund—for the shareholders, corporate democracy was a myth, and the 1980s were the proof.

Time and again, management had been challenged by men who were, with the help of Drexel's "financial alchemy," struggling to give shareholders the profit that was rightfully theirs. Management's response was to try to disenfranchise anyone who threatened the existing order. This was not, Epstein thought, a happy prospect for the future health of the economy.

"Without any real mechanism to assure corporate democracy, the continued dispersion of ownership will gradually lead to the transfer of control over most of America's productive capital from its legal owners to the hands of management groups," he wrote. "This development cannot help but affect the way American capitalism works—as opposed to how it is supposed to work."

Michael Milken couldn't have said it better.

In May of 1987, Milken called Epstein—whose contrarian tendencies included a friendship with Sir James Goldsmith—to wonder if he'd be interested in writing about his business. Although Milken couldn't comment on the "problem," as he delicately phrased it, he was eager to "clear up misconceptions" about his business. "I don't want to become Greta Garbo," he said.

Epstein took the idea of a Milken profile—with Milken's first-ever nonbusiness interview—to *The New York Times Magazine*. An assignment was immediately forthcoming; visions of a cover story danced in many minds. Epstein, the author of nine books, produced a draft that underplayed the government investigation and presented Milken as a protean economic force whose greatest failing was an inability to define "conflict of interest."

Where, the *Times* editors wondered, are the yachts? The planes? Where's all the entertaining we read so much about? Epstein assured them that Milken wasn't like his New York clients—his private life made for dull reading. The *Times* asked for revisions; Epstein withdrew the profile.

The piece ran elsewhere, but something had changed. Not in the writing—in the ownership of the pictures taken by George Steinmetz for the *Times*. "My unprocessed film went to the *Times*," Steinmetz recalls. "The photo editor made his selections, then all the film went to Michael Milken. I got not quite ten thousand dollars for signing over all rights. Later, I saw some of my pictures in other magazines—naturally, the Milken people had sent the most innocuous ones."

So much for media. He wasn't good at it, and he wouldn't get a fair shake even if he were. Better to do what he did best—put his head down and work. But on the way back to his desk, Michael Milken had a question for Gerry Finneran.

"Where's Brazil?" he asked.

"Thirty-seven," Finneran said.

"From what?"

"Sixty-seven."

"That might be a buy," Milken said, and he went back to his desk as Finneran considered the value of Brazil's debt. And then he shivered—that was, he realized, Milken's first suggestion in the two years he'd been at Drexel.

Finneran, a graduate of the Air Force Academy and military intelligence in the Middle East and the Latin American desk at Citibank, had started to doubt there was a directive side to Milken. Well, the man said buy, so Finneran did. In the late spring of 1987, he paid in the high 30s for Brazilian debt. The market rallied quickly to 50. Finneran locked in a profit and bailed out.

Milken registered his approval in his typically off-center way.

"I'd like to go to Mexico," he said. "Next month. For a weekend."

"But no one's there on weekends in July," Finneran replied.

And then Milken uttered the harshest words he ever spoke. *"You don't understand,"* he said.

"Don't understand what?"

"I can leave Thursday night. We can be there until Sunday."

They arrived at 2:30 A.M. Lori had come down on an earlier plane; she had a mariachi band waiting at the airport. On Friday, they had two breakfasts, meetings all day, a dinner that lasted until one in the morning; on Saturday, they had three breakfasts, four meetings, lunch, and another four meetings before dinner. Sunday was designated a day off—there was a tour of the pyramids planned—but Milken slipped in a few breakfasts first.

At one point, Milken mentioned to the chairman of Mexico's second largest holding company that his company's debt was selling for 11 cents on the dollar. "If you could buy it for that," he asked, "why don't you?"* By the end of the weekend, the Mexicans seemed quite excited that a wealthy man like Michael Milken, whether under a cloud or not, was more interested in co-ventures than in cheap labor.

Back in Los Angeles, Milken considered Mexico again. "I'm interested in the Far East, but so is everybody," he explained to Finneran. "Thirty percent of the people in Mexico are nine years old or younger. The question is: Will they have jobs?" Milken found this worth pondering because "how a man feels in Tijuana affects us more than the happiness of a man in Burma—the man in Tijuana can be in San Diego in twenty minutes."

Philosophically, Milken's conclusion was that the stronger Latin America is, the more likely its people are to consume American goods and ideology: "The children who feel disenfranchised by our system are also lost consumers." Practically, the result of all this noodling was a fund. Called DBL Americas, it was Milken the visionary in action—if it was successful, the fund would infuse Mexican businesses with American money, without forcing the Mexicans to become employees of companies they once owned.

Milken personally met with fifty American firms to interest them in this project. His numbers were more persuasive than his ideology; when he said that Latin America would, in ten to twenty years, yield higher returns than any area he could think of, money managers snapped to attention. By mid-October, Finneran had commitments for most of the $200 million fund, with good prospects of getting the remainder before October 31, when the fund was scheduled to close.

On Wednesday, October 14, Michael Milken woke up, decided something was awry, and went to Finneran. "I don't like the market," he said, with uncharacteristic bluntness. "Let's close the fund at the end of the week."

---

*The CEO did. So did many others. By 1990, Mexican debt and other Mexican securities were among the world's most profitable investments.

"We can't," Finneran reminded him. "We've made commitments to hold it open."

You don't understand—I don't like the market," Milken said, giving Finneran a fresh shiver. "Tell them we're closing the fund at the end of the week and to get their payments in."

Finneran scrambled. By Friday, October 16, as the market wobbled, he had collected $170 million. On Monday, October 19, the market crashed outright, losing 508 points in a single day. "We wouldn't have gotten any of the money if we waited," a grateful Finneran reported to Milken.*

A Shearson executive named Elaine Garzarelli predicted the crash and, in that moment, made her reputation; Michael Milken called the crash and tried to hush it up. "I hate to talk about things people find painful," he explained. "But there had been a drop in government bond prices all month. A rational person would say, 'Bonds can't continue to go down like this. Something has to happen.'"

What happened, for Milken, wasn't merely that the bond market gained almost as much as the stock market lost. The import of the crash was that it confirmed what he'd been expounding for years: "October nineteenth reaffirmed how volatile the equity markets are. We're in a period of increased volatility because America represents a smaller share of the world—and we're more affected by what happens in the world."

Such sober analysis was manna to those seeking wisdom in the chaos following the Crash of '87. For Milken, it was an enormous personal reassurance. Seeing into the future—the future of the continent as well as of the market—told him that he still had the touch. He could still blot out all distractions and see the great macro direction of the world economy before it made its global shifts. And then he could reach into the future, and, like so much clay, shape the raw material of things to come to his liking—he could, as few ever had the chance to do, elevate finance to a fine art.

Michael Milken's relationship with a facility for fifty troubled teenagers just a few miles from his home was as accidental—and,

---

*In the next few years, the stock market recovered in fits and starts, and the Dow Jones finally broke the 3,000 barrier. Still, the American stock market underperformed compared with the DBL Americas fund, which, from 1988 through 1991, returned almost 40 percent annually on investment.

some would feel, as suspect—as any of the associations that drifted into his orbit, only to become irrevocably bound to him. At a charity outing in October of 1987, he had seen a boy standing alone and crying. As he hurried to the boy's side, Dr. Barbara Firestone, founder of the HELP Group and Project Six, came over to explain that her charge was crying only because he was hungry. Something that needed doing! Milken hurried off. "I'm Mike," he said, when he returned with an armload of food for the boy and his friends. And then he and Firestone sat down for a chat about her work.

Firestone had no idea who "Mike" was, but she wasn't about to ignore anyone who was interested in supporting her cause. When Milken asked for more information, she dropped everything and prepared a video featuring the children. A few weeks later, Milken called to say a gift for Project Six was waiting for her at the Foundation office, and, oh, by the way, it was for $250,000. "Don't thank me," he said. "I'm only glad I'm in a position to do this."

In the coming years, he'd do much more. Once, at a charity event, he surreptitiously dropped an envelope and suggested to Firestone it must have slipped out of her purse—and, of course, it was a six-figure check. Another time, when he realized the residents of Project Six had to leave their haven on their eighteenth birthday, he funded several residences that combined vocational training and education with ongoing therapy.

The money wasn't, for Firestone, Milken's most important contribution; his personal commitment was. "I need success stories to keep me going," he confided to her, and, here, he found them. More, he generated them. He spent time with the kids, learning their life stories, pet peeves, and private cravings. Once, when he was scheduled to teach a math class, he brought Michael Jackson along, and although the singer wore a red zippered jacket and floppy-brimmed black hat, he soon was just another kid racing to get the right answer first. At sporting events, Milken would show up regularly—more regularly than, in his heyday, he'd made it to the school events of his own children—and shout encouragement to his young friends, calling each and every child by name. And when they felt down, he comforted them: "You're not disabled, you're children with more challenges."

In the middle of a criminal investigation, such goodness smacks of a performance. But no matter what other reasons figured in his involvement with these children, Milken's commitment to them was a return to an earlier time. In this simpler world, Project Six was both his family and his fledgling bond department. Here were the undervalued assets. And here was a leader who would make them shine. For Michael Milken, life had come full cycle.

CHAPTER TWELVE

Even by Wall Street standards, Will Hale had a foul mouth of awesome proportions. "What's the difference between an Ethiopian Jew and a regular Jew?" he once asked a customer. The man didn't know. "The Ethiopian Jew," Hale explained, "is the one with the Rolex around his waist." He fantasized with a Wall Street friend about taking Jane Fonda into the basement and having sex with her together, began a business call with "Hey, sperm breath," and called Sony "the gook stock." His response to rising liquor prices, he liked to say, was to buy cases of vodka and bourbon.

"I'm not a well individual," he'd confide.

But as a trader at Princeton/Newport Partners, Will Hale was, in 1985, well enough to listen to the orders that his bosses were placing. And when he noticed that they were buying Storer Communications stock for their friends at Coniston Partners, he decided to tag along. Not in a major way—he bought, for $275, a single Storer option. If a takeover bid for Storer pushed its stock price through the roof, he stood to make, at most, $2,000.

Hale, who'd been through four Wall Street firms before he was twenty-five, loved Princeton/Newport not just for the information he could appropriate, but for all he could learn. And there was much to learn—its founders, James Sutton Regan and former University of California math professor Edward Oakley Thorp, had produced a 20-percent annual return for their investors for almost two decades without a single losing year or a serious dip in profits. Their method was anything but simple; the traders in the Princeton, New Jersey, office used sophisticated computer programs developed in the Newport Beach, California, office to identify price discrepancies in stocks, bonds, and commodities. Then they used this data to hedge and straddle so aggressively that Princeton/Newport trades sometimes accounted for 1 percent of the total volume on the New York Stock Exchange.

"All those guys at the casinos counting cards," says Thorp, who once wrote a gambling classic called *Beat the Dealer*. "We found an even better way."

Not every Princeton/Newport play was as interesting as Storer. There were also tax trades, designed to avoid the adverse tax consequences of matching long-term losses with short-term gains. As a Princeton/Newport position approached the six-month mark—when profit or loss would be classified as long-term—the firm would sell it to its friends at Merrill Lynch and Drexel Burnham. After an appropriate interval, Princeton/Newport would buy it back at about the same price.

"The tax trades," Jay Regan says, "were the closest thing we had to no-brainers." Because of their low status, they were palmed off on the least accomplished trader—who, in 1985, was Will Hale, then in his second month at the firm. Hale's willingness to do this tedious work was not, according to Princeton/Newport executives, equaled by his manners or his competence. After fourteen months at the firm, they were distressed that he had not mastered the more complicated transactions that were the meat of their business. They couldn't stand his world-class profanity. And they told Will Hale all this when they let him go.

One option purchased on inside information is not usually a concern of the U.S. attorney, but as spring turned into summer in 1987, Giuliani's office was desperately looking for anything that would salvage its case against Freeman, Wigton, and Tabor. And so Neil Cartusciello—the assistant U.S. attorney who had handled the arrests of the "Wall Street Three" and who had, at the dismissal of charges, promised to return with fresh indictments—sat in a document room, day after day, looking through trading records.

Cartusciello was following a tiny lead. When he helped debrief Martin Siegel, Siegel talked about the Storer Communications takeover battle. According to Siegel, Freeman had gleaned his inside information from the firm accumulating stock for one of the bidders. He hadn't mentioned the name, but the trading records would surely show it, and so Cartusciello had hunkered down with these dreary printouts.

At last, he justified the weeks of dull labor; he found the first piece of the puzzle. A firm named Princeton/Newport Partners had made big option buys in Storer, and every option had been bought through Freeman's firm. And something else—one Storer option had been bought by Will Hale, of the same address as Princeton/Newport Partners. Cartusciello had the firm's records subpoenaed. He also subpoenaed Will Hale, who was now working in London at Salomon Brothers.

Michael Lewis, then a trader at Salomon in London and later the author of *Liar's Poker,* remembers Hale as someone who presented himself as a junior "Big Swinging Dick." But with a subpoena on his desk, Hale was spooked. This "bungler with an ego," as another colleague had dubbed him, was sure he was in the middle of a major scandal having nothing to do with Storer and everything to do with the Princeton/Newport tax trades. He rushed to his boss to confess.

"I don't think you have to worry," the managing director said. He understood what Hale didn't: Tax trades were common on Wall Street. "They were part of our business," Michael Lewis confirms. "Regardless of the spirit of the law, people at Solly found ways around it."

Hale had no lawyer, so he hired one—John Gross. As it happens, Gross is one of Rudolph Giuliani's closest friends. Giuliani was best man at Gross's wedding; when Giuliani's first marriage broke up, he moved in for a while with Gross. They had worked together; for a time, Gross was assistant chief of the criminal division while Giuliani was U.S. attorney. And they'd work together again—when Giuliani ran for mayor, John Gross was his finance chairman.

Gross has declined to say how Hale came to be his client. Prosecutors, who have described Gross as a tough negotiator, say Hale's choice of lawyers was a "coincidence." Defense lawyers in the Princeton/Newport case insist that coincidence had nothing to do with it. "There is a long history of cooperating witnesses getting to Gross," one says.

Whatever the genesis of John Gross, a wonderful dance now ensued. Gross told the prosecutors that Hale wouldn't testify voluntarily, though he would entertain an offer of immunity. Fine, the prosecutors replied, what will he tell us? Oh, no, Gross said, we won't give you any previews; it's a take-it-or-leave-it proposition. The prosecutors sighed, but at the end of the minuet, they decided to "gamble" and immunize Hale. And in November of 1987, they brought him into the grand jury.

Bruce Baird's initial questions produced no earthshaking revelations. Then he asked Hale why he had been fired by Princeton/Newport.

"I wasn't comfortable with a lot of the things they were involved in," Hale replied.

"What things?"

"Tax trades," said Hale, who had complained only once and very briefly about the tax trades, and had encouraged several of his friends to apply for jobs at Princeton/Newport. "The tax trades that we did with Merrill Lynch and Drexel Burnham."

"Was there a particular person at either of those firms you dealt with?"

"At Drexel, it was two individuals. It was Bruce Newberg and his assistant Lisa."

Bruce Newberg was a key player in Michael Milken's department. Clearly, the people at Princeton/Newport knew Milken; they might have some great Drexel stories. And Jay Regan might also be of considerable assistance in the Freeman investigation—as Baird already knew, Regan and Freeman had been close friends ever since their Dartmouth days.

Bruce Baird's "gamble" had paid off. For with Hale's testimony, Baird has recalled, "the world changed."

But the world might change again. That is, although Gross had no ties to any other defense attorney involved in this investigation, the prosecutors believed he might decide to share Hale's testimony with lawyers for Freeman and Drexel and Princeton/Newport—and evidence could disappear. It was important, by that logic, to move fast.

In mid-December, therefore, Giuliani's men staged a bigger, more high-tech version of the Freeman-Wigton-Tabor raid. This time, vans filled with federal marshals cruised slowly down the streets of Princeton, New Jersey. They stopped in front of a pleasant brick-and-glass building a chip shot from the university. And then fifty men packing weapons and wearing bulletpoof vests rushed into the Princeton/Newport offices.

The raid had a *Twilight Zone* aspect. The marshals had a video camera; a Princeton/Newport employee grabbed the office camera and started taking pictures of the government's men. The agents found a fake gun; for the first time in recent memory, they noted, they found no drugs. Then they commandeered the conference room, opened their laptop computers, and started typing lists of the material they were taking with them—in the process, they generated so much paper they accidentally left behind an affidavit that stripped the anonymity from their "confidential source," Will Hale.

But what mattered is what they found: hundreds of cartons that contained seventy-two reels from Princeton/Newport all-hearing taping system. This system—fourteen channels wide, holding twenty-four hundred hours of conversation on each giant spool—had been installed a few years earlier to provide a record of every trader's phone conversations in the event of a dispute. Normally, the tapes were recycled every six months. But there were five reels of tape in a cabinet that dated from 1984 and 1985, when Princeton/Newport had a misunderstanding with Nomura Securities over the terms of a deal—the tapes, the firm believed, would prove that Nomura bore some responsibility for a loss of $3 million.

Those tapes provided far more than that. They also featured Drexel and Merrill traders talking about arrangements that any prosecutor in the current environment would find suspicious. Some sounded like classic examples of stock parking. One had Bruce Newberg discussing securities prices with his Princeton/Newport counterpart in a way that invited an indictment for stock manipulation. Another showcased an argument over "cost-of-carry" charges for stock parking.

But the most telling spoke less to criminality than to atmosphere and attitude. In this conversation, Newberg suggested that he'd like the price of a certain stock to fall. Later, Princeton/Newport head trader Charles Zarzecki reported that he'd tried to accomplish this by selling through intermediaries.

"They didn't know it was us," Zarzecki said.

"You're a sleazebag," Newberg replied.

"You taught me, man."

Newberg chortled.

"Hey, listen, turkey . . ." Zarzecki began.

Then Newberg put him away.

"Welcome," he told Zarzecki, "to the world of being a sleaze."

As the prosecutors listened to conversations like this in the weeks after the raid, they recognized what the tapes represented—a human dimension that had been sorely lacking in the investigation. This passage would disgust a jury. And it would appall the public. It was probably the best sound bite since Ivan Boesky told college students that "greed is all right."

"The beauty of the trading records is that nothing tells you it's a phony scheme," an assistant U.S. attorney exulted. "The tapes show what happened: These are extraordinarily bright people, they're very accomplished at what they do, and, when they cheat, they're equally accomplished."

While the marshals were driving toward Princeton, Thomas Doonan was flying to Los Angeles to deliver the day's second surprise. For an investigator who had arrested Dennis Levine, supervised Ivan Boesky's phone calls and slapped the handcuffs on Timothy Tabor, this assignment had the look of a comedown. Lisa Jones—twenty-four years old, pudgy, and sweet-faced, a teenage runaway who'd become softer and less worldly with time and respectability—was hardly worthy of Doonan's expertise.

Perhaps that was why Doonan deviated so dramatically from principles long observed by government investigators. First, he chose to go alone to the home of a young woman who lived alone. Second, knowing that Jones was due at work before dawn the next morning, he went to her home at a time when she was either asleep or preparing for bed. These deviations from accepted practice were, of course, to Doonan's advantage—with no witnesses to the conversation, there would be no one to contradict his version, and with Jones's energies at low ebb, she might unthinkingly incriminate her superiors.

"Government agent," said the voice at the door.

"Come to the window," Jones replied. "Show me your identification."

The muscular, short-haired man did. Jones invited him in. For a single woman making $104,000 that year, she lived modestly; in her sweatclothes, she seemed equally ordinary.

"Still work for Bruce Newberg?" Doonan asked.

"No," she said. "He doesn't work there anymore."

"You've had dealings with a Will Hale, who works out of Princeton?"

She had.

"Mostly about convertible bonds?"

"Yes."

"A number of these transactions—Hale and his people sold them to Drexel, and then, in thirty-one days or thereabouts, you sold them back."

"That's right."

"Those were parks?"

"We do trades like that—but they're not parks."

"Are they for tax purposes?"

At this point, Lisa Jones finally understood where Doonan was headed. "I can't answer any more questions," she said, "until I talk to the lawyer at Drexel."

"Are you aware that Will Hale's offices have been searched?"

"No, no," Lisa Jones said, getting very scared.

"We were hoping you'd cooperate with us," Doonan said, handing her a grand jury subpoena.

"I'm willing to cooperate, but I want to have an attorney present."

"I know you're an Indian, just like me," Doonan said. "The government is interested in the people who told you to do this. So let me give you some advice. If you use a Drexel lawyer, the lawyer won't be looking out for you—he'll be working for Drexel."

"Does my firm know you've contacted me?"

The investigator didn't reply.

After Doonan left, Lisa Jones felt an urgent need to call Kevin Madigan, the lawyer for Milken's department. But she was, after less than fifteen minutes in the presence of a government man, completely terrified. Was her phone bugged? It wasn't worth taking a chance. She got in her car and drove to the nearest pay phone.

A few weeks later, in early January of 1988, Lisa Jones became the first Drexel employee to appear before a federal grand jury. Unsurprisingly, she was accompanied to the federal courthouse by Drexel lawyers Thomas Curnin and Elliot Lauer. And everything that Tom Doonan had said started to become horribly true.

Lisa Jones had lied to Drexel about her age, her birthplace, her education. With Assistant U.S. Attorney Mark Hansen questioning her, she now told the grand jurors an improbable story—she knew nothing about the trades she'd done with Will Hale. Miss Jones, *please*, Hansen said, but the trading assistant was adamant. Furious, Hansen went out into the hallway to tell her lawyers that she was perjuring herself. He was agitated; his voice carried. Inside the grand jury room, Lisa Jones began to cry.

Hard on the heels of the Princeton/Newport raid came an event that seemed to have nothing to do with Michael Milken. That was the indictment of E. Robert Wallach—a flamboyant San Francisco personal-injury lawyer who was Edwin Meese's best friend—for his role in the Wedtech scandal. Here, at last, Giuliani found a non-Wall Street case as compelling as the prosecution of Stanley Friedman; although Wedtech was based in New York, its tentacles reached all the way to the office of the attorney general.

Wallach's role in the Wedtech affair was hardly central. At the beginning of the Reagan administration, he moved his law practice to Washington, the better to bombard Meese with great ideas. These memos touched on many issues, including Wedtech, a Bronx-based military contracting company. It was exactly the kind of company the Reagan crowd could love—minority-owned, and fiercely proud of having made its way without handouts. With some government contracts, Wallach argued, Wedtech could become a showcase for Reaganomics.

For all Wallach had learned about Wedtech, one key fact eluded him. Wedtech's success wasn't based on solid Republican values; it was that old story, entrepreneurship that succeeded because its executives bribed politicians and hoodwinked stockholders. Wallach, a jolly zealot, had been duped along with the rest.

After Wallach had posted more than two hundred memos to Meese, Wedtech decided to compensate him. Wallach's invoice acknowledged payment for legal services; later, he mailed another letter acknowledging payment for legal services.

In the summer of 1987, prosecutors told Wallach he might be indicted—he hadn't performed legal services, they insisted, he'd acted as a lobbyist. In December, Giuliani's men went to

Washington to seek Justice Department authorization for an indictment on "racketeering" charges. A Justice official who attended that meeting told *American Lawyer* editor Steve Brill that no one from Washington could believe how little evidence Baruch Weiss, the thirty-one-year-old assistant U.S. attorney whom Giuliani had assigned to this case, was presenting.

"We'd read all this stuff about Wallach and figured he was a number-one sleaze—and this is all Rudy could get?" the Justice official said. "It looked pretty thin. . . . In another situation, we might have urged them to wait and try harder, or even to forget it. You don't do that with Rudy Giuliani, especially in a case when Rudy's gunning for Ed Meese, or you'll read about it the next day in the paper."

But although the Justice Department approved the indictment of Robert Wallach, the U.S. attorney did not immediately file charges. On December 20, 1987—three days after the Princeton/Newport raid—prosecutors called Wallach's lawyer to give him one last chance. He could, they said, plead guilty to a lesser charge. If, that is, he would help Giuliani indict Ed Meese.

In his years in Washington, Edwin Meese had attracted a great deal of attention, very little of it positive. He'd called the American Civil Liberties Union "a criminals' lobby." He'd suggested that Ebenezer Scrooge, the villain in Dickens's *A Christmas Carol*, suffered from nothing more than bad press—"if you really look at the facts, he didn't exploit Bob Cratchit." He'd failed to disclose an interest-free loan because "it never occurred to me that an interest-free loan was a thing of value." He'd remarked that *Miranda* "only helps guilty defendants," opined that Supreme Court rulings apply just to the case at hand, and endorsed drug testing for everyone who was arrested. And, not least, back in the early 1980s, he'd crossed Rudy Giuliani.

If ignorance were indictable, Meese would end his days in jail; rarely has the Republic had a less qualified, more exasperatingly dense attorney general. But premeditated criminality is another matter. "I have nothing to turn Ed Meese in for," Wallach said, "because there is nothing." Nor could Wallach see himself pleading guilty for providing the kind of client services that, it seemed to him, big-time Washington lawyers perform every day.

And so, just three days before Christmas, E. Robert Wallach—valedictorian of his law school class, former president of the bar association of San Francisco, and a United States representa-

tive to the Human Rights Commission—was indicted as a racketeer.

January blew in with empty courtrooms and no press conferences, but Rudolph Giuliani hoped to change that. Early in the
new year, Bruce Baird met with Jack Arsenault, a lawyer representing Princeton/Newport trader Paul Berkman. Baird was, according to Arsenault, using the occasion to mark the final
flowering of the Giuliani era.

"Look, we have no interest in Berkman and no interest in
Princeton/Newport," Baird reportedly said. "But through Berkman, we can get Regan, and through Regan, we can get Drexel
Burnham and Freeman. We have bigger fish to fry—and we'll
roll over you to get where we want to go."

Baird denies saying anything of the kind. Arsenault swears
his notes are almost verbatim. And, Arsenault says, the proof
Baird threatened him is what happened as a result of that conversation—he never talked to Baird again.

Baird does acknowledge that hostility was the continuing motif of the entire Princeton/Newport case. "Typically, defense lawyers and prosecutors have a dialogue, and there's an effort made
by defense lawyers to convince prosecutors," he says. "We're not
crazy—there's no point forcing a trial no one wants. But in this
case, we're talking about a couple of five-minute meetings. Those
discussions just didn't happen. The defense said, 'The hell with
the government.'"

Baird also acknowledges that some find his "crime is crime"
approach harsh. But he makes no apologies for the way he thinks.
In his first five years at the U.S. attorney's office, he convicted
Joseph Colombo and Carmine Persico. When he was named chief
of the Securities and Commodities Fraud unit in 1986, he inevitably compared those men to the subjects of his new investigation—and the comparison wasn't favorable to Jay Regan and
Michael Milken.

"From the outside, organized crime figures look like devils
and Wall Street people look substantial," Baird explains. "Ninety-
five percent of the people on Wall Street are honest, but the bad
apples . . . I have less sympathy for them than for the Mafia. The
Mafia is immigrants who didn't know better and had no other life;
in cases like Milken, you see real *omerta*. It was almost as if they
viewed themselves as being beyond the law."

Baird feels an equal lack of sympathy for those who represent Wall Street defendants. "Every poor kid who goes through the Manhattan criminal courts in an average day gets a fraction of the due process given to the average white-collar defendant with the best of defense counsel," he says.

Baird is thin and quiet and bespectacled, and he can deliver the most passionately held views in a monotone. Defense lawyers were not fooled by his packaging; they all seem to detest him. "Bruce never lied—he never claimed to have an open mind, he always told us he was determined to crush Milken," one Milken attorney says. Less ironic defense lawyers found Baird simply impossible: aggressive, uncompromising, dogmatic. As an infant, one lawyer insists, he was "never nursed." Another describes Baird as "a real type-A personality, one jab and he's crazed." A third calls him "unrestrained, vicious . . . a cowboy." His colleagues have given signals that they agree. When Baird left the U.S. attorney's office in 1989, one of the first things that his successors told Michael Milken's lawyers was "Look, we're not all like Bruce down here."

But Bruce Baird's quirks alone don't explain why he moved so dramatically on Princeton/Newport in the wake of the "Wall Street Three" debacle, why he may have laid his real cards on the table in a preliminary meeting with a defense lawyer, and why he so enthusiastically embraced the racketeering law and its potential for astronomical financial penalties.

There is also the Giuliani Factor.

Back in September of 1987, Rudolph Giuliani had an important decision to make. He'd been in the job four years. Daniel Patrick Moynihan, the incumbent Democratic senator, looked vulnerable in the upcoming election—was this the time to move out and up? New York's Republican senator, Alphonse D'Amato, thought it was a great opportunity for Giuliani to get back to Washington. And he encouraged Giuliani to run against Moynihan.

But this was not the same Alphonse D'Amato who had stood, in baseball cap and Phil Spector shades, next to Rudy Giuliani on an upper Manhattan street corner in 1986. On that day, Giuliani showed up, his hair combed straight down like Jerry Lewis, his eyes shielded by Ray Bans, and his torso sheathed in a sleeveless leather vest. Buying crack, they were, two highly visible concerned citizens showing the Associated Press photographer how easy it was to score—those were the days.

And then Wall Street completed its leveraged buyout of D'Amato.

It had started, as business deals so often do in Los Angeles, over dinner at Chasen's; at a fund-raiser in 1985, Michael Milken and twenty-three of his co-workers in Beverly Hills each handed over checks for $1,000. By September, D'Amato was asking Drexel and other investment banks how they felt about proposed legislation to curb hostile takeovers. In December, when the bill was introduced, it was not offensive to Drexel; five days later, thirty-six New York Drexel executives, including Fred Joseph, sent the D'Amato campaign their checks for $500 each.

It wouldn't have been so awful that D'Amato was now the "senator from Wall Street" if it weren't for the fact that, just as it had been his prerogative to propose Giuliani to the Justice Department for the U.S. attorney's job in New York, it was his prerogative to recommend Giuliani's successor. And although he didn't tell Giuliani, he had a candidate in mind—Otto Obermaier.

Obermaier had a partner who was working the Drexel case (and would soon add a Princeton/Newport trader to his client list). Obermaier was close to other defense lawyers defending Drexel. Obermaier was no fan of imaginative prosecutions; he had likened ABSCAM to putting Bo Derek into a Notre Dame locker room. Obermaier might, therefore, give Al D'Amato more than a courtesy meeting when it came time to indict the Wedtech scammers—who would soon include D'Amato's longtime friend Mario Biaggi.

Otto Obermaier, in short, was the last man in New York whom Rudolph Giuliani wanted to see sitting at his old desk.

By November of 1987, Giuliani's intelligence had learned that D'Amato had Obermaier waiting in the wings. And so he took the unprecedented step that month of offering the public a portrait of the successor he had in mind. Such a man, Giuliani said, would recognize that the Wall Street cases he and his staff had been developing had to be resolved with indictments and aggressive prosecutions. And such a man should be named soon, so the outgoing U.S. attorney could have him up to speed before he left office.

If, that is, he left his post as U.S. attorney.

All fall, Giuliani waffled. The polls showed him losing hand-ily to Moynihan, but if he ran and lost, the administration would owe him a big favor. What to do? Giuliani had decided he'd have to make his decision quickly. He would, he told intimates, an-nounce his resignation as U.S. attorney on January 19, 1988.

But where was D'Amato? November passed. December passed. And not so much as a peep from the senator about his choice for a Giuliani replacement. That couldn't be. They had to talk. And they did. Twice. And D'Amato refused to tell Giuliani whom he planned to recommend. "I can't walk out of here on that basis," the U.S. attorney replied.

In February, Giuliani made an announcement that came as a considerable surprise to New York Republicans: He wasn't go-ing to run against Moynihan. While his party scrambled to find a candidate willing to fall on his sword in the election, Giuliani returned his attention to the prosecutions of Drexel, Milken, Princeton/Newport, and Wedtech. There was no particular relish in this—the mood in the U.S. attorney's office that season was said to be one of grim determination.

The problem wasn't morale. It was evidence—besides Boesky, the U.S. attorney's office didn't have much. And progress wasn't going to be rapid; as John Carroll, one of the assistant U.S. attorneys on the case put it, he knew so little about the securities business that he'd only recently learned the difference between a put and a call.

How different it would have been if the fall offensive had worked. Princeton/Newport, Lisa Jones, Robert Wallach—had any one of those played out with the speed and ease of Levine and Boesky and Siegel, Rudolph Giuliani would have called this New Year his happiest ever.

But no one caved in. And D'Amato suckered him. Rudolph Giuliani, all dressed up and nowhere to go, had exactly a year—until January of 1989—to step up and announce his avail-ability for mayor of New York, the next office that was up for grabs. It wouldn't take a genius, therefore, to predict that Giuli-ani would want to announce a big arrest, a huge indictment, or a mammoth settlement no later than December.

CHAPTER THIRTEEN

When Michael Milken was introduced to Mikhail Gorbachev in early December of 1987, they hadn't spent a minute together before Gorbachev said he wanted to sell Russian cars in America. Milken had a different idea. "What do the Russians do best?" he wondered. But the question was rhetorical; Milken had an answer ready. "Retinal surgery and cancer research. So . . . the thing to do is convert nonmilitary science into commercial activities through joint ventures with American pharmaceutical and medical companies."

DBL Americas goes to Russia—an idea that Gorbachev seemed to approve. In short order, a Drexel delegation was dispatched to Moscow. Michael Milken began to muse that Reagan and Bush would make very good leaders of the Soviet Union, while Gorbachev might make a better than average President of the United States.

Milken's grimly ironic speculation was colored by current events. All through December, signals had been emanating from *The Wall Street Journal* and the SEC, and they suggested that charges against Drexel, both Milkens, Peter Ackerman, Cary Maultasch, and a virtually anonymous Drexel salesperson named

Pamela Monzert were imminent.* That the charges were coming was unsurprising; the way the SEC had treated Drexel employees had prepared Milken for the worst. "You're presumed guilty," an associate in the High-Yield Bond Department reported after a SEC deposition in 1987. "They assume you had an ulterior motive for everything. They act as if your entire purpose each and every day was to swindle the world."

Other Drexel employees returned to Beverly Hills shaking their heads over the ignorance of the SEC lawyers. In new offerings, there's a provision nicknamed the "green shoe." That is, if a million bonds are to be issued, but there are orders for a million two hundred thousand, the offering may be enlarged by 15 percent; the "green shoe" is where the extra bonds come from. "If you said a word they hadn't heard or didn't understand—and it didn't have to be 'green shoe,' it could be something as obvious as 'syndicate'—they got so excited," a Milken associate recalls. "It's like we were there to train them."

SEC questioning was, on occasion, comical. Toward the end of an unrevealing mid-1987 deposition of Arthur Bilger, the second-in-command of the Corporate Finance office in Beverly Hills, the SEC lawyer, apparently hoping to confirm the lurid stories of wild Drexel parties during bond conferences, wondered about an entry in Bilger's calendar: "Please call Judy. You will like the call." What did *that* mean? "Judy got me tickets to the Academy Awards," Bilger replied, deflating his interrogator.

Milken, though worried by the relentlessness of the SEC investigation, professed to be unsurprised by such stories. The SEC, he said, could decide to target you just for breathing. That the enforcement division lawyers knew nothing about the securities business was, he suggested, only to be expected—if they had a clue, they would never have taken Boesky seriously.

Far more worrisome, for Milken, was the health of Edward Bennett Williams. In December, Williams had looked thin and

---

*In September of 1988, the SEC filed charges against the Milkens, Cary Maultasch, and Pamela Monzert, along with Drexel Burnham, Victor and Steven Posner, and Pennsylvania Engineering Corporation. Peter Ackerman was never charged by the SEC or the U.S. attorney. Cary Maultasch ultimately got immunity from prosecution; the SEC dropped its demands for a seven-figure settlement. Pamela Monzert was never indicted by the prosecutors. Almost four years after filing charges against her, the SEC has taken no action against her; technically, her case is still pending.

drained. But Williams had rallied, and on January 5, 1988, he was the leader of the delegation of Milken lawyers at an SEC meeting to discuss the forthcoming charges. It was quite an assembly: Liman, Litt, and Flumenbaum were seated next to Williams, while John Sturc was accompanied by no fewer than nine members of the SEC enforcement staff.

Sturc did all the talking.

Most of the charges, Sturc began, involved Milken's "fraudulent scheme" with Boesky. That scheme took form in late 1984, he said, when Boesky bought stock in Fischbach at Milken's direction; here, for the first time, Milken guaranteed Boesky that he wouldn't lose money. Boesky next bought stock, and was guaranteed against loss, in MCA. In January of 1985, Sturc alleged, Boesky bought Diamond Shamrock and shorted Occidental Petroleum because Drexel had given him inside information about their upcoming merger. That same month, Milken had Boesky short Wickes, again with a guarantee against loss. In March, Boesky parked Phillips stock with Milken. In the spring, Milken had Boesky take a large position in Harris Graphics; from August to October, Boesky bought MGM/UA and Pacific Lumber on Milken's instructions. Early in 1986, Boesky shorted Lorimar for Milken's benefit. In March, Drexel lied when it billed Boesky $5.3 million for consulting. In April, Boesky bought Stone Container stock to push the price higher while Drexel was managing and pricing a new issue of convertible stock; that same month, he pushed Wickes stock to a particular price to accommodate Milken. And, finally, Boesky bought National Gypsum at a time when Milken and Drexel knew Wickes was about to make a tender offer.

The SEC had flagged only two non-Boesky transactions—a Drexel purchase of Lorimar when it allegedly had inside information, and a possible disclosure violation during the Safeway leveraged buyout. But there was no need for the SEC enforcement team to keep looking. What they cataloged in the Boesky list alone covered all the important violations.

Margin.

Record keeping.

Insider trading.

Manipulation.

The way the commission saw it, Milken and Drexel had crossed every line there was.

Sturc was not precise on the punishment the SEC would seek. Triple damages, of course, for insider trading in Occidental, Lorimar, and National Gypsum. Disgorgement of all illegally gained trading profits and fees. And the SEC reserved the right to seek permanent disbarment from the securities industry—for Drexel as well as for individuals.

When might the SEC file charges?

Anytime after January 19.

What about the U.S. attorney?

Sturc said Giuliani's progress was of no great concern; the SEC would move forward as soon as it was ready. That was a very unusual tack, and the defense lawyers had to suppress their wonderment—for if the SEC and U.S. attorney were not coordinating their prosecutions, that could be very good for Milken. As soon as the SEC filed charges, his lawyers planned to file motions for discovery. With luck, they could review much of the SEC's evidence and get access to the testimony against Milken in time to counter Giuliani's investigation—with a lot of luck, they might even be able to depose Boesky before Giuliani filed his charges.

Why this unusual urgency at the SEC?

Williams didn't ask, and Sturc didn't say. But for the enforcement division, the reasons had far more to do with conviction than credit-grabbing. Lynch and his associates were thoroughly sick of the mergers and acquisitions orgy of the 1980s. They'd never had any respect for the intellectual underpinnings of this explosion. For them, the economists of the "Chicago School"—the high priests of what some people called the Reagan "revolution"—were just political hacks in disguise, outright charlatans who preached dressed-up crap that was credible mostly to number-crunching twenty-six-year-olds.

But the SEC's enforcement lawyers understood why ordinarily sober businesspeople parroted this ridiculous free-market, trickle-down, supple-side ideology: The immense profits washing over Wall Street had made the players crazy. Formerly sane men now talked as if the financial markets weren't just a discipline but an ethic, as if the markets were not just efficient but morally correct.

Large sums of money have often blinded people to questions of right and wrong. What terrified the SEC was the unprecedented scale of the money—which, to them, clearly suggested massive criminality. In Michael Milken, the SEC saw someone more powerful than 99 percent of all the CEOs in America, a man who could command what a public company would or wouldn't do. And why? Because he said so. And because he had a very poorly developed sense of right and wrong, he was destined to win more power and money and control until he was stopped—if he was stopped.

If he wasn't, the future was too black to consider, for at the SEC, some of the enforcement lawyers truly believed that Milken and Drexel could bring about the demise of America. They sounded like zealots when they talked among themselves like this, and they knew it, but they were quite sure it wasn't their fault. From the beginning, they believed that Drexel and Milken had scorned their investigation. "The government's $30,000-a-year lawyers will never crack this case"—that, they felt, was the Drexel attitude.

It rankled. It was bad enough that the least important of these Drexel people had assistants when many SEC lawyers sometimes had none. Or that they had the latest technology while many SEC lawyers were still using typewriters. But for these lowlifes to sneer at people who made less money—as if money were the measure of character—was to throw a gauntlet down.

And so, although they'd never said it before, even SEC veterans found themselves telling each other, I don't care how long it takes, if we have to stay here for fifteen years . . . *let's crush these bastards*.

In the end, that sentiment was why the SEC felt it had to move fast and hard. A criminal prosecution would be welcome. But if it couldn't happen right away, too bad for Giuliani. The most urgent task, the SEC enforcement lawyers all agreed, was to blast Milken—to get the man they considered the most dangerous criminal on Wall Street out of the markets.

"It was hard going," Bruce Baird recalls, of that winter at the U.S. attorney's office. "We had a lot to learn, and we couldn't go outside to learn it—others seemed to feel they'd be viewed as traitors if they helped us. There was a sense on Wall Street that we were the enemy."

Rudolph Giuliani assessed the lack of progress and made a

calculated decision. But he didn't keep it to himself. True to form, he made the announcement where it would have the greatest effect—in front of an audience of securities lawyers, at the Securities Regulation Institute of the University of California at San Diego, on January 22, 1988.

Defense lawyers might call it the criminalization of technical violations, but to Giuliani, it was an insider trading plague. "All you have to do is raise your eyes up from your clients and your books," he said, "and you will realize that we are facing a crisis of unacceptable behavior among people at upper levels of our society."

In such a crisis, you use your strongest weapons. Well, that's exactly what he was going to do. "We won't be shy about using the racketeering law," he said. And not just for overt insider trading offenses, he added. "Related crimes" were equally likely to produce this most serious of indictments.

Ripples of whispered speculation went through the room. The Racketeer Influenced and Corrupt Organizations Act—known more simply as RICO—was the most draconian law on the books. In the hands of a restrained prosecutor, it was a deadly weapon. In the hands of Rudolph Giuliani, it might be the equivalent of the neutron bomb.

In 1970, when Michael Milken was just starting to work full-time at Drexel and Jay Regan was running his trading company out of his apartment, Robert Blakey was putting the finishing touches on RICO. Blakey, then thirty-four, was the son of a banker, but he had very little interest in finance. He wasn't even particularly interested in organized crime, which he had studied for more than a decade. "I have no real ambitions," he would later explain. "I worked on organized crime because, when I got to the Justice Department, they asked me to."

Blakey, a graduate of Notre Dame and Notre Dame Law School, left the Justice Department when Robert Kennedy did, taught law for a few years at his alma mater, then joined the President's Crime Commission, becoming its chief counsel. He worked for Nixon in 1968—"He was interested in crime control, and Ramsey Clark and that crowd certainly weren't"—and, after the election, was asked by John Mitchell to be his assistant. Blakey recommended another man for the job. His name was John Dean.

The Mafia was then infiltrating legitimate companies and nib-
bling at the edges of Wall Street. To counter it, Senator John
McClellan asked Blakey to draft a law that would be "a major
new tool in extirpating the baleful influence of organized crime
on our economic life." But Blakey didn't mean the same thing by
"organized crime" as the men who voted for this law. He had
been deeply influenced by Edwin Sutherland's 1949 study, *White
Collar Crime*, which argued that there was a continuum between
violent street crime and white-collar offenses. The only difference
between mobsters and shysters, Sutherland contended, was "in
the administrative procedures used in dealing with the offenders."

This tough-minded view of white-collar crime found a sympathetic ear in Blakey, who was an aficionado of gangster movies.
"If you look at *Little Caesar* as an effort to understand the rise of
organized crime in the United States, you see that it perceives
only half the problem—the half that deals with *them*," he says.
"But in his rise to the top of organized crime, Rico Bendello apes
the techniques of legitimate business. In an important scene, he's
fitted for his first formal suit, the one he'll wear when he sees
'Mr. Big,' the businessman who lives in the beautiful house on
top of the hill."

Blakey's law, conveniently nicknamed after the title character of *Little Caesar*, makes no distinction between white-collar
and no-collar crime. Under RICO, any defendant can be charged
as a "racketeer" or any business can be indicted as a "racketeering
enterprise" if a prosecutor can identify two crimes—or "predicate
acts"—over a ten-year period. These acts can be murder, extor-
tion, and drug dealing. They can also be wire fraud, securities
fraud, or mail fraud.*

Anyone convicted under RICO faces twenty years in prison
on each racketeering count, even if he has already been tried,
convicted, and jailed for the offenses that qualified him for the
RICO indictment. But an extended stay in jail is not the truly

---

*When Rudolph Giuliani moved to bring charges against Edwin Meese's friend, E. Robert
Wallach, for example, he didn't claim that the lobbying Wallach had done for Wedtech
was illegal. Sending a letter for lobbying but indicating that the bill was for legal services,
however, constituted mail fraud. Sending two letters—less than a minute's work for Wallach—fulfilled the requirements for a racketeering indictment.

remarkable aspect of RICO. Its real power is economic.

RICO hits the white-collar criminal where it hurts him most—in the wallet. the government may force a convicted racketeer to pay triple damages. It may attach his lawyer's fees. And that is just the start of RICO's financial bite. A RICO conviction also entitles the government to seize any property the criminal "established, operated, controlled, conducted, or participated in"—the government can take the whole enchilada.

This financial destruction doesn't wait for a guilty verdict. Under RICO, prosecutors can apply—on indictment day—for a restraint of a defendant's assets in the amount of the anticipated forfeiture. In a classic Mafia case, where organized crime insinuates itself into a legitimate business with the sole intention of looting its till, this provision guarantees that there will be assets to seize at the end of a trial. On Main Street or Wall Street, however, the name of the game is preserving capital and ensuring access to a steady stream of credit. In the case of a legitimate business indicted as a racketeer, these prosecutorial powers strike at the very heart of the enterprise—here, RICO is the equivalent of a rubber truncheon.

So the evidence against him is the *least* important consideration for a businessman facing RICO charges. When faced with financial ruin and subsequent labeling as a racketeer, the legitimate businessman doesn't, as a general rule, have any options: He must plead guilty and settle the case *before* indictment. For the legitimate businessman, the presumption of innocence is, in effect, obliterated—the indictment *is* the verdict.

Rudolph Giuliani, who had attended Robert Blakey's RICO seminars, was among the first to see that RICO could be, as a fellow prosecutor has described it, "our Stradivarius, our Colt .45, our Louisville Slugger, our Cuisinart—and our true love." When he became U.S. attorney, he very quickly used RICO to make mincemeat of the city's Mafia families, taking sole credit for an idea that, as Blakey and other organized crime specialists very clearly recall, did not originate with him.

But RICO was too effective a tool to use only on those whose names ended with vowels. RICO was a perfect weapon to bring Milken and Drexel to their knees. There was only one problem—no U.S. attorney anywhere had ever used RICO against a securities firm. Just as no securities executive knew what its effect would be, neither did any prosecutor.*

After being thwarted for more than a year, it made sense that Giuliani would want to indict Drexel and Milken as racketeers. Still, he knew it was essential to strike a balance between punishment and overkill. His goal, after all, was to exact a plea from Milken and Drexel, not to put ten thousand people—ten thousand voters—out of work and negatively affect all the law firms, investment banks, printers, caterers, and car companies that made a big chunk of their earnings by servicing and opposing Drexel.

Clearly, some sort of demonstration was in order. A dry run. An experience that was, in its way, equivalent to the Spanish Civil War—an exercise that would test tactics and weapons against an unimportant target in the securities business before the first team stepped onto the field. The U.S. attorney's office did not have to search long and hard to find a case like that. It had one right in its sights—Princeton/Newport.

In the spring of 1988, Jay Regan played into Giuliani's hands by summarily rejecting what prosecutors described as their best offer. He wouldn't plead guilty to one count of tax evasion in exchange for total cooperation because, he said, he knew nothing bad about Robert Freeman and hadn't talked business with Michael Milken in five years. And, as he noted, "we didn't think we were guilty."

The government was alleging that fifty-nine Princeton/Newport tax trades were sham transactions, with no economic substance. But on Regan's bookshelf was a volume of United States tax codes, and there, underlined, were sections that seemed to support the validity of those trades. Because, in tax cases, the government must prove that the individual had clear knowledge he was violating the law, Regan felt confident that he and the company faced nothing more than a fine and a recalculation of its tax bill. So he was absolutely

---

*There was, however, ample evidence that the statute could be a death warrant for a legitimate business. In Virginia, for example, prosecutors charged a bookstore owner as a racketeer for selling six smutty magazines and four sex videos for a total sale of $105.30. A judge ordered the seizure of the owner's three bookstores—worth perhaps $1 million. Here, the motivation was explicit. "We wanted to do RICOs," an official said, "to wipe out the business."

stunned when the prosecutors started talking about RICO charges and suggesting that Princeton/Newport's forfeitures might run to $50 million.*

Regan had been in trouble before. At Dartmouth, he put popcorn in a laundromat washing machine and got arrested; another night, he drove a hearse carrying nine friends and a keg of beer across the dean's lawn, ripping out hedges and making himself exceedingly unpopular with the dean. He regarded his present difficulty about as seriously. "According to the government, we started being racketeers in November of 1984 and stopped in February of 1986," he says. "Every other period, though, we were normal guys."

After the grand jury voted to indict Regan, his associates, and Bruce Newberg, the prosecutors still were not quick to file charges. Instead, they decided that Regan's attitude might improve if he had the opportunity to consider the evidence of his criminality, so they invited him to listen to his taping system's greatest hits. This was to take place on a Saturday morning. "Fine," Regan told his lawyer, Ted Wells. "I'll meet you in front of a diner in lower Manhattan."

On Saturday morning, Wells arrived at the diner right on time. Jay Regan was nowhere to be seen. Unless . . . but it wasn't possible. Could he be the one wearing jeans and sitting in a decrepit rocking chair in a vacant lot piled high with rubble? Regan ceased his rocking and walked toward the astonished attorney. As he aproached, Wells noticed the slogan on his baseball cap. SHIT HAPPENS, it read.

Regan wore the cap in the car. He wore it in the elevator going up to the U.S. attorney's office. Just before the doors opened, Wells turned to him.

"You taking that thing off?"

"I don't see why I should."

"You're my kind of client."

---

*Fifty million dollars turned out to be a number favored by the U.S. attorney's office as an estimate of financial penalties in securities cases. When Judge Pierre Leval asked prosecutors to estimate how large Robert Freeman's civil liabilities might be, for example, they indicated that they had no idea. Leval pointed out that "restitution of fifty dollars is a different thing from restitution of fifty million dollars." At that, the prosecutor said he liked the higher range. "I didn't mean to *suggest* that number," Leval said. "I was just pulling it out of the air." No matter, the prosecutor replied; an estimate of fifty million dollars in civil liabilities for Freeman was "fine" with him.

Regan and Wells listened without comment as the prosecutors played a taped conversation that the government considered singularly heinous. When it ended, everyone looked at Regan.

"So?" Regan said, giving prosecutors the verbal equivalent of the slogan on his hat.

That pretty much ended whatever professional courtesy had existed between Princeton/Newport and the U.S. attorney. From there, it was on to the Justice Department, where potential RICO defendants may petition officials to drop or reduce the charges. Because a RICO case can't be built solely on allegations of tax fraud, Regan thought he might get some last-minute relief there.

In normal times, he might have. But these weren't normal times. Two of the attorney general's chief deputies had just resigned, and they'd been quick to suggest that someone might profitably indict Ed Meese. With that, Meese resigned. There was now a vacuum at Justice. In that climate, the old refrain was trotted out once again—who was going to tell Rudy Giuliani not to prosecute?

Jay Regan got this much at Justice: Enforcement chief Paul Coffey agreed to let Princeton/Newport's lawyers present their arguments to William Morrow, of the tax division's criminal enforcement section. But that meeting was hardly worth the trip to Washington. "Morrow is a big guy," recalls Princeton/Newport lawyer Paul Grand. "He came in, took a seat at the end of the table, and kept his head down. After a while, Morrow said, 'This is a manipulation case, there's nothing here to review.' We started shouting: 'This is the first time anyone has mentioned manipulation! What are you talking about?' Morrow headed for the door. Ted Wells, who stands six feet two but looks taller, jumped up. 'We're *entitled* to a tax review!' Wells said. 'You're not leaving until Paul Coffey gets here!'" Coffey was summoned. And he affirmed the RICO.

The next hurdle was negotiating the bond that Princeton/Newport would post at the time of the RICO indictment. Bruce Baird says that he suggested $10 million to $20 million, but that Princeton/Newport insisted it wouldn't put up a dime. Ted Wells disagrees.

"I wrote to Baird, asked for a meeting, and offered a five-million-dollar bond," Wells recalls. "He indicated that we'd meet. I bugged him. He put me off. On indictment day, instead of going

PHOTOGRAPH BY BONNIE GELLER GELD
PHOTOGRAPH BY MARTY KATZ

At a 1983 benefit for the Jewish Theological Semi-
nary, Ivan Boesky (above) played the part of a
great philanthropist. Away from the limelight, he
was less generous; when an employee asked to be
excused from work on the holiest day of the Jewish
year, Boesky told him to conduct business as usual.
Fortunately for Boesky, Harvey Pitt (right) negotiated his plea bargain; the lawyer made Boesky's
greatest deal of all. Pitt's philosophy: "Always do
the counter-inituitive thing."

Michael Milken and Lori Hackel (above) began dating when they were fourteen and married right after graduation from college. After living near Philadelphia for a decade, they moved to a house just ten blocks from Milken's childhood home. Lowell Milken (below) was cast in the role of Michael's hatchet man at Drexel. While his older brother mainlined optimism, Lowell, a lawyer, always asked, "What could go wrong?"

PHOTOGRAPHS COURTESY OF THE MILKEN FAMILY

PHOTOGRAPH BY GEORGE LANGE/OUTLINE

Fred Joseph (upper left) dressed like John F. Kennedy and graduated from Harvard, but the Drexel CEO was no politician; after Drexel went bankrupt, he admitted he had "a problem with aggression." Leon Black (upper right) didn't look like an investment banker— co-workers dubbed him "Pizza the Hut"—but his invention of the "highly confident" letter terrified Wall Street as much as Michael Milken's junk bonds. Jim Dahl (bottom), Milken's best bond salesman, was due to be paid $23 million in 1988; when prosecutors leaned on him, it suddenly wasn't enough. "Jim is for Jim—that's his agenda," an associate says.

PHOTOGRAPH BY ROGER SANDLER/PICTURE GROUP

Rudolph Giuliani (right), U.S. attorney in America's media capital, never met a photographer he didn't like. "I don't cause press coverage," he insisted, but key dates in Wall Street prosecutions seemed to coincide with important moments in his political career. The leaders of the enforcement division of the Securities and Exchange Commission (below) during the Milken case—Thomas Newkirk, Gary Lynch (the unit's director), John Sturc, and William McLucas—believed that Drexel and Milken could cause the fall of America.

PHOTOGRAPH BY THEO WESTENBERGER/SYGMA
PHOTOGRAPH BY MARTY KATZ

PHOTOGRAPH BY AP/WIDE WORLD PHOTOS

Charles Carberry (above), who headed Giuliani's securities fraud division at the start of the Milken investigation, was said to send his new suits out to be freshly rumpled. Defense lawyers found him shrewd and tough, but fair. When Carberry abruptly resigned, he was replaced by Bruce Baird (below). A former narcotics and Mafia prosecutor, Baird's "crime is crime" philosophy strained relationships with Milken and Drexel lawyers. "Bruce was never nursed," one said.

PHOTOGRAPH BY ROBERT DEUTSCH/USA TODAY

Edward Bennett Williams (above left, with Milken) was the dean of American defense lawyers, but by the time Milken became his client, he was dying of cancer. "Next time you have a crisis, call me," he told Milken as they left a congressional hearing; three months later, he was dead. Arthur Liman (below) began the case as Williams's co-counsel, but became the leader of the defense after his death. After years of preparing for a trial, his only chance to confront the witnesses against Milken was at a pre-sentence hearing, where he repeatedly knocked holes in the government case.

Peter Fleming (right) *looked like an Establishment lawyer, but he was the house radical in the Drexel case. "Don't make a fiduciary decision," he advised Fred Joseph when Giuliani was about to indict the firm; Joseph ignored him, took a plea, and was out of business in thirteen months. Arthur Liman's colleague, Martin Flumenbaum (below), was equally committed to fighting it out in court; he endorsed Milken's decision to plead guilty only because he didn't think Milken could endure more battering.*

PHOTOGRAPH BY AP/WIDE WORLD PHOTOS

Oppenheim, Appel, Dixon & Co.

Certified Public Accountants

2029 CENTURY PARK EAST SUITE 1300
LOS ANGELES CALIFORNIA 90067
(213) 277-0400/TELEX 677629/CABLE OABLA LSA

March 21, 1986

Drexel Burnham Lambert Incorporated
9560 Wilshire Boulevard
Beverly Hills, CA 90210
Attention: Lowell Milken

RE: Consulting Services Fee Due Drexel Burnham
Lambert Incorporated - $5,300,000.00

Gentlemen:

There was an oral understanding with Ivan F. Boesky of The Ivan F.
Boesky Corporation that Drexel Burnham Lambert Incorporated would
provide consulting services. There were no formal records
maintained for the time devoted to such consulting services.
There were no prior agreements as to the specific value of such
consulting services to be performed. There was no prior
determination of the specific value for such consulting services
until March 21, 1986, which amounted to $5,300,000.00 due to
Drexel Burnham Lambert Incorporated. Such amount was mutually
agreed upon.

If you agree with the above, kindly sign where indicated.

Very truly yours,

OPPENHEIM, APPEL, DIXON & CO.

By: David Beach
Partner

DB1230043

I have examined the above,

and found it to be correct.

By: _____   5/21/86
Donald Balser - for Drexel   Date
Burnham Lambert Incorporated

By: _____   3/21/86
Lowell J. Milken   Date

---

*Lowell Milken was the only Drexel officer around the night that Boesky's accountants needed
an explanation for a $5.3 million "consulting" bill; although he emphasized that he knew
little about those services, he said he was willing to initial the very general letter they
drafted. "The problem with your guy," prosecutors reportedly told his lawyer, "is that he
stayed too late and signed a letter."*

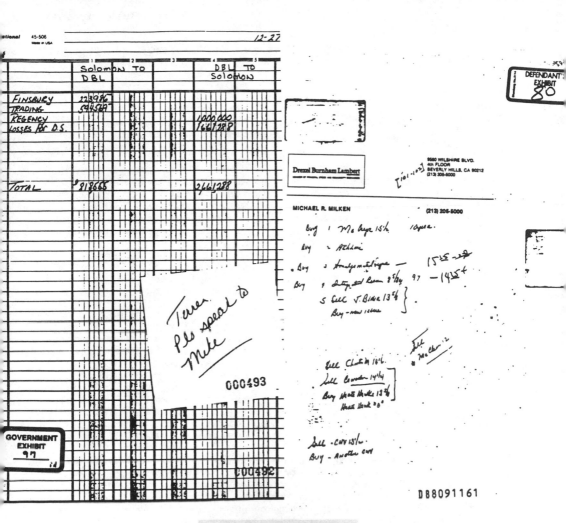

At twenty-five, Terren Peizer had what looked like the best job in America: making $3.5 million a year, sitting three feet away from Michael Milken. When the investigation began, he pasted this childhood picture (above center) onto the family portrait that Milken kept on his desk—even as he was holding onto "evidence" that he could give the government. In 1988, in exchange for immunity, he handed prosecutors a scorecard (above left), which he said had been written by Milken. It looked nothing at all like Milken's actual writing (above right). The judge who sentenced Milken called this misidentification "an innocent mistake."

An Important Message: MILKEN (:30)

VIDEO:

FADE IN TO TITLE:
An Important Message
        from
Drexel Burnham.
FADE OUT.

(As the announcer speaks, his
words appear on the screen in
WHITE LETTERING against a
BLACK BACKGROUND, separated by
appropriate cuts).

AUDIO:

ANNOUNCER # 1 (V.O.):
An important message from
Drexel Burnham.

ANNOUNCER # 2 (V.O.):
You may have heard that the
SEC has made accusations
against our firm, and several
of our employees, including
Michael Milken.

Neither the firm nor any of
our employees have engaged in
any wrongdoing.

The ten thousand men and women
of Drexel Burnham will meet
the challenges of the months
ahead with the same integrity,
dedication and loyalty which
have always been the strength
of our firm. We stand behind
Michael Milken and each of the
employees. And we remain
committed to financing
America's future.

DISSOLVE TO TITLE:
Drexel Burnham
Financing America's Future.

*In the summer of 1988, Drexel planned to spend millions on TV commercials blasting the
SEC charges. But the SEC was slow to act. When it finally did, Drexel lawyers decided to
shelve the campaign, including this script (above) for a commerical in support of Milken.
Once charges were brought, Benjamin Stein (below left), a writer who had asked Milken
for a job, began a violent series of journalistic attacks on him. Michael Thomas (below
right) blasted Milken in his weekly column and went on to write a front-page piece for* The
New York Times Book Review, *praising a book critical of Milken.*

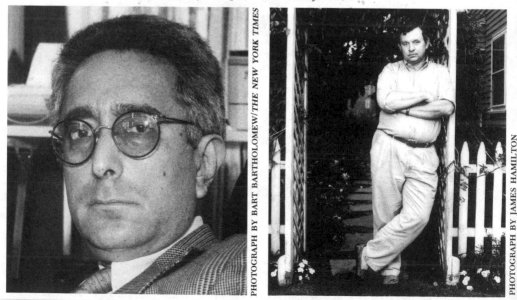

PHOTOGRAPH BY BART BARTHOLOMEW/THE NEW YORK TIMES

PHOTOGRAPH BY JAMES HAMILTON

When Michael Armstrong (left), Lowell Milken's lawyer, saw that the SEC charges were based almost exclusively on allegations made by Ivan Boesky, he decided the smart thing to do was to get Boesky out of the case. The way to do that: prove that Boesky lied to the government. His idea of advertising a reward (below) to people who could provide that damning information was considered inspired, original, and wild—and, for those reasons, not worth trying.

One Million Dollar Reward for
Information Leading to the Conviction
of Ivan F. Boesky For Lying to the
United States Government

Drexel Burnham Lambert and certain of its employees have recently been named in a 184-page civil complaint, filed by the Securities and Exchange Commission, alleging various supposed violations of the securities laws.

These charges are false. They are based almost exclusively upon accusations made by convicted felon Ivan F. Boesky, in an attempt to win favorable treatment from the Government. Boesky was exposed two years ago as the mastermind of a gigantic insider-trading swindle, involving institutions other than Drexel Burnham, in which Boesky made millions of dollars in illegal profits.

The Government, in relying upon Boesky, has been duped by him, just as he duped his victims. We believe that Boesky, in addition to the lies he has told about dealings with Drexel Burnham and its employees, has lied to the Government about other matters, including the following:

-- his own illegal activities, only some of which he has revealed;
-- illegal activities of others, whom he is shielding from the Government;
-- his supposed lack of funds and resources, following payment of the fine he agreed to pay the Government;
-- assets and funds he has secreted with individuals or in confidential foreign accounts.

To uncover the truth about Boesky's false statements to the Government, Drexel Burnham offers a reward of one million dollars to anyone providing information leading to Boesky's conviction for making such false statements.

-- offering rewards to help in the capture of lawbreakers is a time-honored and entirely legal practice, commonly employed not only by the Government but by interested private citizens and organizations;
-- the amount offered is substantial, so as to afford strong incentive for those with information to come forward;
-- from Drexel Burnham's point of view, the amount, while significant, is minor when compared with the enormous expense of meeting the Government's investigation;
-- there is no incentive to give false information since the Government itself stands as the final judge, and the reward will be paid only if the information results in Boesky's conviction;
-- information will, if requested, be treated in strict confidence and used only to provide leads.

Judgment as to payment of rewards is to be made not by Drexel Burnham but by the following professionals experienced in law enforcement. Anyone with information should contact:

Kroll Associates
Attention: Bart Schwartz, Esq.
former Chief Assistant United States Attorney
Southern District of New York

The Investigative Group Inc.
Attention: Terence Lenzner, Esq.
former Special Watergate Prosecutor

Information, or copies of information, may also be sent directly to:

Honorable Rudolph Giuliani
United States Attorney
Southern District of New York
One St. Andrews Plaza
New York, New York 10007

PHOTOGRAPH COURTESY OF JAY REGAN

Jay Regan (above), head of Princeton/Newport, never flinched when the government used his firm as a test case of the racketeering law on Wall Street; he even wore his 'SHIT HAPPENS' hat to a meeting with prosecutors. His firm was forced out of business and he was convicted on 63 counts, but he was later exonerated. John Shad (below), the former SEC chairman who was brought in to lead Drexel after it settled with the government, is seen leaving the building the night the firm went bankrupt.

PHOTOGRAPH BY AP/WIDE WORLD PHOTOS

At the U.S. attorney's office, John Carroll and Jess Fardella (pictured above, left to right) led the Milken investigation and negotiated his plea bargain. In a recent speech, Carroll sounded almost like a Milken lawyer when he called some of the prosecution tactics "novel" and described Lowell Milken as a bargaining "chip." Richard Breeden (right), chairman of the Securities and Exchange Commission, dominated Milken's plea negotiations. "Those boys work for me," he reportedly said of Carroll and Fardella.

PHOTOGRAPH BY ROGER SANDLER/PICTURE GROUP

Ken Lerer (pictured above, at left) *was hired as Milken's public relations adviser when it became clear that Drexel was going to cut Milken adrift. But Milken's guilty plea made it impossible for any PR effort to overcome his image problem. Richard Sandler (above right) was Lowell Milken's best friend and Michael Milken's neighbor. When he became the general counsel for the defense, he took on both of their burdens. Because prosecutors and defense lawyers were hardly speaking, Stephen Kaufman (below), a lawyer famed for his ability to communicate with all sides, was brought in to negotiate the plea agreement.*

PHOTOGRAPH BY DANIEL KRON

addressing what he sees as the major ills in society. In addition
to donating millions of dollars, the defendant has given hours of
his own time and has established a close rapport with many of the
disadvantaged youths with whom he works. The Milken Foundations
are now among the largest charitable institutions in the country.

The popular opinion concerning Milken's involvement in these
offenses is that he was motivated by greed. There is no dispute,
however, that his wealth is the result of legitimate business
activities. In addition, he has contributed a significant portion
of his earnings to charitable concerns, while retaining a modest
lifestyle without the obvious trappings of wealth. Former co-
workers at Drexel cite Milken's inability to refuse anyone anything
and his conviction that he could resolve all problems. The answer
to this offense may lie in part in his own statement namely, "I
wanted to be all things to all people". Among Milken's strengths
are his inability to accept defeat, his total commitment to causes
he considers "just and right" and his vision concerning business
and society. His weakness was that as creator and head of the High
Yield Department at Drexel these convictions were more important
than his responsibilities and obligation to conduct business fully
within the parameters of the law. Yet, despite his fall, Milken is
an individual still able to contribute to society and to create
positive changes in the future.

                              Respectfully submitted,

                              EUNICE R. HOLT JONES
                              Chief U.S. Probation Officer

                              MICHALAH P. BRACKEN
                              U.S. Probation Officer
                              Ext. 7-1072

*Michael Milken's probation report contained
many surprises—Michalah Bracken concluded
that his philanthropy was genuine and longstand-
ing and that he wasn't motivated by greed. Her
favorable conclusion (above) was the biggest surprise of all. Federal Judge Kimba Wood (left)
sounded dispassionate when she sentenced Milken
in 1990. Her husband described his case as another
day at the office for her; this photograph was
taken at a lunch just an hour after she handed
Milken a ten-year jail term.*

PHOTOGRAPH BY ROGER SANDLER/PICTURE GROUP

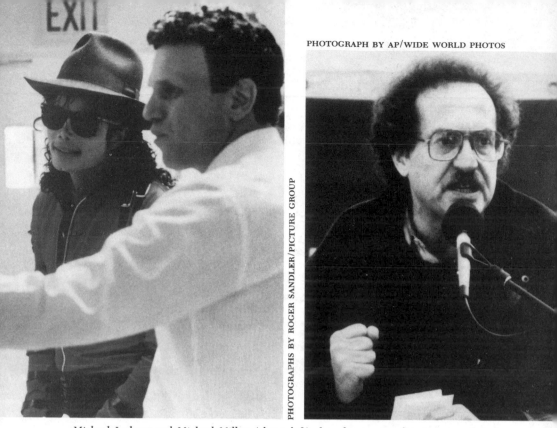

PHOTOGRAPH BY AP/WIDE WORLD PHOTOS

PHOTOGRAPHS BY ROGER SANDLER/PICTURE GROUP

Michael Jackson and Michael Milken (above left) shared a passion for privacy and an interest in children; the singer sat in on math classes that Milken taught. Milken hired appellate lawyer Alan Dershowitz (above right) to improve his image. Other lawyers wondered why. "Never stand between Alan and an open microphone," one noted. Milken now teaches high-school equivalency classes at Pleasanton (below), a work camp in northern California. After completing his sentence, he is to do community service for three years.

to Giuliani's press conference, I waited for Baird for three hours—longer than I've ever had to wait for anyone. Finally, someone came out and said the judge wanted us in his chambers. There, Baird handed me the proposed restraining order. It had a corny paragraph saying that the business would be able to operate normally, but the point was that the prosecutors wanted to freeze *all* of Princeton/Newport's assets—one billion dollars! 'Work it out,' the judge said, 'or I'll sign the government order.' Well, we started so late the court reporter was already gone. We offered to post eight to ten million. Baird objected. When we finally reached an agreement [to $50 million, which the judge later reduced to $14 million], it was one forty-five A.M."

Michael Milken knew that RICO was out there, a circling shark eager to take more than a billion dollars from him in a single chunk, but in the spring of 1988, he was obsessed by something far more immediate. A book, of all things. Books were usually Lori's department; his nonbusiness reading began with newspapers and ended with *Sports Illustrated*. In terms of writing about him, he'd endured—and, perhaps, privately savored—the articles that contributed to his myth. But this was a sustained piece of reporting, and the author was Connie Bruck, who worked at *American Lawyer* for Steve Brill, a writer and editor of legendary toughness. Bruck was also said to be tough-minded. So everything about the project suggested to Milken that it was a hatchet job in the making.

Fred Joseph also had reason to suspect that Bruck was not all sweetness and light. He had first encountered her byline in 1984, when he and Ivan Boesky and their eldest daughters flew down to Duke on Boesky's plane for a college tour. Boesky had read Bruck's *Atlantic Monthly* profile about him on that ride—and although anyone else would find it positive, he was quite specific in his displeasure.

For her part, Bruck was delighted with Wall Street. After writing about lawyers for years, she had discovered a new topic, and it fascinated her. "Milken was just starting to emerge," she has recalled. "I thought he'd be interesting."

Bruck had her champions, among them Drexel public relations adviser Gershon Kekst and Gulf & Western chairman Martin Davis. In 1985, Fred Joseph was particularly susceptible to the Davis endorsement—he hoped to do some business with Gulf

& Western. Letting Simon & Schuster, G&W's publishing arm, put out a book was a step in the door. And the quid pro quo was, quite possibly, mutual—surely, Marty Davis wouldn't let S&S publish anything that might upset anyone at Drexel.*

Michael Milken had once opposed a department newsletter—"We can tell clients everything they need to know on the phone," he'd told the would-be editor—so he was hardly likely to welcome any writer from the outside world onto his trading floor. Early on, Bruck says, he made his unhappiness clear: "I do not want the book to be done." Bruck assured him that his wish was meaningless. Then, she says, Milken made her an offer he thought she couldn't refuse: "Why don't *we* pay you the commitment fee that your publisher would have paid you—except we'll pay it to you to *not* write the book? Or why don't we pay you for all the copies you would have sold if you had written it?"

All this was said in passing, after a speech in February of 1986. Maybe, as Milken has long insisted, it was a throwaway line, a joke. If so, he was a poor judge of Bruck's sense of humor, for she would use this anecdote against Milken when she came to construct a portrait of a man who seemed, on other occasions, to believe that money was the cure for most problems.

Milken got surprisingly little satisfaction from his colleagues in the Bruck matter. Drexel New York treated her like visiting royalty—Corporate Finance types, Drexel clients, and a few former employees were only too happy to tell Bruck of their prowess. "They were their own worst enemies," Bruck has said. "These were the titans of the eighties, men with enormous egos. They wanted to reveal themselves."

Bruck began her work in Drexel's heyday. That gave her an ideal vantage point to learn the inner workings of the firm's biggest deals, to hear the legend of Michael Milken from some of his lesser acolytes, and after Boesky pled, to watch Drexel's culture under siege. In the 1984 *Atlantic Monthly* profile, the real Boesky had eluded her—with Milken facing indictment, she wasn't about to blow a second opportunity.

"When the investigation began, it looked as if Milken had to

---

*Years later, Davis not only declined to involve himself in the dispute over Bruck's dissection of Drexel, but took a run at Time, Inc. without asking Fred Joseph to be his investment banker.

come into the light, or it would appear as if he had something to hide," Bruck has observed. But Milken had no tolerance for her brand of light; he didn't grant her an interview until a Sunday morning shortly before she finished her book. In that three-hour conversation, Milken says, Bruck never once confronted him with the allegations she was preparing to publish. For her part, Bruck found Milken utterly transparent, mouthing banalities that were completely at odds with the behavior she'd studied for two years. "What this sales pitch showed, more than anything else, was Milken's shockingly poor judgment about himself in relation to others," she wrote. What Milken took away from that meeting was the perception that Bruck was a Marxist in a miniskirt.

Bruck had an agreement with Fred Joseph; in exchange for access to Drexel personnel, she would allow him to read the manuscript. If he found errors, she would hear him out, and if he convinced her she had something wrong, she'd make the appropriate changes. But in the winter and spring of 1988, Fred Joseph had—or so he thought—more important issues than Connie Bruck to deal with.

Meanwhile, Bruck's forthcoming book completely unhinged Michael Milken—after reading some of the most inside details of the government's investigation in *The Wall Street Journal* for eighteen months, he had come to feel, like Napoleon, that "three hostile newspapers are more to be feared than a thousand bayonets."

For Milken's advisers and friends, his new attitude toward media was a puzzlement. How could someone who'd ignored the press for twenty years suddenly believe that one book was death to his chances for a fair trial? And not only for its accusations of criminality—what galled Milken most were what he considered bogus accounts of him wearing the miner's light on the bus to New York each morning, or doing magic tricks, or furnishing his home with wicker while he maniacally exploited his clients.

"From our point of view, the Bruck book did very little external damage to Michael," recalls Chuck Winner, who was, that season, gamely working on a media plan to be launched as soon as the SEC filed its charges. "But it did enormous damage to his well-being and internal structure—it consumed him."

Michael Milken wanted to kill the book.

Of the many plans advanced to achieve this, the most desperate was the claim that, because Fred Joseph had an editorial role in the book, he had some right to a stake in its copyright. Perhaps Joseph could advance that claim to slow the publication, force changes, or even submarine *The Predators' Ball*. This sounded like a clever idea—clever, that is, to someone who knew nothing about copyright law, publishing, protocol, or risk-assessment. But Michael Milken didn't care that an effort to damage Bruck's book before publication would look alarmingly like suppression of free speech; all he felt was his own distress. The case scarcely mattered to him—Connie Bruck filled his thoughts like no woman before her.

Efforts were made to derail Bruck. All failed. But Milken did not drop the issue. He did, however, reframe it. The problem, he decided, was that Drexel's public relations team didn't represent him. It was time to find someone who did.

Ken Lerer was a junior at Connecticut College when he heard Ramsey Clark announce on a radio commercial that he would limit contributions to $100 in his campaign against Senator Jacob Javits. Clark wasn't kidding about a shoestring candidacy—to volunteer, Lerer had to call him at his law office, which happened to be Paul, Weiss. A few weeks later, he was, at twenty, deputy manager of the Clark campaign.

Everything clicked. Clark won the Democratic primary and was soon just a few points behind Javits in the polls. Then Javits released a tape recording of Clark and Jane Fonda chatting with the Vietcong in Hanoi at the height of the war. Right there, the Clark campaign ended.

But along the way, Lerer had discovered a small piece of news—a *Daily News* reporter, using another name, owned a neighborhood newspaper that accepted political advertising from candidates he wrote about at the *News*. Lerer wrote up the story, sold it to the *Village Voice*, and, in a matter of months, had a contract as a feature writer for *New York* magazine.* But Lerer had no taste for writing negative pieces; he was not unhappy to leave reporting behind and become assistant to the publisher. A year later, he left to run Bess Myerson's senatorial campaign.

---

*Later, he sat across a desk from Michael Kramer, a political writer who would marry Kimba Wood, a lawyer who would become a federal judge and sentence Michael Milken.

Two campaigns, two losses—Lerer was now, at last, ready to abandon politics. Myerson wrote a letter commending him to Warner Communications CEO Steve Ross, who assigned him to the company's cable TV division. Five years later, Lerer was ready to move on. But where? As it happened, one of his co-workers, Linda Gosden Robinson, was the well-connected wife of American Express CEO James Robinson III. From her days in Washington, she knew Republican consultant James Lake. In 1986, at the peak of the Wall Street boom, it seemed there was enough activity to support one more public relations outfit, so Robinson, Lake and Lerer opened for business in a small office in the Warner building; almost immediately, the much larger advertising and PR firm of Bozell, Jacobs, Kenyon and Eckhardt bought them out.

In April of 1988, Merv Adelson—chairman of Lorimar, a client of Milken's, a client of Lerer's, and then the husband of Barbara Walters—asked Lerer to meet a lawyer named Richard Sandler, who, he said, worked exclusively for Michael Milken. That name didn't mean much to Lerer. Still, he stopped in to meet Sandler on his next trip to Los Angeles.

"We expect an indictment soon," Sandler said, by way of preamble. Then Michael Milken came in and spoke about children. Next, Lowell Milken joined them. And, at last, the Milkens presented their real concerns.

"*The Washington Post* ran a story this morning saying that Mike tried to buy Bruck's book," Sandler began. "If you had this account, what would you do about that?"

"Let me understand," Lerer replied. "This book is coming out?"

"It's done, it's coming out, and the story isn't true."

"The time to deal with this was two or three years ago," Lerer said. "What you can do is go on to the next issue."*

Sandler had interviewed New York public relations experts with bigger reputations, but he couldn't argue with the common-sense approach of this relative unknown. And, from another point of view, Lerer's youth and his background were assets. He had

---

*No sooner was Lerer hired, however, than his advice was disregarded. One of Robinson, Lake's first assignments was to prepare an "error memo" that could be sent to potential reviewers of Bruck's book. Inevitably, this memo had the effect of generating publicity and sales.

no large clients eating up his time. He'd never worked for anyone who needed him to cover up—his credibility didn't have a dent. He knew a great many journalists, and some of them were aware that he had once wielded a pen himself. He could be much nicer than the job description called for; with his dark eyes, long black hair, and casual manner, he was, as *Esquire* writer Tad Friend later wrote, the sort of person who'd be your friend even if he wasn't being paid to. And he had no idea what he was getting into. As he told Sandler, he instinctually felt the bill for every service his office might provide would come to no more than $25,000 a month—a fraction of what he'd eventually bill.

Richard Sandler was hardly calculating enough to list guile-lessness as his first priority in a press representative. But Lerer's innocence, with the residue of boyish idealism running through it, was immediately attractive to Sandler; Lerer embodied the side of Milken that he wanted the world to know. For once, in-genuousness was a plus. In the spring of 1988, Ken Lerer became Michael Milken's public stand-in.

Before the new PR firm could screw things up, Edward Bennett Williams wanted Lerer and Robinson to understand a few simple matters. "This is a criminal situation," he rasped as he sat across from them in his conference room. "And in that situation, I don't believe you have to deal with the press. You don't win in the press. As for me, I have no time for the press. I go into a trial, it's like a prizefight to me—it's all-consuming, and I can't be worrying what my side says to the media. You want to return reporters' calls, fine; if you don't return reporters' calls, I don't care. But if you do, here's what you need to know . . ."

Williams stretched out a bony finger and drew an imaginary line on the conference table.

"On this side of the line, that's the criminal case. You will have *nothing* to do with it. On the other side, that's Michael Milken as a person. Anything you want to do there, do it. This line—it's not fuzzy, it's very clear. You stay on your side of it, we'll get on fine. Any questions?"

There was a brief silence, and then Linda Robinson, who was used to important men paying attention to her, acknowledged that she did have one question.

"Yes?"

"How about an article that explains why stock parking is not a major crime?"

"No!" Williams thundered. "Anyway, you'd never get one that's good enough to mean anything."

If Edward Bennett Williams was in a generally foul mood, he had his reasons. Leaving the SEC offices in January, the strain of acting healthy when his sickness was accelerating had suddenly hit him. "I don't feel so hot," he murmured to Bob Litt. "You're gonna have to take over again."

A month later, much sooner than he would have liked, Williams was called back into service—John Dingell sent Michael Milken a subpoena commanding him to appear at hearings of the Subcommittee on Oversight and Investigations. The subpoena was a grandstand stunt. There was, Dingell knew, no way that anyone facing indictment would answer his questions. But that was the point. The television cameras would catch Milken as he invoked his Fifth Amendment rights, Dingell would get his thirty seconds on the nightly news, and every potential juror in New York would gain one more small piece of information about Milken that the defense could never counter.

John Dingell was smart and tough, but not smarter or tougher than his former law professor. That winter, he agreed that Milken could send an affidavit explaining why he couldn't respond to the subcommittee's questions—he wouldn't have to appear. Then Dingell changed his mind. Milken would have to show up after all.

But when he did, Williams held the trump card. He brought Milken into the hearing room early, so the news photographers could click away. Milken looked tanned and relaxed, and he wore a nervous, goofy smile. Dingell, in contrast, wore two grotesquely black eyes, souvenirs of a weekend spent shooting turkeys in Texas with Treasury Secretary James Baker.

As soon as the hearings officially began, Williams blackened Dingell's eyes once again. He cited an old rule—and the chairman had no choice but to order all cameras and tape recorders to be shut off. A half hour after Dingell had called the hearing to order, the pony show was over.

"Next time you have a crisis, call me," Williams told Milken.

But as Williams now knew too well, all the crises that season were his. He was dying fast, and fighting it every way he could—including denial. If he kept it up, his grand strategy for defending Michael Milken was going to be buried with him. At Williams & Connolly, no one dared suggest that he share his thoughts.

Bob Litt had worked alongside Williams on the case, but rebuffs were much of what he had to show for the association. "I heard you talking on the phone about going up to Giuliani's office next week," Litt might say. "Should I keep my calendar clear for that day?" And Williams would shout, "Dammit, when I want you, I'll let you know." On occasion, Williams did want Litt—that is, late of an afternoon, he'd growl, "Be at the airport at seven tomorrow, we're going to L.A."—but always as an aide, never as a confidant.

From what Litt could intuit, Williams was not sanguine about the outcome of the case; this was one the government couldn't afford to lose. Going to trial made sense if Boesky was the only government witness—but Williams had no illusions on that score. There would be other witnesses, and many of them would be more plausible than Boesky.

Williams was more explicit with Arthur Liman. Over breakfast in 1988, Williams announced that he'd probably take this case to trial. He felt that he didn't have much choice—because of Milken's astronomical earnings, he didn't believe he could obtain a very favorable plea bargain. But paradoxically, the money might be an asset in a trial. If Milken had made $30 million or $40 million a year, everyone would reflexively say he was a crook; at the $550 million level, at least some were sure to think he was another Einstein.

Richard Sandler kept waiting for Williams to tell him what to do next. The lawyer's complaint—an old chestnut, used on many clients—rang in his ears: "Mike, you keep trying to take your appendix out by yourself, you're gonna cut your nuts off." Sandler had a naive belief that Williams would, in the weeks before his death, sit him down and tell him how to handle the case and the client. Instead, Williams's last act in the case was simply to apologize for his unavailability. In mid-August, he was dead.

Michael Milken was desolate. To the end, he'd had a childlike hope that the master defender had one final act of magic in him. Ed Williams truly understood not just the law but the flow of history, the press for innovation and the resistance of those who would stop the innovators—if anyone could

cut through the tangle of disputed facts and see the big picture, he was the man.

As he joined the celebrated and the infamous in St. Mat-
thew's Cathedral for Williams's funeral, Milken remembered Williams's great summation in a decade-old case. "The Unwashed
Window" speech, it had come to be called, for in that summing
up, Williams had challenged the jury to consider the facts without
preconceptions. "If you look at life through unwashed windows,
everything looks a little dirty," Williams had said. "If you look at
life through clean windows, you can recognize the things that are
dirty, the people who are dirty and the people who are clean."

How he had longed for Williams to say that to his jury, to
remind his jurors, as Williams had in that call for an acquittal, of
the pleasure that would be theirs if they returned with a verdict
of not guilty. Now those hopes were dust. For the first time, he
felt lost, truly helpless; he wept like a grieving son.

In moments of stress, style dissolves and character emerges.
And so it was at Williams's funeral, when Michael Milken turned
around to greet a man in the row behind him. The man was important to the defense effort, but his wife had never met the financier; introductions were whispered. When he turned away,
the woman couldn't believe that this was the great and dreaded
Milken. "It's *terrible* what they're doing to him," she told her
husband. "He's just a *boy*." Later that day, she spoke with Milken
at greater length; she came away with a different appraisal. "I like
Mike," she told her husband, "but I wish he didn't feel he had
to sell me all the time." Her husband understood. "She was
right—both times," he says.

"An Important Message from Drexel Burnham" would appear on the television screen. Then, as an announcer read the
text, Drexel's message would scroll down, black letters on a white
background: "You may have heard that the SEC has made accusations against our firm, and several of our employees, including
Michael Milken. Neither the firm nor any of our employees have
engaged in any wrongdoing. The ten thousand men and women
of Drexel Burnham will meet the challenges of the months ahead
with the same integrity, dedication, and loyalty which have always been the strength of our firm. We stand behind Michael
Milken and each of the employees. And we remain committed to
financing America's future."

This thirty-second message was just one of a series of television commercials Winner/Wagner and the Sawyer/Miller Group had prepared for use when the SEC finally moved against Drexel. Another struck at Boesky, "an admitted liar and convicted felon." A third tweaked the government: "The SEC has conducted a twenty-month investigation of our firm. They have found nothing new since late 1986, when Ivan Boesky falsely implicated us."

The "Announcement" campaign was budgeted at $5.6 million. The television commercials were to run on New York local stations and national cable channels like CNN and FNN—as Winner and Wagner wrote, "Everyone watches television . . . when used properly, nothing can outdeliver television's reach." The print ads would appear in local newspapers in large cities, and national papers like *USA Today* and *The Wall Street Journal*.

Drafts of the newspaper ads were at Drexel's New York office in June; by mid-July, the counterattack was ready to be launched. But where was the SEC? Months earlier, Fred Joseph had warned his associates that the commission would give Drexel no more than forty-eight hours' notice before it brought charges; anticipation became the order of the day, every day. But as the pages flew from the calendar, it became clear that something was wrong in Washington. Or, perhaps, in New York, where the U.S. attorney's RICO threats hadn't produced a single significant defection.

If the SEC was waiting for the U.S. attorney to get its act together, people at Drexel thought, Michael Milken might be an old man before he was charged with anything.

CHAPTER FOURTEEN

Of the 712 paragraphs in the SEC charges, 632 were Boesky-related. Of its twenty-one counts, nineteen involved Boesky transactions. But either Boesky didn't understand finance or the SEC hadn't been very discerning—whatever truth the SEC filing of September 8, 1988, may have held in its broad strokes, its details made no sense. No one on Wall Street would have gone long this, short that.

The in-house verdict at Drexel in New York was that the SEC charges were bullshit.

The in-house prognosis was to forget about the commercials and newspaper ads—they might inflame the U.S. attorney—and prepare for the next attack.

Lowell Milken's lawyer had a different idea.

Michael Armstrong was as garrulous and untidy as Lowell was private and fastidious. As a student at Harvard Law, married and a father, Armstrong woke up one night to find his home on fire. The blaze outraced his frantic efforts to save his family—two of his three young children died that night. The hurt was inexpressibly deep, and Armstrong was changed forever. Whatever lay ahead for him, he knew this—nothing so terrible could ever happen to him again.

And so, after graduation, Armstrong went to New York and

became a fearless, uncompromising lawyer. He investigated corrupt policemen for the Knapp Commission, prosecuted white-collar cases for the U.S. attorney, and represented Sunny von Bulow's children in their suit against their notorious stepfather. He drank with judges and he counseled senators, and on every side, on every occasion, he said exactly what he thought—he was the ultimate gunslinger.

Right after the SEC filed its complaint against the Milkens, Armstrong sat down and had a good long think about Ivan Boesky. For all Boesky's secrecy, he concluded, there were people other than his co-conspirators who knew what he was up to. They were mistresses, secretaries, pilots, and stewardesses on his personal plane—people who perform vital functions, then fade into the woodwork. They knew a great deal about Boesky, but none of that information mattered much to them.

When Boesky made his deal with the government, he was obligated to confess every crime, give a full accounting of his finances, and point the finger at everyone who committed crimes with him. Armstrong, like the Milkens and other defense lawyers, doubted that he had done this. More probably, he believed, Boesky told the government one whopper after another, on the assumption that the people who could prove he was lying would never surface.

But what if they did surface?

What if they had proof that Boesky lied to the government?

And what if the prosecutors were forced to admit that Boesky lied to them?

SEC Enforcement Director Gary Lynch told the Dingell committee in 1986 what would happen if Boesky treated the government as he had everyone else: "If he lies to us, if he withholds information from us, if he is not absolutely candid, then the benefits of our settlement agreement are totally off with Mr. Boesky."

Rudolph Giuliani suggested a more apocalyptic scenario. If Boesky hides something and it's discovered, Giuliani said in 1987, "he can be prosecuted for every single crime he's admitted to and also go to prison for a hundred years. And that's precisely what will happen to him if we ever discover that he or someone else hid money from the government."

Lynch and Giuliani left one thing out—the case against the Milkens would come to a dramatic end.

Michael Armstrong wondered how people with vital information could be induced to share their information.

The answer came in a flash—money.

ONE MILLION DOLLAR REWARD FOR INFORMATION LEADING TO THE CONVICTION OF IVAN F. BOESKY FOR LYING TO THE UNITED STATES GOVERNMENT, read the headline of the ad that Armstrong wrote for Drexel. The text pointed out that the SEC charges against Drexel had been based almost exclusively on accusations made by Boesky, "the mastermind of a gigantic insider trading swindle involving institutions other than Drexel Burnham." Those charges were false: "The government, in relying upon Boesky, has been duped by him, just as he duped his victims."

Boesky's lies, the ad continued, fell into four areas:

his own illegal activities, only partly revealed
—illegal activities of other people that he has concealed
—his supposed lack of funds after paying his fine
—assets and funds he has hidden with others or in confidential foreign bank accounts

Offering a reward for information leading to Boesky's conviction, Armstrong wrote, was in the tradition of a time-honored and entirely legal practice. While the reward was substantial, it was small compared with the cost of defending the firm. And, despite the size of the reward, there was no incentive for anyone to invent testimony—the reward would be paid only if the government managed to convict Boesky.

Armstrong originally wrote that people with information should contact Drexel's investigators. He improved this with the suggestion that copies of all information be forwarded to Rudolph Giuliani. Then he topped himself—*all* information should be sent to Giuliani. Let the assistant U.S. attorneys deal with the piles of mail, he thought. It will keep them busy for a while, and if anything does show up, they'll be obligated to turn it over to us.

Armstrong read his ad to the other lawyers working for Drexel and Milken. They thought it was crazy, wild, imaginative, intriguing, brilliant, inspired, and innovative. But they didn't think it should run.

Instead, the Drexel lawyers endorsed Plan B—they'd send

waves of Drexel investment bankers to the U.S. attorney's office to explain how the business really worked.

For John Carroll and Jess Fardella, meeting investment bankers—even from Drexel—was a useful exercise. At the U.S. attorney's office, they'd served their apprenticeship prosecuting drug dealers. They'd been working in securities cases only for a year. Neither had imagined that, in his mid-thirties, he'd be confronting the biggest names in the defense bar in the white-collar case of all time.

Carroll has a genial smile and a pleasant manner; he looks like an investment banker who is too well-bred to don suspenders and Lobb shoes. Banter comes easily to him, as do literary references—he was an English major at Yale, and, he thought, a future professor. If you want to teach literature, that's fine, a sympathetic instructor told him, but you're not likely to do it at Yale.

Steadiness and good humor were, Carroll realized, assets in the law, though he didn't see himself grinding away at a specialty as unglamorous as securities work. At New York University Law School, he took a single course in that area; intellectually, his views about white-collar crime had been influenced most significantly by his senior essay at Yale, which he wrote about William Faulkner's theory of property. His conclusion: Property corrupts.

Fardella, a product of Yale College and Harvard Law, found himself taking the "bad cop" role. He had the intensity and build of a baseball infielder—in fact, he resembled the young Phil Rizzuto—and when he bore in on a witness, you could imagine him getting to a ground ball and completing the double play no matter how hard the baserunner was coming at him. Defense lawyers thought Fardella was an honorable zealot; if they could show him he was wrong about Milken, they told one another, his very identity might disintegrate.

Given the inexperience of these prosecutors, the decision to bombard them with alternate scenarios for Drexel transactions was a shrewd one. In a few months, Carroll and Fardella learned a great deal about the intricacies of investment banking. And they concluded that the SEC-Boesky explanations for several transactions were inaccurate.

But they never doubted Drexel and Milken's guilt.

By the fall of 1988, what defense lawyers nostalgically call "prosecutorial discretion" wasn't an option for Carroll and Fardella. They'd been handed a case trumpeted in the press as one involving major crimes. They'd been challenged by an SEC filing that portrayed Milken as the king of the greedheads. They reported to a supervisor with a reputation as a cowboy and to a U.S. attorney intent on headlines that justified the years of investigation. So Carroll and Fardella, working against the clock, combed the High-Yield Bond Department once again for witnesses who could corroborate Boesky's allegations.

Out of four hundred employees in Beverly Hills, they found two—Jim Dahl and Terren Peizer.

Jim Dahl, the lean blond Floridian who had become Milken's top salesman, stared at the letter from the U.S. attorney's office. It was a formality—a "target letter"—announcing the fact that the government had enough evidence against him to consider filing criminal charges. As such, it invited the recipient to come in and tell his story to the prosecutors, preferably after acknowledging guilt or offering to give testimony against others.

Dahl wondered how much of the government's interest in him flowed from the fact that he was using the same Williams & Connolly lawyers who were defending Milken. All along, those lawyers had told him he was in no danger. Now he was about to be indicted. If that wasn't danger, what was?

I need someone I can talk to, he told Richard Sandler. I have a friend, Steve Andrews, who's a lawyer in Florida. I want to bounce ideas off him. Can I use a private phone in your office?

While he had Sandler's attention, Dahl wanted to talk about another issue of importance—his compensation. He'd seen the Drexel payroll and had been shocked to learn that while he was slated to earn $18 million plus a $5 million bonus in 1988, Peter Ackerman would be taking home nearly $60 million. While $23 million seemed like a lot of money to some people—and had once seemed like a decent living to Dahl—now he couldn't be satisfied with this paltry sum. Months ago, he told Sandler, he'd talked to Milken about a raise. He said that Milken had agreed he should be paid more. But the payroll sheet showed no change, and Milken was denying that he'd ever said it would.

Sandler explained that this wasn't an issue he could resolve. And it might not be the best time to press the point with Mike, he suggested. Dahl disagreed. He had a target letter, he had uncertainty—he wanted money. And he wanted it now.*

Dahl and Sandler next spoke a week later, when they were both in New York. I'm here with Steve Andrews, Dahl said. Can you see him tomorrow?

Sandler called Andrews. They couldn't meet until the evening, Andrews said—he was spending the day with Dahl at the U.S. attorney's office, trying to talk the prosecutors out of indicting him.

When Sandler and Andrews did meet, Andrews told Sandler about Dahl's deal with the government, then returned to Dahl's more immediate concern. Milken had also promised him a bonus of $5 million. He wanted it. That week. Sandler pointed out that in light of Dahl's chats with the U.S. attorney, this was an increasingly awkward subject.

Andrews didn't raise with Sandler an issue that would have been even more difficult to discuss—Dahl's desire to head the High-Yield Bond Department after Milken was forced out. This wasn't a secret, though. Andrews had, in fact, mentioned this fond hope of Dahl's that very day to Drexel lawyer Peter Fleming.

If Jim has committed any crimes, Fleming replied, that will be impossible.

Well, he hasn't, Andrews said.

What about stock parking with Tom Spiegel at Columbia Savings? Fleming asked.

There was none, Andrews insisted. Spiegel sold positions at year end, and, sometimes, he bought them back. But the trades were always done at market risk.

But if Andrews was more forthcoming with Fleming than with Sandler, he didn't exactly make full disclosure. For Dahl had come to a decision. He'd watched the government indict Bruce Newberg, the trustee for his children, as a racketeer. He could see perjury charges coming Lisa Jones's way. He suspected that the grand jurors would someday hear testimony from Gary Winnick, his former boss at the Convertible Bond Department—and he had no idea what tales Winnick might tell in an effort to distance himself from Milken's problems.

---

*Although contemporaneous memos support this account and his lawyer found no fault with it, Dahl says his aim was simply to make sure he would get the $35 to $40 million he claims he'd been promised.

Dahl had been a team player all along. Not by choice, but by necessity. Milken ran the bond department like the Lakers or Michael Ovitz's Creative Artists Agency—it didn't matter who put the ball through the hoop, so long as it got there. Then, Milken wanted his associates to believe, everyone shared in the spoils. But now that he'd seen what Ackerman earned, Dahl no longer felt those spoils were fairly distributed. He could only guess how much Milken was taking out of Drexel each year. In comparison, the $50 million Dahl had stashed away didn't seem like the fortune it once had.

Here Dahl was pressing against one of the key paradoxes of Milken's department. The more money salesmen and traders made, the more autonomy Milken gave them. And yet the more money they made, the more they were tied to him and Drexel. In the end, therefore, the fortunes they were making stripped them of their autonomy. And as they became his dependents, Milken became the ultimate father; he guaranteed their employment and arranged everything from their laundry to their investments.

That paternalism turned some employees into cultists who would have followed him anywhere—"If Mike had said, 'It's time to drink the Kool-Aid,' there were people who would have stepped forward," a Drexel veteran recalls. But there were some employees, though enriched by Milken beyond their most intoxicated fantasies, who secretly resented him for the power he had over them. "It really didn't matter how much he paid you," an embittered former colleague explains. "He could throw millions at you on January first, and it didn't matter, because you made it back for him right away. And, for the rest of the year, you were essentially working for free."

Milken never understood that the more he did for his people, the more he weakened them. And the more he took over their lives, the more he made resentment inevitable—as everyone who works for an all-embracing benefactor must come to suspect, he may be the greatest oppressor of all.

For Dahl, the perception of Milken as oppressor was never far from the surface. He was, according to those who worked with him, the salesman who was most competitive with his mentor. Milken stepped up to the line; so did Dahl. But, unlike Milken, Dahl was almost aggressively unfriendly. "He had no time for pleasantries," one associate said. "Jim is for Jim—that's his agenda."

Once, the money Dahl made with Milken was sufficient to paper over their many differences. But that money no longer bound him to Milken. Just the opposite. Once the government leaned on Dahl, the money came between them, separated them, even made them enemies. It couldn't be helped. If Dahl was indicted as a racketeer, he might lose everything he had.

It isn't shrewd for a U.S. attorney to give immunity to a witness who may be guilty of more serious crimes than the man he's being asked to testify against—if the case goes to trial, juries have a way of smelling a rat. So, before they immunized Jim Dahl, the prosecutors put him through a ritual inquisition; they needed to assure themselves that he didn't have significant criminal liability of his own.

There were, for example, questions about some Boesky trades that appeared in Dahl's ledger; Dahl convinced them that Milken did the trades. There was some concern that Dahl had parked bonds with Beverly Hills Savings and Loan; Dahl convinced them that hadn't happened.

And so, late in September of 1988, the SEC and U.S. attorney immunized Dahl.

The questions began immediately.

Did Milken have the right to trade for Columbia Savings or First Executive without calling them?

Not so, Dahl said. At First Exec, Fred Carr relied on Mike in the beginning, but he became increasingly tough to sell. At Columbia, Tom Spiegel was an easier sell, and if he had a big position in a hot bond issue, he'd let Drexel buy some of it back.

What about Reliance and Saul Steinberg?

An impossible client, Dahl said. Steinberg had a very hard-assed trader who'd buy almost nothing. The guy was so difficult that Drexel had to rotate salesmen.

What about Charles Keating?

A nice guy. An easy account.

Mark Shenkman of First Investors?

An easy sell. When salesmen wanted a good deal, they'd say, "Let's yank the Shenk." He bought bonds "cheap" just like Boesky bought bonds "cheap."

One of the hardest things we're trying to figure out is what Lowell Milken does.

Mike doesn't like confrontation, Dahl explained, so Lowell says all the things Mike might find distasteful. Mostly, Lowell was an administrator—he didn't handle clients.

We're looking at the possibility that Milken and Boesky traded on insider information during the Diamond Shamrock/Occidental Petroleum merger talks. Did you hear any of their conversations?

Yes. After the announcement that the deal fell through, Ivan called, and Mike gave him advice. I got the feeling Mike was trying to help Ivan unwind a bad situation.

But were the Boesky trades really trades for a position he was holding for Milken?

No. It just sounded as if Ivan had lost a lot of money and wanted Mike's advice. He was pretty hot about it. He must have called ten times in twenty minutes.

A few days later, Dahl was interviewed for three hours by John Sturc of the SEC. Sturc asked so many questions about relationships in the High-Yield Bond Department that it seemed the commission was looking to make a failure-to-supervise case against Milken. Otherwise, the questions weren't particularly pointed or probing.

That same day, Dahl appeared before the grand jury—for just fifteen minutes. While there, he had said nothing of consequence. But that was not the significance of his appearance. His real audience was in Beverly Hills. And there, the message wasn't what he'd said, but that he'd said anything at all.

Dahl returned to Drexel early in October and immediately pulled Richard Sandler aside to try to explain his talks with the government. Sandler was, by then, very wary. He knew that Dahl had gone from a target letter to an immunized witness without any warning. He was not about to have a more specific conversation with anyone in that position.

Dahl was eager to have a different conversation with his colleagues on the trading floor. I'm in the clear, he announced at a small meeting of upper-echelon Milken people that week. A bunch of target letters are going out, a lot of you are going to be distracted with lawyers and such. It makes sense, therefore, for me to take more responsibility for trading.*

This was Dahl's first miscalculation. His pirouette had been too dazzling, his transformation from team player to opportunist too abrupt. Milken was in fatal trouble, but he wasn't dead yet. Dahl would have to cool his heels. And he would have to watch as leadership shifted to the logical choice, head trader Warren Trepp, a man who talked to no one, refused to knuckle under to the government, and whose only sin seemed to be the conspicuous ownership of a Rolls-Royce.

For many people in Beverly Hills, the question about Terren Peizer wasn't why he'd turn on Milken but why Milken hired him in the first place. Thin, dark, boyishly handsome, he made no secret of his love affair with himself. He posed, he preened, he batted his lashes at the prettier assistants—he believed the phone operators listened in on his calls so they, too, could thrill to his Beattyesque tones. And yet, at twenty-five, he sat right next to Milken.

How had that happened?

Before coming to Drexel, Peizer was a hotshot salesman at First Boston, where, he liked to say, one of his clients thought of him as "the East Coast Mike Milken." Early in 1985, a Drexel client named David Solomon had complained that his account wasn't being well-serviced; he described Peizer as his idea of a good salesman. So, in July of 1985, Peizer was invited to Beverly Hills to be interviewed by Milken.

Milken says he met with Peizer that weekend for less than an hour; Peizer insists that he spent sustained private time with Milken. "The weekend of my interview," Peizer recalls, "was right out of *The Godfather*."

According to Peizer, Milken—who was never known to reveal his feelings or opinions to anyone on the trading floor—opened up to him, and, in a job interview, confessed to insider trading. As Peizer recalls it, Milken painted his criminal agenda in bold colors, telling this virtual stranger, "You can make more

---

*Although contemporaneous memos support this account and his lawyer found no fault with it, Dahl says he had no interest in heading the department.

money on an underwriting by buying the stock—or having others buy it for you—than by selling the deal."

Lowell Milken hadn't interviewed a salesman since 1981, but at Michael's insistence, he broke his rule about doing no business on weekends and spent an hour with his brother's newest prospect. Someone must have told Peizer that Lowell handled the bottom-line partnerships, for in this interview, he didn't dwell on the big picture.

I make more than a million at First Boston, Peizer reportedly said, for openers. What's my potential here? And a big salary increase was just the beginning for him. I want to make sure I can invest in the partnerships, he told Lowell.*

Yes, Lowell said, you can—in the future.

The future was too far away for Peizer; he wanted to invest in partnerships involving deals that had already been completed in 1985. Lowell had no answer to that. But he did have one for his brother—don't hire this guy.

Michael Milken promptly authorized a $3.5-million-a-year salary for Peizer.

Just weeks after Peizer's arrival in August of 1985, Michael called Lowell again about him—this time to authorize a $500,000 personal loan, payable in sixty days, so Peizer could invest in the partnerships.

But Peizer told me he was making millions, Lowell said.

He was, but he has securities he doesn't want to sell just yet, Michael explained.†

Now that Milken had filled his coffers, Peizer set about imitating every detail of his benefactor's behavior. Milken hated intercoms; so, now, did he. Milken used a special brand of accounting paper; he also had to have some. With his soft voice, it wasn't hard for him to learn to imitate Milken; he got so good at it, he says, that clients would talk to him on the phone and think they were talking to Milken.

Peizer quickly became the pariah of the trading floor. Janet

*Peizer says that he never discussed money with Lowell Milken.

†Peizer had trouble letting go of more than just his stocks. He continued to use a telephone credit card belonging to a former co-worker until a First Boston executive called Milken to demand restitution. Peizer says that he charged no more than $200 to this card and explains the problem as simple forgetfulness.

Chung had looked forward to meeting him; having done so, she told Milken, "You still owe me a boyfriend." More significant, the Syndicate Department hated the way Peizer would announce that his clients would buy a piece of a deal—and then he wouldn't deliver the order forms until he saw how much the other salesmen were committing to.

Prompted by numerous complaints, Milken had a chat with Peizer, though not the one his colleagues wanted. According to Peizer, Milken's only criticism was "Terren, you're not enough of a team player." For Peizer, that criticism was transparent; it was the only way that Milken could justify not giving him a raise.

Whatever their differences, Peizer succeeded in sizing Milken up in record time—all he cared about was productivity. And Peizer, now known as "Terren the Terrible," produced. When his co-workers continued to complain, Milken gave them his standard answer to all conflict: "You can't be critical. You have to learn to get along."

That, according to Peizer, was his philosophy as well. With one exception: He says that Milken tried to pawn Boesky off on him, but he resisted—he had "a feel" for their relationship. Otherwise, he says, he did the job he was hired for. "I covered Mike's accounts so he could concentrate on the next game," he explains. "Mike didn't want to make one to three points when he could make ten."

Soon after the investigation began, there was a change on the family photograph that Milken kept on his desk—Terren Peizer cut out a small picture of himself and pasted it in. Milken, nonconfrontational as ever, left it there.

This gesture might be interpreted as a statement of solidarity. If so, it was the last one Peizer made. Around the time Dahl got immunity, Peizer received a subpoena. Unlike Dahl, he had not been with Milken long. He hadn't made serious money. And because he craved the mystery he generated by keeping his business and social lives separate, he had few ties to anyone in the Beverly Hills office. His decision to become a government witness was, as a result, not a difficult one—he may, in fact, have made that decision as far back as November of 1986.

"In our first meeting, I sensed Terren wanted to settle," recalls his lawyer, Plato Cacheris. "One of his prime concerns was my ability to deal with the U.S. attorney for the Southern District. I had a very sparse history with them. Terren liked that—he didn't want anyone in the old-boy network."

Cacheris, best known for his representation of Oliver North's assistant, Fawn Hall, heard his client out, studied his subpoena, and went out to Beverly Hills to hear Peizer's story at length. There, Peizer had something better than information—although the government subpoena delivered to the Beverly Hills office on Boesky Day had demanded full document production, he'd deliberately held back two pieces of paper.

The first was a Post-It note—"Terren, please speak to Mike"—attached to a page of figures that Peizer claimed was written by Milken himself. This page was dated December 27, 1985. "Losses to DS," was written at the top. Below that were two columns: "Sol to DBL" and "DBL to Sol."

"DS" was David Solomon, head of Solomon Asset Management the Drexel client who'd suggested Peizer to Milken. At the end of 1985, Peizer said, Solomon called to say that he needed to generate some tax losses. He listened when Milken got on the line and told Solomon, "Let me look through my positions." It seemed to Peizer that they'd had this conversation before—he assumed these weren't Solomon's first tax trades.

Peizer didn't understand how to keep track of these trades, he said, so Milken created the "Losses to DS" sheet. Then, Peizer said, Michael directed him to see Lowell. According to Peizer, he saw Lowell—the Milken who despised him and didn't want him hired—several times. The computations were so complicated, he said, that he brought his notebook along. And as Lowell led him through the Solomon arrangement, he too put pencil to Peizer's paperwork.

This paperwork was Peizer's second piece of evidence.

Peizer said he'd also been given a notebook containing the adjustments on the Finsbury arrangements. On the Monday after Boesky Day—the day Peizer was behaving so strangely Milken was convinced that he was a government agent—Peizer said that Milken had asked him for this notebook. Peizer said that he thought about photocopying it, but decided against it. The next morning, he said, he produced the book for Milken, who directed him to give it to Lorraine Spurge, the Syndicate manager. He said he met Spurge in the kitchen, turned on the faucet, and, with the water drowning out any possibility that their conversation might be overheard or tape-recorded, he told her that it contained everything relating to David Solomon. He said he never saw the notebook again.

Cacheris wasn't overly concerned about the missing notebook. "With the scorecard and the detailed sheet, Terren had an ace that I was able to play for him with Carroll and Fardella," he says. "The prosecutors knew very little about Peizer—Dahl had pointed to him as a likely source, but we never learned what Dahl said—and I felt they'd rather talk to Terren than prosecute him. When they learned about the documents, they were more than pleased. One said, 'I feel like a kid in a candy store!'"

He should have. Peizer had rung every possible bell. Here was Michael Milken's handwriting! Here was Lowell's! And here were allegations against Solomon—a second Boesky—that might scare him enough to seek his own deal with the government!

Although Peizer had withheld documents for two years, there was no talk of citing him for obstruction of justice. Very quickly, the prosecutors' questions become more lighthearted.

We've heard that you had sex with at least one woman at Drexel, the prosecutors said.

Not so, Peizer replied. I keep my social life separate.

The prosecutors frowned, fearing they had caught Peizer in a lie.

What about the oral sex you got from ——? they asked.

Peizer laughed. I don't consider that a blow job is sex, he said.

And so, within a month, Peizer had immunity.

In Beverly Hills, Milken's colleagues tended to view the assistant U.S. attorneys as ruthless slimebags pursuing a witchhunt. Peizer getting immunity changed no one's mind. But Peizer felt compelled to enlighten his co-workers. "These guys are just like you and me—young, ethical, and smart," he announced on his return to the High-Yield Bond Department. "They're just trying to do their jobs."

Peizer's endorsement of the enemy did not enhance his popularity. That fall he had a device installed on his BMW 735i that allowed him to start the car from a distance. And he joined the Beverly Hills Gun Club and began taking target practice.

Soon after he became a government witness, Peizer gave prosecutors a briefing so detailed that, his lawyer later remarked, he was hearing some of it for the first time himself. Peizer shared his recollection of Boesky Day, when, he claimed, Michael and Lowell Milken met in the middle of the trading floor and then locked themselves away in Lowell's office. He had a feeling that there had been a shredding party at Drexel the weekend after the Boesky announcement; someone he knew who was no longer employed at Drexel walked in that weekend and was told to get lost.

In recent conversations, Peizer has explained how Milken and Boesky were able to commit crimes on open phones without detection. Over the weekend, Peizer believes, Milken and Boesky called one another at home and made up code names for the companies they might want to buy the following week. On Monday, anyone could listen to them and not know what they were really saying.

Peizer says that he cracked the code during the MGM/Turner transaction. Though the deal had been announced, there was much uncertainty about it, and Milken wanted him on the line to explain a few things to Boesky. But as Peizer has recalled it, Milken and Boesky never discussed the deal. Instead, they talked in their private lingo, referring to MGM as "Lion."

That wasn't the only Boesky conversation that Peizer claims to have overheard. He was also on the line, he says, during the October 1, 1986, call, when Boesky and Milken arranged to meet at the Beverly Hills Hotel the following week. This was, by his account, quite a howler.

If you want to talk about selling the hotel, you have to come to my office, Milken said—suspecting that Boesky was going to be wired, he astutely wanted the meeting to take place far from Boesky's handlers.

No, Boesky insisted. Let's meet at my suite at the hotel.

What to do?

According to Peizer, Milken made a decision motivated by greed. He knew Boesky was shopping the hotel around, he saw a transaction slipping through his fingers, he was outraged.

All right, Ivan, I'll meet you at the hotel, Milken conceded.

If Peizer took the prosecutors through his recollection of the October 1 phone call, they should have been very careful about believing everything he told them—they had a tape of that conversation within easy reach. And as it clearly indicates, Milken *never* urged Boesky to meet at Drexel. Boesky *never* focused on

217

the sale of the hotel as the core issue to be discussed. And, whatever his suspicions, Milken *never* leaned on Boesky in this call; if anything, it is Boesky who pushes Milken to get his way.

Peizer's claim that Milken and Boesky used "codes" is just as puzzling. If they had developed a private language, surely Boesky would have volunteered that information to the prosecutors—and they would have demanded that he use those codes in taped phone calls to Milken, the better to prove the existence of a criminal conspiracy. That wouldn't have alerted Milken to Boesky's status as an informer; if Peizer is correct, Boesky and Milken used codes even when, as in MGM/Turner, the deal was already public.

But Peizer's Boesky stories aren't the only discrepancies between his allegations and what could be verified. There was his certainty about a Boesky Day encounter between Milken and his brother—at a time when Lowell, as medical records submitted to the government indicate, was at a doctor's office. There was Peizer's memory of a former Drexel employee who walked in on a "shredding party" during the weekend after the Boesky announcement—he never materialized. There was Peizer's belief that he had a sample of Michael Milken's handwriting—even the government no longer contends it was Milken's. There was Peizer's assurance that Lowell Milken had written on the Solomon gain-and-loss sheet—once again, the prosecutors no longer share his certainty.

On allegations that could be confirmed, Terren Peizer was batting .000.

"I see every trade Michael Milken does for his own account, every trade he does for the firm, and I can guarantee that not only is Michael straight but he bends over backward to be straight," Fred Joseph had once told a reporter. In the fall of 1988, that seemed like a long time ago to Joseph. Hell, it seemed like ages since August, when he'd told the grand jury he continued to feel "quite comfortable" with Milken's integrity.

In that session, John Carroll had decided to educate Joseph—using the Princeton/Newport tapes as teaching tools. He played a selection from a conversation about a transaction in COMB stock. In this conversation, Newberg and other Drexel personnel watch someone—presumably Minneapolis investor Irwin "The Liquidator" Jacobs—use Jefferies to push the price of the stock up. Infuriated, they responded by trying to knock its price back down.*

Isn't that manipulation? Carroll asked.

In fact, it was a venerable Wall Street practice called "baseball"—one team has a turn at bat, then the other has its chance to score—although Joseph gave it the more dignified term of "stabilization."

Carroll then played a second tape, involving the same stock. On this call, a Princeton/Newport trader told Newberg that the stock would cost him a few cents more per share, as he had to go to another broker to get it.

Tell me, Mr. Joseph—is it permissible to pay a third party to execute a trade?

I can't think of any circumstances that allow this, Joseph replied.

In the weeks to come, those tapes rankled Joseph. Manipulating against a manipulation made business sense; still, it broke the law. Something was wrong in Beverly Hills. Maybe it couldn't be tied to Milken, Joseph thought—but Milken had to know.

Tom Curnin felt these fears even more strongly. It's not just Boesky, he told Joseph. Milken did something. He's got a problem, and you've got a problem.

---

*While prosecutors concede that a manipulation through Jefferies may have occurred here, no one was ever investigated in this matter. The prosecutors' explanation—that this incident was uncorroborated by witnesses—makes no sense: Boyd Jefferies had been a government witness for more than a year. It would appear that only the counter-manipulation was of interest to the government.

CHAPTER FIFTEEN

If you indict us as racketeers, you'll destroy the firm, Fred Joseph told the prosecutors in late November. The plea you want us to take gives us only a fifty-fifty chance of survival. Considering the odds, we'll let *you* put ten thousand people out of work—we won't settle on your terms.

RICO won't put you out of business, the prosecutors assured him. To prove it, they talked to knowledgeable Wall Street executives—George Ball and James Wolfensohn, among others—and were assured that a RICO indictment wasn't automatically fatal.*

Joseph held his ground. Onward ticked the clock. Now it was December, the last month that future mayoral candidate Rudolph Giuliani would be U.S. attorney. Christmas came on a Sunday that year; it would be tacky to announce a major indictment any later than Thursday. The U.S. attorney had until December 22 to bring Drexel to its senses.

At ten in the morning on October 20, 1987, with the market just open and showing no signs of a rebound after the previous

---

*Although the U.S. attorney didn't seek his wisdom, former secretary of the treasury William Simon wrote to the prosecutors to say that no business that ran on credit could survive a RICO indictment.

day's crash, Fred Joseph felt as if he were being cut in half. Surrounded by lawyers, he was preparing for his third command performance at the SEC. But here, on the phone, was a call from Gerald Corrigan, head of the Federal Reserve Bank of New York.

We're not sure how far the market may fall, Corrigan said, so we're asking for help—we want Drexel to be ready to take over a few specialist firms.

The world is falling apart, and on one hand, I'm being asked to help hold it together, and on the other, I have to get ready to see the SEC, Joseph glumly noted when he got off the line.

We'll get a postponement, Tom Curnin said.

In Joseph's presence, Curnin called the SEC enforcement division to make what seemed like a reasonable request.

This is *bullshit!* Gary Lynch shouted. This has been scheduled for a month. You be here!*

According to this account, Curnin next called John Shad, and the SEC commissioner overruled his enforcement director—Drexel could have a week's grace.

Less than half an hour later, Joseph's secretary buzzed him to say that David Vise, the *Washington Post* reporter who covered Wall Street, was on the line.

Joseph took the call.

I hear you've refused to appear before the SEC and will take the Fifth, Vise said.

Joseph was stunned. Vise knew before Curnin had a chance to call the other Drexel lawyers! Lynch—or someone on his staff—had done more than leak confidential information, he'd leaked in a way that sent a message. The SEC *wanted* Joseph to know it had leaked. The commission didn't care about the rules.†

Joseph's agitation was not long-lived; leaks were the order of the day. Years later, Charles Carberry suggested that *The Wall Street Journal's* remarkably detailed early reports came from Oppenheim, Appel & Dixon—the Boesky accounting firm that, presumably, wished to show it had no knowledge of its client's real

---

*Although Lynch remembers the incident, he doesn't remember Curnin's call.

†Later, a confidential SEC memo was leaked to *The Washington Post*. Such incidents outraged Milken's attorneys, who petitioned Judge Kimba Wood to investigate the leaks. She agreed there might be a problem, and ordered an investigation to be conducted—by the government. This investigation produced no culprits.

purpose in paying Drexel the $5.3 million. At the SEC, officials have said the instigators were defense lawyers whose clients were beginning to cooperate and who wanted that cooperation put in the best possible light. Others in the government have made the fantastic claim that Drexel and Milken were, from the beginning, the source of the leaks. In this view, the defense, knowing its cause was lost, hoped that a controversy about "fairness" would draw attention away from the real issues.

Still, the government maintained absolute, pristine secrecy in the Levine and Boesky matters—why was it completely unable to do so in the Drexel and Milken investigations?

In mid-February of 1987, Peter Fleming decided to put that question to the SEC. "Fleming commented that the meeting was fairly fruitful," a Williams & Connolly memo noted that week, "and that the SEC did not deny that they were the source of the leaks."

Harvey Pitt, the Boesky lawyer who had kept a big secret right to the last minute, believes "there may have been a leak in the U.S. attorney's office, although the people I dealt with wouldn't have succumbed to that temptation." But others might have. "I was unequivocally told: 'The leaks are part of our strategy,'" a Drexel client reported after a session with Charles Carberry's successors.

The leaking all but stopped in the summer of 1987. It picked up again in 1988, with *The Wall Street Journal*'s report of the government raid on Princeton/Newport—an event that Princeton/Newport and its lawyers were not likely to want known—and accelerated during the summer. And then, early in December of 1988, the *Journal* began publishing unfavorable Drexel news with the regularity of drumbeats in "Bolero."

First, on December 5, came a report that Drexel's lawyers had been subpoenaed by the grand jury. On December 7, the *Journal* announced that Cary Maultasch would be a "key witness" against Drexel and Milken. On December 9, the *Journal* broke the news of Terren Peizer's cooperation; with Peizer on its side, it noted, the government "toughened its negotiating stand."

Those leaks—either by the government or, as the case may be, by lawyers of cooperating witnesses—weren't sufficient pressure to resolve the Drexel case with a guilty plea. Morale was high at 60 Broad Street, even higher in Beverly Hills. It would take something dramatic to break the firm's will. It would take an event.

Once again, Princeton/Newport would provide that event.

In August of 1988, Assistant U.S. Attorney Neil Cartusciello announced that there might well be a second indictment of Princeton/Newport. The judge set a date in October. The prosecutors weren't ready. A new date was set: November 20.

In the yearly rhythm of Princeton/Newport, November 20 was one day shy of a very key date. Its investors were allowed to withdraw money only once a year—right at the end, with forty days notice. November 21 was the cutoff. In November, though, the prosecutors weren't ready to file their second indictment. So Princeton/Newport decided to give investors until December 10 to withdraw their funds.

When prosecutors heard that, they announced that the superseding indictment wouldn't be ready until January.

"Just tell us if you're going to seek additional forfeitures," defense lawyers begged. Bruce Baird insists that the government was "touching the ground backwards" in its efforts to keep Princeton/Newport alive—although he declined to answer the firm's most urgent question.* That week, Rudy Giuliani's picture went up on the Princeton/Newport bulletin board, with two dark smudges penned over the mouth to create a strikingly Hitlerian portrait.

The U.S. attorney's silence on the question of additional forfeitures was the coup de grace for Princeton/Newport—its investors grabbed their millions and ran. On December 8, Jay Regan announced the death of the firm. "The government has now accomplished the goal it stated when it commenced the investigation—cooperate or be destroyed," his press release asserted. Bruce Baird, in an attempt at damage control, quickly began to claim that any "small business" facing any kind of criminal indictment was likely to fold.

But the lesson of Princeton/Newport was clear on Wall

---

*Three and a half years later, in a talk at Seton Hall Law School, prosecutor John Carroll expressed a dramatically different view of that prosecution. "From the perspective of 1992, I don't think we should have used it [RICO] again in Princeton/Newport," Carroll said. "Our use was certainly a lawful one, and I don't think anybody could find anything that was totally out of the ballpark in whether we used it. I think that the tactic of going after an institution and seeking a very broad freeze order as a way of initiating litigation is a

Street—the government had pushed a seventy-five-employee firm over a cliff without blinking. And Drexel was next.

Stupidly, Drexel had announced it was reserving $500 million to deal with a RICO indictment or a settlement. To give himself negotiating room, Giuliani now demanded as much as $750 million from Drexel—and, to encourage a settlement, he began to hint that he didn't plan to bring just one indictment against Drexel. As with Princeton/Newport, he had a superseding indictment in mind, and it was as vague in its financial penalties as the one that took Princeton/Newport down.

Fred Joseph could predict the magnitude of the financial penalty relating to Boesky charges; he couldn't predict how high a second set of non-Boesky charges would go. Peter Fleming told him that this was the moment when character would be tested on every side. He reminded Joseph about the "two-minute drill" in hotly contested football games—when, with the clock ticking down, the team with the ball runs a series of plays it has rehearsed long in advance. There's no time for huddles, no time to devise new strategy, Fleming said. You've *got* to run the drill.

But Fred Joseph wasn't listening to Peter Fleming any longer. Fleming had doubted the government would use RICO; it seemed he was wrong. Fleming had suggested no jury would bang Drexel for more than $25 million; Giuliani was talking about exponential forfeitures. Fleming liked to go to court; Tom Curnin and his other lawyers were urging Joseph to settle, to get what he could in the way of concessions from Giuliani and move on.

At that moment, Michael Milken suddenly seemed expendable—a major chapter in Drexel's history, but a chapter that was destined to end.

Had Fred Joseph known how the U.S. attorney would handle Princeton/Newport's superseding indictment, he might have fought to the end. But that second Princeton/Newport indictment deliberately wasn't going to be revealed until after Giuliani's deadline for Drexel. As it happened, that gun fired only blank cartridges—the Princeton/Newport superseding indictment was a yawn, containing a few new charges and calling for *no* additional forfeitures.

tactic, years after the fact, I question—I do think it changes the way cases are litigated. I think it does, in some instances, remove the ability of an institution to proceed to a contested judgment."

*   *   *

On a Saturday night in mid-December, Drexel's Corporate Finance Department held its Christmas dinner. Joseph had negotiated with Giuliani all day; he was in despair. But everyone else seemed to him to be in dreamland—spirits were never higher. Chairman Robert Linton sang a ribald "Rudy the Red-Nosed Reindeer" and then, to huge applause, he handcuffed himself to Joseph. Associates offered "I heard it through the Drexel Line/ Not much longer will my job be mine/And I'm just about to do some time/Freddy, Freddy, yeah (no more bonus, no more bonus)." Joseph stood there and smiled, but he was embarrassed. If it makes you all feel better, he thought, sing a song.

The following week, Joseph settled with the government.

"Don't make a fiduciary decision," Peter Fleming had begged Joseph. But, fearing the worst, Joseph abandoned Drexel's culture and two years of adamant defense—he made what he'd later call "simply a business decision."

The terms were terrible. Six felonies. A fine of $650 million. Michael and Lowell Milken would have to leave the firm. Their 1988 compensation would be withheld.

In exchange for all that, the prosecutors made some concessions. Drexel wouldn't have to waive attorney-client privilege and turn over the files from its own investigation to the government. The language of the plea bargain would be watered down. And, although no one had ever suggested that he would be indicted, Fred Joseph would get a pass—not an insignificant fact for a CEO who had once told associates, "My God, in the 1930s, *heads of firms* went to jail!"

Intellectually, Michael Milken had long suspected what Joseph would do. Emotionally, he couldn't believe that men he had worked with all his adult life would sell him out. But there it was—in Arthur Liman's office, his lawyer was telling him that Fred Joseph was on the line.

On his end, Joseph now says, he felt like a man facing divorce. He says he had loved Milken, but he'd become convinced that Milken had betrayed him; as he nursed the hurt, he struggled to remember the love. Milken was caught up in equally complicated feelings—bewilderment shot through with anger—but they were new to him, and he had no way to express them.

So he talked.

About freedom and persecution. About Germany just before World War II. And about Vichy France.

Joseph listened for ten minutes, saying little—he understood this to be the last pitch of a compulsive salesman. But someone was going to walk away here, and someone else was going to prison; stripped of the rhetoric, that was the transaction.

At the Drexel office in Beverly Hills, everyone had left for the day—even those who usually stayed late were driven out by the settlement announcement. But Janet Chung couldn't leave, not until Milken called, not until she knew how he was. Seven. Eight. At 8:30—11:30 P.M. in New York—the phone rang.

"Good evening, Drexel," she said.

"Good evening, Drexel," Milken said, in the singsong voice that always made her smile.

She gave him his messages. Nothing was said about the Drexel plea. Very quickly, they ran out of things to talk about.

"Well, it's very late," Milken said, at last. "And I know you've been there all day and you'll probably be in early tomorrow. I really appreciate that. So please go home and get some rest, okay?"

Janet Chung got to the elevator before she began to cry. Michael Milken went back to the Carlyle Hotel, where he was staying with his wife and children. He didn't cry—he couldn't allow that. But somewhere ahead, down a road he couldn't quite chart, he could dimly see a resolution to the suffering that was now running riot around him and within him.

It too involved a plea.

CHAPTER SIXTEEN

"**W**e've got to derail this train."

Traditionally, this is the sentiment of a defense lawyer anxious to prevent an embarrassing indictment or a trial that promises a guilty verdict and a substantial punishment. But as the Drexel case was coming to a conclusion in December of 1988, that overture was made by Assistant U.S. Attorney John Carroll to Robert Litt of Williams & Connolly. While Carroll doesn't remember initiating this conversation or expressing this sentiment—though who called whom and the exact words that were said don't really matter—what Carroll very clearly communicated was Rudolph Giuliani's great desire to settle the Milken case before an indictment.

Why John Carroll, who, only a year before, didn't know the difference between a put and a call?

Why Bob Litt, who, according to Milken, still thought too much like a prosecutor?

For one thing, Carroll and Litt were friends. When Litt was an assistant U.S. attorney, he had supervised Carroll's first trial. And they had maintained a back channel of communication that involved only one other defense lawyer: Vincent Fuller, Litt's colleague at Williams & Connolly.

While Williams was alive, Fuller and Litt downplayed this relationship with the prosecutors. The closer he came to death, the more Williams wanted total control; he even disdained the joint-defense meetings, calling them "a jerkoff." But Williams was gone now, and the situation, Litt and Carroll agreed, was "crazy"—a word that, increasingly, carried a lot of meaning in this case.

For Milken's lawyers, it was the government that was off-the-wall; having failed to find insider trading, prosecutors were now treating long-held Wall Street customs like parking as if they were capital crimes. For the government, it was Milken who was irrational; he'd done certain things that he had to know would be proved at trial, so why didn't he cut a deal?

For the man in the middle, there was no reason to do anything of the kind. Optimism was Michael Milken's signature; now, more than ever, it was important for him to show confidence in his future. To clients seeking funding, he'd smile and ask, "Where would you like to be in 1995?" To worried investors, he'd say, "If I were you, I'd put one hundred percent of my money in high-yield bonds." As Drexel fell and he stood alone, he now did what he could to keep his lawyers' spirits high.

This took the form of little lectures. The unfairness of the press, the integrity of his business practices in comparison to others on Wall Street, the need for investment capital to make America competitive again—if ever a client was born to be an after-dinner speaker, it was Milken. There was a half-life to these speeches; their potency dissipated quickly. But Milken could manufacture time. And Milken was a very patient teacher. Whatever else he had to do, he could carve a few minutes to take his lawyers through the story behind his prosecution.

"You're sitting in the prosecutors' office," he would say, "and you meet Dennis Levine, who has offshore accounts and an insider trading ring where he recruited people and paid them for their information. And then he leads you to Ivan Boesky, who paid people in cash in unusual places. And Boesky leads you to Marty Siegel, the most prestigious person in the mergers and acquisitions business on Wall Street. And even more than that, since Siegel was on the defense side in M and A, you could assume that the entire business operated with offshore bank accounts, hidden money, large amounts of money being passed, and people selling information from their clients. But since November 1986, neither the Milken case nor any other case has shown any of these effects. And so the media creation that has seen people arrested and dragged from their offices and being put in jail overnight . . . has to be justified by things that have no relationship to the facts and by things that have no relationship to Mike Milken."

The route might deviate, but the conclusion never varied: "Mike Milken has already been sentenced. He was sentenced on November 14, 1986. All that had to be developed was to find the crime."

For Michael Milken, the train that needed to be derailed was the government's.

As Milken talked, Arthur Liman heard echoes of Arthur Miller's *The Crucible*. This drama about New England witchcraft trials in 1692 was a blunt parable about America in the early 1950s, when Senator Joseph McCarthy made wild accusations of Communist infiltration and reasonable people supported him. For Liman, the Milken prosecution was a replay of the Salem and McCarthy witch-hunts. The prosecutors knew Milken was no demon, but they felt powerless to do the right thing. No one could change the way this story would play out; the end was inevitable. It was just as Arthur Miller had written: "Common vengeance writes the law!"

Despite his perspective, Liman too was falling victim to *Crucible* syndrome. While the prosecutors, who saw only the public Liman, couldn't remember when he was so stubborn, so arrogant, defense lawyers saw the opposite—a vacillation in his opinions that suggested he was sometimes hypnotized by his client. "I had conversations with Arthur in which he understood everything, and he had distance and judgment," one lawyer says, "and other times he'd talk about Milken in a way that made you go, 'What *is* he saying?'"

These intellectual swings affected Liman's resolve. He knew that if Milken was going to make a favorable plea bargain, it had best be done quickly; prosecutors don't reward those who make them work hard and long. Milken had sworn he'd fight the government forever, but every damning article in the press set him off, every defection struck him like a personal betrayal. It was hard to believe he could endure a trial.

Meanwhile, the machinery churned. The SEC was constantly turning over boxes of material that required photocopying by a firm in Maryland, indexing by a company in Jamaica, and then reviewing by Paul, Weiss paralegals. There would be one thousand of these boxes before Milken settled—thirty boxes a week for a Paul, Weiss team struggling to keep up with paper generated not just by this prosecution, but by the Princeton/Newport and Lisa Jones cases as well. Before the Milken defense folded, the paralegals would have their own newsletter. After the Milken settlement, they'd lead a cheer at a softball game for "civil Milken"—the civil suits that promised full employment for years to come. Although Liman would be frosted when he learned about that cheer, the paralegals were guilty of nothing more than indiscretion: The government had turned Milken into one of the biggest cash cows that Paul, Weiss had ever known.

In the late summer of 1988, after Williams died and he became Milken's lead lawyer, Liman wanted to summarize what he knew about the case and the client. What were his options? Could the case really be defended at trial? If so, what was the defense?

Michael Milken, Liman wrote in a memo to his colleagues, is a "very precise" person, and "when fees or exposure by Drexel are at stake, he is a man of detail—he would become involved in details even when the issue at stake was whether $100,000 or $200,000 should be credited." Given that, his behavior with Boesky was "totally inconsistent with his normal method of operation when money is at stake."

The list of securities that Milken and Boesky were alleged to have held for one another was started in response to Boesky's complaints—Thurnher had said he decided to chart Boesky purchases when he realized that Boesky was making a list of grievances. Thurnher had seen complainers before, and knew that Milken was a "soft touch with customers; he had taken verbal abuse from them." According to Thurnher, when Milken learned about the list, he called it "bullshit." He never asked to see it.

"The list was a joke," Liman concluded, "though it turned out to be not a funny one."

In a vacuum, the bill for $5.3 million looked premeditated; considering what else was happening at Drexel that week, Liman saw it could be presented as a last-minute improvisation. The night before Drexel sent that bill, Milken had priced a $2.5 *billion* debt offering for Occidental Petroleum. This offering involved four separate issues and required co-managers—it wasn't just the largest financing in Drexel's history, it was immensely complex, and Milken had to stay on top of it all day.

Boesky, in comparison, merited only a few seconds of his time. Milken may have thought: The Boesky deal is closing; he owes us money; let's get paid before he liquidates the old partnership. Very quickly—his mind was still on the Occidental deal and a plane he had to catch for New York—Milken told Thurnher how the fee was to be distributed. And, in that settling, almost all of it went to Corporate Finance and to Research, not to his own department.

Did Milken ever have any control over Boesky's positions?

There was, Liman thought, no conclusive evidence.

Had Milken conspired with Boesky for personal profit?

Implausible for a man making so much money legitimately and who had earned nothing from this so-called conspiracy.

Liman recognized that there were many holes in this defense, the largest being that Boesky's man and Milken's man had fought over the list just before the new Boesky fund went operational—however little the scorecard meant to Milken, it surely was important to his and Boesky's underlings. Still, Liman had found a foundation for a defense. If he had to go to court, there was, at least, a case he could argue.

Bob Litt understood that he had been chosen as the intermediary for reasons considerably shrewder than his relationship with John Carroll. If the plea discussions were unsuccessful, the lawyers involved would forfeit credibility with the client. In effect, those lawyers would have to drop out of the case.

For Williams & Connolly, that was almost a description of existing reality. Although Vincent Fuller was a formidable lawyer, he could never overcome the fact that, for Milken, he was a second-string quarterback. Litt had already earned a reputation as the Cassandra of the defense; from the beginning, he'd believed even more strongly than Williams that the government had too much on the line to allow Milken to prevail. And Litt had little personal stake in the outcome—after Williams died, his brightest prospect was two years of carrying Liman and Flumenbaum's bags. So even if it was probably doomed, why not take a shot at a settlement?

Like Litt and Fuller, the head of the U.S. attorney's securities fraud unit had no confidence that Milken was willing to end the case with a plea. "We said, 'If you tell us that Milken is willing to plead to the five point three million settling with Boesky, we'll talk,'" Bruce Baird recalls. That was indeed a nonstart. Milken insisted there was nothing criminal about the $5.3 million; he'd never change his mind.

The Boesky bill could have been finessed. Cooperation couldn't be; the real core issue was Milken's ability to help prosecutors make more cases. So their first offer was four felonies—at that time, no one could conceive of a plea with more counts than Dennis Levine's. But four counts, they said, wasn't set in stone. Milken could reduce it to three, maybe even two, if he gave the government evidence against significant people: Kravis, Steinberg, Icahn, Perelman, Lindner, Peltz, and others of that ilk.

You believe that every 1980s fortune was built on a crime, Milken's lawyers said. What's the proof? Give us one shred of evidence that the whole takeover game was rigged.

Your client knows what he did—ask him! the prosecutors snapped.

When the acrimony burned itself out, Bruce Baird put the issue in more soothing terms.

It's like alphabet soup, Baird said. The more soup he serves us, the more names we can make.

That's a problem, Litt and Fuller said. Milken doesn't think he has anyone to turn in.

It didn't matter; on the first approach, the prosecutors backed off, fearful that any settlement would find them in the glare of the television lights as John Dingell made them look weak and foolish. A few weeks later, they felt foolish and weak for knuckling under to criticism that might never come. The talks started again. This time, the assistant U.S. attorneys used a bit of psychology.

No one at that office had met Milken, nor had the senior staff at the SEC. But from Milken associates who had become cooperating witnesses, prosecutors were able to form their own profile of Milken's character. "There were aspects that were fuzzy," Bruce Baird says, "but our impression of Milken was that he was *smaller* than life, an idiot savant with a good idea that grew bigger than he or anyone else had expected—and he and others had come to feel bigger in the process." But success, Baird felt, didn't make Milken more decisive. "Witnesses and their lawyers told us he was someone who had a hard time making decisions except under great pressure."

So the government turned up the pressure.

Until February of 1989, Lowell Milken hadn't been a figure of great importance in the case. The SEC certainly didn't think so—despite pumped-up rhetoric that he was an active participant in the illegal arrangement with Boesky, he scarcely appeared in the 184-page SEC complaint. Now, he suddenly became quite important. He became, in fact, key to a settlement.

Lowell Milken had seen that coming.

He'd always felt the government wanted to crush the family; as he saw it, they couldn't leave a single Milken standing. The prosecutors had a Kennedy scenario in mind—they imagined that Lowell would dip his shirt in the blood of his fallen brother, and then, swearing vengeance, he'd pick up the mantle. But the prosecutors had obviously been listening to the wrong people. The truth was that he was removed from the trading floor—so removed that, over the years, salesmen warned him, "Anything happens to Mike, I know that you'll be out of here in five seconds."

Because Lowell always believed he'd be indicted simply because of his name and always knew he'd resist all invitations to plead guilty, he took care to choose a lawyer as intractable as he was. And when Michael Armstrong was asked to represent Lowell early in 1987, he was indeed ready to fight like crazy. First, though, he called Charles Carberry, who had, in his experience, always been straight as a string. Carberry said there was no need for him to come out swinging. In fact, there was no reason for Armstrong to visit the U.S. attorney's office—Lowell wasn't a target of his investigation. Considering that Carberry had spent some weeks debriefing Ivan Boesky, that was, Armstrong thought, a very meaningful rebuff.

I got the small fish, Armstrong told himself. I'm not going to be sending big bills or enhancing my reputation here.

A year later, after Carberry had moved on, Armstrong checked in with John Carroll. As he recalls it, Carroll told him, "Except for the bill for that five point three million, your guy isn't anything. His problem is, he stayed too late and signed a letter."*

*Carroll doesn't recall expressing this sentiment.

On October 10, 1988, with another lawyer and an investigator in his office, Armstrong had another phone conversation with Carroll.

I have no one in the room, Carroll told him.

You have no one in the room? Armstrong repeated, for the benefit of his associates.

That's right, Carroll said, leading Armstrong to conclude that there were no eyewitnesses or documents indicating Lowell Milken had any knowledge that the $5.3 million bill might not be solely for consulting and investment banking services.*

Then Terren Peizer came along, with his story of meetings with Lowell and his assertion that Lowell's writing was on his worksheets. And, for the first time, the prosecutors began to talk of indicting Lowell.

You want to rely on *Terren Peizer?* Armstrong told John Carroll. Come ahead.

Did the prosecutors feel squeamish about banking on Peizer?

It seemed so to defense lawyers, for now, more than two years after they had debriefed Boesky, the prosecutors revealed that their original witness against Michael Milken had also told them about his dealings with Lowell.

What had Boesky said?

That, just days before he agreed to the $5.3 million payment, he and Lowell had talked about it.

Prosecutors insist that they had this testimony all along; defense lawyers insist that Boesky manufactured it in 1988. In any event, the U.S. attorney now said that one charge in any indictment of Lowell Milken would involve his connection to the Boesky payment. But to qualify for a racketeering indictment, there had to be a second "predicate offense." What was it? The prosecutors wouldn't say.

Give me ten hours before you bring charges, Michael Armstrong pleaded. Give me *two* hours—you tell me what you're going to hit him with, and we'll tell you why you're wrong.

Sorry, he was told. We don't do things that way.

*When Armstrong reminded Carroll of this conversation at a Department of Justice conference before Lowell Milken's indictment, the prosecutor did not recall making this remark.

In the end, the U.S. attorney decided that Lowell Milken's second offense was a single moment in a transaction involving the Mattel toy company. According to the prosecutors, Lowell hadn't told representatives of Warburg Pincus—another investment bank involved in the deal—that Drexel held a 200,000 net long position in Mattel series A preferred stock.

The defense found this a remarkably inane accusation. With his brother, Lowell Milken had invested $50 million in Mattel; it was hard to fathom a reason he might have for deceiving anyone in this transaction. Moreover, they contended, the information that the government said that Lowell hadn't divulged could be found on a proxy card in Warburg's files.

As Michael Armstrong would say with a sneer and a shrug, Lowell Milken was being indicted for declining to volunteer an answer to a question that was never asked of him and which wasn't asked because the answer was already in Warburg's possession.

Armstrong never veered from his first statement to the prosecutors: We don't care how many indictments you bring or how big a forfeiture you call for, this is going to end with you dismissing the case or a jury coming back with an acquittal.

But just as the prosecutors weren't impressed by Armstrong's arguments, they weren't moved by his client's single-mindedness. For Lowell Milken wasn't just a potential defendant—he was a hostage.

With talks at a stalemate, Fuller, Litt, and Liman asked for a meeting with Rudolph Giuliani, then in his last days as U.S. attorney. Vincent Fuller is a laconic man with a long memory, and as he sat with Giuliani, he remembered a famous case, when Edward Bennett Williams negotiated with the Justice Department on behalf of Aristotle Onassis. The client came to the meeting. He listened to the lawyers talking until he could bear it no more. Then, in rough English, Onassis blurted, "Enough! What's the ransom?"

Now, listening to Giuliani, Fuller decided he'd heard enough. "What's the ransom?" he demanded.

The reference eluded Giuliani, as did the concept.

"What's the ransom?" Fuller repeated. "How much do you want?"

I want to hear—directly from Milken—everything he knows

about other people's crimes, Giuliani said. And then, maybe, there can be a deal.

What kind of deal?

Giuliani was vague. If he pleads to racketeering, maybe I'll let him have one count. If he can't tolerate a RICO plea, he'll have to take more counts. He wants his brother cut out of the case, another count or two.

The word went back to Milken: The prosecutors want full cooperation, no chiseling. You must not only tell what you believe is the truth, you must tell a truth *they* believe—you must become the government's animal.

Michael Milken listened. And said nothing.

John Shad came to Milken's home to talk with him one Sunday afternoon in mid-March of 1989, a visit of such excruciating awkwardness that Shad must have wondered more than once why he ever asked for this meeting.

Milken could have ticked off some reasons for the tension in the air. Shad's long career on Wall Street had been followed by an unmemorable term as ambassador to the Netherlands. It was as the SEC chairman who presided over the most controversial investigation of Wall Street in its history that he was best known—an achievement that didn't sit well with Shad or his Wall Street friends. But now Shad was about to become chairman of Drexel Burnham, and if he could help Fred Joseph lead the firm out of the wilderness, he might be regarded as a miracle worker.

From Milken's point of view, it would take a miracle for Shad's SEC record to be forgotten. Although he had left the commission two years earlier, his lieutenants were still pursuing Drexel's employees. They were installing former SEC commissioners on the Drexel board. And, in what looked very much like a government takeover of an investment bank, Shad's associates had seized upon an idea that Gary Lynch suggested as a joke—that in order to separate the High-Yield Bond Department from Milken's influence, it ought to be relocated to New York—and presented it as a serious demand to Drexel officials.

What *did* this man have to talk about with Michael Milken?

His own fears, mostly.

Shad was afraid that the most talented people at Drexel would regard the plea bargain and Milken's upcoming departure from the firm as a signal that its feisty and contrarian culture was dead. If they broke away from Drexel and formed their own boutiques, the firm would be seriously weakened. Shad wanted Milken to help prevent that.

You know, Michael, my wife died fifteen months ago, Shad said. I'm not afraid of dying, but I am thinking of my legacy. I gave a chair at Harvard; they're already changing it. I see your legacy as more stable—I see your legacy as your department at Drexel.

No, my children are my legacy, Milken said. If they're happy and productive, that's all I want.

This reply unsettled Shad, who thought he was coming to see a financier, not the Sage of Encino.

Well, I see it as Drexel, he said, gamely trying to recoup. It's what you've spent your life building. If it falls apart, your life's work goes up in smoke. I want to preserve Drexel. What can I do to ensure unity?

You can *listen* to people, Milken replied. You can show them you *care*. You can say that you *won't* let them be called into the U.S. attorney's office or be hauled before the grand jury for weeks on end.

Lori Milken thought Shad was embarrassed. But it was worth it—Michael was speaking out at last. She dared to hope the days of turning the other cheek were finally over.

There are three kinds of clients, a lawyer involved in the Milken defense effort explained. One lets you do your work, but gives you no assistance; he gives you no input, yet leaves you with all the responsibility. A second kind of client listens, works with you, tells you what you need to know—that's Lowell Milken. And then there's the third variety.

The lawyer sighed.

The third kind of client has his own ideas about everything, and he feels strongly about those ideas. He wants to analyze the case from every angle, so he demands five hundred things at once—you'll never satisfy his demand for information. He wants to be involved in everything, so you spend a lot of time negotiating with him. For all that, he doesn't have a particular point of view about his options. He likes to know everything, and then decide.

That client is Michael Milken, the lawyer said.

Other lawyers on the case agreed.

Milken's busy all the time, working hard on the case, so hard that you start to wonder, another defense lawyer mused. Was this the most farsighted criminal ever—a guy who consciously broke the law, covered his tracks, created documents to minimize detection, asked his colleagues to perjure themselves, and now tied his lawyers up with thousands of little questions? Or is Milken simply a panicked control freak trying to run the defense the way he did the bond department? Is this, in the end, the story of a vendetta against a brilliant nerd by prosecutors and deceitful, self-serving clients and subordinates who made up a story at the first hint of trouble?

The lawyer ultimately decided that Milken was a panicked control freak. But, he realized, it didn't matter what he concluded. Whether Milken was guilty or not, he realized, a long investigation was bound to push him toward a psychological collapse. And the symptoms would be a particular kind of paralysis—an active, even frantic effort to delay.

By February of 1989, Litt and Fuller had long since done all the negotiating they could, assembled all the options, presented all the information. John Carroll moved deadlines up, pushed them back. Milken remained mum. At length, with the indictment looming, Litt became convinced the many issues still to be resolved could never be settled. Just before the March 29 deadline, he took his family to Disneyland.

Still, as a courtesy, Carroll called Litt the day the grand jury was to vote—was Milken having a last-minute change of heart?

As a courtesy, Litt called Milken at home.

This is it, Michael, he said. We've got to have a decision.

Lori Milken was in the room with her husband. For weeks, she'd been urging him not to give in. But if Milken was convinced by her arguments, he certainly didn't communicate that—or anything definitive—to the frustrated Williams & Connolly lawyer.

Litt's next call to Carroll was yet another report that he didn't have an answer.

Then I've got to let the grand jury indict him, Carroll replied.

Arthur Liman was so certain Milken wasn't going to plead guilty that he was at the airport, about to leave the country on vacation, when the message reached him—his client would consider a deal. Like a reporter frantic to file a late-breaking story, he called the U.S. attorney's office to blurt out the news. But the grand jurors had already voted. The press conference announcing the indictments of Milken, his brother, and Bruce Newberg, the Drexel star of the Princeton/Newport tapes, was about to begin.

Michael Milken, who liked to take decision-making down to the wire, had not only dawdled just a bit too long, he had given the government a signal he hadn't intended to send. In his mind, he was merely exploring his options, stopping the clock while his representatives had value-free conversations with the prosecutors. Those prosecutors, though, took Milken's last-minute decision as a change of heart: The man who'd sworn he was innocent was willing to acknowledge his guilt. More, it confirmed their impression that he had trouble making decisions—if they wanted a plea from Milken, the way to extract it was to keep pressuring him.

Most of the ninety-eight-count indictment was, for devotees of the case, old news. Boesky charges were the order of the day—but lined up, what an order they made. Ninety-eight felony counts. A potential 520 years in jail. Racketeering charges. And, because of RICO, the "criminal enterprise" was defined as Drexel. If convicted, Milken might forfeit every dollar the firm paid him for his work from 1983 through 1986—a sum that came to $1.1 billion.

Of all the staggering numbers in the indictment, one was especially unbelievable: In the last of those years, the indictment noted, Milken's earnings topped $550 million.

If you took crisp $100 bills and began to stack them, you would reach $100,000 when your pile was six inches high. A million dollars would reach the hairline of a very tall jockey. Five hundred and fifty million starts to make the pile significant—that stack would reach half a mile into the sky. That's twice as tall as the Empire State Building, or about the height of Donald Trump's proposed Television City tower (with just enough room overhead for Trump's ego).

Five hundred and fifty million dollars was a fact the press loved. If Michael Milken had been a publicly held company, *The New York Times* noted soberly in its front-page account of the indictment, his 1986 pre-tax earnings would have placed him sixty-fifth on the *Forbes* magazine list of after-tax earnings, just ahead of McDonald's. But Milken was not a company. And this sum, awesome though it was, didn't include Milken's earnings from outside investments and Drexel partnerships—according to a confidential financial statement that Milken submitted to the government a few months before he was sentenced, he actually reported gross earnings of $714,850,538 in 1986.*

Adjusting for inflation, Milken had vastly outearned Al Capone, the previous *Guinness Book of World Records* record holder for gross income in a single year—a comparison that was soon noted. It needn't have been for the point to have been made. Even Americans who had no idea what Milken did—even people who persisted in pronouncing his name as "Milliken"—knew his salary. And many of them didn't buy the Reagan argument that America's greatness was that any man could become rich here. They knew better: No one could tell them that Milken made that kind of money legally.

Within Drexel, Milken's earnings had long been kept a secret. Only four people at the firm knew the total—his immense compensation was, even in the early years, broken down into smaller amounts and paid from different accounts so the clerks wouldn't catch on. In 1987, Milken and Joseph had discussed what would happen if the public ever learned what he made. Milken was sure that would never happen; Joseph was sure it would. Worse, Joseph suspected it would be leaked.

The possibility of premature disclosure of Milken's earnings was something that the U.S. attorney for the Southern District thought about as well. And a policy was developed there to keep these epic numbers secret—Milken's compensation was the supreme sound bite, the ultimate smoking gun, the capsule characterization that would stick to him for the rest of his life. So although assistant U.S. attorneys learned this most potent fact about Milken as soon as they joined the investigation, it was not disclosed to the SEC in Washington.

And—for once in the case—there were no leaks.

"It is obvious that she is beautiful," Senator Alphonse D'Amato said as he introduced Kimba Wood to his colleagues on the Senate Judiciary Committee. "It might raise the question, in

---

*His federal and state taxes for that year were $205.9 million.

terms of her youth, how is it that someone so youthful in appearance should be placed before this committee as a nominee to the prestigious court of the Southern District Federal Court."

Kimba Wood, the daughter of an Army officer who wrote speeches for generals and a mother who named her for a small town in Australia, didn't wince at D'Amato's paternalism. She had, in her forty-four years, often encountered condescension and paternalism—and she had, in her quiet way, defeated it by sidestepping it. At Harvard Law, a schoolmate recalls, many men had a mild obsession with her, noting whether she wore corduroys or skirts, whether she wore her hair up or down; she strode across the campus and into the classroom apparently unaware of the attention, as if all she cared about was knowledge. She graduated from law school at a time when women lawyers were oddities; she plowed ahead. With the exception of a failed first marriage, in fact, Wood's adult life was an unbroken series of successes: *cum laude* from Connecticut College, a master's degree from the London School of Economics, Harvard Law, a partnership at LeBoeuf, Lamb. "Kimba is a perfect person," a friend enthused. "She has a perfect brain and she's perfectly beautiful."

That friend was Julie Baumgold, a writer married to Edward Kosner, editor and publisher of *New York* magazine. It was hardly surprising that the Kosners introduced Wood to columnist Michael Kramer, or that she would take a writer as her second husband. Despite her delicate features and soft voice, she liked issues and people involved with them. Once she married Kramer, Wood became one of the most media-connected young lawyers in New York—upper-echelon writers, editors, and literary agents knew "Kimba" and spoke warmly of her ability to manage career, marriage, and motherhood without slighting anyone. Clearly, this woman wasn't going to spend her life litigating general commercial disputes for $200,000 a year.

Wood was a registered Democrat. She had once worked on behalf of the poor at the Office of Economic Opportunity. At the start of the Reagan administration, she was co-counsel with the American Civil Liberties Union on a discrimination suit. But the Senate Judiciary Committee was pressuring the Reagan White House to appoint more female judges, and so, despite what a conservative Republican might call her glaring defects, Wood submitted her application for a seat on the federal bench to Senator D'Amato early in 1987. A year later, D'Amato presented her to his colleagues for confirmation.

Senator Patrick Leahy noted that Wood had never participated in a jury trial. "Are you worried about that?" he asked.

"I am not," Wood replied. "I believe that with the help of the other judges on the Southern District, I can quickly come up to speed on the practical aspects of trying cases. I have already sat with one judge for a day and I will be doing so with others in the next few months . . . there is definitely learning that I need to do in the next few months on that."

Wood's nomination was speedily confirmed, and she became the youngest member of the federal bench in New York. That made her intriguing both to prosecutors, who sensed that her inexperience might make her more deferential to the government, and to defense lawyers, who hoped that the judicial novice might also be something of a maverick. And so the defense didn't protest when the government steered the Milken case to Wood, who was then closing out the Drexel settlement.

A forty-five-year-old judge, a forty-three-year-old defendant: one baby boomer passing judgment on another.

How would Kimba Wood rule?

The Milkens first raised that question early in 1989, when they had to decide what to do about money. Their money. Money they had earned at Drexel in 1988, and which the government had refused to let them be paid. The government argued that it was improper for Drexel to pay hundreds of millions to the Milkens while the firm was settling charges for offenses that the brothers allegedly committed. That the prosecutors hadn't found any illegal activity by the Milkens or Drexel in 1987 or 1988 seemed not to be of great concern to anyone outside of Drexel, the Milkens, and their lawyers.

And that enraged the brothers. RICO was sentence before trial, punishment before conviction—but it was at least the law of the land. For the Milkens, this was something else, something far more frightening: unconstitutional seizure of property. It had to be fought.

They had indirect encouragement to fight from Fred Joseph, who spoke on the subject—in a talk taped by Milken sympathizers—over the Drexel Line hookup in early January of 1989. "The section imposed on us that we won't pay Mike's 1988 contract:

clearly unfair," Joseph told the firm's employees. "Our policy has been that indicted employees take a leave of absence, and usually we compensate them. They treated Michael differently—it's unfair. I frankly don't see any reason for Michael to be less innocent until proven guilty than other people."

But as important as the money was, its confiscation presented a far more intriguing possibility to the Milkens—fighting to recover it might be a way to get the entire Drexel plea thrown out. For in that same Drexel Line talk, Joseph had clearly stated what most knowledgeable Drexel people suspected: The government's contention that the plea was "voluntary" was a lie. If ever a settlement had been coerced, this was it.

"Negotiating with these guys is a strange experience," Joseph had said. "It's not like trying to do a business deal. You're sitting with a very powerful government agency that tells you what you are going to do and you try to take back what pieces you can and walk away, as we did. . . . We ultimately concluded that the firm absolutely had to settle—a financial institution cannot stand up to a RICO indictment."

A young judge wasn't likely to make any ruling that went against public sentiment. To brainstorm this delicate matter, Arthur Liman turned to Laurence Tribe, professor of constitutional law at Harvard. Tribe had known Wood since her Harvard days; they talked occasionally about law clerks and legal conundrums. As he wrote Liman, "She has a fascination with analytical puzzles in constitutional law and a thirst for thoroughly documented paths through whatever mazes she or her law clerks may conjure up."

In February of 1989, Tribe sent a memo to Liman suggesting a stunning line of attack, far more aggressive than a breach-of-contract suit against Drexel. The Milkens might also be able to sue Gary Lynch and Rudolph Giuliani—as Tribe wrote, "the actions of Lynch and Giuliani may well have been beyond the scope of absolute prosecutorial immunity."

The Milken lawyers went to work finding applicable cases on the salary issue that they could cite to Wood. And they presented their argument to her. But before she could rule on their motion, Michael and Lowell Milken were indicted.

Milken had removed his personal possessions from Drexel long before the indictment. Some thought his place at the center of the famous X-shaped desk should be left empty forever. Warren Trepp, the head trader, didn't agree—he took Milken's place right away.

"You can't know how sorry I am to be sitting here," he told a co-worker as he began his first day in Milken's chair.

"Not as sorry as we are to see you here," he shot back.

But personal feelings on the trading floor were soon eclipsed by the first High-Yield Bond Conference ever held without Michael Milken. His absence hung over the conference—the good cheer and free spending had an end-of-an-era feeling. Milken holed up in Richard Sandler's office, just one floor away from his old desk; friends came to see him there. The general expectation was that he'd show up at the dinner the DBL Americas group was throwing at the Bistro, but when the government passed the message to Fred Joseph that Milken wasn't welcome at Drexel events, Milken promptly withdrew. The only sign of defiance was a short video assembled from snippets of Milken speeches that was, Milken's friends made clear, going to be shown no matter what.

As the conference began to take on the air of a wake, Michael and Lowell Milken headed to New York to be arraigned. Lowell sat quietly with his wife. Michael did something uncharacteristic—he slept. That night, the Milkens and their wives, along with Harry Horowitz and his wife, watched *Tucker*, the Francis Coppola film about the upstart automobile inventor who was forced out of business by an unholy alliance of competitors and the government.*

The following morning, the Milkens and their lawyers rode to the federal courthouse. The caravan seemed vaguely funereal until the Lincoln sedans stopped at a traffic light. There, a man in a wheelchair called out for spare change. A window in the lead car was lowered. Lowell Milken leaned out and handed the man something. As the riders in the second car passed the astonished beggar, they saw him waving a fifty-dollar bill.

---

*Some of Milken's inner circle could almost recite verbatim the conclusion of Preston Tucker's closing statement at his trial: "If big business closes the door on the little guy with a new idea, we're not only closing the door on progress, but we're sabotaging everything we fought for, everything the country stands for. One day we'll find ourselves at the bottom of the heap instead of king of the hill, having no idea how we got there, buying our radios and cars from our former enemies." In comparing Milken to Tucker, Milken's friends overlooked the fact that Tucker lost.

Downtown, the sense of unreality continued, as the Milkens began their morning in court with grimy formalities: mug shots and urine tests. The brothers had to sit in the hallway next to prisoners in handcuffs, then wait their turn in line—unlike some celebrity defendants before them, they weren't given access to a private room. Michael was dazed and depressed by the spectacle playing out in front of him. Lowell was equally distressed, but his feelings took another form—he was seething. A man who had sworn never to end his case with a plea bargain had just been given another reason not to settle.

In the courtroom, more strangeness. Judge Wood conducted the proceedings as though reading from a manual. She was—and from the wrong page at that. "How do you feel today, physically?" she asked Milken, reading from the procedure for entering a guilty plea. "Are you under the care of a physician or psychiatrist?" "How do you plead?" Milken gave the expected monosyllables, his answers becoming stronger and clearer as he did. By the time he said "Not guilty," there was something like conviction in his voice.

As the prosecutors and defense lawyers were standing around afterward, John Carroll made a plea for a reasonable conclusion to the case. We need more direct dialogue, he said. We need to calm down. We need to find a way to resolve this.

Across the continent, Milken supporters were holding a solidarity rally at the bond conference. One Drexel client urged the crowd to send "vibrations" to Milken in New York. Others passed out T-shirts and buttons that proclaimed MIKE MILKEN, WE BELIEVE IN YOU—the same sentiment that headlined a newspaper advertisement placed by clients and supporters.

Orchestrated by Selig Zieses, chairman of Integrated Resources, this ad was signed by ninety people, including media billionaire John Kluge and MCI Chairman William McGowan. The high-profile New York clients—Henry Kravis, Ronald Perelman, and Saul Steinberg—were noticeably absent. Zieses had contacted them, but they had pointedly declined to return his calls.

These ads in *The New York Times*, *The Washington Post*, *Los Angeles Times*, and *The Wall Street Journal* attracted considerable attention—mostly for the names of the signatories and the $150,000 they had shelled out. In the fascination with names and advertising costs, no one commented on the curious wording of the headline. WE BELIEVE YOU would have done the job nicely: a simple statement of support for a friend and benefactor. WE BELIEVE IN YOU, however, evoked religious imagery. It suggested that some of Milken's clients regarded him—and, perhaps, that Milken regarded himself—as the founder of the Church of Alternative Capitalism, a latter-day messiah. For a man who insisted that he didn't want to be a symbol or have his name turned into a cause, Michael Milken tolerated phrasing in this ad that made it seem he was now being crucified, but soon, very soon, he would be reborn.

That tent-revival expectation could be felt in the courtroom when Milken proclaimed his innocence. It could be felt outside, where the marshals said they'd never seen so many supporters pressed against the sawhorses that lined the steps. Hours later, on the plane back to Los Angeles, the mood was still upbeat. "This is like working for the Dukakis campaign!" squealed the daughter of a Milken associate.

She wasn't the only Milken supporter who saw the indictment as positive and liberating for the defendant. Many friends longed for him to come out swinging, and soon. In their dream, he was not the man of the predictable press releases and the corny life story and the Abe Lincoln homilies—he was the conscience of American finance. If he'd just show his real self, they believed, people would finally get what the fuss was all about. All he had to do was forget that he hated to reveal himself in public and had, only days earlier, authorized his lawyers to explore a guilty plea. All he had to do was fight back.

CHAPTER SEVENTEEN

One curiosity of the Milken case is that the most widely publicized business story of the 1980s was shaped by just a handful of writers. While every newspaper and magazine of consequence covered the story, only two newspapers—*The Wall Street Journal* and *The Washington Post*—consistently got inside the investigation. And for those who wanted the story in context, there was only *The Predators' Ball*.

This reporting, with its implicit message that Milken was badly in need of prosecution, had enormous impact on journalists and editors across the country. It deserved to; those writers had terrific credentials. James Stewart, of the *Journal*, won the 1988 Pulitzer Prize for his articles on the Crash of '87 and the Wall Street insider trading scandal. The *Post*'s Steve Coll and David Vise would collect a Pulitzer for their exhaustive series on the SEC. Connie Bruck had been the star reporter for *American Lawyer*.

Until the indictment, these few writers defined the perception of Milken for most readers. But when Milken was indicted, he achieved across-the-board celebrity status—the $550-million-a-year man. It was inevitable, therefore, that he'd move from the business section to the editorial and cultural pages.

Bruck, Stewart, Vise, and Coll were influential because even their most one-sided work seemed authoritative. The second wave of Milken-watchers—and there were just two of consequence, Benjamin J. Stein and Michael Thomas—couldn't have been more different from these highly credentialed writers. From the outset, their work was blunt, intensely personal, and violently hostile to Milken.

Whatever effect Stein and Thomas had on readers, they had a remarkable effect on Michael Milken. Friends warned him: This stuff will disturb you. Don't read it. But Milken couldn't help himself. Just as he'd been obsessed with the negative writing that had come before, now he couldn't live without reading the bombs Thomas and Stein lobbed at him.

For Milken, these two writers became crucial figures. They unnerved him, they made him feel that anyone could now write anything about him and get it published and have it believed. In the end, they helped break him—and even then, as it turned out, they weren't satisfied.

No sooner had Michael Milken stepped off the plane in Los Angeles than Benjamin J. Stein smashed him in the face. From the opening line of his piece in *Barron's*—"This is a story of a man who masquerades as a friend of investors"—Stein threw one punch after another. Citing statistics, making analogies, lapsing into slang, Stein's expertise seemed vast. He wrote like a Renaissance man possessed. No doubt about it, he didn't wish Milken well.

Milken's alleged crimes, Stein argued, had a common theme: "the perversion and betrayal of principals by agents." For Stein, Milken was a monopolist who set bond prices to suit himself, a dictator who gave mere lip service to the values he claimed to champion. He created no jobs, hurt productivity, damaged American competitiveness. He was the enemy of all who tried to work and invest with integrity.

The writer who delivered up this broadside is mild-mannered, sad-faced, and watery-eyed—a skinny Henry Kissinger. Because Stein speaks in a monotone that reminds director John Hughes of "every teacher we've ever hated," he has made many appearances in movies (*Ferris Bueller's Day Off*) and television shows (*The Wonder Years*), often cast as a teacher delivering a boring lecture on economics.

This is, in fact, a subject he knows well. The son of Herbert

Stein, former chairman of the President's Council of Economic Advisers, he is a graduate of Yale Law School and the Nixon White House, where he worked as a speechwriter. In the mid-1970s, Stein left law and politics behind and moved to Los Angeles, where he hoped to make his way as a screenwriter and producer.

Stein wasn't a great success in Hollywood—although his ideas seemed to be. As Stein saw it, soon after he would embark upon a project, someone would come along and, without compensation or credit, separate him from it. In 1985, he sued film producer Brian Grazer, alleging that Grazer had entered into a partnership with him to develop a CIA spy comedy, only to dump him when another CIA comedy came along. In 1986, at a time when he believed that he had an exclusive relationship with Linda Fairstein, head of the Sex Crimes Unit at the Manhattan district attorney's office, another Fairstein project was announced; Stein sued the writer and the producer, claiming that they appropriated his material.

Although suing producers is generally regarded as an excellent way to short-circuit a Hollywood career, Stein had no doubts about the rectitude of his path. "Getting anything done here," he wrote in 1986, "means either a lawsuit or a threat of a lawsuit." Hollywood wasn't the only source of his legal ire; he was also pressing a suit against a company in which he owned stock. "Eventually, I'm going to win and give back to those suckers what they and all their pig kind have dished out to me," he wrote.

In one instance, Stein found himself on the wrong side of the law. While passing through a checkpoint at the Burbank Airport in the spring of 1983, the Smith & Wesson 2.5-inch blue steel revolver and six .38 rounds he was carrying in his duffel bag set off alarms. Stein told the policeman who arrested him that he didn't have a permit for this gun. And, according to the police report, he said, "I didn't know it was against the law to carry a gun in a bag."*

---

*Early in 1992, after it was learned that President Bush was taking Halcion during his trip to Japan, Stein published an op-ed piece in *The New York Times* about his own experiences with that drug. He had been taking prescription tranquilizers since 1966, he wrote, and Halcion was the worst of them all. In that column, Stein used a literary device to explain his arrest: "A friend of mine took a small dose of Halcion—less than what the President is reported to take—and then carried a gun through a metal detector at an airport. He had forgotten not only that he had a gun with him but also that guns are illegal at airports."

Stein didn't leave prose behind when he moved west. In the fall of 1985, Stein ventured to Birmingham High School in Encino—Michael Milken's alma mater—to begin research for "a book about high school and why kids come out not knowing anything." While he didn't write that book, he did publish *Hollywood Days, Hollywood Nights: The Diary of a Mad Screenwriter*, in which he mused about Birmingham High, Hollywood, and women. The subject that most concerned him in those pages, though, was money.

"I have not earned any real money in a good long time," he noted. He hated "the fucking stock market" and bemoaned "the perpetual crisis of my life: If I'm so smart, why aren't I rich? Why can't I even figure out a way to make a decent living?" This lack of money had a predictable effect on his self-esteem; he lived in "my cell of ambition and self-loathing." And so his New Year's fantasy on the first day of 1986 was that "Michael Milken will call from Drexel and tell me they will fail without my insight."

Stein achieved fame, but not fortune, in December of 1987, when he published a column in *GQ* under the pseudonym of "Bert Hacker." The author—who began his piece with the line "I have known Joan Rivers for more than twenty years"—wrote that he'd had dinner with the comedienne ten days before the suicide of her husband, Edgar Rosenberg. Later, he said, he went to her home to sit *shiva* for Rosenberg.

There were problems with this piece, all of the hallucinatory nature: Stein had *never* met Joan Rivers, much less been invited to her home to grieve with her. But now it appeared they would meet, in court—Rivers filed a $50 million libel suit against Stein and Condé Nast Publications.

With that, Rivers says, Stein's lawyer contacted her to deliver a threat: If she didn't withdraw the suit, the world would soon know she was a lesbian who gave her husband the pills he used to kill himself. Rivers says she challenged Stein's attorney to go public—and told him how much she was looking forward to announcing that it was Stein's wife who lured her out of the closet.

Stein had no comment until his appearance on the CBS *This Morning* show in February of 1988, when Kathleen Sullivan suggested his reporting techniques leaned heavily on hearsay. Not at all, Stein said—his reporting methods were the norm. "The entire Watergate coverage was based on hearsay, and they gave the people who wrote that the Pulitzer Prize," he told his astonished interviewer. "If you look at any day's front page of *The New York Times* and *The Washington Post*, the huge majority of what is reported is hearsay."

Condé Nast chose not to support this position. In 1989, it settled the Rivers suit for an undisclosed sum and printed an apology in *GQ*.

Burned in Hollywood, Stein turned his limpid gaze more frequently on Wall Street. In June of 1988, he lauded Michael Milken in an imaginary commencement address: "Milken said he began his career by telling his bosses that he was not sure he was smarter than anyone else applying for the job, but that he would work twenty-five percent harder. The results are obvious: It's smart to work hard."

His praise for Milken was short-lived. That year, he has said, an unnamed Drexel employee—apparently upset with articles he'd written attacking leveraged buyouts—called and threatened to kill him. But the writer chose not to alert the police. Instead, acting on what he has described as advice from an unnamed lawyer at Cahill Gordon, he wrote Milken a two-page letter on November 23, 1988, in which he proposed that Milken engage him as an ombudsman, "an in-house analyst of the fairness of the deals you put together."

In normal times, Michael Milken rarely dealt with his mail; he wrote so few letters in the 1980s that his signature is already a collector's item. By November of 1988, he was off the trading desk and considering a different set of legal issues than the ones that intrigued Stein. Stein's letter, a low priority, was promptly filed and forgotten.

Historically, rejection without so much as a reply didn't sit well with Stein. About two years earlier, he had written to Barry Diller, then CEO of Fox Entertainment, offering his services. Diller hadn't replied. A few months later, the first of a series of biting personal comments about Diller began to appear in Stein's pseudonymous *GQ* columns. So Michael Milken was, at the very least, destined for some toupee jokes.

Stein had to know that the Drexel job was, at best, a longshot. But in the spring of 1989, a TV film about three civil rights workers murdered in Mississippi looked like a surer thing for him—with a partner, he'd sold the story to Warner Brothers. According to what he describes as an oral agreement, he was slated to get a producer's credit and $100,000. Then the same old thing happened: His partner sold him out and teamed up with a more established producer. Stein, who had spent five years nurturing this project, filed a new round of lawsuits.*

At about the same time that Stein was discovering the latest in a series of personal betrayals by the powerful, the man he'd come to consider a betrayer of capitalism was about to be indicted. Once again, Stein offered his services—this time to *Barron's*, the weekly financial paper that is, like *The Wall Street Journal*, owned by Dow Jones. Here, he got a positive response. Very positive: From his first piece, Ben Stein was *Barron's* writer of choice on matters Milken.

Once he had a platform that gave him an estimated 1.2 million readers, Stein went to work in earnest. Milken's junk bonds, he would write, were "a boiler room scam," sold through a "complex Ponzi scheme" to a fraternity of buyers who formed "the Drexel daisy chain." These clients were not just greedy, but irrationally euphoric: Their "use of drugs . . . explains much about the willful refusal of the whole gang to see that the scam had to come to a bad end." But despite obvious criminality and apparently widespread cocaine abuse, the fix was in: Milken had "a number of well-known journalists" on his payroll, while Drexel backed so many politicians it constituted "an alternative government."

Shocking, unsubstantiated, never-proven assertions made with absolute certainty. Gloom so deep it finds no bottom. Was Stein breaking news? Or was there, in Stein's own writing, a simpler explanation?

"I felt depressed and often suicidal for days after taking it and more or less permanently depressed if I took it continuously," Stein noted in his 1992 column on Halcion, without saying how long he had taken the drug. "It clouds judgment and forecloses careful analysis. It makes the user alternately supremely confident and then panicky with an unnameable dread."

---

*According to Benjamin Stein's lawyer, all of the movie- and television-related lawsuits were settled amicably and to Stein's satisfaction.

*   *   *

Two weeks after Ben Stein weighed in, Milken was convicted by Michael Thomas, whose "Midas Watch" ran in the *New York Observer*. Weekly newspapers delivered free are not usually devoured, but Thomas's column had become essential reading for those who loathed the Upper East Side's junk bond jillionaires, feared that their names might be mentioned, or who were just plain delighted by high-octane writing that took no prisoners—in short, by almost everyone of influence in the most media-conscious part of New York.

If Stein wrote like a woman scorned, Thomas sent his thunderbolts from a higher plane. He had impeccable East Coast credentials, and he never let his readers forget it. He was the son of an investment banker who'd been the youngest partner ever at Lehman Brothers. He'd graduated from Yale. His first wife was the daughter of Leland Heyward, the legendary Hollywood agent and producer. He'd worked at Lehman Brothers, labored briefly for Burnham & Company, and served on the board of Twentieth Century Fox. And then, in his mid-forties, Thomas left business and became a novelist and commentator.

Although Thomas was a kind soul among friends, he could be a terror when unleashed in public. Epigrams came naturally to him: "—— did to offshore tax shelters what pantyhose did to finger-fucking" and "Businessmen writing on serious subjects are to the *Times* Op-Ed page what women with a grudge are to Knopf" are throwaways from a single evening. In print, he was more prone to caricature: Donald Trump was the "Prince of Swine," Henry Kravis the "Little King," and Ralph Lauren the "Wee Haberdasher." He had no nickname for Milken, but he didn't lack for a characterization: Milken was a crook.

Thomas had sent some scattered shots in Milken's direction over the years, but with the indictment in hand and Milken's compensation on the airwaves, he now began blasting in earnest. "For the last five or six years," he wrote in mid-April of 1989, "it was plain to anyone with half a brain that Drexel wasn't being run out of New York." He suggested that Milken might have "diverted" more than $100 million from Drexel bonus pools to his own account. And, noting that crack cocaine hit the streets the same year that billion-dollar junk bond takeovers began, he wondered if there was a connection between Los Angeles becoming the drug money-laundering capital of America and Milken's compensation.

In comparison with what was coming, those sentiments were mellow. A potential RICO forfeiture of more than a billion dollars wasn't harsh enough for him: "All of Mr. Milken's loot earned subsequent to 1980, including fees on fees, interest on interest, should be seized. Oh, leave the fellow, say, a million for a fresh start." Before Milken was sentenced, Thomas stated his dissatisfaction: "Whatever Judge Wood gives Mr. Milken won't be enough."

Months after Milken went to jail, Thomas was still steaming. Because Milken had been sent to a minimum security facility, he argued, Milken now had little incentive to tell all to the prosecutors: "A stretch in Leavenworth might have proved useful, since I am reliably informed that the prospect of having one's sphincter enlarged to the circumference of the Holland Tunnel by the rigors of the prison social calendar often works wonders when it comes to refreshing memories clouded by the Fifth Amendment."

A wish for a man to be stripped of his assets and then gang-raped in prison—for a self-proclaimed defender of civility, those are extreme sentiments. But for Milken and his inner circle, who took this small-circulation weekly newspaper as seriously as if it were *The New York Times*, there was another level of Thomas's attack that was even more disturbing.

In his column of mid-April 1989, Thomas had sounded off about the "Mike Milken, we believe in you" advertisement: "The list of signatories looked like the membership roster of the new golf club being built up the road." To some readers, that flip, throwaway line was a vintage Thomas dismissal of second-raters. Other readers, though, may have taken it for code. For the membership of "the new golf club" was predominantly Jewish. In fact, it was so Jewish that, in the sporting circles Thomas favored, it came to inspire a wry joke. Usually, when golf clubs wish to avoid the accusation of prejudice, they invite a few Jews to join. For once, as the joke about the new Long Island club had it, a golf club was courting Christian members.*

---

*This new golf club has, in fact, come to be known in sporting circles as "Hebrew National."

Michael Thomas has said that he has never written an anti-Semitic sentence. But in his remarks about the *Mike Milken, we believe in you* signatories, there was, between the lines, a characterization that might be taken as a slur. Milken didn't understand that crack—the reference was too inside for him. But he recognized it as a blow, and he understood that as long as he was a target, his critics were going to hit at him with any weapon they could find.

CHAPTER EIGHTEEN

Mike is 100 percent of our profits, we won't do anything to hurt him, Fred Joseph had promised Milken's lawyers—and then he'd cut Milken adrift.

Mike could be useful to the country, send him to Washington, make him solve the drug problem, just don't put him in jail, Joseph had begged Giuliani—only to hear the almighty prosecutor say he was sorry, but he didn't have that power.

Now Leon Black and Peter Ackerman, two key executives who'd threatened to quit if Milken were forced out of the firm, were doing deals Milken would never have financed—and these deals weren't working out.

Why didn't I listen to you? Fred Joseph asked his favorite witch doctor.

Because, Ned Kennan said, you don't listen to anyone.

What can I do?

Milken's glory is evaporating fast, Kennan said. The Milken lovers are turning into Milken haters. They're doing crazy deals just to earn fees—they're piglets, they're money-mad. You've got to turn these piglets into *mensches*. You've got to get them to understand other people, to have compassion, to share.

Fred Joseph had always loved encounter groups. They cleared the air. They helped clarify goals. The idea of financing LBOs had been born at one, financing hostile takeovers at another. Perhaps a get-together could now unify the firm.

In March of 1989, with morale in a free fall, Joseph convened a "Socratic Seminar." Herbert Schmertz, the veteran public relations consultant, was the organizer. Arthur Miller, a professor at Harvard Law School, was the moderator. The format was role playing.

You're an account executive at Drexel, Miller said, pointing a finger at a Drexel investment banker. You're Rudy Giuliani. You're a reporter at *The Wall Street Journal*. Okay, how do *you* feel about Drexel?

Within minutes, the role playing dissolved and the psychodrama began. Soon the plea bargain was described as "cowardly" and "awful" and "a copout." Then it was Fred Joseph's turn to share.

"You negotiated this settlement, then voted against it—what process puts that together?" Professor Miller asked.

"I negotiated a bad settlement," Joseph said. A few minutes later, though, he was looking toward a better future. "As soon as we settle with the SEC, people will see we're the safest firm on Wall Street to deal with."

Schmertz was dumbfounded by Joseph's refusal or inability to hold a single point of view. At one level, Schmertz ranked this as one of the best Socratic Seminars he'd done; the emotional involvement was high. But because the firm's leader kept flip-flopping, it produced no clear direction for the future.

"As a leader, Fred Joseph wasn't effective," Schmertz concluded. "I asked him: 'You said we shouldn't pay this fine and take this plea, yet you did—you can't be a leader in that situation. Leaders don't have a right to personal views. How do you explain it?' I didn't get an answer."

In April, Drexel formally settled with the SEC. "All this will be compliance—government and business working together, hand in hand," a Drexel employee said bitterly as he led a visitor around thousands of square feet of raw space in Beverly Hills. Proof that the firm's new masters were firmly in control came later that month, when Milken met with some Boston shipyard workers and their Drexel advisers. It was a blatant violation of the new Drexel rules: Talk to him, you can't do business with us. To placate the SEC, Milken was hurriedly shunted aside.

And yet, at almost the same time, Fred Joseph may have

tried to circumvent the SEC agreement. Joseph spoke nostalgically of Milken's protean intelligence. Mike has such great ideas, he reportedly told Richard Sandler. The hardest thing about losing him is losing access to those ideas. Is there some way you can talk with him, and then you and I can talk? Sandler emphatically told him that was impossible.*

Milken added this incident to the mental list—a chronicle of offenses against him—that he had started recently. The list was not a good sign. Milken always catalogued, but in the old days, his lists were about tasks. This was about grievances. And the more he collected, the more his emotional balance was impaired.

Terren Peizer's reward for cooperating with the government was an unexpected leave of absence. Though he was still collecting his $3.5 million salary, Peizer wasn't happy to be paid for nothing. He complained to the prosecutors, who complained, in turn, to Drexel, which, reluctantly, welcomed him back to the office. But not to the trading floor—Peizer now worked in a drab, windowless office, with no real assignments and no one to talk to.

At the bond conference in early April of 1989, Peizer pulled a client aside. He was losing weight, he said. He didn't feel well. He wished that Milken weren't so stubborn. He didn't want to testify against Milken—he hoped someone would convince him to plea. I *can't* talk to you, and I *won't* talk to you, the client said, and he walked away.

Two weeks later, anxious to have some impact, Terren Peizer had dinner with Laurie Cohen, a *Wall Street Journal* reporter who began covering Milken when James Stewart became the paper's page-one editor. That dinner paid off immediately—in late April, Cohen broke the story of Milken's connection to money manager David Solomon. Soon, she wrote, Solomon's violation of the federal tax laws would be presented to the grand jury. But Solomon was negotiating with the U.S. attorney in an effort to win immunity by testifying against Milken.

This article demoralized Milken. Right after they indicted him, the prosecutors had announced that it was only their first strike—as they did to Princeton/Newport and threatened to do to

*Joseph says he told Sandler that he was sad to lose Milken's brilliance, but insists that he never suggested violating the SEC agreement.

258

Drexel, they would bring a second, superseding indictment against him. Those additional charges, Milken suspected, were really the primary charges. He felt that the prosecutors had come to understand that the Boesky case would never stand up, and now they were casting about for new witnesses who had nothing to do with Boesky.

To create this second front, Milken believed, the government had once again turned for help to *The Wall Street Journal*, the publication that veteran business editor James Grant called "the useful idiot" of the prosecution. "The train is leaving the station, get on board or you won't make it to the Promised Land"—that was, Milken believed, the message the *Journal* piece about Solomon really delivered to the handful of readers who could get its special meaning. For those potential witnesses, he felt, this wasn't journalism; it was a help-wanted ad.

So Milken braced himself. There was, he knew, more coming.

Suddenly, the dam broke, and every day brought fresh disappointment.

A man who identified himself as a *Wall Street Journal* reporter called Joni Noah to say he had seen Michael Milken drive her home in a chauffeured Mercedes. He'd watched Milken hug and kiss her. He was pretty sure Milken had slipped her some money. When Milken drove away, he'd gone up to the mailbox and learned her name.

I'm going to do an article for the paper revealing that Mike Milken, the so-called family man, is having an affair, he said, but if you talk to me, I can protect you. Trust me, we can work something out.

Are you insane? Joni Noah replied. Michael Milken is my *brother*!

Then a Drexel friend of Milken's was about to retire. A dinner was planned. Milken was invited. The word came down: Mike shows up, Drexel won't pay the bill.

Rejection was all he was going to get from Drexel, it seemed. That summer, just before the issue would have been argued in court, the government dropped its insistence that Milken's 1988 compensation be withheld. But what had he earned? Richard Sandler believed there was $150 million in the high-yield bonus pool after everyone had been paid. Gerald Tannenbaum, a lawyer with Cahill Gordon, told Sandler that $50 million to $60 million was more like it. A few months later, though, Tannenbaum was talking about $5 million.

Last time, the number was around $60 million, Sandler said.

I never said that, and if I did, I wasn't authorized to, Tannenbaum replied.*

Another Cahill lawyer, Irwin Schneiderman, now became involved.

Forget everything anybody's said so far, Schneiderman told Sandler in September of 1989. Drexel's in such desperate shape that it can't pay Milken the kind of money he's looking for. Perhaps we can give him stock—if that doesn't violate the SEC agreement.†

For the moment, that ended the conversation. It never resumed. When Drexel went out of business, Milken was among the unpaid.

Schneiderman's admission of financial crisis wasn't surprising to Milken—everything the firm did now looked like a breakneck drive toward self-destruction. Ever since 1987, when he moved away from fundamental responsibility for trading and financing, Drexel had enthusiastically welcomed the wacky and unscrupulous; the Corporate Finance team in New York seemed determined to underwrite every possible deal.

There was the Native American who had excited Drexel's New York investment bankers with his tales of success as an oil driller using a secret science called "close-ology." It wasn't until he arrived in Beverly Hills that he was pressured to define his method. "I go out to the oil fields and I see where other companies are drilling," he explained, "and then I try to drill as close to them as possible."

The close-ologist was sent packing. He was soon followed by Barry Minkow, the whiz kid who started a business called ZZZZ Best, turned it into a scam, and was eventually shipped off to jail.

"I was brought into a conference room where this boy was

*Gerald Tannenbaum did not respond to repeated requests for comment.

†Irwin Schneiderman did not respond to repeated requests for comment.

sitting on the floor, in shorts and a T-shirt, drinking Coke from the can as he talked on the phone," a Milken associate recalls. "A guy from Corporate Finance whispered, 'Barry doesn't want any covenants.' I said, 'Well, we always need a couple.' Barry said, 'You didn't hear right: I don't want any fucking covenants.' I said, 'You know, son, in some cases, covenants protect *you*.' They took me outside and told me, 'You're irritating our client.' I said, 'Okay, tell him anything you want.'"

Minkow didn't make the grade, but many others—too many others—qualified for Drexel's support. "No one would face the fact that the place was brain-dead as soon as Mike left," a Drexel veteran says. "When we put twenty million dollars into Stars to Go, it sounded good—the company supplied videos to Seven-Eleven stores—but as soon as you looked at the numbers, you saw there was no cash flow, no future. It didn't matter. By then, Drexel was a casino: Any game you wanted to play, they set up a table for you, gave you chips and left you there, unsupervised. Some of us tried to convince Fred Joseph to shut the casino down. He'd say: 'Are you *sure* these deals won't work?' Well, you know, shit floats for a long time, then it sinks. The only question is when. Six months, twelve—these deals were definitely going to crater."

Milken watched, horrified, at Drexel's financing for Braniff at a time when everyone else was shunning airlines. He cringed when the firm dropped $60 million in an oil operation. Neither company made its first interest payment. Clients like Ralph Ingersoll and Bill Farley, once so attentive, now ignored Milken's advice and plunged deeper into debt. The junk bond world seemed to have gone mad.

In Washington, the legislators were making decisions that seemed to Milken to be as crazy as Drexel's choices. Congressman Tony Coelho, the majority whip who was a likely character witness at any Milken trial, had accepted a loan from Milken client Thomas Spiegel so he could make a $100,000 investment in a Drexel bond offering. The news of this compromising relationship had been known for a while—John Dingell, who'd been quite friendly with Coelho, is said to have learned it more than a year earlier—but its public announcement shocked a city already reeling with scandal. Coelho, sensitive to the changing reality, promptly resigned.*

Milken, Drexel, junk bonds—the Coelho resignation turned these unpopular topics radioactive. In July of 1989, with almost no opposition, Congress struck a far heavier blow to the Milken cause. Four months earlier, the General Accounting Office had reported that no savings and loan had ever failed because of its investment in junk bonds—according to the GAO, junk bonds produced *higher* returns than home mortgages, Treasuries, and investment-grade bonds, even when defaults were factored in. But now, in a ruling inspired more by politics than by economics, Congress ordered S&Ls to dump their junk bonds over the next five years.

Whatever trouble had been caused by bad junk bond investments at a handful of S&Ls, the lawmakers now multiplied tenfold. Few S&Ls waited to sell. Most bailed out, dumping their portfolios at fire-sale prices. Supply swamped demand; the junk bond market plummeted. This affected, in turn, insurance companies that held huge portfolios of junk bonds. Within months, junk bonds were almost as unpopular as George Steinbrenner.

Companies that seethed when Milken and Drexel prospered now fearlessly went public with their loathing for Milken's battered product. That summer, the Dreyfus Fund ran an advertisement of a wastebasket overflowing with scrunched-up paper. "Junk has always had a place in our company," the ad read. "Just not in our portfolio." Another ad was more subtle. In it, as two men walk through the marble atrium of a corporate headquarters, one remarks, "You wouldn't think one person could cause a loss of this magnitude. Just be thankful our bank is insured through Chubb."

In media circles, Milken fared no better. Whittle Books had commissioned Edward Jay Epstein to write an eighty-page text on Milken for its "larger agenda" series, which was not only sold in bookstores but distributed free to America's most influential executives. This project was innovative and controversial—Whittle kept the cost of its books low by including full-color advertising between chapters—and, in what he considered the spirit of the venture, Epstein turned in an outline that cast Milken as an

*Coelho was later exonerated of all wrongdoing.

innovator who was guilty mostly of offending the established order.

This was not an argument Whittle could live with. The book was shelved. The following year, Whittle published a book about "financial euphoria" by John Kenneth Galbraith, who dispatched Milken in a single paragraph as an example of financial schemers who appear, almost on cue, every twenty years or so. "Milken's competence and superior diligence as a salesman, sometimes called promoter, is not in doubt," Galbraith wrote, "but the discovery that high-risk bonds leveraged on limited assets should have a higher interest rate hardly stands on a par as an invention with the electric light."

To provide at least the semblance of activity, Milken formed a new company—International Capital Access Group, a name that conveyed great public spirit—where he expended modest energy on behalf of clients he wouldn't have had time for in the old days. But not much got done. Milken would start a project, and then the case would intrude or an article would appear, and he'd lose focus.

His most sustained effort at ICAG that summer was to direct research for a book that would chart his contribution to the American economy over the last two decades. "Some people collect art, I've devoted my life to helping people build businesses—I want my children to have something that shows what I've done," Milken told a visitor, sounding tired and fragile and doomed.

Some days, he sought out causes as if he were a prophet or a politician, although he still preferred to work unnoticed by media—he was sensitive to accusations that his interest in Afro-Americans and the poor was a calculated effort to create sympathy among those who were most likely to sit on his jury. At a New York conference organized to create new alliances to access capital, he was overshadowed by Jesse Jackson, his newest friend, leading the group in prayer: "Steve Ross, let me hear you say 'A-men!'" Another night, he honored Milken Scholars—minority students who were, sometimes with a boost from him, college-bound—with a show at the Apollo Theater and dinner at a Harlem restaurant, where Jesse Jackson emerged from the kitchen carrying a tray piled high with meals for the delighted teenagers. He went public only once, in Indianapolis, where he addressed an Afro-American group called 100 Black Men: "What is a junk bond? What it really is is America. It's every single one of you in this room."

Michael Milken may have been frustrated, a workhorse without work, but there was plenty of work to be done—settlement talks had started again. Speed was of the essence. Milken was concerned by Drexel's imprudent deals; he feared that, if the firm collapsed, he'd have even more trouble getting a fair trial or an equitable plea bargain. For his part, Liman believed that the plea bargain they'd failed to achieve during Giuliani's tenure had to be concluded during the tenure of Benito Romano, Giuliani's cherry-picked interim successor—once Romano left the U.S. attorney's office, Otto Obermaier would finally have his day.

Obermaier's firm had become even more involved with white-collar cases, so Obermaier would have to recuse himself from any involvement in Milken plea discussions. And that would create a vacuum. A momentary vacuum. Then men from Washington—men who could be counted on to screw up delicate negotiations they didn't understand—would rush in and take over. Whatever plea bargain Arthur Liman could get from Romano was better than that.

Michael Milken authorized this latest exploration of the U.S. attorney's willingness to deal, then held himself aloof from the process—as ever, he regarded these settlement talks as a nonbinding exploration of possibilities, not as a commitment to take a plea. Meanwhile, from a distance, he awaited the Princeton/Newport trial. If his friends did well, he could see himself following in their footsteps.

In July, the Princeton/Newport defendants went to court, footnotes to history at last on center stage. Jay Regan, fearless in his own defense, took the stand. A former IRS commissioner and an emeritus tax professor from Yale, who would have testified that Regan had reason to believe he'd committed no tax crimes, were denied that privilege—according to the prosecutors and the judge, their testimony might have confused a jury. "You don't need a fancy tax expert," Mark Hansen said in his summation. "Common sense tells you it's fraudulent, it's phony. . . . If it sounds sleazy, it's because it is sleazy. Your common sense tells you that."

The absence of confusing testimony and the presence of the tape recordings led the jury to convict the defendants on sixty-three of sixty-four counts. The prosecutors had never mentioned "racketeering" during the trial; when the jurors learned about RICO, their reaction was strong. Instead of allowing the government to take $22 million from defendants convicted of evading $96,000 in taxes, the jurors demanded $3.8 million. At sentencing, even that figure was too high. Judge Robert Carter essentially threw out the RICO verdict, directed the defendants to spend no more than three to six months in jail and pay fines of $1.8 million—and he suggested that some defendants petition him for a further reduction.

The most stunning moment of the Princeton/Newport trial didn't occur in the courtroom. In mid-trial, the Justice Department issued new RICO guidelines that all but announced—in prose that sounded almost as if it had been written by Princeton/Newport lawyers—there'd never be another prosecution like this.

"To have your own organization release that kind of statement was dispiriting," Mark Hansen recalls. "We had to go to the judge and say, 'We're not a rogue band of prosecutors off on a frolic.' It would have been more intellectually honest for the Department of Justice to pull the case."

Hansen may have been puzzled by the new guidelines, but there was one thing he understood very well: the daily presence of Milken lawyers in the courtroom. "At that time, there was substantial sentiment that the government didn't have the horsepower, that the defense lawyers in these cases could run circles around us," he says. "Had the government lost this case, Milken would have been a trial or at best a weak plea. We made John Carroll's work much easier—after Princeton/Newport, there was a very good chance he'd win without ever fighting it out in court."

There was another trial that summer in federal court in New York, and while the prosecution of E. Robert Wallach didn't directly concern Milken, it had symbolic meaning in his home. That season, Lori was reading Simon Schama's *Citizens*, a study of the French Revolution that focused less on the grievances of the peasants than on schisms among the elite—rivalries that seemed painfully similar to the ones buffeting her husband. A revolution fueled by a mindless hunger for victims: that wasn't far from the explanation of Michael's prosecution she'd given to her children. "Your father is a genius, and has totally revolutionized the finance industry," Lori had said. "People don't like change, and they're trying to get rid of your father, and if you'll look in your history books, you'll see that people who have tried to make change have had this happen." More than children believed that—Michael had begun to talk of the Russian dissidents.

As it happened, Robert Wallach had been Avital Sharansky's chief American aide in her struggle to get her husband freed from a Soviet prison; although her mother was near death, the Sharanskys had flown from Israel to New York to repay the debt at his trial. They were due to fly back to Israel that night to resume the death watch—Mrs. Sharansky had just one day to appear as a character witness for Wallach.

Then Assistant U.S. Attorney Baruch Weiss objected. Mrs. Sharansky's appearance, he said, would be "an appeal to sympathy of a prejudicial nature"—that is, in an echo of the prosecutors' argument against letting the tax experts testify for the defendants in the Princeton/Newport trial, the jury might be inclined to believe the defense witness.

Judge Richard Owen, who had been visibly disdainful of Wallach from the beginning, said he wanted to consider the matter overnight.

Wallach's lawyer, reminding the judge that the Sharanskys had to leave that evening, asked if he would at least allow Mrs. Sharansky to give a deposition.

"If she can come here from Israel, she can stay one more night in the United States," Owen replied. "Maybe the fact is she *ought* to go back, and maybe the fact is she should *never* have come in the first place."

The Sharanskys returned to Israel that night, and the jury was never tainted by Avital's testimony. But as he left the courthouse, Natan Sharansky couldn't resist a sardonic comment. "I have seen only one trial in the Soviet Union: my own. And now"—and here he actually smiled—"now I have seen one in America."

In Encino, as Milken read the tea leaves, they all spelled plea bargain. As the judge had ruled in the Wallach trial, your character witnesses might not be allowed to testify. As the Justice Department had decreed in Princeton/Newport, there might be a change of rules so no one would ever again be threatened by the kind of indictment that had brought you to court. And, perhaps most ominously, the prosecutors seemed willing to cross every line, crush every pawn, in their campaign to bring you down.

This last home truth was made abundantly clear to Milken later in August of 1989, when Bruce Newberg's young assistant Lisa Jones was sentenced in New York. The trial had been a mismatch; her Drexel-chosen lawyer, knowing that the prosecution would pick apart her many misstatements and untruths, unaccountably failed to soften this testimony by bringing it out in his own questioning of Jones. Under brutal questioning from Mark Hansen—who'd go right on to the Princeton/Newport trial—the young defendant was made to look like a cornered liar. No one was surprised when she was convicted of five counts of perjury and two counts of obstruction of justice.

After her conviction, Jones replaced her lawyer with Daniel Bookin, a former assistant U.S. attorney in New York. At sentencing, he tried gamely to place her case in context. "This investigation, which was aimed at sophisticated, educated men of enormous wealth and power, has now resolved into the conviction of this young woman who was none of these things," Bookin began. He pointed out that a psychiatrist favored by the U.S. attorney's office in Los Angeles had examined Jones and concluded that jail could harm her. He asked that she be sent to a woman's camp and then to a facility with psychiatric counseling.

Another prosecutor might have agreed. But Mark Hansen is, as he says, "as straight an arrow as you'll ever see." He'd "never smoked a joint." Instead of a bachelor party, he retraced, on foot, Hannibal's march over the Alps. His worldview came from Voltaire: "Fight injustice where you see it, love those who love you." In that cosmology, mercy had no priority. "Each and every lie Lisa Jones told was the result of a deliberate and calculated choice," he argued. "What is the system of justice to do with a person like that?"

The judge's answer was: eighteen months in jail, two and a half years of supervised work afterward, and a $50,000 fine. In court and in Beverly Hills, Milken supporters were stunned—this was half as long as Boesky's sentence! The fifth longest sentence in Wall Street cases thus far! Where was the judge's sense of proportion?

After the Jones sentence, the equation changed. Now, if Milken was going to win at trial, he would need to walk in with something spectacular, some evidence that couldn't be kept out, some revelation that would detonate the government's case. And that meant only one thing—someone had to prove that Ivan Boesky, still the linchpin of the prosecution's case, had lied.

CHAPTER NINETEEN

Did Boesky lie to the government?

At a time when absolute truth was called for, Boesky—a prisoner of his character—most likely withheld, fudged, skewed, and even outright invented. He would not have been the first to fib about small things. But what about larger matters? Did Boesky, for example, lie not only in his debriefings but in order to get the deal in the first place?*

By the fall of 1986, his lawyers have claimed, Boesky would never have considered bamboozling the government. The last thing he'd do, they have said, was hide money, minimize his crimes, or give false testimony. Ivan Boesky, by their account, was an emotionally shattered, financially ruined man struggling to rebuild his life.

"All this [settlement money] came from his own pocket," Harvey Pitt said in November of 1986. "And there ain't a lot left after this."

Leon Silverman, another Boesky lawyer, painted an even more tragic portrait. "For a year and a half, he has done nothing except cooperate with the government," Silverman told the judge

---

*Ivan Boesky did not respond to repeated requests for an interview.

who was to sentence Boesky. "He faces bankruptcy. He has parted with his sustenance."

Remarkably, the government was the institution least likely to know if this was true. In order to keep its negotiations with Boesky a secret in the summer of 1986, the SEC made no independent investigation of his finances—according to *American Lawyer*, Boesky was never even asked to give the enforcement division a full list of his assets. The government simply accepted Boesky's contention that he didn't have enough cash to pay his fine and allowed him to hand over $50 million in stock instead. "We did have access to his tax returns," Gary Lynch explained, "and that gave us a pretty good idea of what he was worth."

That explanation is laughable—it doesn't take a genius accountant to keep a tax return from revealing net worth. But Lynch, like other government officials in other crises, could not admit a truth that Washington seems to believe is too shocking for the public to handle: Life is deals. The bottom line of the deal between the SEC and Boesky was that the SEC was so eager to hear him talk about Milken its lawyers turned a blind eye to his quaint impersonation of a repentant sinner. In the government debriefings, a key question—did you move money out of the country?—was probably never asked.

Like everyone else on Wall Street, Michael Milken and Drexel's top brass believed that Boesky had socked many tens of millions away in a Swiss bank of impeccable discretion.

Unlike everyone else on Wall Street, Milken and Drexel had a reason to find the missing money—it was the one piece of evidence that would force the government not only to prosecute Boesky, but to drop him as a witness.

Reconstructing Ivan Boesky's movements was assigned to different detective agencies at different times. A squad of former Mossad agents submitted at least one report, replete with one intriguing code name in Hebrew: "The Fiddler." An independent operative was brought in—at an outrageous fee—to crack the message ("Conf. Luigi @ 9") found in Boesky's wastebasket on one of his postsettlement trips to the Bahamas. Luigi, it turned out, wasn't a Mafioso but a maître d'hôtel who was merely confirming a reservation for Boesky.

The most sustained digging was done by Kroll Associates and

the Investigative Group, headed by Terry Lenzner, a sleuth best known for his work on behalf of the Watergate prosecutors. Kroll and Lenzner were well staffed and, certainly, well funded. Right away, they got their hands on Boesky's office diaries; if these weren't rich in clues, they at least provided a lot of entertaining reading.

Beginning in 1984, the investigators learned, Boesky was treated for baldness by Dr. Norman Orentreich. He was scheduled to meet with "Mr. Wheat," an alias favored by Dennis Levine, and "Token Wasp," who has never been identified. He attended an exhibition of new sculpture by George Segal. He flew to Nevada by private jet with a dozen passengers, including several beautiful women, and traveled by helicopter to visit prep schools for his sons. On vacation in Nantucket, he called singer Paul Anka several times. There were several references to meetings with Henry Kissinger, although an employee noted that Boesky never left messages when he called Kissinger. There was the occasional reminder to send a check to his sister, whom he supported but hardly ever saw. And there were intriguing mentions of visits with investment bankers at highly respected firms, whose names never surfaced during the government's investigation of Wall Street.

In 1986, as the government was closing in, Boesky's public profile changed considerably; he stopped flying to Washington by private jet and began taking the shuttle. He didn't completely abandon his love for power and privilege—his September calendar indicated a dinner engagement at Harvard with the prince and princess of Wales and a lunch in Washington with Senator Jesse Helms.

In November came the plea. But shame and disgrace didn't, for Boesky, mean a change in his spending habits. That winter, he took his sons to Islamorada, Florida, for a week of fishing. In the spring of 1987, he was scheduled to host a lunch for some Japanese men at New York's most expensive restaurant, The Quilted Giraffe. That fall, Boesky had a standing reservation on the Saturday-morning Concorde to London. He continued to reserve tennis courts for several hours at a stretch, so he would never have to wait to play.

Not a bad life for a man whose lawyers had recently prepared a confidential financial statement for the government indicating that his net worth was negative $4 million.

*   *   *

Ivan Boesky went off to prison in late March of 1988. Once again, good fortune was running with him—he was sent to the facility that was his first choice. And, once again, he got everything his way.

The Lompoc prison is set north of Santa Barbara, California, near a charming all-American town eight miles from the Pacific Ocean. The hills famed for their flowers are also dotted with cattle, and much of the prison activity involves their care—healthy, wholesome work, though not the kind that Boesky would find amusing for very long.

For the benefit of his family, Ivan Boesky adopted the role of the martyr. He told visitors that he hated his work at the prison dairy, but he didn't want to complain. He hadn't—thank God—been subjected to violent assault or sexual abuse, though that was such a constant fear he took pains to avoid the shower room. He didn't have "special privileges," he insisted, and if anyone back home said he did, he wanted it known that was a fantasy.

But Boesky seems to have understood the politics of prisons from the beginning. After being assigned to the facility that was then second only to Allenwood for good living and comfy accommodations, he abused most of the rules of this minimum-security prison. Considering that high-profile cases are supervised more by Washington than by individual jails, it is likely that the administrators at the highest level of the Bureau of Prisons knew what Boesky was up to.

That, anyway, is the conclusion of some of the inmates who knew Boesky best.

"Ivan was actively courted by the feds," says an inmate who lived in Boesky's dorm. "He was able to go into town when he wanted, and he was allowed to use the administrators' phones."

Former inmates recall that access to unmonitored phones and the freedom to come and go as he pleased were only the beginning of Boesky's abuses of prison rules. The work assignment to the dairy didn't displease Boesky for long; he was soon stationed in the visitors' room, where he had little to do. He was rarely seen in the mess hall, preferring to eat steaks and fresh fruit—two items not on the general menu—in the relative privacy of the visiting room. On several occasions, according to a former inmate, a blonde in her early thirties picked Boesky up in a blue

Honda, and, he believed, took him to a Lompoc motel.

None of this increased the prisoners' respect for Boesky, not that he had much chance with his fellow inmates in the first place. "Milken was everybody's hero—he was going to fight the system," a former inmate says. "The idea that you do a patriotic duty by cooperating with the government isn't a popular notion in prison, especially if you're like Ivan and you seem to go out of your way to ruin a lot of lives in order to save yourself maybe a year."

In the beginning, Boesky kept his head down and his conversations cryptic. It didn't matter; everyone gave him a wide berth: "The joke was that if you're working in the visitors' room with Ivan, don't stand between him and the road, or you might take his bullet." But as Boesky's perks became known and accepted, he began to open up to the Jewish inmates. These men had formed a kind of congregation, and Boesky enjoyed attending the services led by a traveling rabbi. "We each contributed as much as we could," the leader of this group recalls. "Some gave the rabbi twenty dollars a month, some gave two hundred dollars. Getting money out of Ivan was like pulling teeth. I finally had to sit him down and explain it to him. 'Look, Ivan,' I began, 'this is a poor rabbi with *nine* children.' Ivan stopped me cold. '*I* didn't tell him to have nine kids,' he said."

After that, Boesky's social life was pretty much reduced to the guys at the weight pile and the inmates in his dorm. Some of those inmates were brilliant pranksters, not pleased to be in prison and eager to embark on projects that would embarrass their jailers and, possibly, win their early release. So they were more than ready to tell the Milken investigators who showed up in 1989 a thing or two about Boesky that wouldn't sound pretty in a courtroom.

Those revelations, naturally, were about sexual activity that violated prison rules. According to one of these inmates, Boesky may have preferred women but, once in prison, he became an active homosexual. This inmate went on full-time Boesky-alert and could soon cite times, places, positions, and partners: Boesky on his knees in a bathroom stall, Boesky on his back in a cubicle, Boesky in the visitors' room lavatory. Another inmate then spread the shocking stories. It didn't take long for the dorm to be rife with rumors: The FBI man who frequently visited Boesky was really his lover; Boesky had brought a stud into prison to live with him for a few days; Boesky routinely paid younger inmates for sex.

Although some of these stories, a former prisoner recalls, were told "by people who don't ordinarily tell rumors," there was a problem with these tales.

They were difficult to verify, and, in all probability, they weren't true.

"I heard the rumors about Ivan being gay," says an inmate named in the investigative reports as one of Boesky's targets. "The thing is, none of those stories about me in the reports ever happened. He never approached me in the shower, and he never offered me money. The guys who talked to the investigators were interested in nailing Boesky any way they could. I think they believed that lawyers would pay them for their testimony."

"In prison sex, there are pitchers and catchers," a Lompoc veteran says. "Ivan wasn't hip enough to pitch, and he certainly wasn't attractive enough to catch. On the other hand, if there's a sighting in the south of France of 'X'"—his references were to a prisoner who was rumored to have acquired an expensive gold watch shortly after meeting Boesky and a house near Cannes that Boesky owned—"you've got the story."

The investigators found all this fascinating. They also found it useless—for all Boesky's indiscretions, he hadn't said anything about money he might be hiding from the government.

There was one man not bound by attorney-client privilege who might know Boesky's secrets. His name is Houshang Wekili, and he is, in all probability, Boesky's only true friend. They'd met in Detroit as children. As young men, they'd traveled together to Iran, fueling speculation that Boesky had some CIA involvement. When Boesky became successful, he put Wekili on the payroll for a rumored $1 million a year.

Wekili was silent and sullen, pale and skinny, and he made little effort to sparkle—on Boesky's plane, while others enjoyed multicourse meals, it was said that he went to sleep on the floor. No one at Boesky's office knew what he did to earn his money; his co-workers tended to avoid him. His sole function was as an occasional go-between. When Boesky was in an unreasonable phase, Wekili could sometimes be persuaded to try to calm him down.

If anyone knew Boesky, it was Wekili. But there was no way for investigators to crack Wekili's silence and learn a single fact about his finances.

Fugitive financiers love Switzerland, and Ivan Boesky was no exception. What's unusual is that Boesky didn't wait until his fall to think about that attractive alternative to jail—he made his first moves in that direction in 1983, when he and Martin Siegel were committing their most outrageous crimes.

As ever, there was some deception involved, starting right at home. When Boesky obtained a residence permit for himself and his family in Fribourg, Switzerland, in 1983, he told his wife that he was concerned about an armed right-wing group living just five miles from their home. This group marched. This group may have been responsible for anonymous mailings of anti-Semitic pamphlets. Because he had long been connected to Jewish causes, Boesky felt at risk—he wanted a safe haven and a dual passport.

That wasn't what he told the Council of State in the canton of Fribourg. There, as required, he indicated that he would make Switzerland the center of his business and family life; the Boesky Investment and Financing Corporation would be headquartered there. But his apartment at Beauregard 9 was never occupied; this was, as a Swiss lawyer delicately put it, "a fictitious domicile."

There were rumors that some of Boesky's trips to Paris may have included a quick flight to Switzerland, whispers that Boesky offered to set up a Swiss bank account for Martin Siegel. Those leads didn't pan out. For most investigators, the tantalizing suggestion of hidden money turned into ozone.

For twenty-two years, Marvin Sontag was a special agent in the criminal investigation division on the Internal Revenue Service. He was a very good agent, which is why the Organized Crime Strike Force of the U.S. attorney's office in the Southern District of New York often borrowed him. There, he was said to be responsible for the conviction of more career criminals than any agent in the history of American law enforcement, including Elliot Ness.

Unlike the other investigators, Marvin Sontag had no national reputation, no staff of investigators—he worked with his daughter, Barbara. Because Milken lawyers brought him onto the case after the other investigators had been hired, he stayed around mostly to study what Kroll and Lenzner had found and to dig through the mountain of Boesky material that the government had turned over to defense lawyers. And so it came to pass that Marvin Sontag was the investigator who may have figured out what Ivan Boesky was really doing with a shell company called Cobalt Holdings.

As those who worked with him knew all too well, Boesky would, if not stopped, go hog-wild and buy up every available share of any stock that struck his fancy. That created havoc for him with the regulatory agencies, for he'd spend so wantonly that he was in constant jeopardy of violating the net-capital rules. The way he got around them was to park stock—to make it appear he'd sold the securities in order to have more cash on hand and stay within the law. Naturally, Boesky didn't inform the regulators that he was planning to repurchase these securities at about the same price.

When Drexel financed Boesky's new fund in 1986, Milken and others insisted that there be restrictions on this wild investor—he couldn't spend more than $400 million on any one security. Boesky may have seen these restraints coming. And he may well have known how to get around them.

In 1982, Michael Collins, a Boesky associate in Bermuda, set up a Panamanian company called Cobalt Holdings. Collins was also a director of Farnsworth & Hastings, a snooty-sounding Boesky company that had, in truth, been named after streets in his native Detroit. Farnsworth & Hastings was owned by an English company called Cambrian, which was in turn controlled by Boesky. The odds that Cobalt was also used by Boesky were thus very high.

In January of 1986, according to *The New York Times*, Boesky found a use for Cobalt. Although the *Times* concluded that Boesky used Cobalt to avoid investment restrictions, it appeared to Sontag that Boesky had an additional use for Cobalt—as a parking lot.

Michael Davidoff, Boesky's head trader, pleaded guilty to parking securities through Boesky's London broker, Robert Harris. In a typical parking scheme, profit and loss are usually infinitesimal—the point isn't to make money from these sales and repurchases, just to send the securities on a little trip.

But in the trades Davidoff pleaded guilty to, Seemala lost $7 million.

Given the timing and nature of the trades, it appeared that they involved Cobalt. By the time Boesky's firm closed its doors, at least $5 million had not been returned to Seemala. If there really is a discrepancy here, the ultimate recipient of those Cobalt millions has never been identified.

Boesky's American felonies led the English authorities to probe his London activities and prompted the Guinness scandal. By mid-1987, investigators from the London Stock Exchange were interviewing Robert Harris. Over the course of the next year, these investigators and detectives from Scotland Yard met with prosecutors from the U.S. attorney's office in New York and enforcement lawyers from the SEC in Washington. They sent documents to the U.S. attorney. And they interviewed Boesky.

No charges were ever brought against Robert Harris. Friends of the London broker describe the Cobalt trades as a "vanilla event," a scenario that might be illegal in America but common and acceptable in England. Although Robert Harris declined repeated requests for an interview, he did point a finger at Boesky. "I was duped," he told a *New York Times* reporter. "Boesky used me as his straight guy."

To some investigators, the Cobalt trades suggested that Boesky may have stolen money from his company and defrauded Drexel and his investors; to Giuliani's men, Cobalt wasn't a Boesky crime and, therefore, wasn't relevant or worthy of much attention. Perhaps that is why, although some lawyers have insisted the prosecutors were legally obligated to turn this material over to defense lawyers in both the Mulheren and Milken cases, the U.S. attorney didn't do that.

Despite the government's insistence that Cobalt didn't constitute an unacknowledged Boesky crime, something clearly happened here. Boesky never advised the New York Stock Exchange that his firm traded through Cobalt. When congressional investigations asked Harvey Pitt about Boesky's overseas accounts in 1988, he made no mention of Cobalt; Pitt, who informed his clients they'd damn well better tell him everything they did, had never been briefed by Boesky about Cobalt. If it had not been for two articles in *The New York Times*—*The Wall Street Journal* somehow missed the Cobalt story—the public would never have heard of this Boesky sideshow.

Was Cobalt grounds for throwing out the Boesky plea?

Perhaps.

True, it may have been "only" $5 million, an insignificant sum when billions are at stake. On the other hand, $5 million is more of a cushion than most people will ever enjoy. What was once beer money may have looked to Boesky like a nest egg.

But the amount doesn't really matter. If Cobalt represents a Boesky lie to the government, he violated the foundation of his plea. And the prosecutors—who knew about this scam both because the English authorities gave them the evidence and because Boesky trader Michael Davidoff pleaded guilty to Cobalt trades through Harris—then became, in effect, Boesky's co-conspirators.

If Milken's lawyers had this proof, why didn't they petition the U.S. attorney to prosecute Boesky? Why, at the very least, didn't they leak the story in a way that would have impacted public opinion?

Because, they say, they wanted to get Ivan Boesky on the witness stand before they unveiled their Cobalt allegations.

There was no trial, and so Cobalt remains what it was all along: a tantalizing detail, a metaphor for Boesky's character, a small monument to all that will never be fully disclosed about the Wall Street scandals of the 1980s. If Ivan Boesky hid money from the government and his creditors, he got to keep it. And in that same vault, Boesky also got to bury Michael Milken's last frail shot for freedom.

CHAPTER TWENTY

"**W**arm up your fingers," Michael Milken said. "You're going to have to go very fast."

The fifth- and sixth-graders crowded into a classroom at the M. L. King School in Los Angeles waved their arms and snapped their fingers, ignoring the sign over the blackboard: WE READ SILENTLY FOR 17 MINUTES EVERY DAY. WE DO NOT WRITE, TALK, OR GET OUT OF OUR SEATS.

"Nine times twelve," Milken said, over the din.

"Hundred 'n eight!" many shouted.

With a smile that could have sold a million bonds, Milken called a dozen children to the front of the room. He handed six of them pocket calculators. The other six, he said, were going to represent people. They'd have to figure out the answers in their heads.

"Let's see who's faster—people or machines," he said. "Sixty-five times sixty-five."

The front of the room buzzed.

"Who won?" Milken asked.

"People!" the class shouted.

"Pretty tough to beat the people," Milken said. "Your brain is *much* faster than a computer."

After the people won a few more games, Milken held up a hand for silence.

"We're very lucky today. We have Mr. Wizard Alan with us."

Alan Flans, a dentist by profession, had the good sense to marry into Milken's family and agree to work at Drexel. One Christmas, the resident humorist of the High-Yield Bond Department created a collection of fake greeting cards. The one he had Flans sending to Milken read: "Happy holidays, Mike, from one guy who's not getting divorced next year." Although Flans was no longer at Drexel, he was still married. His current assignment was to race from school to school with Milken, don a conical hat that Milken had worn one Halloween, and play the role of the trickster.

In secret, Flans wrote a number on a sheet of a paper, folded it, and gave it to a student for safekeeping. Milken had the other students put some number through a series of changes. Then he had Flans take the paper and unfold it. There it was: the same number the students had reached. "To be a wizard," Flans said, "you have to be more than a good-looking face."

Milken asked if anyone had a favorite basketball team.

"Lakers," many cried.

"Anyone like Chicago?"

A few did.

"Let's have some Chicago and Laker fans up here." A dozen kids raced forward. "Are these people trustworthy?"

"Only Jessica!" a boy in back shouted.

"Do they know what the score of the Lakers-Bulls game will be?"

No one did. Milken showed them how they could discover the score. "When you go home this weekend," he asked, "will you do a whole lot of math?"

"No!"

"I bet you will—and you won't even know it. And because you're all so good at this stuff, you're now members of Mike's Math Club. You get your shirts today, and if I hear you guys continue to do great, you get calculators."

The class ended. Milken went into another, where the thought for the day was "keep our thoughts positive" and the daily word was "network." When that class ended, he hurried on to the Thirty-sixth Street School. He taught three more classes while his driver and Alan Flans searched in vain for candy bars and a cool drink. By two in the afternoon, he had taught several hundred Hispanic and Afro-American children, eaten nothing, and taken no bathroom break—and as others looked at their watches and muttered about the long drive back to their homes on the west side of Los Angeles, he slowed the schedule again. In the gym, twenty girls wanted him to watch them tap-dance to "Tequila," a song that, in his distant childhood, he would have known not only by year and group, but by label and flip side.

As the girls tapped away, children arranged themselves around Milken.

"You like the Simpsons?" he asked.

"Sure."

"Do they teach you anything?"

"No."

"They teach me something—they care about people," Milken said. "What's your favorite book? Mine is *The Giving Tree*."

"I like that one, too."

"What did you learn from it?"

"Not to be greedy."

"That's a good thing to learn," Milken said, benignly.

"Mike, did you play baseball?"

"I played third base and left field."

"Were you good?"

"I was a good hitter, but I wasn't a good fielder—I made errors."

Milken caught a visitor's eye, and blushed. Three thousand miles away, they both knew, his lawyers were crafting the language of a plea that was all about error.

Mike's Math Club and Milken's work with his family foundation and his attendance at baseball games in the company of less than privileged children made other people—particularly writers covering the Milken story—uncomfortable. His passion for philanthropy was, they said, freshly minted; criminal investigations have a way of turning defendants into humanitarians. That skepticism was understandable. Milken's philanthropy made him even more difficult to fathom. He consorted with Boesky, and, at the same time, he was a hopeless idealist? It was easier to conclude that what Milken did for others was part of a public relations campaign, cooked up to impress a judge or jury, and destined to end as soon as his case was settled.

But the uncomfortable fact is that Milken had urged his colleagues to volunteer time to charities as early as 1980. Milken and his brother had started giving money away in an organized way in 1982. They had contributed some $66 million to their foundation *before* the investigation started in 1986, and they had established substantial programs with the University of California, the University of Pennsylvania, and the Simon Wiesenthal Center well before Ivan Boesky turned himself in. And giving money to institutions was only the beginning for Michael Milken. If friends were in trouble, he devoted time and resources; if there was sickness, he couldn't do enough.

Mike's Math Club was typical of these efforts; it emerged, unplanned, from an afternoon he'd spent at Project Six in 1988. He'd tossed out some math questions, and the kids had faltered; addition was the outer limits for them. Milken applied his standard formula for problem solving—like all people with more challenges than others, what these kids needed was some focused attention. Meeting once a week, he coaxed them into doing mathematical puzzles. In less than a month, he had them doing algebra. The world beckoned.

Milken began teaching in Los Angeles public schools in 1989, and then, when visits to his lawyers had him spending more time in New York, he took on classes in inner-city neighborhoods. As ever, he had a scary power to remember names and histories, to size up ability and target his questions accordingly; the energy he once brought to business he now applied to teaching.

"Is this what he'd like to do for his punishment?" a teacher asked, after seeing him in action.

"This is what he does for *pleasure*," a friend replied.

And, he might have added, for therapy.

While Milken taught and fretted, Rudolph Giuliani ran for mayor of New York, using his prosecutorial successes as his shield. He entered the race a heavy favorite, and, for a while, it looked as if he'd get a free ride to City Hall. But certain of his prosecutions—most notably of Bess Myerson and of Wigton, Freeman, and Tabor—came back to haunt him. Then White and Case, the law firm that was paying him close to $1 million a year for the privilege of the association, was revealed to have represented General Manuel Noriega's government in Panama; four months after Giuliani signed on at the firm, he resigned. After that, it took only some news flashes about the annulment of his first marriage—he claimed he didn't know he'd married his cousin—to make him look evasive and small.

The low ebb of Giuliani's campaign came as the direct result of his questionable judgment. In a city steaming with ethnic division, Giuliani invited comedian Jackie Mason to serve as a warm-up act. At that time, Giuliani hadn't been concerned with Mason's free-swinging Borscht Belt humor. Nor had Mason cared that the men Giuliani prosecuted on Wall Street were almost all Jewish: "A guy sticks a knife in somebody, what is that, Jewish crime? No, that's *black* crime; a guy steals downtown, *that's* Jewish crime." What occurred next was probably inevitable—at a luncheon with reporters in attendance, Mason jokingly used the term *schvartze* to describe Giuliani's opponent, David Dinkins. It was only when the story surfaced, however, that Giuliani realized that he'd have to abandon the comedian.

As election day approached, Giuliani also abandoned his high-minded campaign themes. His campaign workers put a New Year's advertisement in a Jewish newspaper that juxtaposed two photographs: their candidate with George Bush, and Dinkins with Jesse Jackson. And, lapsing into the familiar mode of indictment day press conferences, he began hurling charges at Dinkins as though he were about to prosecute him.

"His eyes are hot and his mouth is cold," Murray Kempton wrote of Giuliani's public appearances, "and there is no combination of features more apt to set any small child except one's own to shrieking in his mother's arms." Less high-toned were an opponent's commercials that capitalized on the harshness of his character: "Why are New Yorkers afraid of Rudy Giuliani?" they asked. "Because they ought to be!"

On election night, as Giuliani was heading toward a narrow defeat—he lost, one wag said, by as many votes as there were employees of Goldman, Sachs and Drexel Burnham—the crowd at his headquarters cried, "Recount! Recount!" Some thought they heard something different: cries of "RICO! RICO!" And they felt a certain relief that the Savonarola of the 1980s had, for now, been denied a job that required as much compassion as savvy and skill.

But although Giuliani was gone—a Captain Ahab who'd speared his whale, only to beach himself in the process—his prosecutions had a life of their own. On August 4, 1989, *The Wall*

Street Journal reported that the long-promised expanded indictment was coming Milken's way in September; three days later, the prosecutors announced that they were actually aiming for October 1. On September 12, the *Journal* ran an item that suggested a second indictment would be filed in October; on September 26, John Carroll assured Judge Wood that while there'd be some delay, it would be only a matter of weeks. On October 12, Carroll moved the filing date back to November. In mid-January of 1990, when no indictment seemed forthcoming, the *Journal* reported that it was expected the following week.

To Milken, it was all fake drama, designed to ratchet up public expectation and pressure potential witnesses to seek immunity before it was too late—the Giuliani method, still going strong. Confession, contrition, cooperation: Those virtues were all the prosecutors understood. And wanted. For then, like their former boss, these holy men could trade the scalps on their belts for political careers or, at worst, jobs that paid in the deep six figures.

Milken was, belatedly, coming to understand the process.

The superseding indictment, though real, was not something the prosecutors had much enthusiasm for. Shortly after the first indictment, they approached Milken's lawyers suggesting "peace with honor."* One of the prosecutors told Arthur Liman: We're not trying to strip Milken of his dignity. We just want everyone to put down these weapons and move on.

Because there was no common understanding of the most basic facts of the case, Arthur Liman asked yet another lawyer, the highly respected Stephen Kaufman, to join the settlement talks on Milken's behalf. Still, the negotiations were protracted and painful. There was only one agreement that wasn't difficult to reach—the talks would be kept secret from the SEC.

For the U.S. attorney's office, the reason for secrecy was understandable. Richard Breeden, the new SEC chairman, was a former deputy counsel to then-Vice President Bush. When Bush ran for President, Breeden played the part of Jack Kemp in some debate rehearsals. After Bush became President, he supervised the administration's legislative effort to bail out the savings and

---

*The prosecutors insist that it was Milken's lawyers who approached them, using that phrase as their calling card. The two sides differed on everything, as usual.

loans. His reward was the SEC, which he was quickly transforming into a hard-charging financial version of the FBI. Taking over the U.S. attorney's office in New York was not in his charter, but it wasn't out of the question—Breeden was so peremptory that he had quickly earned the nickname of "King Richard."

That nickname was deceptive. For all his ambition, the lean, serious, forty-one-year-old lawyer had won Bush's affections through team play and slavish loyalty—qualities much prized in an administration that took its values from the President's time on the playing fields of Andover and Yale. Breeden shared the Bush economic philosophy: Don't overregulate, but what you do keep on the books, enforce with a vengeance. And in a city that found it hard to get excited about this President, he'd collected so many pictures of Bush that he had to hang some in his bathroom at home.

Did the administration believe that Michael Milken was as essential to America's economic welfare as fur hats?

If so, Breeden would volunteer to lead the death squad.

The Milken lawyers didn't need Breeden's presence to mistrust the SEC. "This agency is as much out of control as the National Security Council was during the Iran-contra affair," Arthur Liman wrote in an internal memo just as Breeden was arriving at the commission. "The SEC condoned leak after leak in the Milken case, thus encouraging its staff to believe they were above the law." It was only to be expected that, after so much error, the SEC's new head would consolidate in a single persona every wrongheaded idea the commission had been trying out for years.

This sort of political intrigue maddened Michael Milken. Wall Street was less complicated. And less ambiguous. For sometimes, if he closed his eyes, he couldn't tell if the voices he heard belonged to his lawyers or the prosecutors.

But there was no tuning these voices out.

Late in 1989, the drumbeats grew louder. The prosecutors sent out target letters, threatening head trader Warren Trepp, veteran salesman Alan Rosenthal, and a junior salesman named Peter Gardiner with RICO indictments. Two other Milken salesmen, Roy Johnson and David Sydorick, were offered immunity. And then, in late 1989, the prosecutors conferred immunity on Gary Winnick without even putting him in front of a grand jury and hearing him refuse to testify.

This blew Milken away.

Winnick had dreamed of working closely with Milken. But once he arrived in California and began running the Convertible Bond Department, everything changed. He was one of the few department heads to use a private office. And he was the only department head besides Milken to publish his own newsletter.

Winnick loved Milken for the power of his intellect and his genius at creating and nurturing markets, but he feared what he describes as Milken's need for total control. And so, in 1985, he left Drexel to form Pacific Asset Management, backed, in part, by the Milkens. Since then, he'd been off the map—even the investigation passed him by.

Winnick had little to tell the prosecutors, but for Milken, who saw betrayal even where the facts suggested that the government had played a wild card, that wasn't the point. Winnick was, if not a friend, at least a comrade. For him to go over to the other side was, for Milken, a sign that people with no legal exposure had decided that they had to join the prosecution or be crushed.

One more hurt.

And one more reason to teach.

School was now Milken's haven, the only place where he could express his hope and optimism, his single opportunity to create value. Because of that, school had to be taken away. All it took was for the New York papers to get wind of his volunteer work. One article later, and the schools that had welcomed him now felt foolish and awkward.

At seven in the morning after the story of his teaching made the news, Milken called his sister Joni. You'll have to lead the classes today, he said. There's been a problem in New York. I can't do this anymore.

They're killing him, Joni thought. They're taking away something positive he likes to do.

But Milken wasn't being killed, just hunted down and cornered.

After Drexel settled with the government, many wondered who the board would bring in to run the firm. But Fred Joseph's competitive spirit wouldn't allow him to make the expected gesture and fall on his sword. Instead, he decided to transform Drexel and make peace with the Establishment.

Joseph shed businesses. He cut the payroll. He gave inspiring talks that some employees even believed. He was, however, never able to find a product more compelling than Milken's junk bonds. And he was unable to strike a balance between the sheep and wolf—in himself or in the firm.

It was as a crisis manager that Joseph's decisions proved fatal. Fearful that Black and Ackerman would leave, he guaranteed them Milkenesque bonuses. To justify those bonuses, Black and Ackerman pushed through deals that made scant economic sense. Because those deals were so wretched, Drexel had to invest its own funds in them. When the deals failed, the downward spiral accelerated. In the process, the firm became a hotbed of greed, petulance, and finger pointing.

"I see daylight," Joseph told *The Wall Street Journal* early in February of 1990. "The worst is behind us." Days later, with the worst staring him in the face, Joseph was desperately seeking an infusion of capital from a new partner. And anyone with cash would do.

Just before the end, Leon Black decided to ignore the SEC strictures against discussing business with Michael Milken. Black, who had recently collected a bonus of some $15 million that he wasn't about to throw back into the Drexel kitty, was no diplomat: When he called Richard Sandler, he bluntly asked if Milken would care to increase the chances that he'd live to see all the money Drexel owed him by investing as much as $100 million in the firm. Milken, suppressing the urge to lecture, declined.*

Way too late, Joseph came to understand the Wall Street wisdom of getting along by going along—for his fate was ultimately in the hands of Nicholas Brady, who had run Dillon, Read when Fred Hartley was fighting the Drexel-backed raid on his oil company. Now the secretary of the treasury, Nick Brady was walking proof that Drexel was a friendless institution everyone in Washington and on Wall Street wished dead.

On February 13, 1990, Joseph made them all happy and declared bankruptcy.

"The government takes no satisfaction—I know I don't—in seeing people lose their jobs. But Drexel was manipulating the high-yield bond market in a systematic way for years, and it's a

*Leon Black did not respond to repeated requests for comment.

good thing that's been stopped," said Bruce Baird, who, in all the years that he prosecuted Drexel, had never once accused Milken or the firm of a single crime involving high-yield bonds.

In New York, Drexel's executive elite talked of conspiracy. Of the many improbable stories making the rounds, the wildest had John Gutfreund, then the head of Salomon Brothers, in Washington days before the Drexel bankruptcy, rushing around Capitol Hill in a last-ditch lobbying effort—in this version of events, he wanted to make sure there would be no eleventh-hour bailout of his firm's most hated rival. Other investment banks, Drexel executives said, knew a day earlier about this blessed event. For the conspiracy theorists, the proof that certain people were told, "Don't worry about trading junk bonds; do it, there will be liquidity" was that the market held level after Drexel's announcement.

In Beverly Hills, Drexel employees who were too numb for paranoid scenarios stepped into the unaccustomed daylight, blinking at the street life they'd never noticed before. The traders, salesmen, and Corporate Finance executives scurried for new positions; their assistants called Milken for help. That month, on top of everything else, Michael Milken became an unpaid personnel consultant.

Another burden.

Michael Milken's ninety-two-year-old grandfather wore hearing aids, but he could hear a knock at the door.

FBI, the men said, flashing badges.

We hate to bother you, sir, they said, but we'd like to know about your investments. Could you tell us—where do you have your brokerage accounts? What stocks do you own?

Michael Milken had been having trouble getting through the day for a while; he walked with a stoop, he no longer rushed everywhere. His friends, his family, and his lawyers all asked the same question: How do you think he is? And, privately, they told one another that he was failing, that this prosecution might exact a fatal toll. One day, he said it himself: I don't know how much more of this I can take.

The FBI visit came on top of all that bad feeling, and it crushed Milken. His grandfather had absolutely nothing to do with the case, and the FBI knew it. The only reason the prosecutors had to aim the FBI at his grandfather, he thought, was to humiliate him in front of his family, to make everyone afraid.*

In the aftermath of that FBI visit, Milken cycled the same questions: When will it stop? What comes next? Is there any trick too low and dirty for these people? What can I do to put an end to this?

Just what the government wanted him to think.

Every time the prosecutors talked to Michael Armstrong, they heard the same old song.

This is fucking outrageous, Armstrong would say.

C'mon, Michael, be reasonable, the government men would say. There's another indictment coming.

Come ahead, Armstrong would reply.

The U.S. attorney got the idea—Lowell Milken wasn't taking any plea. And he was rather enjoying the way his lawyer was letting the government know where it could stick its threat of a superseding indictment.

In January of 1990, though, when the prosecutors sensed that Michael Milken was almost beaten down enough to plead guilty, they took a fresh look at his brother. To make Michael's decision easier, they proposed a deferral of Lowell's indictment. Armstrong wanted something more: an agreement that any evidence in Michael's plea agreement couldn't be used in Lowell's trial. The U.S. attorney's office, hopeful that this was the start of settlement talks with Lowell as well as Michael, agreed. And the prosecutors suggested to Arthur Liman that Armstrong really ought to come downtown for a friendly chat.

Armstrong was still operating on the assumption that Lowell would never take a plea, but he decided to see if this opportunity might be exploited a bit more fully. Soon he devised a limitation of charges and penalties—a cap. He'd ask the government to make Lowell its best offer. At any point within six months, he could accept it. Or he could go to trial.

There was another incentive to explore a plea: to help Paul, Weiss. No matter what they came up with, Michael's lawyers feared they couldn't produce an agreement their client would ac-

---

*Prosecutors in New York, though aware of the FBI visit to Milken's grandfather, say they didn't request it. Prosecutors in Los Angeles say they are "99 percent sure" that they didn't ask the FBI to conduct this interview.

cept—Michael didn't want to do anything that would leave Lowell alone and exposed. But if he knew Lowell's situation had a clear solution, he could then concentrate on his own dilemma.

Lowell found this incentive very dubious, but he had Armstrong call the prosecutors and present them with a memo, outlining a preliminary agreement. They discussed an acceptable charge—perhaps an accessory after the fact to one of the counts against his brother. And they agreed to talk again.

Then there was silence.

The prosecutors' next call to Michael Armstrong was very different in tone.

Two felonies, they demanded.

It was one last month, Armstrong pointed out.

Well, it's now two, he was told.

I can't bring this to Lowell, Armstrong said. Forget the whole idea of a cap.

But of course he called Lowell.

You're no longer authorized to talk to these people, Lowell said.

Silence descended again.

Pleas are always compromises. The defendant abandons his insistence on innocence; the prosecutor adjusts the offenses to indicate his appreciation of that admission. As a general rule, it makes sense to assume that the defendant was guilty of more charges—and more serious charges, at that—than the plea agreement indicates.

There is one exception to that generalization, and it is insider trading. Prosecutors regard insider trading the way district attorneys regard murder. If a defendant has traded on inside information and a federal prosecutor has him cold, that criminal had better be prepared to sing like Boesky or Siegel if he hopes to be cut any slack.

Michael Milken was never going to cooperate like that.

If he was guilty of insider trading, therefore, he was going to have to plead guilty to that charge.

But Michael Milken wasn't going to be found guilty of insider trading.

For three and a half years, the prosecutors had tried mightily to make that case. In all that time, with all their subpoena power and RICO threats, they never got beyond Ivan Boesky—and

Boesky never pointed out pre-announcement trades that netted Milken a quick $20 million, or foreign bank accounts, or bags of cash, or code names in diaries. Still, the prosecutors told Milken's lawyers that any plea bargain would require Milken to take one count of insider trading. The defense lawyers refused. And the prosecutors promptly dropped that demand.

What the prosecutors could document were conspiracy, aiding and abetting net-capital violations, aiding and abetting others in the false filing of their tax returns and SEC filings. These were serious charges. They were also less serious charges than the government had claimed it would prove at trial.

Late in 1989, prosecutors proposed that Milken plead guilty to six felony counts and pay a fine of $650 million.

Never, Milken's lawyers replied. That was Drexel's plea. Michael wasn't the same as Drexel then, and he's not the same as Drexel now. Six counts, maybe, but not $650 million.

The number of counts in a multiple count plea is meaningless, the prosecutors replied. We all know that judges give concurrent sentences if one count is conspiracy and the others are overt acts.

Historically, yes, said the defense lawyers. But we can't take a chance that Judge Wood will hand down consecutive sentences. You've got to make her understand that you're not looking for an enhanced sentence. We know nothing you say is binding on her, but you've got to send her a message.

The prosecutors and defense lawyers spent the next two sessions working out the language of that message. In January of 1990, they reached tentative agreement on a settlement—six felony counts and a $500 million fine. Because Milken's version of the facts and the government contentions were miles apart, there was no advantage in having him meet with prosecutors before he was sentenced. If he debriefed the prosecutors before sentencing and they concluded that he had told them nothing worthwhile, they might well ask the judge at sentencing to set aside his plea—and if she agreed and called for a trial, Milken would go into court branded as a self-admitted criminal who was, for good measure, a liar.

The prosecutors had no interest in seeing Milken punished at sentencing for his failure to make cases for the government, and they agreed to let him begin debriefings afterward. But the solution to that problem intensified the importance of another problem—their recommendation to the judge. Because cooperation wasn't a factor here, they agreed not to recommend any sentence. That, they said, was the comfort that defense lawyers required, that was the message everyone involved believed the judge would understand.

Not the best deal, Milken lawyers said. And not the worst. But a deal that Michael can probably live with—if he decides not to go to trial.

It was now time to deal with the SEC.

The prosecutors understood that tempers hadn't improved at SEC headquarters in Washington. So they devised a plan that covered what appeared to be any eventuality. Milken's lawyers would make an offer of a financial settlement to the SEC. If the commission accepted it, simultaneous settlements would end the case. If the commission rejected it, Milken could settle with the U.S. attorney and litigate with the SEC.

Or so it was agreed in January, before the Drexel bankruptcy.

Unfortunately for Michael Milken, the tentative agreement wasn't submitted to the SEC for its approval before Drexel's bankruptcy.

And, after the Drexel bankruptcy, the SEC was quite sensitive about the public relations aspects of any Milken settlement. If Milken paid less than Drexel, it might look as if the SEC had taken too much from Drexel—it might look as if the SEC bore some responsibility for Drexel's failure. So Milken should, Breeden thought, pony up *more* than Drexel.

A billion dollars was a figure Breeden liked a lot.

Then Breeden did something novel: He went to the attorney general of the United States to complain that the U.S. attorney for the Southern District of New York had gone soft on Milken. Attorney General Dick Thornburgh understood that Breeden and Treasury Secretary Nicholas Brady were in alignment on this issue—they believed that Milken had committed the equivalent of murder in the financial markets.

That winter, Thornburgh sent word back to the prosecutors: Milken would settle with the SEC and the U.S. attorney at the same time, or there'd be no deal. They were not to give the judge any signal that would encourage her to give Milken concurrent sentences. And the deal he'd have to take was nonnegotiable.

Six felonies, six hundred and fifty million dollars, and not a penny less, Breeden reportedly said.*

Arthur Liman had inaugurated the Securities Fraud Division for the U.S. attorney in New York. For three decades, he'd seen U.S. attorneys enjoy a charmed and independent existence. Never had he known the attorney general to overrule a deal made by that office. Never had he witnessed the SEC, or any other agency, dictating terms to the Southern District.

If Giuliani were still in command, Liman thought, this would never have happened. Zealot or not, Rudy ran the office. He shook your hand, you had a deal. Now, it seemed to Liman, the U.S. attorney's office was being run out of the SEC in Washington.

Later, Breeden would say that directly.

"Those boys," he would tell Liman and Kaufman, referring to the assistant U.S. attorneys in New York, "work for me."†

In April, the U.S. attorneys met with the defense lawyers to announce the new terms of the deal. Alan Cohen, John Carroll, and Jess Fardella sat on one side of the table; Arthur Liman, Stephen Kaufman, and Richard Sandler lined up on the other.

There's good news and bad news, the prosecutors began.

Let's start with the bad news, Arthur Liman said.

The bad news, the prosecutors said, is that Breeden changed the terms of the deal and the attorney general agreed with him. We can't signal the judge about the sentence, Milken has to settle with us and the SEC at the same time, and it's six felonies and $650 million.

What's the good news?

If Michael settles, Lowell's indictment will be dismissed, they said. He'll be banned from the securities industry for life, but the SEC will let him sign a consent decree saying that he doesn't admit or deny its allegations—he will be, completely and forever, finished with the government.

---

*Richard Breeden says that he never made this remark. The SEC did allow Milken to settle for $50 million less.

†Richard Breeden says that he never made this remark.

We'll see, Liman said, a very modest reaction.

The other defense lawyers were just as noncommittal.

As Milken's team was leaving, John Carroll put a hand on Richard Sandler's shoulder and whispered, "Come back with something."*

No defense lawyer spoke until they reached the elevator. Then Sandler turned to Liman and Kaufman. "Welcome to Iran," he said.

On the way uptown, the defense lawyers tried to imagine why Lowell had suddenly become a bargaining chip. For years, they decided, the government had persisted in believing that a plea could be beaten out of Lowell. Recently, the prosecutors realized that Lowell wasn't kidding—he'd fight to the death. And someone important said: At this rate, Michael Milken is never going to plead, so let's make him an offer he can't refuse. Who gives a shit about Lowell? It's Michael we want. We're looking at one of the great settlements of all time, and we're going to let it get away because of *this* guy? Forget him.

The defense lawyers had it almost right. Only the dialogue was different. What actually happened is that the proposed Milken deals once again went to the highest law officer in the land. And what Attorney General Dick Thornburgh said was far more succinct, blunt, eloquent, and cruel than defense lawyers could imagine.

"A brother for a brother," Thornburgh told his deputies.†

The government believed that Robert Freeman, who had agreed to plead guilty to one felony count, had actually committed at least twenty more crimes. It said as much in its sentencing memo. Judge Pierre Leval had the option of calling a Fatico hear-

---

*"The brother issue is an interesting issue," John Carroll said in his Seton Hall Law School talk in April of 1992. "One sees family members charged in cases together all the time. . . . Any time I'm in a case and I see family relationships in the case, I recognize that as a leverage point. I think that Lowell Milken, like his brother, was fairly in the case. We would not have indicted him if there wasn't a basis to indict him . . . but it would be naïve to say he wasn't sort of a ready chip in the negotiation."

†Dick Thornburgh, who recalls that the idea to drop Lowell Milken from the case came from the prosecutors in New York, denies making this remark. A close former associate at the Justice Department, however, says, "That sounds like Dick."

ing—a short, informal trial, with reduced rules of evidence—to determine the validity of those allegations. He did not. In mid-March of 1990, he announced that he was going to ignore the government's sentencing memo. He would sentence Freeman for a single felony—just as the plea bargain indicated.

The prosecutors weren't about to let this happen again. They'd conducted a long investigation. As in the Freeman case, they believed they had identified many offenses that weren't going to be acknowledged in the plea agreement. They didn't want Milken to be sentenced only for these six felonies—they were terrified that Milken's crimes had been so watered down he might get a lighter sentence than Boesky. And so they told defense lawyers that they would present evidence of what they believed was additional wrongdoing in their sentencing memo. Judge Wood might accept the allegations. She might call for a Fatico hearing. She might ignore the allegations of additional offenses. But she was damned well going to read them in their brief.

If you present those allegations, we'll contest them.

That's your right, the prosecutors said.

Then everyone cooled down. Perhaps the thing to do was exchange sentencing memos before they submitted them to the judge. Maybe Milken could acknowledge something. With luck, a collision could be avoided.

Boesky had provided three felony counts so far: two offenses plus conspiracy. The deal called for three more. The prosecutors said there were dozens to choose from. What were they? The prosecutors suggested a few. But Michael Milken denied that those were criminal acts. And there was nothing in the trading records to make him change his mind.

"If you take ten years of trading records from anyone on Wall Street, you can find something," a defense lawyer said. So ten years of trading records were hauled out of the Paul, Weiss document room. The indictment was scoured again. Late at night, the lawyers walked the corridors, picking and choosing.

Alright: MCA. Steve Wynn wanted to sell, Boesky wanted to buy. The fact was that Wynn sold less than half of his MCA stock to Boesky, then dribbled the rest into the market. Still, Boesky had been guaranteed. One more Boesky felony.

The prosecutors needed a non-Boesky felony. All right: Finsbury. This was a fund that had been created to allow Europeans to invest in high-yield securities. Drexel paid a 1-percent commission to its salesmen for selling this fund to foreigners; unknown to Milken, Drexel charged this commission to his department. Milken, who fought tooth and claw for considerably smaller sums, saw this as one more example of Drexel New York taking a bite out of his profits, providing fees to the firm but not to the High-Yield Bond Department. He went to David Solomon, one of the fund managers who traded for Finsbury, and solved the problem—Solomon would make fractional adjustments on the price he paid Drexel for junk bonds. That is, with the approval of Drexel New York, his customers would pay slightly more than they might have—though the price was still within the range of the market—in order to compensate Milken's department.

This was a fairly classic example of the "soft-dollar" practices that are common on Wall Street, but Solomon hadn't disclosed the adjustment to his customers—and in that failure to disclose lay a crime. Really, it was Solomon's crime, but why split hairs: It was what the prosecutors sought, a non-Boesky crime. That it was an invented crime didn't really matter. It was felony number five.

David Solomon would also provide felony number six. In December of 1985, he had asked Milken to help him generate some tax losses. Milken found securities with a wide gap between the bid and asked prices. Solomon bought high and sold low, locking in an impressive tax loss. Meanwhile, Milken promised him investment opportunities in 1986 that would more than offset his losses.

The U.S. attorney found these felonies acceptable.

The news went south.

The felonies were acceptable in Washington.

For the lawyers, at least, the deal was done.

Now it was all up to Michael Milken.

A plea, any plea, would be the worst mistake of your life, Lowell told him. You've always said: Risk is a function of knowledge. When you started in business, you were extremely risk-averse. But as you went up the knowledge curve, you came to understand that some deals aren't such big risks. This is different. You've learned a few things about the criminal process, but not enough—you're risking a lot if you think you know what you're doing. You want this to end. But a plea won't be an ending.

These people are into total destruction. Fight them. If you believe in yourself and you lose in court, you can still say: I did nothing.

Having watched Milken react badly to the smallest events of the investigation, Richard Sandler felt the plea made psychological sense. At the same time, he wanted Milken to go to trial and confront his accusers. But how much battering could one man take? That was Milken's decision; if he could accept it, the plea was the right thing to do.

Ken Lerer was torn. Although this is the best deal you're going to get, he said, it's hardly the deal of a lifetime. In the long run, the public reaction will be so terrible that it might hurt you more than fighting on and losing in court. That's a reason not to settle. But the psychological damage was becoming so great that Lerer didn't see how Milken could hold out another day.

Imagine this picture, Harry Horowitz said: a man with a gun to his head, on his knees, sucking a goat's cock. Only when they publish the picture, they crop it so nobody knows about the gun. That's how it's going to be for you if you take a plea—you do a terrible thing, and everybody gets to think it was your idea.

Michael Armstrong and Martin Flumenbaum were, given recent experience, skeptical about any agreement that involved the SEC. They felt that Bill McLucas, the new enforcement chief, was a straight shooter, maybe a Carberry in training. The problem was McLucas's boss. Do a deal with someone like Breeden, they felt, and you can kiss all agreements good-bye—once Breeden had Milken in his clutches, the torture would begin in earnest.

But Flumenbaum had to agree with Arthur Liman that their client couldn't go on. Milken had no filter, he was like a child—every press leak, every negative article, every accusation cut like the first one. In three and a half years, he'd grown no wiser about the judicial process. For the sake of his sanity, he had to end the war.

Milken was going to have difficulty making up his mind—if there was anything his lawyers knew, it was that. So they brought in Judge Simon Rifkind, the patriarch of the firm, to make sense to the client and his wife. "You're crazy if you don't take this plea," Rifkind said. "Only religious fanatics feel they *have* to go to trial."

Michael Milken went home to Encino to think it over.

*　　*　　*

"You're tearing yourself up. You're thinking about it too much," Arthur Liman said, a few days later. "It's like you're on the end of a diving board, looking down. Either jump or don't. But don't keep looking."

"You're wavering, Mike," Steve Ross said.

Michael Milken, up for days, went through the pluses and minuses once more. He never wanted to be a public person; now Ted Turner's helicopters—helicopters he'd financed—flew over his house, invading his family's dwindling privacy. At a trial, the press would be in his face every day. For what? Princeton/Newport, GAF, Paul Bilzerian—all the trials so far had ended in convictions. It hardly mattered that the Princeton/Newport defendants were sentenced to tiny jail terms and minuscule fines; it had taken them a year to get to that point. They also lived near New York—he'd have to uproot his family for six months or more in the event of a trial. And this trial wouldn't be the last. The government had one stick left, and it was beating him with it: In the South, so long as there were charges that could be brought, he would be hounded by litigation. Just the other day, a judge in Texas handed down a thirty-year sentence in an S&L case. With RICO, it might be worse for him; if convicted, he could end up in a facility where he was the only inmate wearing a white collar. And what about Lowell? If he hadn't flown to New York that day in March of 1986, Lowell would never have signed that letter for Drexel; he'd be far from all this trouble.

You can't go to dinner.

You can't save anyone.

You hurt anyone who speaks up for you.

No member of your family will be spared.

Everyone who refuses to lie about you will be indicted.

You're told that you can win at trial. Okay, you may survive—but how many people can you take with you?

So you look at the Wall Street guys who took plea bargains. Robert Freeman, who hit the press about the same time you did: four months. Sandy Lewis: nothing. Boyd Jefferies, who pled to parking and books-and-records violations very similar to what's been negotiated for you: probation. With sentences like that, why fight?

And you're bone-tired. Depressed. Frightened. All your life, you've mainlined optimism—now you're so submerged in despair that your heart tells you one thing and your head another, and you don't know what to think anymore.

All you want is an ending.

When Larry Shamhart pulled the Mercedes into Michael Milken's driveway that April morning, the light was on in Milken's study. Through the window, he could see people pacing. No one emerged. By nine, he realized that Milken wouldn't be going to the office this morning.

Inside the study, Milken's wife and mother sat with him, talking quietly. The family had voted the night before, with Lori and Ferne favoring a fight and a trial. The boys' opinion was split. Bari was too young to be consulted. What Michael felt, no one quite knew.

The phone rang. It was Bill Tatum, publisher of the *Amsterdam News*. Three years earlier, he had wanted to buy the *New York Post*, but no investment bank would take his call. Drexel backed him to the tune of $35 million—a gesture that looked suspiciously like an effort to get an Afro-American installed at a paper read by a lot of people who serve on juries. Today, with perhaps another hundred counts being added to the charges against Milken, he wanted his friend to know that a New York jury would never convict him of anything.

Thank you, Bill. Talk to you.

Jesse Jackson was next to call. Jackson had called often on missions of mercy: children who needed help came begging to him, and he, in turn, went begging to Milken. Today, he began to talk about a girl who needed an operation.

Not today, Jesse. There's something going on here.

That was the last time the Milkens ever heard from Jesse Jackson.

Other callers had a more personal message: No matter what you do, Mike, we love you, we'll always be with you.

In New York, as the deadline approached, lawyers gathered in Arthur Liman's office. Richard Sandler. Martin Flumenbaum. Stephen Kaufman. Robert Litt. Ken Lerer sat ready to handle calls from the press.

Five minutes before the deadline, Liman asked his secretary to call Michael Milken in Encino.

Michael, I've got Richard on another extension.

Hi, Arthur. Hello, Richard. Did you get any rest?

Liman couldn't be diverted today: It's time, Michael. We have to decide.

There was dead silence in Liman's conference room for the next five minutes.

Milken's conversation was rambling and cryptic. He went over the pros and cons. He talked about his anguish. He said he wanted to end the struggle, but if he did, he feared that everything he stood for would be questioned. He kept coming back to that thought: a lifetime of contribution wiped out with a word. With that, he began to sound like a man undergoing amputation without anesthesia.

Toward the end, Liman covered his eyes with his hand.

"Okay," Milken said suddenly, "we'll take their offer."

Liman was stunned. He'd had no idea how this monologue would end.

Are you positive?

Yes.

Gently, Liman ended the call and contacted Alan Cohen, Roger Hayes, John Carroll, and Jess Fardella at the U.S. attorney's office.

My client, he said, has authorized me to proceed.

In Encino, the client and his wife and his mother hugged one another. They cried bitter, hysterical tears. And then, because the women were now so much stronger than he was, they put Michael Milken to bed.

CHAPTER TWENTY-ONE

In the jury room on April 24, 1990, Lori Milken cast a cold eye on John Carroll and Jess Fardella. They said they were pleased to meet her and sorry about the circumstance. They shook her hand. But the prosecutors couldn't, she noted, look her in the eye.

Her husband was calm, almost detached. In the car, he'd talked about America's small companies and wondered where they'd find financing now. Arthur Liman listened, saying nothing, aware that defendants, like patients facing surgery, often focus on unrelated issues to distract themselves.

Now the moment was at hand. Milken checked his pockets. There was one personal item, a picture of his children. And a bulkier item, token of his new status as an admitted felon: a seventeen-hundred-word chronicle of his crimes.

This allocution, as it was known, was the work of many pens. Although the U.S. attorney's office was putting out a statement of its own, it was essential that Milken stand up and admit his crimes. The prosecutors knew how difficult that would be for him—if he had the chance, they suspected, he'd make his offenses sound insignificant. So they'd made his allocution subject to government approval, and they'd haggled over every word. No improvising, they reminded him. You read this exactly as written.

In the courtroom, Lori took a seat next to Lowell, who put an arm around her from the moment the preliminaries began.

There were titters at Judge Wood's questions about Milken's ability to pay the largest individual fine in the history of Wall Street. And there were giggles when Wood said she'd appoint a lawyer if he couldn't afford one.

At last Milken spoke. His tone was thin and flat, a shock for those whose idea of a Wall Street voice was Ivan Boesky's arrogant baritone. What I did was wrong, Milken said, and I knew it at the time. Boesky was not a social friend. Our businesses and philosophies were much different. But Boesky was a major factor in the securities markets and he had the potential to become a significant account—what started as an "arms length and correct" relationship eventually involved "reciprocal accommodations."

Milken rolled through the transactions. I guaranteed Boesky against loss in Fischbach. I guaranteed Boesky against loss in MCA. I assisted Boesky in evading the net-capital rules by holding Helmerich & Payne stock for him. I made adjustments in the price of securities bought and sold by David Solomon for the Finsbury Fund, which wasn't disclosed to the fund's customers. I helped David Solomon lower his taxes by arranging unprofitable transactions.

Two themes ran through all five offenses: a commitment to clients that failed to acknowledge legal limits, and crimes that had nothing to do with junk bonds. "My plea is an acceptance of personal responsibility," Milken emphasized. "Our business was in no way dependent on these practices."

He had one paragraph to go when he cracked.

"This investigation and proceeding are now in their fourth year. This long period has been extremely painful and difficult for my family and friends"—here his voice wobbled and his neck reddened—"as well as myself." He paused for breath. "I realize that by my acts I have hurt those who are closest to me." He began to sob, a surprise to many, though not to his wife, who'd seen him weep at innumerable movies. "I am truly sorry," he blurted, lurching forward. Liman put an arm around him. A glass of water was produced. "I thank the Court for permitting me to add this apology and for its fairness in handling this complex case," he concluded.

Although a crowd of spectators and press photographers waited behind sawhorses on the steps of the courthouse, Milken and his wife decided to exit through the front door. Halfway down the steps, as nervous grins drifted across his face like fast-moving clouds, silence gave way to scattered applause. Only one man cursed: "They should have taken all your money away!"

The Milkens flung themselves into their car, and the Lincoln pulled away quickly. The scene in court and the minor indignity on the steps no longer mattered. On October 1, there would be a sentencing. At last, Milken thought, the agony was almost over.

To Richard Breeden, it didn't matter that the U.S. attorney couldn't nail Milken on insider trading—for Breeden, he'd done that, it wasn't even a close call. Milken was a cheat. A thug specializing in kickbacks. A pickpocket. Who stole, among other things, fifty thousand work hours from the professional lives of the men and women of the SEC.

The SEC chairman contained his apparent loathing of Michael Milken until Judge Wood had accepted Milken's guilty plea.

Then he called a press conference.

"Mr. Milken has been portrayed as wrongly accused and as having simply devoted himself to the financing of small or emerging businesses," Breeden said. "Despite the efforts to mold public opinion, his admissions today demonstrate that he stood at the center of a network of manipulation, fraud, and deceit."

Breeden was now going to set public opinion right—that is, he was going to focus it squarely on Judge Wood.

"Contrary to some reports, the government will not recommend concurrent sentences," he said, as if he knew nothing of the paragraph in the plea agreement that committed the government not to recommend any sentence. "In our view, a substantial period of incarceration should be imposed."

As the defense lawyers saw it, the chairman of the SEC had just breached the plea agreement.

Arthur Liman believed that it had all been arranged—John Carroll and Jess Fardella would speak for the government. The SEC, having won every concession it demanded, would be silent. If Breeden felt compelled to comment, he could shout into his pillow. But he could not call for Judge Wood to ignore the agreement Milken had made with the U.S. attorney.

And so Liman got right on the speakerphone and gave Alan Cohen, the third head of the securities fraud division since the start of the case, the tongue-lashing of his life.

Don't you *remember* all the hours we spent on that one paragraph? Liman asked. Don't you *remember* how important that was to us—don't you *remember* how we said Michael would *never* take a deal if the government was going to call for consecutive sentences? Don't you remember the script we all read this morning? I said, "The government has agreed that it will make no specific recommendation as to the sentence of incarceration. That means the government will not ask the court to impose consecutive sentences in this case." Judge Wood asked John if that was correct. And John said, "That is correct. It's the general practice of our office not to recommend specific sentences, including consecutive sentences, although on certain occasions we have done so." It couldn't have been clearer. Now I find out that you had a copy of Breeden's press release *before* we went into court this morning! Why didn't you say anything to me? What's *happened* to the U.S. attorney's office? We shook hands with you—what is your handshake *worth*? Is integrity just a *word* to you? Don't you care about your *honor*? Is there *nothing* you won't tolerate?

According to Liman, Cohen admitted he had said Breeden wouldn't do anything inconsistent with their understanding. Now he offered to review the SEC's sentencing letter to make sure it wouldn't repeat this error.

The problem is, Liman replied, that you said Breeden was under control. The solace you offer for the future doesn't make up for the prejudice Breeden has already caused—and the damage he's done to your office.

Arthur, we'll make it up to you.*

But Liman wouldn't be appeased. Neither would Kaufman, or Sandler, or any of the lawyers who had participated in the plea discussions.

They fucked us, some said. Let's fuck them—let's withdraw the plea.

But the bright flame of outrage is difficult for lawyers to harness; it burns too near the irrational for comfort. Over the next few days, angry men became reasonable again. Only no one forgot—on either side. And soon the admission of guilt that looked to the world like a declaration of peace became merely the beginning of a harsher war.

---

*Alan Cohen says he made none of these admissions, had no reason to give Liman any solace, and didn't offer to make anything up to Liman.

*   *   *

Michael Milken's picture ran, in color, on the front page of the *Los Angeles Times* the day after the plea. Lori got to the paper first. She read it all the way to the garbage can. By the time she dumped it, all she could think was Michael, Michael, I could slap you for pleading guilty.

Three days later, fifteen-year-old Gregory Milken ran in a school track meet. Lance had said to take the plea, get it over with; Gregory had been all fight, fight, fight. In recent days, he'd been upset by the news coverage. Now, as he neared the finish line, running the fastest race of his life, he had a seizure.

Ignoring Lori's screams, Michael Milken jumped over a fence and ran onto the field. By the time Lori reached them, Gregory's head was cradled in his father's lap. He had stopped shaking. He's okay, Michael said. *He's okay.*

The next day was the annual fund-raiser at Bari's school. Today, Lori had a new upset: Bari knew about the plea, a friend called her and said, hey, your dad was on TV for being a crook. Lori was shattered—she couldn't get out of bed. So Michael took Bari to the fund-raiser. They participated in every event.

That week, Milken made his regular appearance at Project Six. "I want the kids to know I won't disappear," he told Barbara Firestone. With his young friends, everything seemed the same; the conversation was all about them.

"I'm so afraid you'll go away," a girl blurted out, breaking the spell. "I lost my father, and . . ."

"Sometimes friends have to be separated," Milken said, so calm that only Firestone saw the start of tears. "It doesn't mean the friend doesn't care. Or that the friendship won't continue. Or that the friend won't be back."

Still later that week, Michael Jackson had a visit from Milken. The singer seemed to be unaware of a change in his friend's situation. It had to be explained to him. Didn't bother him at all. "I never read the paper," he said.

In May, Michael Milken met his probation officer. Her name was Michalah Bracken, and she was very senior. Also very tough—she had written a probation report on convicted investor Paul Bilzerian so devastating that it was said to have singed the paper.

Tell me about yourself, she said.

He talked about his family.

Lowell particularly interested her.

What does he do? she asked.

Milken started to talk about Lowell, but went right on to the family's foundations. In 1983, he said, he saw a child who lived near the University of Pennsylvania draw a picture of the school—as a fire-breathing dragon. That led to the community outreach program at Penn, paid for by one of his foundations.

How much money do the foundations have?

He responded: $170 million in the Capital Fund; $120 million in the Milken Family Foundation; $60 million in the Medical Foundation; $20 million in the Institute for Job and Capital Formation.

The money didn't seem to throw her.

He had come here alone, Milken said, because he was tired of having his lawyers do all the talking. He had a lot of pent-up energy; he talked at length about his work, about his understanding of his crimes. He had come to feel that he was a poor manager who took responsibility for everything and made promises he shouldn't have.

I've thought about this a hundred times, he said.

Keep thinking about it, she said, challenging him to dig much, much deeper. Understanding is the key.

The next day, Lori Milken had her first visit with the probation officer. Michael's greatness is part of his tragedy, Lori said, echoing her husband. He loves to help people. He has incredible energy. He is the most optimistic person I've ever known.

Michael's problem, as Lori explained it, was that he couldn't stop helping people. We had a housekeeper, she told Bracken. She'd been with us since New Jersey, and we brought her out here with us, and now she was getting on. She had to stop working, but I couldn't tell her. Michael went out and bought some Danish and went to her house. He sat with her for an hour, and he couldn't do it either. She worked for us until she was seventy-six, and then she decided she'd like to enjoy life a little more, so Michael retired her on full pay. And that's how he was with everybody—he couldn't say no.

What mostly concerned Lori, though, was the health of her children. She said Michael had everybody's medical history in his head. Before every doctor's appointment, he called the doctor to bring him up to speed on the family's latest problems. Whenever there was a medical emergency—the recent track meet, for example—he handled it.

It's inconceivable to me how I will ever be able to cope in such stressful circumstances if Michael isn't there with me, she said.

Michalah Bracken told Lori that she was quite sure the medical condition of her three children would be a factor with Judge Wood, who was, after all, a parent.

In August, Michalah Bracken submitted her report to Judge Wood. In it, the judge got her first look at Milken's wealth. According to a financial statement he submitted, he had $550 million in eight bank accounts, $14 million in nonmarketable securities, and $505 million tied up in more than seventy private investments. The wizard alleged to be worth $5 billion had actually banked about $1.1 billion.

Then came the bigger surprises.

Bracken appreciated that peers talked of Milken as a business "iconoclast" and "visionary." But, she emphasized, he still made time for family, friends, and causes. "The Milken Foundations," she noted, "are now among the largest charitable institutions in the country."

Bracken understood popular opinion held that greed was Milken's primary motivation. She found, however, that "his wealth is the result of legitimate business activities." Greed played less of a role in this case than a need to solve everybody's problems. "The answer to this offense," she suggested, "may lie in part in his own statement: 'I wanted to be all things to all people.'"

Then Michalah Bracken delivered her biggest surprise.

"Among Milken's strengths are his inability to accept defeat, his total commitment to causes he considers 'just and right,' and his vision concerning business and society," she wrote in her conclusion. "His weakness was that, as creator and head of the High-Yield Bond Department at Drexel, these convictions were more important than his responsibilities and obligation to conduct business fully within the parameters of the law. Yet, despite his fall, Milken is an individual still able to contribute to society and to create positive changes in the future."

If Milken had written it himself, this report couldn't have

been more favorable—this was not the grinning criminal master-mind, raping the innocent, but a fallible idealist who had merely gone too far. Between the lines, this characterization gave Judge Wood plenty of ammunition to give Milken a mild sentence.

It was not what anyone expected from Michalah Bracken.

Such was the incredulity in government circles, it is rumored, that Ms. Bracken was encouraged to change her report. If that happened, Bracken piled one disappointment on top of another. Her report stood.

He took care of people.

That was what many of the letters his friends wrote to the judge said, and that was the theme Arthur Liman developed in the sentencing memorandum he submitted to Judge Wood on September 10, 1990. When Milken coached his sons' basketball teams, he cared more that everybody contributed than about winning. An associate was diagnosed with anorexia; he read up on the disease, offered unlimited Häagen-Dazs, called often. He comforted strays, rewarded teachers, sought no credit.

As with individuals, Liman argued, so with his business relationships.

Prior to 1986, Liman pointed out, no criminal prosecution had ever been brought for the offenses that, for Milken, were felonies. No one had ever been charged with aiding and abetting the filing of a false 13(d) schedule by another party. Prior to 1986, no one had been prosecuted criminally for aiding and abetting books-and-records violations by another broker. To the present moment, Liman had never heard of anyone being prosecuted for failing to disclose an attempt to recoup expenses from a portfolio manager. And the other offenses that were felony counts for Milken were once subject only to civil charges.*

---

*"Many of the prosecution theories that we used [in the Drexel case] were novel," John Carroll acknowledged in his talk at Seton Hall Law School. "Many of the statutes that we charged under weren't novel statutes, but they hadn't been charged as crimes before—I guess if the government is only supposed to do what it's done before, we're guilty of criminalizing technical offenses. But I think that's sort of a misguided approach to the problem. . . . I think it's a misguided use of our resources to just fight the last war. From a policy point of view—and this is very much a part of our enforcement program— we're looking to fight the next war. We're looking to find the next area of conduct that is willfully wrong, that meets any sort of statutory definition of what criminal conduct is, but that hasn't been prosecuted."

According to Liman, Michael Milken—who paid more taxes on earned income than anyone else in the country from 1984 to 1988—committed these dubious crimes not for personal gain, but to accommodate clients.

The problem was a character flaw, not greed.

In this case, Liman noted, "public debate has taken on the appearance of a heresy trial." He asked the judge to return proportion and fairness to Milken's case—to treat him as an individual, not as a symbol. Consider the history of white-collar sentences in the Second Circuit, Liman urged. Consider that Milken didn't personally profit by his crimes. Consider that he has already been stripped of the presumption of innocence for almost four years. Six hundred million dollars represents nearly all of the after-tax income Milken made at Drexel from 1983 to 1987—consider what that means as punishment.

Consider his gifts: his rapport with the young, his passion for community service. And then, Liman said, consider Charles Atkins, who founded a business solely to generate phony tax losses. His frauds cost the government hundreds of millions of dollars. To conceal them, he perjured himself and obstructed justice. And yet, although the judge who sentenced him felt his crimes threatened the integrity of the financial markets, Atkins got two years plus 500 hours of community service—and, later, the judge substituted another year of community service for the jail time.

Turn this man, who did so much less, over to the Los Angeles Police Department, Liman pleaded. Chief Gates would welcome him at DARE, the Drug Abuse Resistance Education Program. Let him work in the drug program, let him help reduce the dropout rate. Sentence him to community service, Your Honor. Hold him accountable, but don't send him to jail.

"Milken's crimes formed a pattern of calculated fraud, deceit and corruption of the highest magnitude," the government's sentencing memorandum began. "In a highly sophisticated and systematic way, Milken endeavored to enhance his power and enlarge his wealth."

Carroll and Fardella's rhetoric was consistent. Milken behaved like "the kingpins of other sophisticated criminal enterprises." His business had "the appearance of normality." He enforced "a code of silence." His objective was simple: "power and wealth." His offenses were "crimes of greed, arrogance and betrayal." He viewed himself as "above the law." He "corrupted the very market he is sometimes credited with creating."

Nothing aberrational about it, "Milken's criminal activity was a significant and necessary component of the growth of his power." His decision to plead guilty thus indicated only "surrender, not contrition." By delaying cooperation until after sentencing, he may have moved the crimes of co-conspirators behind the statute of limitations—this, after fighting so long that he had, in effect, conferred immunity on who knows how many associates.

Milken, the prosecutors argued, wants it both ways. On one hand, he built an industry; at the same time, he asks us to believe that he was weak and distracted and easy to bully. Nonsense. He had an "apparent obsession with accumulation," he was "driven to capture every profit." In the years 1983–1987, his compensation ranged from 43 percent to 81 percent of Drexel's profits— how can he claim a disinterest in wealth? He was, in fact, so obsessed with making money that he was largely responsible for Drexel's bankruptcy: "The excesses in Drexel's corporate culture that Milken fathered hastened the collapse of the company."

In April, the prosecutors wrote, they anticipated cooperation from Milken that would bear "certain fruit." Now, they expected less: "Milken has indicated that he has little intention truthfully to cooperate." He should be punished "as the unreconstructed and unapologetic man that he is"—with no credit for his "many post-investigation social and charitable good works."*

For punishment to be just, the prosecutors concluded, Milken should be judged not only for the crimes he has admitted, but for many others he hasn't acknowledged—for "the enormity of his crimes." And that meant prison. Prison for a long, long time.

Judge Wood was a very popular pen pal that season. Some letters came from those who hated Milken: "We wish to express our desire to see him hung by the balls until death." Some came from readers of the *Los Angeles Times*, which published her ad-

---

*Judge Wood asked the probation officer to investigate this last charge, and learned that Milken's good works began long before November of 1986. In court, she passed this information on to John Carroll, who seemed puzzled by the accusation in his memo: "I can't, off the top of my head, think of where that was. It might well have been in there, but it was not intended."

dress for the benefit of "people interested in writing to the judge about Milken before he is sentenced."

Several hundred came from friends whose names the world would never recognize. A woman with multiple sclerosis told of the times when she was sick and despairing, and the Milkens would uncomplainingly take care of her young son. Another woman's daughter had been hit by a car, and the brain damage had caused her to lose all sense of appropriateness; for more than a decade, Milken had looked after her. Childhood friends who swore he'd never changed, teachers who still knew him, charity volunteers who had seen him give his time without seeking any privileges or rewards—these letters spoke of a man working hard to qualify for sainthood.

Men of power and position also weighed in. Vice Chairman Howard Gittis of Revlon wrote that Milken had often recommended bank financing for his company's transactions, although that meant a huge loss of fees for Drexel. Armand Hammer, viewing the 1980s as "a time of the greatest transition in human history since World War II," believed that "Michael Milken led the charge which helped to assure that American democracy could thrive." Roger Stone—chairman of the container company that the SEC alleged had been defrauded by Milken—called him "one of the most outstanding individuals I have ever known." Peter Magowan, chairman of Safeway Stores and grandson of the founder of Merrill Lynch, had once opposed Milken, but later became his client and friend: "If I had a son, Mike Milken is everything I would want my boy to grow up to be."

The clergy of several faiths also wished to be heard. Isaiah Zeldin—Milken's rabbi, and his counselor in sessions that were as close to psychiatry as Milken would allow himself to come—felt Milken's "punishment to date has been severe enough." And Roger Mahoney, the Roman Catholic cardinal of Los Angeles, endorsed Milken's plea to work in the city's antidrug program.

Milken's upper-echelon Drexel colleagues also wrote. Chris Anderson—in 1984, he'd introduced Dr. Ned Kennan to Fred Joseph—argued that any guilt of Milken's ought to be spread around. Milken was my product, he said. On the East Coast, we invented him and packaged him, we put flesh and fur on a myth, we told our clients "Mike says" when we'd never talked to Mike, and when he faltered, we created new products to replace him. And now we're sentencing our creation.

Charles Huber, who'd known Milken since 1972, came closest to summarizing Milken's refusal to judge and his unexpected passivity when he likened him to Billy Budd: "He would rather bow to an unreasonable request from an alleged friend than either challenge the friendship or deny the request. . . . If Mike had a fault, it was that he would do business with anyone."

The picture that emerged was of a socially committed genius who didn't know when to stop helping people. It was the old theme: His greatness was also his weakness. And it popped up so often in these letters that a reader was confronted with the old dilemma: Michael Milken, villain or victim.

Judge Wood had plenty of time to read these letters, and the probation report, and the sentencing memos—by her edict, all government and defense documents were to be in her hands twenty days before she pronounced sentence on Milken, so everyone would have a chance to reply and she would have a chance to reflect.

But when it came time to reflect, Wood found that she was still dealing with completely opposite descriptions of reality. She was unable to decide which was true. She was, she suggested, not going to be able to sentence Milken on October 1. Instead, she was thinking of convening a Fatico hearing in order to gather more evidence.

The way out was for the defense and prosecution to find some common ground. Wood had noted that, in his April allocution, Milken had admitted "other accommodations of a similar nature between the Boesky Organization and Drexel, some of which were wrong." Now she requested that Milken be more specific.

On September 26, Arthur Liman messengered a letter to Judge Wood that listed those accommodations. From May to July of 1985, he wrote, Boesky had parked ABC and Ensearch securities at Drexel. That January, when Boesky complained of losses in Fischbach and MCA, Milken advised him to buy Diamond Shamrock stock and indicated that he should get 50 percent credit for any gains in that security. As it turned out, Boesky lost money; that winter, Milken put Boesky into eight bond issues in order to make up losses in Fischbach, MCA, and Diamond Shamrock. And, that May, Milken recommended that Boesky make his debut as a corporate owner by buying a company called Harris

311

Graphics, with a portion of any profits he made being credited to Drexel.

These admissions gained Milken nothing. On September 27, Judge Wood ordered a Fatico hearing. In this hearing, Wood said, the U.S. attorney would select two to five instances of alleged wrongdoing that Milken hadn't admitted, and then the defense would respond. Each side would have twenty hours.

"All I am looking for," she explained, "is insight into defendant's character."

On September 27, unaware that Judge Wood was walking into court to order a Fatico hearing, the chairman of the SEC express-mailed a letter to her about Milken.

Richard Breeden—who had, with great success, already staged one takeover of this case—had not allowed himself to be controlled by the U.S. attorney in New York.

If anything, his ten-page, single-spaced letter represented what defense lawyers considered a further breach of Arthur Liman's understanding with the prosecutors. For while some of this letter was the April press conference warmed over—"Michael Milken has engaged in an array of illegal conduct that is unparalleled in the history of the federal securities laws"—Breeden now made fresh and unproven allegations.

Milken used Boesky, he said, to trade on inside information in the Diamond Shamrock/Occidental Petroleum, Storer, National Gypsum, Lorimar, and Viacom transactions. Milken's victims, he argued, included "financial institutions . . . that have suffered enormous economic losses which will have to be borne by investors and taxpayers alike"—code for the S&L crisis. For Breeden, the only way to avoid "a double standard of justice" was to impose a sentence equal to Milken's massive, cynical crimes.*

This time, Arthur Liman communicated his displeasure directly to Judge Wood. He was astonished, he said, that Breeden deliberately sent his letter at the last minute in an effort to deny the defense any chance to respond before the anticipated sentenc-

---

*For all Breeden's verbiage, he didn't mention that, at the time of the settlement, Liman and Kaufman proposed to him that Michael Milken come to Washington and talk about his business with the SEC chairman. According to Liman and Kaufman, Breeden recoiled so violently he appeared to have been shot; according to Breeden, this conversation never happened.

ing date. With the sentencing postponed, though, he had the chance to tell the judge a few things Breeden omitted to tell her.

First, Liman said, Breeden's assertions bore no relationship to facts—the U.S. attorney never charged insider trading in those transactions. Moreover, Breeden didn't acknowledge that Milken would gladly have defended these SEC charges, but that the SEC chairman had personally insisted on a joint settlement in April. Finally, Liman called the letter "a political document, meant for the press, appealing to the political sentiment against mergers and acquisitions, leveraged buyouts and investments by savings and loans in high-yield bonds, all of which Mr. Breeden conveniently forgets were expressly authorized by legislation." The Breeden letter, Liman concluded, "deserves to be rejected by the Court."

Events soon overtook Breeden's letter, rendering it a kind of historical oddity, an expression of Milken's all-purpose use as political football and symbol of the 1980s. If Wood considered Breeden's views, she never mentioned it. For the first time since he'd injected himself into the Milken case, the chairman of the SEC was the one who had to learn a lesson—timing is everything.

For prosecutors and lawyers, who had less than two weeks to prepare, the prospect of a Fatico hearing was dismaying. For Milken, it was far worse. He'd spent the summer preparing himself for sentencing—he was primed like an athlete for October 1. Now, all the efforts of his lawyers were meaningless; only the hearings counted.

This could be good, Arthur Liman had told Lori Milken when the possibility of a Fatico hearing was first mentioned.

This is awful, Liman confided to her, when possibility turned to reality. I don't think Michael's up to this.

That was an understatement. Milken felt bewildered and betrayed. They blew it, he told family and friends. The lawyers didn't do a good job, and now we have this.

Milken's family and friends were unaware of his inability to play a game he didn't dominate, and all the flawed strategy that flowed from that—the waffling, the grudging admissions, the provocative refusal to give the prosecutors his immediate cooperation. And so they took up a new theme—Milken had been martyred twice, first by the government, and then by his own lawyers.

You make a plea agreement, Milken's friends now said, and you don't get *anything* in return? You think the government's out to screw you, and you don't tie their hands? You settle because you don't think Mike can go on, and then you put him in a position where he gets killed if he doesn't take the stand? What kind of no-deal deal is this? What does $600 million buy these days? And what happens from here? How bad can this thing get?

CHAPTER TWENTY-TWO

Michael Milken usually had a driver take him from the Carlyle Hotel to Arthur Liman's office. Now, he liked to walk, with a bodyguard rushing to keep up. For some on the vast support staff, wondering why he walked was something to do. Fresh air, one thought. Exercise, another guessed. Normal life, something he's never known, suggested a third. Then, in the elevator, some assistants saw the fear and confusion. It had never occurred to them that Michael Milken was human, and they suddenly felt bad about all the double-billing of time by junior people, the personal cab rides charged to his defense, the useless databases that answered no real questions.

Liman, with just two weeks to prepare for court, had no time for the client. Milken turned to machines, docile companions that fed him trivia and filled the hours. He punched up Drexel trades on Lexicon, examining them from every possible angle. He spent half a day at the microfilm viewer, searching *The Wall Street Journal* for minutiae. Once, he called for a computer run twenty categories wide in an effort to compare convertible bonds for a certain period. Another time, he asked for articles about stray bullets killing kids.

What is he doing here? someone asked.

The answer came back: He's fighting for his life.

*   *   *

Judge Wood had explicitly ruled that there be no opening statements, but John Carroll gave one anyway. It's not just the transaction, he began, it's the context. Milken and Boesky invented the crimes; subordinates carried them out. By the time they got to Wickes, there was no clean slate.

Until January of 1985, Milken and Drexel didn't have a significant relationship with Wickes. But that company was coming out of bankruptcy, and its CEO, Sandy Sigoloff, was known to be interested in expansion and acquisition—Milken wanted his business. He got it. Over the next three and a half years, Drexel collected $118 million in fees from Wickes. The way Milken cemented that relationship, Carroll contended, was by ingratiating himself with the client through an illegal favor.

In 1985, Wickes preferred stock paid a large dividend. This was good for preferred stockholders, bad for the company's cash flow. But this was not written in stone. If Wickes common stock traded at or above 6⅛ for twenty out of thirty consecutive trading days, those who owned the preferred would have to redeem it for common—and Wickes would save $15 million in dividends.

On April 22, 1985, Wickes common had hit the target price for nineteen of the past twenty-eight days. All Sigoloff needed was one more good trading session. This, thought someone at Drexel, is a job for Ivan Boesky. The very next day—starting just twenty minutes before the close of the market—the Boesky organization bought 1.9 million of the 3.5 million Wickes shares purchased during that trading session. The stock closed at 6⅛. Wickes lost the dividend.

We contend that Milken was behind the manipulation, Carroll concluded. He had the relationship with Wickes. He could guarantee Boesky against loss. And he had the hunger for fees.

We don't dispute the manipulation of Wickes by Boesky and Drexel, Arthur Liman began. But my client didn't do it. Not everything that happened at Drexel is his fault.

My client had a great deal of contact with Ivan Boesky, Liman continued, but you won't see Boesky here. He's not being called by the government because you can infer he wouldn't claim my client ever asked him to buy Wickes.

There was a much better reason for the prosecutors to keep Boesky as far from this courtroom as possible. A few months earlier, Boesky had testified for the government in the Mulheren trial. There, he had trouble remembering anything. He didn't recall what his plea bargain required of him. He didn't remember transferring money to his wife's account shortly before he made his deal with the government. His memory was only slightly better on post-settlement events—asked if he'd broken the rules while in prison, he said, "There were a couple of chaps who did laundry there, and I gave them a few quarters to do my laundry." When Boesky was finished, Mulheren's lawyer called him "a pile of human garbage." No one rushed to disagree.

"Had Milken gone to trial, you would have had to put Boesky on the stand," former prosecutor Bruce Baird said later. "In his absence, he would have been the lion that didn't roar." But in a hearing like this, with lawyers invited to roam through issues of character, John Carroll's hands were tied; no prosecutor in the land would want Arthur Liman and his investigators' reports near this reptilian amnesiac.

If ever a courtroom understood Carroll's dilemma—and Liman's—it was this one. These were professional Milken watchers; they knew the players, caught the nuances, and retained every detail. Most of the newspaper journalists seated in the jury box had been following the case from the beginning. In the spectators' section, there were many Drexel graduates, still sleek and alert, sitting with the California clan. Heads moved in unison as lawyers and prosecutors traded shots; it was like watching serve and volley at the Open.

And Arthur Liman, on his feet for the first time, had just hit what might be an ace.

Michael Davidoff had been Boesky's trader, but Boesky barely figured in his testimony. Nor did Milken. The request to buy came from Cary Maultasch. In the frenzy of Wickes buying, Davidoff had called his boss. Do what Maultasch asks, Boesky had said. Jess Fardella didn't press; Davidoff was only an order taker.

Martin Flumenbaum stepped up to cross-examine.

Had Davidoff ever met Milken?

"I'm not sure. I have seen a lot of pictures of him."

Ever had a call from Milken directing him to buy Wickes? No.

Did Maultasch mention Milken's name?

No.

Did Milken ever call directing him to buy any stock?
No.

Milken called you, though, about MGM bond trades?
Yes.

Look at this chart. Milken was working on the MGM restructuring at this time. If he wanted you to trade on inside information and make up some of Mr. Boesky's huge losses, would it have made sense to buy some then?

Yes.

But Mr. Milken didn't call you, did he?
No.

Poor Cary Maultasch.

Way back in the winter of 1987, when Boyd Jefferies agreed to plead guilty to two felonies, some of his offenses were frighteningly familiar to Maultasch. He had his lawyers call the U.S. attorney. But nothing Maultasch could tell them was good enough for him to get immunity. Over the next few months, his lawyers tried again, and each time, they stalled at the same hurdle.

In February of 1988, Maultasch decided the problem was his lawyers. He hired Reid Weingarten, a Washington lawyer who'd been a federal prosecutor for a decade and was now serving as special prosecutor of Richard Secord in the Iran-contra proceedings, and Nashville lawyer Aubrey Harwell. They immediately called the prosecutors to see if they could do better.

He's going to jail, John Carroll assured them.

Come on, this is a *witness*, they countered.

No way, Carroll said. If anything, this guy is a candidate for a RICO indictment.

When the prosecutors got their hands on the Princeton/Newport tapes, they took an even harder line. It was Maultasch's misfortune to have filled in at the Beverly Hills office over Christmas of 1984. During those three days, Maultasch took a call from a Princeton/Newport trader—and to the prosecutors, one equivocal sentence at the end of this short conversation was grounds for a second RICO.

Shocked, Weingarten called Rudolph Giuliani, whom he knew and respected.

When we determine someone is worthy of prosecution, Giuliani told him, we do whatever it takes.

Shortly after this call, Jim Dahl got immunity.

Maultasch's lawyers were appalled.

If you immunize Dahl, they told the U.S. attorneys, you ought to give Cary a reward and a public apology.

Giuliani's response was to lay out the case against Maultasch for the Justice Department. Washington affirmed the two RICO indictments against Maultasch; Harwell and Weingarten went back to Giuliani one last time. And, early in December of 1988, they made the best deal they could—the government would defer prosecution. At a later date, the U.S. attorney would review Maultasch's cooperation, his truthfulness in any testimony he might give, and his culpability. If the government still wanted to prosecute, he had a choice. He could plead guilty to a one-count, nonfraud felony that had never resulted in a jail sentence and would not require him to pay a civil penalty—or he could go to trial.

That satisfied everyone but the SEC.

We want "seven figures," the enforcement division said.

No seven figures, no nothing, Weingarten told Giuliani.

Giuliani now made a call of his own. When he was finished, Maultasch owed the SEC not a penny. Though he would be banned from the securities business, that ban could be reversed without a financial penalty.

In the fall of 1990, the government suddenly noticed it needed Cary Maultasch to testify at the Fatico hearing. It hadn't been the U.S. attorney's idea to put anything in writing, but Maultasch's lawyers had been firm: no letter, Cary takes the Fifth. The prosecutors' need was great. Overnight, two RICO indictments dematerialized.

Two and a half years after he first approached the government, Cary Maultasch had—thanks to Fatico—wriggled off the hook.

In his preparation for Fatico, John Carroll had been very general with Maultasch—he sensed that his line of questioning, if not his actual questions, would immediately make their way to Liman. Carroll's prediction was off. It took three days for his briefing of Maultasch to reach Liman's desk.

Now, Maultasch slouched in the witness chair, tie loosened, as if he'd warmed up for the occasion by shooting some baskets

319

in the park behind the courthouse—with immunity in his pocket, it seemed he was finally expressing his disdain for the feds.

After leading Maultasch through his purchases of Wickes stock, Carroll turned his attention to a more damaging scenario, the events of October and November of 1986. The phone calls from Los Angeles about Milken's meeting with Boesky. His advice to Milken to "be careful" with Boesky. His trip to Los Angeles, and his whispered conversation with Milken in the Drexel conference room.

As a witness on the Wickes manipulation, Maultasch was like clay—on cross-examination, he gave the defense everything. Yes, he'd asked Davidoff to buy Wickes. No, he'd never been asked by Milken to do so. Nor had he told Milken what he'd done. He had, he said, acted at the request of Drexel trader Peter Gardiner—laying the burden of proving Milken's involvement squarely on Gardiner.

And yet, despite Maultasch's inability to tie Milken to the crimes the government alleged, his stories of paranoia and intrigue set a tone for the testimony to come: light on incriminating evidence, heavy on atmospherics. If the prosecutors kept this up, Milken was in danger of being damned on a charge that had never been seriously pursued before—obstruction of justice.

Peter Gardiner lacked the sharp-eyed hunger of many Milken associates, which may explain why he was the low man in the pecking order in Beverly Hills, earning $71,000 in his first year. The most he made there as a salesman and trader was $1.3 million—he had no economic reason to protect Milken.

And yet he lied to the grand jury. And to the SEC. And, perhaps, to the New York Stock Exchange.

"I lied to exculpate myself," Gardiner told Judge Wood. "I lied to protect others who were as yet untouched by the investigation. I lied as a function of having lied to myself for a long time about what had gone on at Drexel."

But after Milken pled guilty, Gardiner—who had received a target letter from prosecutors advising him of an imminent indictment for insider trading—said that he began to fear his former boss would turn him in. Belatedly, and in exchange for immunity, he now said he would tell the truth. And this truth was damning—on the day Boesky bought all that Wickes stock, he testified, Milken pointed to his computer screen and said, "Peter, Wickes, six and one eighth."

Liman went after that story on cross-exam.

You heard all that over the din of the trading room—where Gardiner sat about forty feet from Milken—and then you called Maultasch and told him to load up on Wickes?

"I can't answer yes or no, I just don't know. It's possible, but I just don't have any recollection one way or the other."

"Did you know that Boesky was buying shares?"

"I don't recall."

"You don't recall asking Mr. Maultasch to have Boesky buy a million shares?"

"No, I don't."

"You don't recall asking Mr. Maultasch to have Boesky buy another five hundred thousand shares?"

"I don't recall it."

"And you don't recall having another conversation with him and asking him to have Boesky buy another three hundred thousand shares?"

"That is correct."

All Gardiner distinctly remembered, it turned out, was Michael Milken smiling after the close of the market. "Looks like we lost the dividend," he quoted Milken as saying.

Judge Wood listened attentively. Reporters scribbled. But they didn't write what the prosecutors would have liked. Giving immunity to an admitted perjurer months after Milken's guilty plea hadn't produced the desired result—the first case of Milken's alleged additional wrongdoing had just fallen apart.

"The witnesses in this case are under a horrible burden," John Carroll told Judge Wood, in an effort to explain the weak testimony the government was presenting. "They are testifying against a man they worked for, who was their boss, who is today one of the most powerful people in the financial community. These witnesses are not happy to be here. You have seen that. These witnesses have mixed allegiances. You have seen that. I sit with these people in my office, Your Honor. They are intimidated to a large extent."

Michael Milken dashed off another note and pushed it to Arthur Liman. He had generated hundreds of these messages already, most on matters that were trivial. And then at night, when

Liman was preparing for the next day's witnesses, Milken would appear with more details he wanted his lawyer to bring out. He couldn't see that Judge Wood grew impatient with Liman when he focused on the technicalities of the bond business—but then, he really couldn't see himself in a courtroom, bound by customs over which he had no control. In his crisis, Milken retreated internally to the world of the trading floor, where statistics could be marshaled to support his side of the story. If the judge were a bond buyer, he could sell her some; he just had to move her into his world.

Michael, I don't have time to present her with all these statistics, Liman would moan. We have to stick to the issues.

He *is* the client, Richard Sandler would say.

Let me spend a few minutes gathering my thoughts, and then we'll talk, Liman would tell him.

Before the hearings began, Michael Armstrong had sent Liman a memo with a dozen suggestions. One was about the importance of putting Milken on the witness stand. The issue for Judge Wood is Milken's character, he wrote; to reveal that, Milken would have to speak for himself.

"He's going to have to testify pretty soon anyway," Armstrong reasoned, "and the government may possibly be a little leery of crossing him too hard because they still have some hope he will be a witness for them. It will be much tougher for the judge to sentence Michael to a long period of incarceration if she gets to know him a little bit. . . . The one great danger is that the judge will not believe him. That is a matter for preparation."

Arthur Liman had a team of lawyers and paralegals in the courtroom. While John Carroll and Jess Fardella typed their own memos and pushed their own evidence carts into court, he had only to make a request and an assistant would rush over from a special downtown war room with another museum-class exhibit. Insofar as a lawyer could be prepared, Liman was ready.

But Michael Milken was not. Nor would he be. Day after day, he wrote his notes. Night after night, he stalked the Paul, Weiss halls, hectoring, obsessed, burned out. This was no intimidator, this was no powerhouse; this was an emasculated defendant whose best witnesses had been systematically eliminated by target letters and who faced prosecution for perjury if he testified in his own behalf and wasn't believed. He was befuddled, indecisive, and easily rattled—although Liman agreed with Armstrong in theory, he saw no way to put this fragile and miserable man on the witness stand.

When Henry Kravis first met Michael Milken, he didn't get a word in. Milken talked, he listened, and twenty minutes later, although Kravis didn't know what the hell Milken was saying, he was quite clear that this unusual creature was capable of raising vast amounts of money. Drexel soon began to finance some of the leveraged buyouts that were the signature transactions of Kohlberg Kravis Roberts, known on Wall Street as KKR.

In 1985, KKR went after Storer Communications, a cable television company that had attracted the attention of several other bidders. Kravis was fearless when he thought a deal was worth it—three years later, KKR bought RJR Nabisco for $25 billion—and, to him, Storer was. He secured a "highly confident" letter from Drexel, raised his bid, and flew off to Wimbledon with Fred Joseph and other Drexel executives while Milken focused on raising the money.

That was not so easily done. A new bidder appeared, driving the price higher. Now the deal was very rich—according to some knowledgeable investors, too rich to be successful. In order to make it more attractive, Milken had to devise some novel securities. But even they weren't magic—because KKR had not yet hit the towering home runs that are now associated with its name, investors were skittish. Still, Milken believed in Storer. Believed in it so much that, when Drexel refused to invest its capital, he said he would commit $261 million of his own money to the preferred stock.

Drexel had told KKR, early on, that "equity sweeteners"—warrants—needed to be made available in order to make the sale of this preferred stock more attractive. That was fine with KKR. "Just sell the deal," Kravis reportedly said. What Drexel had not told KKR was that employee partnerships in Beverly Hills were buying the preferred and getting the equity.

Because Milken and his associates were so keen on having these warrants, they weren't generally made available to investors. And so, by the time the dust had settled, Michael and Lowell Milken, their families, and the employee partnerships owned 82 percent of the warrants. The rest came to be owned by some institutional buyers, some executives—and some fund managers who were among Drexel's better customers. Three years later, when these warrants were converted to cash, cable properties had become so successful that the total profit was $172 million.

From the government's point of view, Storer was a classic example of Milken greed. To make money now, he'd defrauded KKR—even asking, at the last minute, for KKR to reduce the price of the Storer warrants from $10 million to $5 million. To make more money in the future, he'd bribed customers. Along the way, he'd violated Drexel policy.

Even Milken's staunchest allies feared these days in court. Milken might have been justified in taking a big dip in exchange for his mammoth commitment to buy the preferred stock. KKR, the most sophisticated of all Drexel's clients, might well have understood that the transaction would never have gone forward without those warrants. And Drexel policy didn't demand disclosure to the client.

None of that mattered. In hindsight, it didn't seem pertinent that Milken was willing to take a major financial risk here—or that he had, in his view, committed more of his own money to the deal than KKR had. What stood out was how much he made, and that it looked like a sure thing, and that fund managers who did business with Drexel were now indebted to him. Whether Storer was criminal or not, it looked indisputably sleazy.

If Terren Peizer was supposed to bolster the government's claim that Milken had bribed fund managers by offering them the chance to buy Storer warrants, he was another dud. But he provided damaging testimony on a topic that kept bubbling under the surface of this hearing—obstruction of justice. In his interviews with the prosecutors, he had recalled that Michael and Lowell Milken rushed toward each other and met a few feet from his desk after they heard the Boesky news; today, he remembered only that Michael hurried into his brother's office.

Peizer was most expansive on the subject of a blue ledger book with a record of Finsbury trading. He had, he claimed, handed it over to Lorraine Spurge, Milken's Syndicate manager, at Milken's request. He did this, he said, in the office kitchenette, with the faucet running. "It seemed like everyone was talking and running faucets," he recalled.

In his cross-exam, Arthur Liman began gently. Then he produced the paper that, Peizer had told prosecutors, was written by Milken. Was this Milken's writing?

Peizer thought so.

Liman handed over a sample of Milken's actual script. The difference was striking. Could Peizer comment on that difference?

"I don't know how to articulate this—in terms of the writing, it is a different format," Peizer said of the sheet that had been so instrumental in winning immunity for him.

You've told us a story about my client going to his brother's office after the Boesky announcement, Liman said. Didn't you tell the grand jury that Lowell came out of his office and they met sort of halfway?

"That sounds familiar."

Is it a fact that Lowell was sick and out of the office that day?

"Anything is possible. It is hard for me to believe."

Liman took Peizer through another inconsistency—the writing he'd given the government that he said was Lowell Milken's but turned out not to be. He noted that Lorraine Spurge had sworn that Peizer had never given her a trading book. He showed Peizer the certification he'd signed for Drexel attorneys attesting that he'd turned over all documents when, in fact, he hadn't. He brought out that, to Peizer's knowledge, Milken never bribed fund managers, which was the crux of the government's charge in the Storer case. And he got Peizer to admit that Milken had never asked him to destroy or suppress documents, and never asked him to lie to the prosecutors or cover anything up.

Liman's delicate cross-examination didn't lead the prosecutor to ask follow-up questions that could have lured Peizer into unknown territory. By the same token, he had scarcely dented Peizer's story about the Finsbury notebook.

Judge Wood, a devoted reader of grand jury minutes, had one question that the prosecutors had, curiously, failed to ask.

There was a time when, as Michael Milken watched, you cleared out your desk drawer in order to give documents to the Drexel lawyers? Did Milken say anything?

"'If you don't have them, you can't provide them,' Milken told me." And then, Peizer said, Milken opened his own desk drawer. It was empty.

The government next called Fred Joseph. The courtroom tensed. This was the kind of great confrontation that only a trial can provide—former partners at odds with one another, each holding who knows what cards.

On the witness stand, however, Fred Joseph offered low-key testimony about the Storer transaction. He said that Milken had violated Drexel policy by giving favored treatment to individuals. He testified that Drexel had been denied an opportunity to buy Storer warrants for its own account. He was quite certain that Milken hadn't told the truth when he said there were no fund managers in Drexel partnerships.

But Fred Joseph didn't remember Milken loaning the firm $27 million at the end of 1985, around the same time as the Storer deal. He didn't remember that, just before Storer, Drexel's Corporate Finance Department had invested in a leveraged buyout for Calvin Klein; some of his closest associates took equity in that. He didn't remember that fund managers had been invited to invest in Drexel partnerships before—including one partnership in which his wife and a Drexel lawyer were investors. Nor did he remember, until Liman confronted him with his grand jury testimony, that when Drexel declined to buy the Storer preferred he authorized Milken to buy it and the warrants. At that time, he had indicated that, far from being angry with Milken, he was grateful to him—Milken's investment enabled Drexel to complete the deal and obtain huge fees.

Fred Joseph, who had been expected to be an exciting witness, turned out to have a memory problem that rendered his testimony dull and meaningless.

Kindercare provided responsible child care for working mothers—was there anything more socially useful than that? Not to Drexel. Milken mentioned Kindercare often in his speeches. He considered opening a Kindercare facility in the Beverly Hills office. The firm showcased Kindercare in its commercials. Kindercare returned the affection: Ninety percent of its $120 million investment portfolio passed through Drexel.

Now John Carroll was calling a surprise Storer witness—Richard Grassgreen, Kindercare's portfolio manager.

Would you, Carroll began, identify this document?

It's an application for immunity.

Have you entered into a cooperation and plea agreement with the government?

Yes.

What are your obligations under this agreement?

To plead guilty to two counts of felony and to return all the money I received to the company. To testify fully . . .

Grassgreen had defrauded his own company, he said, but Milken was unaware of that. And yet, although Grassgreen had stolen whatever wasn't nailed down from his own company, he insisted he had asked Milken whether Kindercare—and not him—should buy these warrants. This drew a rare laugh in the courtroom. From Judge Wood, this clinched the impression she was forming of Grassgreen: He wasn't credible. Once again, the prosecutors had given favorable treatment to a confessed crook in exchange for testimony against Milken that the court couldn't believe.

By the laws of drama, the climax comes at the end. Perhaps that was why John Carroll, the former literature student, chose for the third and final transaction of this Fatico hearing an incident that would, he said, prove Michael Milken traded on insider information—the charge that wounded Milken the most, for he always insisted that he never abused a confidence.

In press reports and in congressional committees, the golden age of insider trading is said to be 1984–86. On the wings of hostile takeovers, it was widely believed, confidential information flew across the land, and so many people were so indiscreet with this information that most significant corporate events were preceded by dramatic stock run-ups. But for its example of Milken's alleged insider trading, the government reached deep into the past—all the way back to 1983.

At that time, Milken dropped in on a meeting with Caesars World, a Nevada-based casino company that was not then a Drexel client. They talked about a business relationship, but no clear commitment was made. Before and after that meeting, Drexel traded in Caesars World securities—in the government's view, on material, nonpublic information.

The first witness was Jim Dahl.

Some of the information in this case was awkward for the government—at one point in the suspect trading, Milken and his wife were wandering through used bookstores in the Lake District of England. And some of the information was technical. It turned out the prosecutors hadn't quite mastered the facts of the Caesars World case.

"If you had known there was going to be an exchange offer announced—" Liman began, at one point in his cross-exam.

"I don't think there was evidence that there was a swap," John Carroll interjected.

"I will show you," Liman said, with some bite.

Dahl blanched. "Your Honor, could I take a short break?"

Arthur Liman couldn't recall when he had last seen a witness suffer such sudden bladder trouble so soon after a break.

Worse still for the claim that Milken had traded on inside information was that a customer from whom Dahl had purchased some Caesars World bonds—at Milken's request, he alleged—had made and kept notes of his conversation with Dahl. These notes totally discredited Dahl's version of that transaction. Once again, the prosecutors had been embarrassed by their immunized witness.

But the most interesting part of Dahl's testimony came when he was asked about the events that followed the Boesky announcement. This was the same subject that had provided Peizer with the opportunity to give damaging testimony against Milken. Dahl's story was just as damning.

"I was at home," Dahl testified, recalling the Sunday after those Friday headlines. "Mike gave me a call and said he would like me to come into the office. . . . I went in, and sat at my desk. Mike was at his desk, working. I recall Janet Chung was in the office helping Mike, and I don't recall anyone else being there."

"I did some work at my desk. After two hours, I was getting a little impatient and wanted to go home. I said, 'Mike, if there's something you want to talk about, let's do it, because I am out of here soon.' He got up from his chair and walked out of the trading room and into the men's room. He went over to the sink, turned on the water, started washing his hands, and said, 'There haven't been any subpoenas issued. Whatever you need to do, do it.' He looked at me for a response. I said okay, and I walked out and I went home."

Under cross-examination, Dahl said he didn't believe Milken was asking him to destroy documents after that conversation, or withhold evidence, or coordinate stories with anyone. But those admissions didn't inspire anyone to question the foundation of his anecdote. Only Janet Chung—Michael Milken's assistant—could have done that.

*   *   *

You shove those canvas boating bags under your desk, Janet Chung used to tell Milken, and they have silent sex there, and when it's time for me to empty and sort them, there are a dozen where there used to be eight. Milken blushed—any mention of sex embarrassed him. Which delighted Chung and only made her mention it more.

On Sunday, two days after Boesky's announcement, Chung went to the office to sort Milken's bags with his other assistant, Sue Cochran. Usually, the office was deserted on Sunday, but as she wrote in her diary that evening, Cary Maultasch was there. The most memorable event in her brief entry for that day was that Milken was "distracted," and yet Sue "chose to bitch about our lunches." That she said little more is telling—as Milken has joked, Chung's diary was so fanatically detailed that if she'd shredded anything, she'd surely have mentioned it.

Two years later, the government subpoenaed Chung's diary, and prosecutors began to wade through daily entries that began in 1984 and ended late in 1988. It was a punishing task—Chung's writing was as exhaustive meditation on two subjects, men and Milken. In January of 1989, some assistant U.S. attorneys and an SEC investigator had revived sufficiently to want to question her about this diary. When they did, they were particularly interested in her impressions of those two days in November of 1986.

Under their questioning, Chung said that she arrived at Drexel around 9:30 on Sunday morning. She ate bagels with Cary Maultasch and gossiped with him about her love life, and then she and Cochran dragged almost a dozen canvas bags filled with prospectuses, annual reports and memos into the glass-walled conference room. As it always did, organizing her packrat boss's paperwork took hours.

That morning, she told the prosecutors, Milken gave her four Lakers' tickets; that night, she and two other women from Drexel took Maultasch to the game. The seats were terrific, right under the basket. But Maultasch fell asleep.

Did you, the prosecutors wondered, go through any other containers?

No.

Get any instructions from Milken?

No.

Did you sort through any other documents?

329

No.

See anyone shredding documents?

Not to my knowledge.

The prosecutors turned next to the cast in the Drexel office that Sunday.

Was Richard Sandler there?

No.

Charles Thurnher?

No.

Jim Dahl?

He would *never* be there on a Sunday.

In February of 1989, when Chung was debriefed at the U.S. attorney's office, Jim Dahl had already become a government witness. In all his interviews with defense lawyers, he had never mentioned that Milken ever suggested that he destroy evidence. There was no reason, early in 1989, for Chung to believe he was now telling stories to that effect—her response to the prosecutors' question about Dahl was spontaneous and direct.

But Janet Chung, the unofficial historian of Milken's trading floor, didn't testify that she never saw Jim Dahl in the Drexel office that Sunday. Her memory was just fuzzy enough that she couldn't be absolutely certain. And if she was wrong—or if the prosecutors chose to believe that she was wrong—she might be the next Lisa Jones, an assistant doing prison time for perjury. The risk was just too great. And so Judge Wood never heard anyone say that the Milken-Dahl conversation in the men's room might not have happened.

In the face of thirteen hundred pages of testimony and two sets of memos from each side, Judge Wood felt obliged to give a full analysis of each transaction and each witness.

In the Wickes transaction, she found circumstantial evidence linking Milken to this manipulation, but it was "too thin" to justify any enhancement of his sentence. She paid no attention to Gardiner's testimony: "His failure to recall key facts, coupled with his prior perjury, render it difficult to credit any of his testimony."

In the Storer transaction, she didn't find that Milken bribed fund managers by inviting them to purchase warrants—the government's central charge. What did trouble her was Milken's failure to disclose his purchase of the warrants to KKR. Milken didn't want KKR to know what he was doing, she concluded, because KKR would very likely have wanted to renegotiate Drexel's fee.

As for Caesars World, she decided Milken didn't have insider information before or after he attended a meeting with the casino's executives. Milken had every right to trade in its securities.

If Fatico had only been about the three transactions that the prosecutors had selected for the hearings, the government would have suffered a resounding defeat.

Obstruction, the uncharged offense, was something else.

Obstruction of justice: The term was so forbidding that lawyers discussed it with Michael Milken only because the prosecutors wanted him to plead guilty to it. His refusal to consider that was complete and absolute. But in September, when Arthur Liman, Martin Flumenbaum, and Robert Litt were writing their sentencing memo, Litt thought about raising that subject once again.

Look, you *didn't* obstruct justice, the Williams & Connolly lawyer wanted to tell Milken, but it might be smart to admit to obstruction in the sentencing memo, or the judge may come to believe it on her own and crucify you. Here's what you should say: "In the days after the Ivan Boesky announcement, I was scared. I panicked. I destroyed evidence and I encouraged others to. It was the biggest mistake I ever made, and I am truly sorry."

But Milken couldn't hear that, so Litt didn't say it.

And Judge Wood found it on her own and nailed him for it.

Wood wrote that she paid close attention to Terren Peizer's "demeanor and manner of response" in court, and she believed him when he said Milken opened an empty desk drawer and made a cryptic suggestion to destroy evidence. As for Peizer's misidentification of Milken's handwriting and his faulty memory of an encounter between Lowell and Michael Milken on the trading floor soon after the Boesky announcement—both were "innocent mistakes." In her view, Peizer testified "forthrightly, carefully, and credibly."

Despite the client witness who produced documents that flatly contradicted Jim Dahl on the key point of his Caesars World story, Judge Wood also found Dahl "highly credible." In particular, she was impressed by his account of the bathroom conversation two days after the Boesky announcement: "Milken directed

Dahl to come into the office that Sunday for the sole purpose of signalling to him, clandestinely, the advisability of removing or destroying documents damaging to Michael Milken."

Although Peizer and Dahl didn't destroy evidence, she concluded, Milken still obstructed justice. "Michael Milken's pattern of wrongdoing, as shown in the crimes to which he pled guilty, is to step just over the line into unlawful conduct, and to do so in a way that preserves his 'deniability' and minimizes the risk of detection. His clandestine and subtle messages to Dahl, and his slightly veiled message to Peizer, are characteristic of this way of operating."

Kimba Wood was not thinking about community service for Michael Milken.

CHAPTER TWENTY-THREE

Larry Shamhart rode downtown with Michael and Lori Milken for the sentencing. It was the day before Thanksgiving, a time for family, and Shamhart was glad to be included in Milken's. But despite the symmetry, there was a sickly feeling in the air. All morning, friends and lawyers had been ghosting around Milken, as if they had come for a funeral and found that the corpse had stepped out of his coffin.

When they reached the courthouse, Shamhart turned to shake Milken's hand. "I got a nice letter from your Mom," Milken said. "Please thank her for me." Shamhart didn't know what to say. Milken had never met his mother, she was nothing to him. And yet, at the biggest moment of his life, he was still thinking about other people.

The Milkens had arrived early, but Richard Sandler had beaten them—Judge Wood had released her Fatico findings that morning. They were not grim, but the obstruction sections didn't bode well; as Sandler stood outside the judge's chambers with Arthur Liman and John Carroll, he asked Carroll for a favor.

Would you go easy on him? Sandler asked.

Jess is going to do the talking today, Carroll said. I've had the limelight.

Will he go easy?

Carroll nodded.

Now came the hard part, the milling around, the waiting. Tom Curnin, the Drexel lawyer, glided like an undertaker from group to group. No one knew what to say.

At last, in the largest courtroom in the building, Judge Wood took her seat. Before her arrival each day at the Fatico hearings, regulars had amused themselves by guessing if she'd wear her hair up or down. Today, her face drew all the attention. It read inscrutable.

Sentencing day orations are purely for press, spectators, and the clients; judges don't have last-minute changes of heart. Yet Arthur Liman spoke for nearly an hour, ringing every bell, bringing his client, at least, to tears. Then Fardella described Milken's crimes and called for substantial imprisonment. These phrases had been heard so often they had, like Liman's Ciceronian cadences, long lost their power. But Fardella was true to Carroll's word—he was concise, on and off in a few minutes.

Wood, in contrast, delivered a long preamble. But it was almost pleasurable to hear—hers was a beautiful style, the sentences balanced, the thoughts lucid, the organization suitable for some future textbook—and, as in the best writing, the force of her thought tuned her listeners to her pace. Perhaps the Milkens cared only for the result; for others, that concern was displaced by the intellectual thrill of watching a very smart person think her way to a conclusion.

Wood explained why she had called a Fatico hearing. She summarized her findings. She assured Milken that she wasn't delivering a verdict on what letter writers and editorialists liked to call a decade of greed.

Then she got to the issue at hand.

That Milken's crimes benefited his clients wasn't the point; those crimes may have solidified his clients' loyalty, increasing the likelihood that they'd pay additional fees in the future. Moreover, Milken's offenses were no less criminal for being technical; technical crimes, she argued, were his style. While his attorneys had argued that most of his business was conducted lawfully and he would have prospered without breaking the law, she found the evidence before her "sparse and equivocal." That judgment, she said, quoting Liman, would require a historian; her concerns were deterrence, retribution, and rehabilitation.

And here, her view of his offenses was harsh: "You committed crimes that are hard to detect, and crimes that are hard to detect warrant greater punishment in order to be effective in deterring others from committing them." For that reason, she found no reason why his sentence should be compared with any other—particularly with that of Ivan Boesky, who, she noted, gave the government what it called the most extensive and remarkable cooperation in the history of the securities laws.

She appreciated Milken's desire to work with disadvantaged children. He'd have that chance. "Because changes are likely to take place in community programs between today and the day you are released from prison, it would be inappropriate to select a particular program for you today," she said.

That was the signal, and if Michael Milken didn't catch it, his wife did—behind her dark glasses, Lori lowered her head.

Judge Wood called for Milken to rise.

For months now, commentators had been handicapping this moment. Benjamin Stein was unsure of the length of Milken's sentence, but he was certain that Milken would go to prison in Danbury, Connecticut, a prison that, as it happened, Milken had not requested. Stein was positive that Milken's eldest son would enroll at Yale, a college to which, as a matter of fact, he hadn't applied. And Stein was reliably informed that Milken's family would move to a mansion in Greenwich, a town that, in the entire decade, Milken had never once visited.

Alan Abelson, Stein's editor at *Barron's*, was confident enough of this information to go public on NBC with that completely inaccurate jail, school, and real estate news. On a roll, Abelson then compounded these errors by assuring viewers that Judge Wood would hit Milken with five years.

In the Milken camp, the most widely guessed number had been four years—Boesky-plus-one. What do you anticipate, how bad could it be? Lori Milken had asked Arthur Liman last night. I don't want to tell you, he said, turning away, but she'd held on to four, held on to it until just now, when she knew: It was going to be beyond belief.

But what astonished was how matter-of-fact this moment felt. All the symbolism would have to be pumped in later—Wood stepped briskly up to the job and, quickly and what certainly sounded dispassionately, dispensed what she thought was justice.

Probation on one count, two years in prison on each of the five other counts, to be served consecutively—ten years in all.

And when that was over, eighteen hundred hours of full-time community service a year for three years.

The courtroom just stopped. No one had expected anything like this. Liman and Milken stood so dumbstruck Wood had to tell them to sit down.

Court was adjourned a few minutes later, and Milken was led out. The reporters were frozen in place, getting it all down. Lori, head still lowered, moved fast, arriving in the judge's hallway just after her husband. Everything felt small and cramped, and there were people around—ten years wasn't a number the Milkens could absorb here. Someone led them to a small waiting room and closed the door.

And the madness began.

The cries of Lori and Michael Milken—hysterical, unashamed wails and shrieks, the kind of sound that would, in isolation, make you think of animals caught in traps—cut through the chat in the judge's hallway and stopped traffic all the way out by the elevators. People looked at one another, suddenly uncomfortable, hoping for an end. But the cries built, the animal hurt finding new timbres, until the curious did the smart thing and beat it.

Outside the witness room, Richard Sandler paced. More marshals arrived: fingerprint time for Milken. Someone had to open the door. Sandler, who'd taken every blow along the way, volunteered to take this one too. He saw quickly that oxygen was more urgent than ink—Milken was having trouble breathing. The marshals produced a tank. By then, there was some uncertainty whom it was for, the man on the table or the woman who watched and shrieked.

At the airport, the situation was no better. In addition to Lori, Lowell, and Lowell's wife Sandy, Milken had brought several friends from California for the sentencing. After court, they had hurried back to the plane, stowed their luggage, taken their seats—everyone wanted to be airborne as soon as Michael and Lori pulled up. Then came a call from the courthouse: Mike's in bad shape, he needs to lie down. It was decided that three or four friends would deplane and fly commercial, though no one knew how that was going to be managed on the eve of Thanksgiving.

At this, Milken arrived. No one had ever seen him look so bad. No, don't take anyone off, he said. We brought them, we'll take them back. This was no favor. As soon as they were aloft, he began to cry again. All the way to Los Angeles, Lori held him, but he was broken now, and inconsolable.

Below him, as he flew, the news was crossing the land, making its way into the homes of people he had never met. But some of them thought they knew him. They knew him because the insurance companies and pension funds that represented their future had, without asking them, invested their money in junk bonds. They knew him because the savings and loans they had always regarded as the safest places to put their nest eggs had bought high-yield issues. Or because the companies they worked for had been taken over by raiders whose primary interest was slashing and burning their way to the bottom line. Or because their employers, in beating back a raider's attack, had taken on so much debt that survival required massive layoffs.

They'd lost money and security and jobs and certainty, and they didn't want to hear anything to the contrary—they didn't want to be told that Michael Milken had created businesses and enriched investors or that Michael Milken was not solely responsible for their distress. As his plane cast its shadow over them, there were many Americans that day who said, in one form or another, "Good! The greedy bastard got his." And in this way, Michael Milken came to be what Kimba Wood's sentence seemed to say— that he was a villain three times guiltier than Ivan Boesky, the biggest criminal in the history of Wall Street.

"It was the correct sentence."

Of the many commentators whose opinions mattered, none was more eagerly sought than Rudolph Giuliani. He chose the forum for his extended interview well: *Barron's*, the publication that was home to Ben Stein and, years ago, the journal that had engaged him as its lawyer. FROM MILKEN TO THE MAFIA: A TALK WITH RUDY GIULIANI was the headline of the piece that appeared just four days after the sentencing.

And, as Giuliani saw it, Milken and the Mafia had a few things in common. Like other men involved in "a major criminal activity," he gave considerable thought to his crimes—thus their subtlety. And, because he was "the fellow at the top," he used subordinates to do the dirty work. Levine and Boesky touched money. Milken didn't. "That's the difference between the courier and the kingpin."

337

What distinguished this case from others, Giuliani believed, was media: "I think I'm probably in a unique position to know the amount of pressure that was exerted in this case. Public relations of all kinds. Trying to affect the reporters who were reporting on the case. Trying to affect political people. It was like a major political campaign rather than a criminal case."

Giuliani—the *Barron's* reporter called him Rudy—was asked not a single rough question. Had he manipulated the press? "There were leaks to *The Wall Street Journal* . . . but they certainly weren't coming from me or my office." Was RICO unfair? "It is the most carefully handled procedure that I can think of in the Justice Department." Did he feel good about the Milken sentence? No, though "I felt very good about the plea."

Giuliani felt less good two days later, when Michael Armstrong's letter arrived at his office. Armstrong wrote "to bring to your attention . . . that it is improper for a former prosecutor to comment publicly and prominently about a matter with which he was involved and which has not yet been resolved." And this wasn't just an ethical problem. Armstrong reminded Giuliani of a case in which a court found comment from counsel "not only subject to regulation, but highly censurable and worthy of disciplinary measures."

Do it again, Armstrong all but dared Giuliani, and I'll have you brought up on charges.

Maybe Armstrong was kidding. Maybe *Sheppard* v. *Maxwell* (384 U.S. 333 [1986]) didn't apply. But after disparaging the Milken lawyers only days earlier, Giuliani decided that maybe he'd rather not test them. After that *Barron's* interview, he was mute on the subject of Milken.

Mirror, mirror on the wall, who's the meanest of them all?

According to the joke that made its way around the courthouse in the weeks after Milken's sentencing, the mirror said it was Idi Amin.

And that angered Saddam Hussein, for he had wanted to be the numero uno bad guy. Upon hearing the mirror's verdict, he immediately ordered the murder of a thousand Iranians. Then he asked the question again.

This time, the mirror said that Manuel Noriega was the meanest man of all.

Furious, Hussein ordered ten thousand Kurds to be rounded

up and gassed. And again, he asked the question: Mirror, mirror, on the wall, who's the meanest of them all?

The mirror said . . . Kimba Wood.

And Hussein wondered, Who's Kimba Wood?

Kimba Wood was, overnight, America's most popular judge—not a bad credit for a woman who was said to be eager to move on to the court of appeals, and, down the line, to the Supreme Court—but she wasn't particularly beloved by her brethren in the Second Circuit for her Milken sentence. Some snickered at Michael Armstrong's comment that no one would ever plead guilty in her courtroom again; it would serve her right to confront a calendar jammed with trials. For she had violated the code of proportionality—in hitting Milken with consecutive sentences, she made judges who ruled on more blatant insider trading cases look like wimps.

As a result, although Wood's husband had told *The New York Times* that this Milken sentencing was just another day at the office for her, the Bureau of Prisons didn't see Milken as just another defendant. Milken had asked to serve his time at a facility in Nevada—he wanted to be near first-class medical facilities, in case something happened to one of his children during a visit. Wood had endorsed that request. But in Washington, the Bureau of Prisons overruled her, ordering Milken to report to a minimum-security work camp called Pleasanton, located just far enough from Oakland to make for an exciting ambulance ride.

As the criticism from judges and lawyers mounted, Wood scrambled for a face-saving gesture. She found it in a hearing to determine the financial loss Milken had caused with his crimes. The government claimed that the damage was $3,445,800, an amount that elevated Milken to a category requiring more jail time before parole. Inexplicably, the prosecutors didn't try to validate that figure—after all their non-negotiable demands, they either didn't care about this claim or doubted they could prove it.

In the absence of the government's proof, Wood ruled that the economic consequences of all the crimes that Milken admitted to totaled $318,000—a third of a day's pay for him in 1986.

This was mighty strange. On national television, Ben Stein was insisting that Milken's junk bond empire had been a scam from the beginning, and that its cost to the American people would be "on the order of seventy-five *billion* dollars." But if all the judge could find was damage amounting to $318,000, Milken had either gotten the screwing of the twentieth century or he and his lawyers had masterfully outwitted the government.

Either way, something was off.

Milken and his lawyers thought so, too. Following Wood's logic at sentencing, five years might have made sense; ten was like a train wreck, an event so unexpected you couldn't really point a finger at anyone. But Milken did—this was an outrage, he wanted relief.

Arthur Liman got right on the phone to the Harvard Law School, and Laurence Tribe whipped up a memo. He didn't consider withdrawing the plea; he was seeking grounds for appeal. In reaching her conclusions, he noted, Judge Wood had read the Boesky sentencing memo, a sealed document damning to Milken; she had an obligation to disclose that she was considering it. The notion behind Fatico—that a man's entire character can be determined on the basis of a few episodes selected by the government—struck him as a violation of due process. And in judging Milken harshly for "crimes that are hard to detect," Wood displayed what Tribe described as a fundamental misunderstanding of Wall Street crime, which is, Boesky and Siegel and Levine notwithstanding, inherently subtle.

Other lawyers were more concerned about finding the best way to deliver Tribe's message—the key was to make Judge Wood see her error without feeling her competence had been attacked. Robert Litt, of Williams & Connolly, came up with the most viable approach: "The overall theme should be that a conscientious (and, we hint subliminally but not overtly, inexperienced) judge was simply overwhelmed by prejudicial material, such that a dispassionate and fair sentence was not possible. In other words, blame the government."

The lawyers talked lawyer talk, circles upon circles. Milken craved a dramatic solution. Restlessness and desperation ruled his household. And in that moment, Lori Milken went to the movies.

Reversal of Fortune is a film about Alan Dershowitz, the Harvard Law professor and "lawyer of last resort" for clients like New York hotelier Leona Helmsley and convicted murderer Dr. Jeffrey MacDonald. The movie was co-produced by Dershowitz's son; it starred Ron Silver, a friend of Rudolph Giuliani. But although they were ideologues of every stripe, the cast and crew

understood that they had come together for a commercial purpose: to create a fact-based, but hardly literal, account of Dershowitz's defense of Claus von Bulow in the attempted murder of
his wife. The film was outrageous—its narrator was the comatose
Mrs. von Bulow—and brilliantly directed. Of its many achieve-
ments, it made the frizzy-haired, bespectacled law professor into
something of a hero.

Lori Milken watched this movie as though it were a docu-
mentary.

A few weeks later, the Milkens met Dershowitz at the Carlyle Hotel in New York. After the sentencing, they'd given up
the suite they'd been renting by the year—it usually cost $2,000
a night, but they got a deal—and were now staying in a small,
relatively austere room. Dershowitz liked that; these people reminded him of his friends from Brooklyn. And Milken liked
Dershowitz; here, at last, was someone who said he liked to fight
and had the record to back the claim.

Alan Dershowitz did not consider that the Milken he was
meeting was, no matter what he said, a very different man from
the one who ruled the financial world in 1985. And Milken did
not consider that the lawyer might, in person, be much different
from the basketball-shooting, Chinese-takeout kind of guy he'd
seen in the movie.

Image met image. A deal was struck. Michael Milken would
go to prison, and Alan Dershowitz, while not promising any mira-
cles, would see what might be done to spring him.

In the weeks before he went to jail, Michael Milken sometimes seemed manic in his martyrdom. He taught for the last
time and, on a whim, had Michael Jackson join him. He called a
great many people to thank them for their kindness. He went
shopping for an inexpensive wristwatch, sweat pants, and shorts—
and a baseball cap, for he wasn't going to be allowed to wear his
toupee in jail.

He was due to report to Pleasanton on Monday, March 4,
1991, but he knew there would be photographers outside the facility, and he wasn't about to let them have a shot they could sell
to the tabloids. Sunday was visiting day; he might get lost in the
crowd if he surrendered twenty-four hours early. This was a confidence the government could keep.

On Sunday afternoon, Milken said goodbye-for-now to his

children. He had a moment with Lowell—a difficult, painful moment—and then, with as little fanfare as possible, he went to the airport with Richard Sandler and Lori.

Larry Shamhart was the driver again. There was nothing to say. At the airport, Shamhart hugged Milken, told him he loved him, said he'd do anything he asked.

There was silence on the plane, and silence again in the rental car on the drive to Pleasanton—all the emotion had been spent. Milken didn't want an emotional transition, and Sandler and his wife honored that, hugging him quickly and letting him go. They sat in the car, watching him walk to the glass door at the main entrance, growing smaller and less distinct, until he was no longer Michael Milken, childhood friend and childhood sweetheart, but just another man in jeans and sneakers and a baseball cap.

Can't we go in and get him? Lori said.

She knew better. Michael Milken was 16126-054 now, a piece of government property. The feeling was chilling; she couldn't talk about it. The closest Richard Sandler came to sharing his emotions was with one of the prosecutors. Everyone in your business, he told John Carroll, should have to do what I did Sunday.

CHAPTER TWENTY-FOUR

Pleasanton is no Lompoc. That's clear as soon as you drive through the gates—beyond the wood-frame offices and undeveloped fields of Camp Parks are row after row of what were once two-story barracks. Now they're looming hulks, blasted by weather, their windows long shattered. What they need is to be torched. But that's impossible; the walls are loaded with asbestos, the cost would be prohibitive.

The motif of ruin ends on 8th Street, where there is a real prison. Its strong walls catch the eye; the antiseptic building just across the street from it escapes notice. But here, in a modern version of those abandoned barracks, is where Michael Milken came to reside in March of 1991.

There are no locks, no armed guards; the facility has the feel of government housing or a dorm at a poorly endowed college. This informality goes only so far. Friends and family on an approved list may visit only a few days a week, and children aren't allowed to bring sporting gear or games with them. Journalists may see Milken during the week, but they must send a formal request long in advance, and prison officials, aware of Milken's sense of privacy, tend to reject media inquiries as a matter of course—I had to write a second, more explicit letter to make it clear that Milken actually wished to see me.

A month and a half after Milken has walked through the

doors of the security check-in, I retrace his footsteps. The processing for visitors is correct and thorough—after expressing concern over my wallet, which holds more cash than the regulations allow, a guard leads me to Milken's dorm. I sit at one of the two tables in the visitors' area and idly study the vending machines while my escort goes into the inmates' quarters. Somewhere back there is a cafeteria, a television room, and a library where prisoners can meet with their lawyers. And there are bedrooms for the eighty men who live here. Small bedrooms—Milken shares his with three other men.

More to the point, the prisoners' area has five pay phones. After Milken finishes his work for the day, he can often be found here, calling his lawyer's office in Los Angeles and then having a secretary bounce him on to his lawyers in New York. In this way, he is as well connected as he ever was. Perhaps even more so—because his workday is shorter here than it was at Drexel, his "visits," as he calls them, are much longer.

In the evening, Milken's calling has a different pattern. While his fellow prisoners watch TV, he retreats to the phones once again and makes collect calls to the remnants of his world. But the prison routinely tapes calls from these phones, and while no one could possibly be interested in monitoring hours of Milken's drone, there are topics that are best addressed in person. Thus, this visit, Milken's first jailhouse meeting with the press.

Milken appears. He wears a navy turtleneck, jeans, and sneakers. And a baseball cap. He is tanned from working outside—in addition to cleaning bathrooms and mopping floors, he has been tidying up the trash area and scouring rust off signs—and thinner than before. Physical labor and the absence of his name from the front page seem to have calmed him somewhat. But this calm is deceptive; from our phone conversations, I'm aware that frustration and bitterness have been loosed within him, and he's struggling to keep these feelings from dominating him.

As Milken takes a seat across from me, the guard presents him with a form. He scans the standard permission sheet. At the same time, he leans back and, very casually, removes his cap. A thoughtful, obviously premeditated gesture; my adjustment occurs while he's otherwise engaged. But little adjustment is necessary. As with many men who wear toupees, Milken looks better without one.

Milken's decision to remove the baseball cap strikes me as his way of announcing that he has nothing to hide. After years of evasive conversations and unenlightening interviews, he wants to be heard. He's said he wants to confront all the issues. No topic is forbidden.

Milken speaks. His voice is clear, his gaze direct. And the subjects are understandably large—outside this cheerless facility, Milken is being blamed for almost everything that is going wrong in the economy.

It's not only that he believes the blame is misplaced; it's that he feels as if the country is just catching up to his own views. The well-publicized bankruptcies of 1980s companies that fell in love with leveraged buyouts—he'd warned that disaster was in store for many of them, but they didn't listen, and now their failures are attributed to him. Ditto the fall of Drexel—he'd told his associates and stated publicly that the age of LBOs, takeovers, and debt deals was over and equity was the new king, but they went right on playing the only game they knew, and now, some of them would like to believe, that he sank the firm.

"My business was about helping companies and having them be successful; I thought that was the difference between Drexel and other firms," he says. "And I thought others at Drexel also cared about people and companies, that they too believed in getting capital to people with ability. Many did, but management apparently did not."

At the same time that he was forced off the field and Drexel was limping, he feels that real problems—Third World debt and bad real estate loans, for just two—were being ignored. People began to decry "loose credit standards" and "the excesses of the Milken years" as if these other problems didn't exist. Overly restrictive credit standards on successful businesses followed, he continues, and the suffering of American business was soon extended to the nation: "Companies are interrelated. When you deny credit to young or smaller businesses that create jobs and grow the economy, they can't buy from larger companies. After a while, it doesn't matter that these larger companies can get credit—the fact is, their business shrinks and everyone suffers."

We have covered much of this in previous conversations. While it's not an uninteresting monologue, it does eat up the clock. But Milken can't sit down and just answer questions. He needs to warm up, making general statements and then moving on to cases. These half-hour monologues aren't just the release of pent-up thoughts, they're also a kind of dam, holding more painful subjects at bay.

For millennia, prisoners have had scant interest in what they've done wrong—and an obsession with the wrongs they feel have been done to them. Milken shares that preoccupation. And so his conversations tend to gravitate toward an all-purpose one-liner: His offenses aside, his biggest blunders were his naïveté and his insistence on maintaining a code of honor in a dishonorable world. Because he never spoke up and never fought back, he says, he is now paying the price.

"I believed in giving anonymously, praising others, and only speaking well of others," Milken says. "You can't live in this country today with those beliefs. Not to confront falsehoods for twenty years—that was a mistake. The truth keeps leaking out, but in the short run, it doesn't shine through. Operating behind the scenes, always giving the credit to others and never explaining why you did what you did—another mistake. Giving help anonymously— also an error. When people find out, your philanthropy becomes tainted, you did it 'for some other purpose,' and because you have no public history, you have no standing. All those years, I thought the marketplace or the customer was the final judge. I was wrong. In the short run, it's the media. And in the media, nothing means anything unless it's negative."

He took the plea, he says, because he couldn't take any more of the RICO threat hanging over his family and the incessant battering coming his way from the government, the press, his own firm, and his competitors. In his mind, the plea should have put an end to the assault. Just the opposite has occurred: "Certain people, at the Fatico hearing and elsewhere, moved further from reality. The only solution is to address their credibility."

He means not just the writers he's never met, but people closer to home—some of his former colleagues, beginning with Jim Dahl and Terren Peizer, whose testimony he finds riddled with error.

"In a deposition Dahl made just before the Boesky news in

1986, he described himself as a senior salesman with a great deal of autonomy. When he took a massive position in this particular security—something he had the authority to do—he describes me as being worried by his boldness, since I'd been unaware of major financial commitments he'd made on behalf of the firm. After the investigation began, he went through some changes in identity. For almost two years, he had a consistent memory of his responsibilities and his business. Then he discovered another man's salary and decided he was underpaid. After that, he wanted to replace me. When that didn't work out, he told the government I had to approve his trades. And that's Jim. He spins stories.

"So when the government says, 'We need to present an inside trading case at Fatico,' they remembered that Jim had told them about Caesars World. Well, that's a dream transaction, isn't it? You're looking for insider trading, but you exclude every major transaction of the 1980s. You don't choose Phillips or Unocal or even Pacific Lumber. You don't choose a transaction that involves a merger or an acquisition, you don't choose a takeover stock, you don't choose energy, which is the area that started the backlash in the first place. All those names we've been reading about in *The Wall Street Journal* since 1984 or 1985—you pick none of them, and nobody asks why. Instead, you choose Caesars World, a case from 1983, because Jim's told you a story. What Jim doesn't know is that one of his clients wrote a memo at the time, and that memo contradicts him. So, at Fatico, Jim tells his story, he's presented with the facts *and he changes his mind.**

"But no one remembers when a witness changes his story. People remember the accusation. You can be in Great Britain, the way I was during the key events that Jim talks about, but words put you at the scene of the crime. You're only safe in rural Mexico in a town where there are no phones and you're in a deposition all day. In the transactions we're talking about here,

---

*Dahl, who was found credible by Judge Wood at the Fatico hearing, was the government's prime witness in its investigation of Thomas Spiegel, the Milken friend who headed Columbia Savings & Loan. In November of 1991, just before the statute of limitations expired, the assistant U.S. attorneys for the Southern District put considerable pressure on Spiegel, urging him to make a deal before they brought their indictment. Spiegel didn't blink—and, perhaps expressing their lack of confidence in Dahl, the prosecutors didn't indict. At some point along the way, the government's prime witness may have changed his mind again. Dahl now says that he had long told the U.S. attorneys the real criminal act would be to indict Spiegel; in his view, Spiegel violated no laws.

there are no bags of cash, no people who don't report all their income on their tax returns—there are just words. Here, someone gets the time wrong, for example, and the case goes forward. It's not just sticks and stones that hurt—words can, too."

"The difference between Jim and Terren Peizer is that Jim makes it up as he goes along. He's so glib he thinks he can make it work out later. Terren had two years to plan his reconstruction of the past, and he gave the government many stories that couldn't be corroborated.

"I now understand why he said what he did. For all the 'information' he gave the prosecutors, I think Terren held back something more important than writing that wasn't Lowell's or mine. In the first few months of 1985, Drexel worked on Coastal and National Can as well as others, and David Solomon didn't receive any information or invest in these transactions for his own account—that kind of thing wasn't our business. It was then that Solomon began to complain about the coverage of his firm's account. He told me he not only wanted a new person, but that he wanted Terren Peizer, who covered his account at First Boston. Based on the recommendation of this major client, we saw Peizer, we hired him, he came to Drexel. We didn't know it, but suddenly Solomon was buying almost every deal for his personal account for the next nine months."

Here, Milken's not simply pointing a finger at a colleague in order to divert attention from himself; even before Peizer came to Drexel, his trading on Solomon's behalf seems to have had some curious aspects. As trading records indicate, Solomon bought Texas International subordinated notes in early May of 1985—through another broker—at an average price of 53. Just four days later, Solomon sold those bonds back to the broker at 59⅞, giving him a fast six-point profit. On the same day, that broker marked the bonds up a fraction and sold them to Peizer at First Boston at 60, which neatly covered the broker's cost. At the end of May, using the same broker as an intermediary, Solomon again bought Texas International bonds and sent them on a one-stop trip to Peizer. On July 12, 1985—Peizer's last day at First Boston—the firm emptied its inventory of Texas International bonds, selling them to the broker at around its cost; a few days later, Drexel bought the bonds. Solomon's estimated profit from these seemingly riskless trades: $595,000.*

Peizer's move to Drexel only increased Solomon's investing success. Two weeks after Peizer joined Milken's staff, Solomon made $700,000 on MGM call options and stock. Through other brokers, he bought National Gypsum, he bought Beatrice—at the end of that nine-month period, Solomon's personal account was up about $2 million.

Did Peizer cross the line? Some people had their suspicions. In an interview with the prosecutors, a Drexel client said that on April 8, 1986—prior to the announcement of Wickes's bid for National Gypsum—Peizer recommended that he buy National Gypsum stock. In his debriefing by the prosecutors, Gary Winnick said that Peizer advised him that he'd "tipped" a client on either Beatrice or Storer.† Independently, a former Drexel employee has said that a client reported being tipped by Peizer to buy Beatrice.

Terren Peizer insists he was unaware that Drexel was involved with Beatrice and National Gypsum—and so, he says, he couldn't have tipped Solomon or anyone else to buy into these deals. He admits he made a comment to Solomon about Turner bonds when Turner was working with Drexel on the MGM deal, but he insists that he would never have given non-public information to a client. He claims he spoke with the prosecutors about all this before he received immunity. He was required to, he says—they assured him he couldn't get immunity if he had committed serious crimes.

Had their target been anyone other than Michael Milken, would the prosecutors have immunized Terren Peizer and, later, David Solomon? Milken wonders. And as he considers Peizer's pleasant life in Los Angeles and his own grimmer days at Pleasan-

---

*Interpretations of these trades differ. Some say that when same-day trades turn out to be this profitable, there's a strong suggestion of a prearranged accommodation. Others say that this is simply professional trading. Peizer insists that if any impropriety occurred, it wasn't on his end; he says that Solomon told him he was selling off bonds he'd held for a long time.

†As of late 1990, the government hadn't verified whether Winnick's information was accurate.

ton, it's not surprising that he's more than a little miffed.

The guard reappears. The time has passed so quickly, and there is so much more to talk about. Still, this has been a bracing conversation—despite Milken's pain at raking up bad memories and ugly emotions, there is the satisfaction of breaking through a barrier. That inspires him to give me some homework.

"Next time," he says, "let's talk about what I pled to, as compared to Siegel, Levine, Jefferies, Freeman, and Boesky."

"I have an assignment for you, too," I reply. "If you saw trouble brewing in New York and Washington in 1985, how come you stood there and got run over?"

"Look, I made mistakes," Milken says. "And setting aside for the moment what I pled to, I also made the mistake of speaking out primarily at Drexel and to clients when I should have left and stated my beliefs publicly—loud and clear."

But there's a better answer, rooted in his family history. The analogy isn't exact, he emphasizes, for while his father died from his mistake, he still has his health. Still, the familial connection—what he calls "the habit of thinking of yourself last"—is resonant.

"Why don't you ask my mother," he says sadly, "why, when my father got an infected toe, he put off going to his doctor—because he was too busy with the business and family problems of his friends and clients—until it had turned into a fatal cancer?"

Before Milken went to prison, friends encouraged him to ignore the books and articles that repeat old untruths, work on interesting projects that keep the mind sharp, and, above all, focus on large issues that bring out his best. But it's hard to think big thoughts when you're being sued for $10 billion by some of the nastiest litigators on the planet. And that's Milken's situation. In addition to the $600 million he's already handed over to the government, the Federal Deposit Insurance Company has filed suit against him for his alleged crimes against the savings and loan industry. And the FDIC has chosen as its lawyers Thomas Barr and David Boies of Cravath, Swaine & Moore.

In the mid-1980s, Cravath was the New York firm that vouched for Robert Campeau, who promptly laid waste to two great retailing chains and almost single-handedly caused the junk bond market to crash. Now it's as if the 1980s never happened. The big law firms that once made their fees boosting deals have done a predictable flip. Their new specialty is "workouts"—wringing money from bankruptcies and related disasters that they helped create.

Barr and Boies, both master litigators, have warmed up by launching some wildly overstated suits against Drexel, making claims the prosecutors never did. In November of 1990, representing the Federal Deposit Insurance Corporation, they filed a RICO suit against Drexel, claiming that this defunct firm with $3.1 billion in assets should pay $6.8 billion for its role in the S&L mess. The next day, representing Columbia Savings, they sued Drexel for an additional $4.5 billion, contending that the firm was responsible for losses in Columbia's junk bond portfolio.

But the FDIC suit against Milken is the one most likely to produce big revenues. For one thing, Milken actually has money. And that means Cravath might be very well paid. By the terms of the deal Barr and his senior associates have made with the FDIC, they may each bill $600 an hour—$200 an hour more than Barr usually charges his clients—if they bring in more than $200 million for the government. If they fail, Barr will have to settle for $300 an hour.

Cravath is, in effect, operating as a bounty hunter, going after the one deep-pockets defendant for every last million. David Boies admits that's the firm's intent: "It's almost certain that we could never recover all of the amount that we have damage claims for—Milken doesn't have that much. In theory, he might run out of money before we run out of lawsuits."

To save time, Cravath lawyers and their affiliates at Milberg Weiss adopt the divide-and-conquer tactic perfected in the criminal case. In May of 1991, Melvyn Weiss sends a letter to former Drexel executives: "These litigations will constitute a relentless pursuit to recover money from any source where there is believed to have been wrongful conduct. We are writing to you because we believe you have information that may be of assistance to us. In addition, we believe you are one of the people whose activities bear investigation. We ask you to consult with your attorney and consider voluntarily cooperating with us. Such cooperation will be considered by us in our dealings with you."

That was the letter. In person, some Milken friends say, these lawyers are even less subtle.

This continuing pressure against the financier and his handful of supporters is underscored by what is, for Milken, a heart-

351

breaking irony. For at the same time that one part of the government works to strip him of every penny, another is sending him the message that he was a fool to plead guilty. In June, the Court of Appeals for the Second Circuit notes that the testimony of tax experts has a certain relevance in tax cases and overturns the RICO conviction of Princeton/Newport. That same month, it reverses the conviction of John Mulheren, whose trial had produced Ivan Boesky's only court appearance. "Rudolph Giuliani," begins a *New York Times* article that analyzes these stunning reversals, "is a man of fewer and fewer convictions."*

All this weighs heavily on Michael Milken. He has come to feel that he has made a great mistake—no, that his lawyers have made a great mistake. In his version of events, his lawyers pushed him into taking the plea. They told him it made sense. They assured him it would work out. Now everyone who fought the government is free, and John Mulheren, who never wore a tie and rarely wore socks to his trial, gets to tell the press, "If you give an inch on a principle, ever, that's the end." These are, Milken believes, his own sentiments. Somehow, they have been stolen from him. He wants them back. Something must be done.

And so Milken reaches out for Alan Dershowitz.

"Milken's entire career was premised on keeping the public in the dark about what was going on in the junk bond market," Dershowitz wrote a year earlier. "His plea bargain should not be shrouded in the same veil of darkness."

Dershowitz, author of a recent best-seller called *Chutzpah*, no longer feels this way. In fact, he regrets ever writing these words—and not because Milken is paying him $400 an hour. Back then, he says, he didn't know what an innovator Milken was, or how the government had scapegoated him. Now he thinks that some of Milken's practices shouldn't have been legal—but, he adds quickly, they were at the time. His view is that the government has, for Milken, made new law without notice.

According to other Milken lawyers, Dershowitz has been hired purely to provide a media presence for a client determined

---

*"The court of appeals is not a political body," remarks Giuliani, eager to head off criticism that might follow him around when he next runs for public office. "This whole search for meaning—it really is a little silly."

to have a visible and celebrated attorney speak up for him. This is not what Dershowitz believes. He's convinced that he's been hired as an "option arm"—to see how the case might have been defended and to explore how it might still be defended. Milken himself has told him that: There are no limits on your exploration. But, practically, there are, and at every turn, Dershowitz feels he's running into them. He perceives that Arthur Liman is freezing him out by processing his requests for documents with painful slowness; in his view, no one connected to Liman wants him near the motion for sentence reduction.

Because he has nothing meaningful to do and is infatuated with his new client, Dershowitz dreams of the most dramatic function he might perform for Milken—withdrawing the guilty plea. There are, traditionally, only three arguments for such a motion. A defendant can claim his lawyer was incompetent. Or a defendant can claim he didn't understand the consequences of his plea. Or a defendant can claim that his plea was coerced. This, Dershowitz feels, is the claim to make: Milken was put into a *Sophie's Choice* position because of the pressure on his brother.

In July, Milken has been in jail just four months. But the world has moved on—and not in his favor. Just before junk bonds begin a rousing recovery, the government seizes Executive Life and Columbia Savings, two of his best customers. Jim Dahl, who was in charge of trading with savings and loans at Drexel, makes his second deal with the government, turning over 90 percent of his stake in Drexel partnerships to the FDIC and becoming a witness in the FDIC suits against Milken; in exchange, twenty lawsuits against him disappear and he gets to keep the approximately $50 million he made at Drexel. Freedom from prosecution, it seems to Milken, is only the first step in an ongoing process that leads to a well-paid career as a government witness.

In the background, playing against all this, Milken hears Alan Dershowitz murmuring that, if he'd gone to trial, he wouldn't have gone to jail. Thus encouraged, Milken tells stories to Dershowitz that make an already incendiary lawyer eager to fight. And then he allows Dershowitz and his Boston colleague, Harvey Silverglate, to explore the most radical motion of all—pulling the plug on Liman and withdrawing his plea.

Dershowitz doesn't know what one of the lawyers advising

Milken has said: "I've never seen anyone with a better instinct for the capillaries." He doesn't know that, from day one, Milken has encouraged every lawyer to present him with options, sworn he'll consider even the wildest proposal, and then, when the moment comes for a decision, he has invariably chosen the seemingly safest route. Because he is a neophyte, Dershowitz takes Milken's talk of drastic action seriously. He broods. He and Silverglate consult legal tomes. And while Dershowitz finds the proposition tempting, he also finds that the risk is just too high. Nothing he knows about Kimba Wood tells him she'll be sympathetic to his motion. If Milken allows him to move forward, he'd make a lot of noise. He'd scare the government. And then he'd hurt his client when it came time for the more meaningful application—the motion to reduce his sentence.

I can't do better for you than your present lawyers, Dershowitz tells Milken.

What once looked like tragedy is turning into farce. That, anyway, seems to be the view of Stephen V. Wilson, the judge in the United States District Court in Los Angeles who has drawn the Milken civil suits that have been filed in California. But how can Wilson not giggle? He looks out into his courtroom on September 13, 1991, and sees a wall of well-paid pinstripes. Fifty-eight lawyers await him—the roll call alone fills five and a half pages of transcript.

Thomas Barr begins by moving to disqualify a lawyer who represents the Drexel partnerships. Barr has just been handed some invoices that show how much this lawyer's firm earned for representing two savings and loans.

"These invoices," Barr intones, "total in number some $185 million—I'm sorry—*thousand* dollars."

"Mr. Barr, you got those confused with *your* bills," Judge Wilson says, getting in the day's first dig.

Alan Dershowitz makes his presence known a few minutes later. His motion is a riposte to Barr's—he wants the Cravath lawyers disqualified. Columbia Savings & Loan, he alleges, lost more money in junk bond deals represented by that law firm than it did in Milken deals. In fact, he proposes to show that Cravath has produced prospectuses for its clients that are identical with prospectuses it now claims are fraudulent.

"You're very eloquent," Wilson replies, "and I hate to derail you, but I was thinking here—could you say something really outrageous? Because you haven't done it so far. I was thinking how I can ask Professor Dershowitz if what he said might be characterized as 'chutzpah'—and notice I say 'hu' not 'chu'—but you haven't said anything sufficiently outrageous to allow me to do that."

"I apologize, Your Honor."

Later, Wilson, though still amiable, moves to stop the billing clock. "When this is all over and everyone's rich enough, we'll have to try the case," he says. "I want that sooner than later. I'm not on a commission basis, you know."

Wilson's point slowly becomes clear. Nobody may care much about the defendant—nobody here may care much about anything beyond billing—but he does. And so, with jibes and jokes, he puts every lawyer on notice; the trial they all want in 1998 will begin in 1992.

Farce turns back to tragedy for Milken in September of 1991, with the publication of *Den of Thieves*. James Stewart, the *Wall Street Journal* reporter who has dogged him from the day of the Boesky announcement, delivers the hardest blow yet in this book, which focuses on Levine, Boesky, Siegel, and Milken. Before his fall, Boesky was a great source for Stewart, while Siegel was not only a source but someone Stewart seemed to admire. Milken, in contrast, has never met Stewart and has long been his favorite villain. So Milken expects that Siegel will be well treated in this book, that Boesky will be taken seriously, and that he will be regarded as the dark prince of Wall Street.

Milken has been wondering which of his associates talked to Stewart. Reading the book, it all becomes clear: of the very few former colleagues who talked to Stewart, the key sources seem to be Fred Joseph, Jim Dahl, Terren Peizer, and Gary Winnick. These are, for Milken, the men who might have the most urgent personal reasons to point the finger at him. Here, unsurprisingly, what they have to say about him is overwhelmingly negative.

Stewart's conclusions are even more unfavorable. For him, Milken used takeovers and mergers to solidify his position as ringleader of "the greatest criminal conspiracy the financial world has ever known," threatening not only the markets but "the sense of justice and fair play that is a foundation of civilized society." The government men, in contrast, were overworked and ill-paid patriots. That they didn't convince Judge Wood of Milken's guilt in the three transactions they presented at the Fatico hearings isn't of much interest to Stewart—those hearings, which he describes as "anticlimactic," merit one paragraph in footnotes set in small type at the back of the book.

Den of Thieves is so unfavorable to Milken that even Rudolph Giuliani, months later, will comment, "I get the feeling that Jim Stewart could find Mike Milken responsible for World War II." Still Ken Lerer counsels silence. Rise above it, he advises. Let's not make this a rerun of *The Predators' Ball*.

Arthur Liman agrees. Alan Dershowitz doesn't. He sees anti-Semitism on every page, starting with the title, a biblical reference to Jesus kicking the Jewish money lenders out of the temple. Then Michael Thomas—the writer who has, week after week, filled his column with violent personal attacks on Milken—announces that he will heap praise on *Den of Thieves* in the all-important *New York Times Book Review*. This is too much for Dershowitz; he *has* to do something. He tries to disqualify Thomas as a reviewer, fails, and then goes public with his charges. *Den of Thieves* immediately soars to the top of the best-seller list.

And Milken focuses anew on Ivan Boesky and Fred Joseph, whose handiwork, he believes, dominates Stewart's book.

Everyone who saw *The Big Chill* remembers the scene. Kevin Kline, as the CEO of the Running Dog Footwear Center, is jogging early one morning with his old pal William Hurt.

"I'm about to tell you something I'm not supposed to tell anyone," Kline says.

"Then maybe you shouldn't," Hurt replies.

Kline isn't deterred. "In a few months," he says, "a very large corporation, a conglomerate, is going to buy a very small company, and anyone who has our stock is going to triple their money. . . . I was thinking maybe you could use the information to get into another line of work."

"You never learn, do you?"

"By telling you this," Kline notes, "I just violated about sixteen regulations of the Securities and Exchange Commission. Don't repeat it."

"Don't repeat what?" Hurt asks, and they smile at one another and jog on, their friendship deeper than ever.

That is a textbook example of insider trading. During the heyday of leveraged buyouts and mergers and takeovers, this kind of conversation was a remarkably ordinary event—in 1983 and 1984, according to *Business Week,* 72 percent of the companies involved in those transactions saw their stock price rise in the month before an announcement of a deal. The general public surely believes that Michael Milken and Ivan Boesky traded inside information every week, if not every day. Even Norman Pearlstine, executive editor of *The Wall Street Journal,* believes this. In a letter to a reader a year after Milken's sentencing, he confidently—and erroneously—states, "Milken pleaded guilty to insider trading."*

If Milken could make only one point, it's that he never shared inside information.

"Boesky wasn't a factor in my business," he says. "If Drexel had never done a trade or a financing for Boesky, it wouldn't have had a noticeable impact on the High-Yield Bond Department or its earnings. So what reason did I have to share information with Boesky? None. It never happened.

"Ivan Boesky made tens of millions of dollars buying stocks with inside information he got from Marty Siegel and Dennis Levine. And yet he loses six-to-eight million dollars on Occidental Petroleum and makes no money on MGM or Pacific Lumber—what kind of 'arrangement' with Mike Milken is this?

"Look at Pacific Lumber. The government says I told Boesky to buy the stock. They forget that Boesky, unbeknownst to me, first bought ten thousand shares before the announcement—through Jefferies—and *sold* them three days before the announcement. Why would he do that if he knew anything?

"Look at MGM. Boesky couldn't have paid more if he tried. If I had an interest in his three million shares of MGM common stock, all I had to do is whisper in his ear and make twenty million dollars. If I was so greedy, why was this illegal relationship so unprofitable?

"But it's even simpler than that—if Boesky had Mike Milken, why did he need Dennis Levine? If I 'controlled' Boesky,

---

*When his error was pointed out to him, Pearlstine acknowledged that he'd been mistaken.

why didn't I even know about his relationship with Levine? If I was so eager to park stock for Boesky, why did he go to Jefferies to park twenty-to-thirty million dollars' worth when Drexel had a trading inventory of four billion? Why were Jefferies and others his principal broker?

Here's how much control I had over Ivan Boesky: *I couldn't get him to buy my product, the bonds I believed in and encouraged everybody to buy—and if I controlled him, don't you think I could have succeeded in that?"*

In the fall of 1991, Fred Joseph disappoints Milken anew. It's not just that, in *Den of Thieves,* he casts himself as Milken's greatest victim—it's the way he ignores the fact that, in any business, the CEO has final responsibility for policy decisions. Milken was off the trading desk as early as 1987; when he officially left the firm, it still had $1.3 billion in capital. Under the terms of Drexel's settlement with the government, no one at the firm was allowed to talk to him. Tell me, says Milken, how did I induce Drexel to erode that position and go bankrupt less than a year later?

Whatever Fred Joseph's answer to that question, it won't be to Milken's liking. For, irony of ironies, Joseph has a new job—a two-year appointment as Drexel's "institutional memory," at a salary of about $300,000 a year. Joseph is thus, in Milken's view, a "paid witness," a man whose livelihood depends on giving testimony against him in Drexel's RICO suit. Considering what he believes has happened to Joseph's memory, this is almost the worst news yet.

"Fred's reconstruction of history is unbelievable," Milken says. "He's forgotten *everything.* His mind's a blank slate—all truth comes as a revelation to him. It was Fred who wanted me to make money for people running funds and companies. Fred was one of the Drexel people who told me to go easier on Ivan's covenants. It was Drexel New York—not the High-Yield Bond Department—that had direct phone lines to Ivan. It was Fred's decision that Drexel should buy five percent of Boesky's new fund. It was Fred who wanted to hire every takeover artist in America. Now Fred says he had 'moralistic feelings' about arbitrageurs talking to me—and yet he hired Dennis Levine and Marty Siegel, and built a department around them. If he's nervous about arbs, why did he set up a Drexel arb account with Marty Siegel, a guy who has the biggest connection to them?*

"At Fatico, you could see that Fred had a chip removed. But many things are connected to that chip—an entire two-week period. At the same time that he can't recall asking to borrow twenty-seven million dollars from me and I told him about Storer warrants, some of the people who were buying those warrants and thirty to fifty senior Drexel executives bought Southland warrants—and they went up one hundred percent in six months. That's not a bad return, Fred *might* have remembered that.

"And he certainly might have remembered that while the firm hadn't wanted to commit its own funds to the Storer deal, he was delighted when I committed to invest $261 million of my own. I committed to buy Storer warrants that might have cost me $145 million more, so you could say I was on the hook for $406 million. I guess if you put up that kind of money, you're not eligible to share in the up side—but if I'd personally lost $400 million, that would have been okay.

"As for disclosure, there was no issue. The Drexel lawyers who had worked on previous KKR deals told us what to do. When it came time for Fatico, though, nobody remembered anything, but everybody knew just what to say. It was like a script: You say this, I'll say that. What Fred left out was that I wanted to protect the Grail—he and some of his Corporate Finance crew just wanted to consume it."†

---

*Fred Joseph denies telling Milken to go easy on the convenants for Boesky's fund. Joseph says that he and Milken never discussed taking care of fund managers—although many of the fund managers who bought into the Storer deal had also bought into Prime Cable of Georgia, a transaction that Joseph was so intimately involved with that he even talked to some of the buyers. Joseph says that he wanted more stellar names in the mergers and acquisitions area because Drexel was thinly staffed there. At the same time, Joseph acknowledges that he was afflicted with a competitive drive so intense that, a year after the government investigation started, he would gladly have financed Ronald Perelman's controversial bid for Salomon Brothers. Milken, in contrast, was appalled by Perelman's bid for Salomon and called his vice chairman to urge him to drop it, just as he'd called Perelman a year earlier—before Boesky's plea was announced—to argue against his planned takeover of Gillette.

†Fred Joseph now remembers the $27 million loan; he says he just didn't remember it at the Fatico hearing. He believes that Milken committed $150 million to the Storer deal. Technically, that is correct. But this sum represents Milken's final commitment; four months earlier, when the deal was first structured, Milken did indeed commit $261 million.

*   *   *

From where Milken now sits, even good news carries a sting. The junk bond market has a remarkable year in 1991—the high-yield fund that *Forbes* magazine rates highest returns 67 percent profit on investment, while the lowest yields a still impressive 30 percent. "In the end, the thing they were attacking was the only thing that stood up," Milken says. That reminds him of Stein and Thomas, and their certainty that his bonds were a Ponzi scheme—a fraud in which the first investors are repaid with the money of the suckers who invest later. Ponzis, by definition, can never recover once they collapse; junk bonds were 1991's best investment.* And yet the critics repeat the same tired accusations.

But the enduring value of junk bonds is just one irony. For Milken, there are many, many others:

- Salomon Brothers, the firm that wished him vaporized, is now both the biggest buyer of junk bonds and an adviser to the government agency that's selling the junk of seized S&Ls. This is a cushy arrangement that Washington would never have allowed Drexel to enjoy. And although Salomon finds itself at the center of a bid-rigging scandal in the summer of 1991, no one in Washington or on Wall Street suggests that relationship ought to be reexamined.
- In January of 1992, the SEC allows ninety-eight brokerage firms and banks to plead guilty to civil charges that they routinely lied to get undeservedly large allocations of government-backed securities. "These firms were creating crib sheets and other false records to make sure that when they lied, they lied consistently," SEC chairman Breeden says. "The practice of exaggeration was nearly universal." Although these practices were similar to some of the crimes cited in the Milken plea, there is no criminal prosecution; the brokers were asked neither to admit nor deny the charges, merely to pay their fines and never do it again. No charges were filed against any individuals. The total fines that the ninety-eight firms will pay come to $5.2 million—between $5,000 and $100,000 per firm. Despite the mild-

---

*High-yield bond funds have continued to perform better than any other mutual fund investment in bonds. In the first quarter of 1992, junk bond funds gained 8.01 percent. The average bond fund, in contrast, gained just .07 percent.

ness of the punishment, the *Washington Post* describes this as "one of the most sweeping enforcement actions in history."

- That same month, the Federal Reserve Board clears the path for banks to invest again in junk bond deals without charging their borrowers higher fees for their loans. Junk bonds, apparently, are no longer so risky that banks must be actively discouraged from buying them.
- Also in January of 1992, First Boston becomes the first investment bank to decide that its funds no longer need to limit their junk bond holdings—junk bonds, it seems, have been rehabilitated far more rapidly than their greatest promoter.
- In February of 1992, at the height of a Japan-bashing frenzy in America, Prime Minister Kiichi Miyazawa responds to criticism of his country's trade practices by attacking the 1980s on Wall Street. "Junk bonds, just as their name implies, are very dangerous," he says, in a speech before the Japanese Parliament. "We have these leveraged buyouts where those without their own money can buy up things, and then, unable to pay their interest on their debts, the companies fall into bankruptcy. It should be obvious to anyone that such a situation could not continue long. Yet, over the past ten years, this very situation has continued. I have long felt that this might involve something like a lack of a work ethic."
- In April of 1992, nine senators on the Judiciary Committee write to the heads of the Resolution Trust Corporation and the Federal Deposit Insurance Corporation to complain about the government's arrangement with the law firm it selected to handle the Milken civil suits. Cravath, Swaine not only charged higher fees than comparable firms, the senators allege, but had negotiated "unwarranted and unusual" bonuses for itself. These bonuses were triggered if Cravath collected a relatively modest sum from Milken—given his wealth and his willingness to pay huge fines in the past, "It was obvious that a recovery of $200 million would not demand exceptional legal expertise for a competent law firm." And yet it had, according to Cravath's bills, required 53,200 billable hours—6,600 by partners of the firm—to produce this settlement. Barr and Boies, the two senior partners, would each make at least $1.3 million for a year's effort. Surely, the federally funded corporations that are "the largest employer of lawyers in the country" could have negotiated more forcefully with Cravath about its bills; it should now

renegotiate those fees. This was a detailed, politically provocative letter—but it got no play in the press.

It's all so clear to Milken. "People were yelling fire in a crowded theater—only there was no fire," he says. But the cry worked. One player and one team were removed from the game, everyone else divvied up the spoils, and then Japan, our chief foreign rival, discouraged the kind of financing that would enable us to be more competitive.

In March of 1992, weary of the legal process, Milken agrees to pay another $500 million to settle the civil suits. Some of that money will come from his stake in Drexel partnerships. How much are those interests worth? Milken says $300 million, the FDIC says $200 million. In a remarkable about-face, the government asks Milken to oversee the sale of these securities. From his prison room, Michael Milken—who was once considered so dangerous he couldn't be allowed to be near the financial markets—will, once again, be allowed to undertake his lifelong quest for undiscovered value.

A door closes, a window opens. For those not in jail, life moves on.

For Rudolph Giuliani, currently marooned at a New York law firm, that means another race for mayor. This time, he thinks he's found the secret.

"I've learned to reveal more of myself," he says. "It took months of campaigning to realize I didn't need to be that reserved. Like the other day, I was in a wild Hawaiian sports shirt. Everyone loved it. I loved it."

Richard Breeden has also changed.

His campaign for a Cabinet position has been derailed—it seems that he was carrying out an agenda at the SEC that was at odds with the President's. As the economy has faltered, Breeden has scrambled to regroove himself as a champion of easier financing for small businesses. He wants Congress to drop securities fraud from the RICO statute. Some days, he even wants to make it easier for dissident shareholders to take on entrenched management.

Others who worked on the Milken prosecution have also found their situations changed. After a frenzied courtship by many firms, former SEC enforcement chief Gary Lynch chose prestigious, white shoe Davis Polk, where his starting salary was said to top $700,000. In 1992, he is hired by Kaye, Scholer, a law firm under attack from regulators for the work it did in behalf of Charles Keating and his failed S&L. The regulators are "looking for a scapegoat—pursuing Kaye, Scholer for advocating a legal position taken in good faith stands our legal traditions on their head," charges Lynch, sounding very much like the most rabid of the Milken defense team.

Charles Carberry, Lynch's counterpart at the U.S. attorney's office, is doing the Lord's work by supervising the reorganization of the Teamsters; he is harried but happy, and his reputation is unblemished. Bruce Baird, who followed Carberry as chief of the Securities Fraud unit, is now a defense lawyer in a venerable Washington firm. John Carroll, who closed out the Milken case, now heads the Securities Fraud unit. Jess Fardella, his partner, headed a narcotics unit for a year before deciding to join a law firm.

Fardella's decision makes a certain sense—Otto Obermaier, the U.S. attorney for the Southern District of New York, has all but suspended high-profile Wall Street investigations. To the consternation of the New York defense bar, which has been twiddling its thumbs for a year, his efforts to prosecute securities violators are focused on small-scale, traditional fraud. The U.S. attorney's office, as a result, is said to be running on "Otto-pilot."

For Representative John Dingell, old habits die hard. Once, his invitations to appear before his subcommittee terrorized Wall Street; now, he's moved on to expose unwarranted perks and overcharges at American universities. "Had matters stopped here," a *New York Times* editorial notes, "Mr. Dingell would be a hero." But in the Dingell tradition of swinging a big ax, government auditors follow his lead and suggest that the offended universities deserve to lose much of their funding.

Loss of funding is a reality for Drexel survivors, who have not only seen their jobs disappear but have had to pay millions of dollars to settle civil suits. But don't weep long for them. Leon Black's new firm recently bought $6 billion worth of a busted firm's junk bonds for just over $3 billion—at this rate, it's said, he'll soon be among the richest men in the country. Terren Peizer runs an investment company in Los Angeles and doesn't look back, though Milken is, he admits, sometimes in his dreams. Jim Dahl and his family have moved back to Florida. Fred Joseph, while still a Drexel consultant, also consults for others.

It's the criminals' lives that have changed most dramatically. Martin Siegel, whose Wall Street career once seemed limitless, still lives in Florida; although he is never seen, his expensive beach house is sometimes shown on television news clips. Dennis Levine wrote a book and preached the gospel of rehabilitation right up to the minute that *60 Minutes* exposed him as a reflexive hustler. Ivan Boesky, whose most pressing business involves his effort to get alimony from his soon-to-be ex-wife, spends most of his time in Europe—"visiting his money," as Arthur Liman likes to say.

In this checkered pattern of gain and loss, it's not easy to place Michael Milken.

That is partly due to the circumstances of his plea; it's hard to be sure a man really is a major criminal when his chief accuser has significant credibility problems, when he has been beaten silly by the RICO stick, and when lawmen have assured him that his brother will swing from the highest tree if he doesn't do what they want. It's harder still to cast a man as the prince of darkness when, after all that, he pleads guilty to crimes that are miles away from early government and press claims, and continents removed from his primary business. And it's more difficult yet to comprehend the evil in his genius when the court that sentenced him finds that the extent of his economic damage is less than $320,000.

The behavior of the U.S. attorney and the SEC lawyers only deepens the mystery. If Milken only committed second-tier felonies, how do the government men justify a $600 million fine? Beyond Boesky's claims, did they ever have reason to believe Milken had committed major crimes? If so, who gave them this information? Why, after the biggest manhunt in Wall Street history, were they able to build only a narrow, technical case against Milken? Did they blow the investigation?

Their press leaks are the least of the subjects they might profitably be asked about under oath—prosecutors leak to the press all the time, and as a journalist, I would be a hypocrite if I didn't bless them for it. What's telling in the Milken story is that prosecutors and the reporters who served them have gone to such great lengths to deny the leaks. It's as if any admission, even of the obvious, would cause the case against Milken to collapse.

What the prosecutors and SEC lawyers are really sensitive about, I suspect, is the revelation that they were as "highly confident" as Drexel and Milken. Investment bankers weren't the only ones who swaggered through the 1980s—if it was a time of excess, that virus reached far beyond Wall Street. Encouraged by Wall Street competitors and Washington legislators and confronted by an infuriating defendant, lawmen saw that advancement, reputation, and future prosperity depended on their success in the Milken prosecution. And, like Milken, they had a sense of holy purpose. In the certainty that they were breaking important ground and saving the Republic from ruin, they may have thrown accepted rules of conduct out the window.

If there were prosecutorial excesses, they don't excuse Milken and his defense team. Following traditional paths in a time when media is sometimes even more powerful than the government, they chose not to make an affirmative presentation of Milken's innocence during the investigation. Instead, they focused on Milken's philanthropy and on discrediting the witnesses against him, insisting that he would fight it out with the government in the only forum that mattered—the courtroom.

At that time, Milken's public image was a blank screen upon which prosecutors and reporters alike could project their own fantasies of greed. Against that onslaught, Milken found nothing to say that changed any of those perceptions. And when his supporters talked about his charitable work, his feelings for children, and the $25,000 that his foundation gave to each of three hundred outstanding teachers, they left many people with the impression that he was some Wizard of Oz figure, who hid behind a screen of surrogates so no one could see what he was really like.

It was essential, therefore, that Milken go to court, take the witness stand, and stare his accusers down. He never got there. And, afterward, he never stepped forward to explain himself. In the vacuum that he and his advisers created, it was inevitable that the press would take his silence as more proof that he was the arch-criminal of our time.

In jail, where no one can see, Milken is still a creator of success stories. Half a year into his sentence, he is relieved from menial chores and allowed to teach. His students find him a compelling and committed instructor. As well they might—to better understand those who are in prison for drug offenses, he goes through the Narcotics Anonymous program.*

In public, though, all anyone can see are the defeats. And, through that prism, nothing Milken does works out. He hires an appellate lawyer who is a lightning rod for controversy, only to be shocked and disappointed when that celebrity ambulance chaser adds Mike Tyson to his client list. He settles civil suits that he might well have won, leaving his family with an estimated few hundred million dollars, but because the financial agreement is kept from the public, many continue to suspect that he still has as much as $4 to $5 billion left. His lawyers have concentrated their efforts on this civil settlement, hoping that Milken's gesture of conciliation here will impress Judge Wood when she considers his application for a reduced sentence; they finally file that motion just two months before a trial of the only Drexel employee to be indicted after Milken pled. This delay gives the prosecutors the opportunity to request that the judge postpone her ruling until they decide if they want Milken to testify at his friend's trial.

What impresses about this unbroken record of losses is not that $100 million or more was spent on lawyers and public relations consultants, but how little it availed the client. As a bond salesman, Milken never had to sell himself to his customers—he overpowered them with ideas validated in the marketplace, overlaid with a dusting of charisma. But a legal battle fought in the media capital was beyond him, and he fell back, as people do, on an old habit: in his case, letting others define him. It was hardly surprising, therefore, that observers found Milken and his defense team so grating—arrogant, disrespectful of the intelligence of others, and apparently convinced that money and delay could sabotage every confrontation. Few outside the Milken circle would ever know how much those attitudes were less a mark of character than a reflection of how far this bond salesman was out of his league.

---

*Unnoticed by the media, Joni Noah—Milken's sister—and her partner, Robin Leach, have turned Mike's Math Club into one of the most potent tutoring programs in the nation. By 1991, they are using problems created by Milken to teach math to twenty-one hundred fifth- and sixth-grade students in ten inner-city schools in Los Angeles. They try to write to each student who sends them a letter; at last count, they were corresponding with fifteen hundred children.

Michael Milken is continually aghast at the ways the press gets him wrong. He doesn't see that what looks to him like a code of service may look to others like a need to manipulate friends and clients, if not outright control them, first by doing favors and then by asking for some in return. He doesn't see that his incessant quibbling over small factual errors may come across as a refusal to acknowledge larger truths. He doesn't see—and that's the problem. He's trapped in his worldview, a universe away from the emotions and conflicts that rule other people. For a man who seems genuinely to care for people, he got very far in life without discovering that they are not merely recipients of his help or obstacles to be surmounted.

That myopia is, for me, at the root of Milken's troubles. Milken is a tragic figure not because, with all his talent, he had criminal intent—he's tragic because it never worried him that he might be breaking some law. In his heyday, he threw off great ideas all day long. It was the ideas he lived for. Goony as it sounds, the mental excitement those ideas generated—and, of course, their ability to bring him hundreds of millions of legitimately earned dollars—blinded him to such mundane considerations as bookkeeping and disclosure regulations and other, seemingly trivial securities laws.

There are usually many hands on the tiller in any situation that ends in disaster; in the fall of Drexel, the list of culprits is long. Milken's responsibility is more cultural than criminal. In his zeal to achieve his radiant mission, he turned Drexel into a work machine with many of the trappings of a cult. As so often happens when a people stay together for a dozen hours a day, five or six days a week, the group achieved liftoff—its norms appeared sane while the world's appeared insane. Few at Drexel stopped to wonder, therefore, why there was always another deal, another client, another reason not to go home. Fewer still seemed to understand that even a guru can't manufacture time, that speed and pressure almost always leads to corner-cutting.

What was the avatar's mission? No one penetrated that secret. They couldn't. Long before, Milken had crossed the border between privacy and secrecy—he seems to have wanted to be the most powerful man in finance without the public ever knowing who he was. This obsession with personal obscurity, I believe, wasn't to conceal his true goals from others; it was to keep important knowledge about himself from himself. In twenty-five years of reporting, I have never encountered a man with less interest in his own psyche. I can only conclude that Milken ran so fast and worked so hard to keep some deep personal pain at bay.

Had Milken taken time for himself and confronted his demons, he might have wondered about his insatiable appetite for work and achievement and his distorted sense of entitlement. He might have looked into the hole in himself that nothing ever filled. He might even have questioned his hunger to dominate the world of finance in order to give the fruits of his success back to us in the form of charity. But because he didn't, he and his entire operation marched right off a cliff, victims of a mass disconnection from reality.

And so the Drexel juggernaut had to die—not because it was a criminal enterprise, but because it was an unnatural one. In the end, it was as simple as this: Michael Milken needed to slow down and consider the world beyond his trading room, but he wouldn't, so he had to be stopped. If it hadn't been Rudolph Giuliani and Gary Lynch, there would have been others who welcomed the opportunity. "Things refuse to be mismanaged long," Ralph Waldo Emerson writes in his essay on compensation. "Nature hates monopolies and exceptions."

"And yet the compensations of calamity are made apparent to the understanding also, after long intervals of time," Emerson also says. "A fever, a mutilation, a cruel disappointment, a loss of wealth, a loss of friends, seems at the moment unpaid loss, and unpayable. But the sure years reveal the deep remedial force that underlies all facts."

Pleasanton's asleep. But not Michael Milken. At his desk, a solitary worker in the predawn hours, he sits with his pencil and his legal pad, seeking that deep remedial force. So far, it eludes him—nothing he has learned has shown him how bright a light there must be to cast so dark a shadow. But someday, perhaps, he will look into himself, square his shoulders, and, in taking genuine responsibility for whatever it was he did, free himself from the special pleading that has been the hallmark of his defense. In that moment, he may not only be rehabilitated as a man, he may start the long journey back. And then, at last, he may begin to be worthy not just of our curiosity and our compassion, but of our respect.

SOURCES AND
ACKNOWLEDGMENTS

In 1985, after reading a piece in *The New York Times* about the training of new recruits at Salomon Brothers, I decided to chronicle a group of young people going through boot camp on Wall Street. In short order, I had a contract to write a book called *Salomon's Choice*. There was just one problem. Salomon Brothers wasn't interested in cooperating—too much of what I would learn, I was told, was privileged information. (Salomon much preferred, it seems, to have an insider write a far more devastating book, which is what Michael Lewis, a graduate of the Salomon program, did in *Liar's Poker*.)

As an idea, *Salomon's Choice* made the rounds on Wall Street in the spring and summer of 1986, becoming in turn *Goldman's Choice*, *Merrill's Choice*, and *Morgan Stanley's Choice*. When all these firms had turned down my request for access, I pitched *Drexel's Choice*. And, at Drexel, I survived a first meeting and actually had a second before the proposal was again rejected.

I heard a great deal about Drexel's star junk bond salesman along the way, and so, rather than return money to my publisher, I decided to write a book about Michael Milken. That July, I called him. "He won't talk to you," an assistant said. I suggested that I might write him a letter. "He won't read it," I was told. And with that, my efforts to write a book about Wall Street languished.

I wrote an occasional magazine piece about investment banking, and then, in the spring of 1988, I had my first break. Riding down one morning in the elevator of the Manhattan apartment building where my family and I live, I noted that one of my neighbors, Ken Lerer, looked unnaturally wan. I asked if anything was wrong. "No," he said. "I've just agreed to handle the press for Michael Milken."

Location, location, location—the gospel of real estate salesmen is also how I got my foot into Milken's door. Once there, however, I promptly inserted it in my mouth, for as a trio of Milken's intensely devoted representatives met with me to solicit my views, I offhandedly said that my quest was to discover whether he was a "beleaguered angel" or "the prince of darkness." Some three weeks later, they decided that my shocking proposition was, perhaps, an expression of candor and open-mindedness, and we met again.

Why did Milken give me access that so many sought? It didn't hurt that Lerer believed I was passable. It probably helped that I'm not known for my expertise in finance. It certainly helped that, even before my faux pas, I offered to show Milken a transcript of our interviews, so that he could correct them for accuracy and clarity.

This offer was not, I should emphasize, a clever ploy to reassure a media-shy financier. I had been sending interview transcripts to my subjects and sources since 1983, when Robert Gottlieb, then editor-in-chief of Alfred Knopf, requested one. Far from taking control, Gottlieb proved to be a more forthcoming conversationalist; as an experiment, I began to send transcripts to almost everyone I interviewed. The results were overwhelmingly positive, and I quickly made transcript review a cornerstone of my magazine writing. I have continued the practice in this book; I sent interview transcripts to hundreds of people. Although transcript review added time and effort to my workday, it minimized the possibility of misquotation and factual error. I will be eternally grateful that I had reason to call Robert Gottlieb.

Once the ground rules had been established, I spent some sixty to eighty hours during the summer of 1988 interviewing Milken about his background and his views. The following year, when Milken was indicted, I began to focus on the then-untold story of the criminal investigation and prosecution. At that time, no one knew how the story would end. Nor did I know what I would write. I am particularly grateful, therefore, to Michael Milken, who made what is for him an entirely unnatural decision and allowed me to hang around in rooms where other writers were barred.

I am almost equally grateful to Tina Brown, editor in chief of *Vanity Fair*. I have worked for many talented editors over the years; Tina is fearless, demanding, unreasonable, and altogether inspiring—without trying to, she changed the way I approach my work. She is also immensely supportive, and her personal kindnesses over the years have helped me endure more than a few difficult moments and impossible people. My *Vanity Fair* colleagues were ever-ready with help, notes, sources, and advice; in particular, I want to thank Marie Brenner, Fred Dannen, Dominick Dunne, Caroline Graham, Reinaldo Herrera, David Kuhn, Pam McCarthy, Joan Montgomery, Maria Ricapito, Jane Sarkin, Michael Shnayerson, Krista Smith, Wendy Stark, and Mary Turner. Special thanks to Kim Heron and Elise O'Shaughnessy for their willingness to read a work-in-progress, and to Ann Schneider for photo research.

At William Morrow, I am indebted to Howard Kaminsky and Adrian Zackheim, who took on this project at a time when the world thought it knew the Milken story. Their support has been unwavering, their humor pointed, their editorial expertise vast; a writer can't ask for more. I appreciate the efforts of Robert Aulicino, Scott Manning, Suzanne Oaks, Richard Sugarman, Deborah Weiss Geline, and Meryl Zegarek. And I am also indebted to Elizabeth McNamara, who provided legal wisdom and human understanding in refreshingly equal doses.

This book would not exist without Kathy Robbins, who has, as my agent, coach, and friend, run this six-year marathon with me. Even when she must have wondered why we persisted, she encouraged me to continue. Her associate, Elizabeth Mackey, delivered this message with great style and barbed wit on an almost daily basis while I was finishing the book; together, they made an ordeal seem like an adventure.

Others who helped mightily along the way are Steven M. L. Aronson, Fenton Bailey, Catherine Bailey, David H. Dreyfus, Beth Feinman, Bea and Neil Herbert, Nicky Kentish-Barnes, Laura King, Tom McCambridge, Dr. Melvyn Schoenfeld, and Andrew Tobias. In California, Liane and Richard Kornbluth and Kitty Wise and Robert Smith stood in for the home team, and the angelic Judy Resnick uncomplainingly watched me pace a groove in her carpet as I talked through contradictory ideas. Robinson, Lake & Lerer has the single largest repository of media clips about Drexel and Milken I know of; there, Ann Brackbill, Liz Maas, Meghan Myers, Debra Rudich, and Christie Smith cheerfully handled my requests. At Drexel, Steven Anreder made it possible for me to study similar files. I was greatly assisted by the ground-breaking work of Connie Bruck and Steve Brill in *American Lawyer*. I can't recall who suggested that I read Oscar Wilde's play, *An Ideal Husband*, but thank you; it's the best explication of the human dimension of securities crime that I've encountered.

Thanks to Roger McGuinn for the opening line. The idea of Milken looking over the edge of the world on page 91 was inspired by a passage in Peter Reich's *Book of Dreams*. On page 201, the idea that, in moments of stress, style dissolves into character comes from a conversation with Warren Bennis. The notion on page 368, that the source of light also is the source of shadows, is borrowed from a poem by Richard Tillinghast.

As ever, I am indebted to my wife, Annette Tapert, who, in addition to cheerleading, browbeating, and editing, functioned this time as a second agent, saying the right thing to the right person at the right time. And special thanks to Georgia and Nicholas Tapert, who pretended that they really were frightened when I threatened to cut off their hands if they came near my computer with refrigerator magnets.

INDEX